Cyber Law in Australia

Cyber Law in Australia

Second Edition

George Cho

This book was originally published as a monograph in the International Encyclopaedia of Laws/Cyber Law.

Founding Editor: Roger Blanpain
General Editor: Frank Hendrickx
Volume Editor: Jos Dumortier

Wolters Kluwer

Published by:
Kluwer Law International B.V.
PO Box 316
2400 AH Alphen aan den Rijn
The Netherlands
E-mail: international-sales@wolterskluwer.com
Website: lrus.wolterskluwer.com

Sold and distributed in North, Central and South America by:
Wolters Kluwer Legal & Regulatory U.S.
7201 McKinney Circle
Frederick, MD 21704
United States of America
Email: customer.service@wolterskluwer.com

Sold and distributed in all other countries by:
Air Business Subscriptions
Rockwood House
Haywards Heath
West Sussex
RH16 3DH
United Kingdom
Email: international-customerservice@wolterskluwer.com

ISBN 978-94-035-2102-2

e-Book: ISBN 978-94-035-2135-0
web-PDF: ISBN 978-94-035-2172-5

The Author

George Cho, PhD, is Professor of GeoInformatics and Law at the University of Canberra. George was the Chair of Academic Board (2008–2013) the peak academic body on quality and standards and in 2018 he was Acting Deputy Vice-Chancellor Research and Innovation at the University of Canberra. He obtained an Honours degree in Arts from the University of Malaya, Masters from the University of British Columbia and a PhD from the Australian National University. He also gained a Graduate Certificate in Higher Education from the University of Canberra and an LLB from the Australian National University. He was admitted as a barrister and solicitor of the Supreme Court of the Australian Capital Territory and the High Court of Australia and is a barrister-at-law in New South Wales. He practises law *pro bono* for the Welfare Rights and Legal Centre Night Time Legal Advice Service in Canberra. George was made a member of the Order of Australia in 2005 for his services to higher education and to the study of geographic information systems. He has published numerous books and journal articles on law and geography topics, including *Geographic Information Science: Mastering the Legal Issues* (John Wiley 2005); *Marketers and the Law* (LBC Sydney, 2000, with Clark and Hoyle); *E-business: Law and Management for the 21st Century* (Info-Sys International Publications, Canberra 2000, with Clark and Hoyle); *Y2K: Avoiding the Legal Byte* (Prospect Publications, 1999, with Clark and Hoyle); *Geographic Information Systems and the Law* (John Wiley, 1998) and fifteen other prior book publications. George has also written book chapters in various texts including *Commercial and Economic Law in Australia* (Griggs et al. Kluwer Law Intl. Alphen aan den Rijn, 2018); 'E-commerce law' in *The International Encyclopedia of Laws*; and 'E-commerce: Legal and Policy Framework' in the book *Managers and the Law: A Guide for Business Decision Makers*, edited by Griggs, Clark and Iredale (Sydney: Lawbook Co, 2009); and *Australian Commercial and Economic Law* (The Hague, Kluwer Law International, 1999). He is an International member of the editorial boards of the *Journal of Law and Information Science, GIS Law, International Journal of Geoinformatics*, and *Coordinates*. He has delivered papers to international and national conferences on topics related to information systems, intellectual property and e-commerce. His e-mail address is george.cho@canberra.edu.au.

For this volume, George has rewritten the whole text. He is grateful to the contributors of the previous work *Cyber Law Suppl. 50* (2015) by Eugene Clark, George Cho,

The Author

Arthur Hoyle and John McLaren for their work in addition to Paul Hynes on 'Part I. Telecommunications Regulation' and 'Part V. Non-contractual Liability'. Further, the present work has adapted material from previously published works by: E.E. Clark (2003), 'Managing the Transformation to e-Government: An Australian Perspective', *Thunderbird International Business Review*, Vol. 45(4), July-August, pp. 377–397, John Wiley & Sons ISSN: 1096-4762; E.E. Clark & M. Sainsbury (2002) *Privacy and the Internet*, Sydney: Thomson/LawBook Co.; E.E. Clark & G. Cho (2001) 'Privacy in an e-Business World: A Question of Balance', *Journal of Law and Information Science,* Vol. 11(1), pp. 7–37, ISSN 0729-1485; E. Clark & R. Prentice (2000) 'Circuit Layouts' in Butterworths, *Halsbury's Laws of Australia*, Vol. 15, Intellectual Property; and, K. Stewart 'Privacy' in E. Clark, G. Cho & A. Hoyle, (2000) *E-business: Law and Management for the 21st C* (Canberra: Info-Sys Law).

Table of Contents

The Author 3

List of Abbreviations 23

Preface 31

General Introduction 35

Chapter 1. General Background of the Country 35

§1. Geography 35

§2. Cultural Composition 35

§3. Political System 36
I. The Constitution and System of Government 36
II. Judicial Power 38
III. Political Parties 39

§4. Population 39

§5. Economy 40

§6. Social and Cultural Values 41

Chapter 2. The Information Communication Technology (ICT) Infrastructure 42

§1. Cyber Law Concepts 42

§2. Australia's Competitive Position and Challenges in the Knowledge and Information Economy 46

§3. Current State of the Australian Economy 47

§4. Australia's Digital Economy 48

§5. Participation of Australians in the Digital Economy 50

I. Internet Activity 50
II. Household Use of IT 51

§6. Emerging Markets and Potential Growth of Australia's Digital Economy 52

Chapter 3. ICT Market and e-Government 54

§1. Definition of E-Government 54

§2. Law and E-Government 54

§3. Government's Role in Promoting E-Business 55

Chapter 4. Australian E-Government Initiatives 57

§1. Introduction 57

§2. Government Policy Framework 57

§3. Infrastructure Challenges 58

§4. Australian E-Government in a Global Context 59
I. Australia E-Government Leadership 60
A. National e-Conveyancing 62
B. Developments in e-Health Records 63

§5. Conclusions 64

Part I. Regulation of ICT Market 65

Chapter 1. Introduction and Background 65

§1. Geography and Market 65

§2. Background to the Legislation 66

Chapter 2. Industry Structure and Regulatory Entities 69

§1. Service Providers and Network Units 69

Chapter 3. Access Regulation: Part XIC CCA 72

§1. Introduction 72

§2. Object 74

§3. Service Declaration 75

§4. TAF 75

Chapter 4. Regulation of Anti-competitive Conduct: Part XIB CCA 76

§1. Introduction 76

§2. The CCA 77

§3. The Competition Notice Regime 77

§4. The Telecommunications Market 78

Chapter 5. Regulation of Consumer Protection in Telecommunications Sector 81

§1. Introduction 81

§2. Universal Service Obligation 82

§3. CSG 83

§4. Telecommunications Industry Ombudsman 84

§5. Broadcasting Services 85

Chapter 6. Telecommunications Reforms 88

§1. Introduction 88

§2. Structural Separation of Telstra 88

§3. Reforms to the Competition Regime 89

§4. Consumer Safeguards 89

Part II. IPR in the ICT Sector 91

Chapter 1. IPR in ICT 91

§1. Introduction 91
I. IPR 91

§2. IPR Protection in Australia 93

I. Copyright 94
II. Databases and Compilations 94
III. Patents 94
IV. Business Methods and Systems 95
V. Designs 95
VI. Trade Marks™ 95
VII. Moral Rights 96
VIII. Geographical Indications 96
IX. Protection of Other IPR 96
A. Trade Secrets and Confidential Information 96
B. Photographs 96
C. Fonts 97

§3. IPR International Environment 97
I. IPR Conventions, Agreements and Treaties 97

§4. Copyright © and ICT 101
I. ICT Data on the Internet 102

Chapter 2. Legal Protection of Computer Software 104

Chapter 3. Legal Protection of Databases 106

§1. Electronic Databases 106
I. Authorship of a Database or Compilation 107
II. Database Rights in Derivative Works 107
III. Revisions 108
IV. Compilations and 'Sweat of the Brow' 108
V. Maps as Factual Compilations and Mere Representations 110
A. 'Thin' Copyright Protection 111

§2. European Union Database Directive 112
I. Sui Generis: Database Right 112

§3. Conclusions 113

Chapter 4. Legal Protection of Circuit Layouts 114

§1. Introduction 114

§2. Background: Circuit Layout Protection 115

§3. Relationship with Other Areas of IP 116

§4. Protection under the CLA 117
I. Criteria for Protection 117

II. Nature of Protection 117
III. Length of Protection 118

§5. COMMERCIAL DEALINGS 118
I. Assignment and Licence of EL Rights 118
II. Prospective Ownership 118
III. Advantages of Marking 118
IV. First Sale Doctrine and Parallel Importation of Integrated Circuits 118
V. Parallel Importation of Software 119

§6. ACTS OF INFRINGEMENT 119
I. Elements of Infringement 119

§7. DEFENCES 120
I. General 120
II. Statutory Defences 120
III. Common Law Defences 121

§8. REMEDIES FOR INFRINGEMENTS 121
I. Who May Bring an Action 121
II. Available Remedies 121
III. Groundless Threats of Legal Proceedings 121

§9. PROCEDURAL MATTERS 122
I. Limitation of Actions 122
II. Proof of Facts 122
III. Jurisdiction and Appeals 122

Chapter 5. Other IPR in ICT 123

§1. MORAL RIGHTS 123
I. Moral Rights 124
II. Sui Generis Rights 124

§2. BUSINESS METHODS AND GEOGRAPHIC INFORMATION PATENTS 125
I. Business Methods 125
II. Geographic Information Patents 126

§3. THE DIGITAL AGENDA 127

§4. ATYPICAL DEVELOPMENTS AND OTHER LEGAL ISSUES 128
I. The 'Copyleft' Movement and No Rights Reserved 128
II. Addenda to FOSS 130
III. Geographical Indications 131
IV. Photographs 132
V. Fonts 133

Chapter 6. Business Names and Internet Domain Name Registration 135

§1. Registration of Business Names 135

§2. Domain Names 136
I. Definition 136
II. Typology of Domains 137
III. Administration of Domain Names 138

§3. Registration in Australia 139
I. Unassignable Licence 140

§4. Domain Name Dispute Resolution Procedure 140
I. Australian Domain Name Dispute Resolution Procedures 140
II. Domain Name Versus Trade Mark 141
III. Critique of the UDRP Cybersquatting 141

§5. Reform 142
I. Australian Reforms 142
II. Reform of ICANN 142

Chapter 7. IPR: Infringements, Defences and Remedies 145

§1. Infringements 145
I. Territorial Copyright and Parallel Importation 145
II. Substantiality Requirements 146
III. Reproduction in Material Form 147

§2. Defences to Infringement 147

§3. Remedies 148

Chapter 8. Summary 150

Part III. Contract Law and ICT 153

Chapter 1. Introduction 153

§1. Principles of Contract Law 154

§2. Elements of a Contract 155
I. Offer and Acceptance 155
II. Valuable Consideration 159
III. Consensus 160

§3. Requirements for a Written Document 160

§4. Terms of a Contract 161
I. Express Terms 161
II. Implied Terms 163
III. Shrink-Wrap and Web-Wrap Terms 166

§5. Contract Issues in E-Commerce 168

Chapter 2. Hardware Contracts 170

Chapter 3. Software Contracts 173

§1. Bespoke Software 174

§2. Personnel Contracts: Employee Versus Independent Contractor 176

Chapter 4. Turnkey Contracts 178

Chapter 5. Software Distribution Agreements 180

Chapter 6. Maintenance Contracts 181

Chapter 7. Facilities Management 182

Chapter 8. Network Services 183

§1. Computer Service Bureau Contracts 183

Chapter 9. Government Contracts 185

§1. Simple procurement 185

§2. Semi-complex Procurement 185

§3. Government Outsourcing 186

Chapter 10. Damages 187

Chapter 11. Collateral Issues 191

§1. Liability and Ownership of Property 191

§2. Minors and Agents 192

§3. Consumer Protection 193

§4. Remedies 194
I. Anton Piller Orders 194
II. Mareva Injunction 194

Part IV. Electronic Transactions 197

Chapter 1. Legal Status of Electronic Transactions 197

§1. Introduction 197

§2. E-Commerce and the Internet 198

§3. The ETA: Background 201

§4. Future Developments 205

§5. A Note on Digital Signatures 205

§6. Summary and Conclusions 207

Chapter 2. Cryptography, Certification and Security Tools 208

§1. Introduction 208

§2. The PKI 208
I. Development in Australia 208
II. Definition 209
III. Workability of PKI 210

§3. Digital Certificates, E-Procurement and E-Tendering 210

§4. E-Commerce Trust Mechanisms and Security Tools 212
I. SSL 212
II. SET Protocol 212
III. Virtual Private Networks (VPN) 213
IV. Passwords 213

§5. Export of Encryption Technology 213

Chapter 3. Legal Aspects of Electronic Banking and Payments Systems 214

§1. Introduction 214
I. Need for Third-Party Assurance of Web-Based E-commerce 215

II. Electronic Financial Transactions and Payments Systems 215
III. Areas Needing Assurance 220

§2. ELECTRONIC PAYMENTS SYSTEMS (EPS) 221
I. Internet Banking 221
II. Electronic Payments Systems (EPS) 222
III. Digital Cash (DC) 223
IV. Digital Cheques 225

§3. SECURITY AND CONTROL OF PAYMENTS SYSTEMS 225
I. Characteristics of Payments Systems 225
II. Clearing and Settlement 226
III. Netting Arrangements 226
IV. Exposure Risks 227
V. Herstatt Risks 227
VI. Application to Digital Cash 227
VII. Control of the Payments Systems 228
A. Australian Solutions 230
B. e-Crime 231
C. Other Criminal Activities 231

§4. AUSTRALIAN REGULATORY RESPONSES TO E-CASH 232

§5. CONCLUSION 233

Chapter 4. Consumer Protection of ICT Users 234

§1. INTRODUCTION 234

§2. OVERVIEW OF CONSUMER PROTECTION REGIMES 234
I. In General 234
II. CCA and Fair Trading Legislation 235
III. CCA and Australian Consumer Law (2010) (Cth) (ACL) 236
IV. CCA and Enforcement, Remedies and Statute of Limitations 236
V. CCA and Defences 237
VI. Other Consumer-Related Commonwealth Legislation 237

§3. CONSUMER LAW GOVERNING THE QUALITY OF GOODS AND SERVICES 238

§4. CONSUMER CREDIT 238

§5. VOLUNTARY CODES 239

§6. INTERNATIONAL STANDARDS FOR CONSUMER PROTECTION IN CYBERSPACE 239
I. Consumer Protection in Electronic Commerce 240
II. Australian E-Commerce BPM 240

Chapter 5. ICT and Civil Procedure 242

§1. Introduction 242

§2. Jurisdiction: General Principles 242
I. Definition 242
II. General Versus Specific or Special Jurisdiction 243
III. Jurisdiction Clause 243
IV. Territorial Restrictions on Laws 243
V. In Personam and In Rem Jurisdiction 243
VI. Subject-Matter Jurisdiction 244

§3. Jurisdiction in an ICT Context 244
I. In Australia 244
II. A Technological Solution? 246
III. The Internet: A New and Separate Legal Frontier? 246

§4. Venue 246

§5. Choice of Law 246

§6. Conflict of Laws 247
I. Nature of the Conflict 247
II. Categorizing the Cause of Action 247
III. Applying the Conflict Rule 247
IV. Recommendations for Reform 248

§7. Discovery and Rules of Evidence 248

§8. Dispute Resolution 249
I. Use of Technology by Australian Courts 249
II. Mediation and Arbitration 250

Part V. Non-contractual Liability: Roles and Responsibilities 253

Chapter 1. Civil Obligations: Negligence 253

§1. Introduction 253

§2. Nature of Tort 253

§3. Liability and Jurisdiction in Tort 254

§4. Categories of Tort 254

§5. Intentional Torts 255
I. Definitions 255
II. Fraudulent Misrepresentation 256
III. Defamation 256
IV. Passing-Off Goods 258
V. Trespass 258

§6. Negligence 258
I. General Civil Remedy 258
II. Doctrine of Negligence 259
III. Negligent Misstatement 260
IV. Defences 261

§7. Breach of Statutory Duty 261

§8. Remedies 262

Chapter 2. Liability of Network Service Operators and ISP 263

§1. Introduction 263

§2. Statutory Duty 263

§3. Defamation Action 264

§4. Negligent Provision of Information 265

§5. Liability in Special Contexts 266

§6. Conclusion 266

Chapter 3. Product Liability 267

§1. Introduction 267

§2. Product Safety Laws 267

Part VI. Privacy Protection 269

Chapter 1. Regulating Personal Information and Data Protection 269

§1. Introduction 269
I. Definition of Privacy 269
II. Privacy, Technology and the Internet 271
III. Privacy Abuse 272

IV. Balancing Interests 274
V. Australia's International Obligations 275

§2. Commonwealth Privacy Act 277
I. Scope of Privacy Act 277
A. New Privacy Law 278
B. Summary of New Provisions 278
C. Other Provisions 280
II. Privacy and the Private Sector 282
III. Importance of Consent 282
A. Automated Collection by Cookies 283
B. Behavioural Ads 283
C. Cyber Attack 283
IV. Data-Matching and Data Sharing Guidelines 283
V. Privacy Codes 285
VI. The Privacy Commissioner 285
VII. Other Commonwealth Legislation Impacting Privacy 286
A. Financial Data 286
B. Health Records 287

§3. Privacy Legislation in the States and Territories 287

§4. Related Laws 287

§5. Industry Codes 289
I. Industry Codes 289
II. Third-Party Verification 290

§6. Non-legal Means of Privacy Protection 290
I. Technical Solutions 290
II. Education 290

§7. Conclusion 291

§8. Freedom of Information Legislation 291
I. Commonwealth FOI Act 291
II. State and Territories FOI Acts 292

Chapter 2. Privacy in Telecommunications 294

§1. Introduction 294

§2. Telecommunications Act 294

§3. Other Legislation 295

§4. Criminal Laws 296

I. Commonwealth Criminal Laws 296
II. State and Territory Criminal Laws 296

§5. Industry Codes 297

§6. Specific Applications 298
I. Spam Legislation 298
II. Combatting Spam 300
III. Cookies 301
IV. Web Bugs, Spiders, Data Aggregation or Screen Scraping and Data Mining 302
V. Unauthorized Access to E-Mail 303

§7. Conclusion 304

Part VII. Cybercrime Law Enforcement 307

Chapter 1. Legal Developments in Cybercrime 307

§1. Introduction 307

§2. Definition of Criminal Acts and Punishment 307

§3. Sources of Criminal Law 308

§4. Principles of Criminal Liability 308

§5. Establishing Criminal Liability 309

§6. Capacity 309

§7. Criminal Procedure 310

Chapter 2. Cybercrime: Substantive and Procedural Law 312

§1. Introduction 312

§2. Definition and Reach of Cybercrime 312
I. Definition 312
II. Nature and Extent of Cybercrime 313

§3. Commonwealth Cybercrime Legislation 315
I. Commonwealth Cybercrime Laws 315
II. State and Territory Cybercrime Laws 317

§4. Telecommunications Crime 319

§5. SPECIFIC CYBERCRIMES 319
I. Theft 319
II. Computer and/or Internet Fraud 320
A. In General 320
B. Computer Fraud as a Civil Wrong 321
III. Identity Theft 322

§6. COMMON 'MISCHIEFS' 324
I. Hacking or Cracking 324
II. Criminal Code: Commonwealth, State and Territories Models 324
A. Western Australia 325
B. Queensland 325
C. Tasmania 326
D. 'Unauthorized' Access 326
E. Privacy 326
F. Computer 327
III. DDoS 328
IV. Viruses 328
V. Password Sniffing 328
VI. Spoofing 329
VII. Pagejacking 329
VIII. Phishing and Key Logging 330

§7. CYBERSTALKING AND CYBER-BULLING 331

§8. ONLINE GAMBLING 333
I. Extent of Gambling in Australia 333
II. Interactive Gambling Act 333
III. Interactive Gambling Act Reforms 333
IV. National Consumer Protection Framework 334
V. Enforcement 335
VI. Penalties 335
VII. Role of ACMA 335
A. Interactive Gambling Industry Code 336
VIII. Gambling Reforms 337

§9. OBSCENITY AND PORNOGRAPHY 338
I. Summary of Issues 338
II. Online Privacy Protection of Children 338
III. Industry Codes and International Cooperation 339

§10. SUICIDE-RELATED MATERIAL 339

§11. ANTI-VILIFICATION LAWS 340

§12. ANTI-TERRORISM LAWS 340

Chapter 3. Cybercrime Law Enforcement and Criminal Procedures 342

§1. INTRODUCTION 342

§2. NEED FOR COOPERATION BETWEEN INDUSTRY AND POLICE 342

§3. PREVENTATIVE PRIVATE ACTION AGAINST CYBERCRIME 343

§4. INTERNATIONAL DEVELOPMENTS 344
I. International Cooperation 344
II. Racist Websites 344
III. Convention on Cybercrime 344

Part VIII. Environmental Law Issues 347

Chapter 1. Cyber Law and Environmental Law 347

Chapter 2. Information Technology and E-Waste 348

Chapter 3. E-Waste Issues: Global and National Initiatives 351

§1. REDUCTION OF E-WASTE GENERATION IN AUSTRALIA 351

§2. NEW ZEALAND 353

§3. EUROPEAN UNION AND UK 353

§4. CHINA 355

Chapter 4. Role of Environmental Law in Cyberspace 356

Chapter 5. Governance and Regulatory Framework for Environmental Law 358

§1. FRAMEWORK FOR E-WASTE LEGISLATION 360

Chapter 6. Summary and Conclusions 361

Part IX. Technological Developments 363

Chapter 1. GIS and Cyber Law 363

§1. GIS IN A CYBER LAW CONTEXT 363

§2. Data and Information 363

§3. Definition of GIS 364

Chapter 2. GIS and Cyber Law Legal Issues 365

Chapter 3. GIS and the Law of Contract 366

§1. General 366

§2. Geospatial Information: Products and Services 366

§3. Contract of Service and Contract for Service 368

Chapter 4. GIS and Property Rights 370

§1. Characteristics of Property Rights and GIS 370

§2. Protection of IP in Australia 370

§3. Protection of IPR and GIS 371
I. Ownership Rights 371
II. IPR Protection Framework 372
III. Legal Risks 375
IV. Functional Characteristics 376

Chapter 5. GIS and Privacy 379

§1. Overview of Privacy Issues 379

§2. Nature of LBS 380

§3. Legislation and LBS 380

§4. Implications 381

Chapter 6. GIS and Liability Issues 384

§1. Legal liability and risks 384
I. Legal Responsibilities 384
II. Contractual Liability 384
III. Tort Liability 385
IV. Liability of Network Hosts 385
V. Mitigating Circumstances 385
VI. Volunteers as Good Samaritans 385
A. Common Law Cases 385

B. US Legislation 386
C. European Rescue Laws 386
VII. Other Tortious Liability 386

Chapter 7. GIS: Emerging Issues 388

Chapter 8. GIS: Cloud Computing and VGI 390

§1. Cloud Computing 390

§2. VGI 391

Chapter 9. Robotics Industry and Artificial Intelligence 393

§1. Robotics and Cyber Law 395
I. Legal Definition of Robot 395
II. Impact on Employment 395
A. Jobs Most at Risk 396
B. Jobs Least at Risk 396

§2. Artificial Intelligence and Cyber Law 396
I. Autonomous Vehicles: Driverless Cars 397
II. Legal Challenges and Privacy Issues 398

§3. Other Legal Issues 400

Part X. Conclusions 403

Selected Bibliography 415

Index 419

Table of Contents

List of Abbreviations

2LD	Second Level Domain Names
AAT	Administrative Appeals Tribunal
ABA	Australian Broadcasting Authority
ABACUS	Australian Business Assessment of Computer User Security
ABC	Australian Broadcasting Corporation
ABN	Australian Business Name
ABS	Australian Bureau of Statistics
ACA	Australian Communications Authority
ACCC	Australian Competition and Consumer Commission
ACDC	Australian Commercial Disputes Centre
ACICA	Australian Centre for International Commercial Arbitration
AACIP	Australian Advisory Council on Intellectual Property
ACL	Australian Consumer Law Act 2010 (Cth)
ACMA	Australian Communications and Media Authority
ACN	Australian Company Name
ACORN	Australian Cybercrime Online Reporting Network
ACS	Australian Customs Service
ACSC	Australian Cyber Security Centre
ACT	Australian Capital Territory
ADMA	Australian Direct Marketing Association
ADR	Alternate Dispute Resolution
AFP	Australian Federal Police
AFS	Australian Financial Services
AGIMO	Australian Government Information Management Office
AGPS	Assisted Global Positioning System
AI	Artificial Intelligence
AIC	Australian Institute of Criminology
ALRC	Australian Law Reform Commission
AML/CTF	Anti-Money Laundering and Counter-Terrorism Financing Act 2006 (Cth)

List of Abbreviations

ANZ	Australia New Zealand
APCA	Australian Payments Clearing Association
API	Application Programming Interface
APEC	Asia-Pacific Economic Commission
APMC	Australasian Police Ministers' Council
APP Code	Australian Privacy Principles Code
APP	Australian Privacy Principles
apps	Applications
APRA	Australian Prudential Regulation Authority
APS	Australian Public Service
AR	Augmented Reality
ARNECC	National e-Conveyancing Council
ASADA	Australian Sports Anti-Doping Authority
ASCII	American Standard Code for Information Interchange
ASD	Australian Signals Directorate
ASIC	Australian Securities and Investments Commission
ASIO	Australian Security Intelligence Organization
ATF	Approved Treatment Facilities
ATM	Automated Teller Machine
ATO	Australian Taxation Office
AUD	Australian dollar
AuDA	auDomain Administration Ltd. (Australian)
AUSTRAC	Australian Transaction Reports and Analysis Centre
AWBC	Australian Wine and Brandy Corporation Act 1980 (Cth)
B2B	Business-to-Business
B2C	Business-to-Consumer
B2G	Business-to-Government
BIS	Bank for International Settlements
bot	Robot
BPM	Best Practice Model
BSB	Bank State Bank
C2G	Consume- to-Government
CA	Certification Authority
CAL	Copyright Agency Ltd.
CAUCE	Coalition Against Unsolicited Commercial e-Mail
CCA	Competition and Consumer Act 2010 (Cth)
CCC	Copyright Clearance Centre (US)
ccTLD	Country code top level domain names
CCTV	Closed Circuit TV

CERT	Computer Emergency Response Team
CGDN	Community Geographic Domain Names
CHESS	Clearing House Electronic Sub-Register System
CISPA	Center for IT Security, Privacy and Accountability
CLA	Circuit Layouts Act 1989 (Cth)
CLAA	Cybercrime Legislation Amendment Act 2012 (Cth)
CLI	Calling Line Identification
CLRC	Copyright Law Reform Committee
CND	Calling Number Display
COAG	Council of Australian Governments
COTS	Commercial off the shelf
CSG	Customer Service Guarantee
CSP	Carriage Service Provider
Cth	Commonwealth
CUECIC	Convention on the Use of Electronic Communications in International Contracts (UN)
DaaS	Data as a Service
DBCDE	Department of Broadband, Communications and the Digital Economy
DBMS	database management system
DC	Digital certificates / digital cash
DCFS	Designated Collection Facilities
DDoS	Distributed Denial-of-Service
DDSO	Digital Data Service Obligation
DEC	Digital Equipment Corporation
DGPS	Differential Global Positioning System
DMCA	Digital Millennium Copyright Act 1998 (US)
DOE	Department of Environment (UK)
DOHA	Department of Health and Ageing
DRM	Digital Rights Management
DSC	Digital Signature Certificate
DTA	Digital Transformation Agency
DTS	Distributor Takeback Scheme
DVA	Department of Veterans Affairs
ECEG	Electronic Commerce Expert Group
EDI	Electronic Data Interchange
EDR	External Dispute Resolution
EEA	European Economic Area
EEE	Electronic and Electrical Equipment

List of Abbreviations

EFA	Electronic Frontiers Australia
EFT	Electronic Funds Transfer
EFTPOS	Electronic Funds Transfer Point of Sale
EGDI	e-Government Development Index
EL	Eligible Layout
EMG	Environment Management Group
EPC	European Patents Convention
EPIRB	Emergency Position Indicating Radio Beacon
EPO	European Patents Office
EPS	Electronic Payments System
ETA	Electronic Transactions Act 1999 (Cth)
EU	European Union
FOIA	Freedom of Information Act 1982 (Cth)
FOSS	Free Open Source Software
FSR	Financial Sector Reform (Amendments and Transitional Provisions) Act (1998) (Cth)
G2B	Government-to-Business
G2C	Government-to-Consumer
G2G	Government-to-Government
GAC	Government Advisory Committee
GATT	General Agreement on Tariffs and Trade
GCC	Geospatial Cloud Computing
GDP	Gross Domestic Product
GDPR	General Data Protection Regulation (EU)
GIF	graphics interchange format
GIS	Geographic (geospatial) information system (science)
GNSO	Generic Names Supporting Organization
GNU GPL	GNU General Public Licence
GNU	GNU's not UNIX (recursive acronym)
GPKA	Government Public Key Authority
GPS	Global Positioning Systems
GST	Goods and Services Tax
gTLD	Generic Top-level Domain Name
HBCI	Home Banking Communication Interface
HCA	High Court of Australia
HCPIL	Hague Conference on Private International Law
http	hypertext transfer protocol
IaaS	Infrastructure as a Service
IANA	Internet Assigned Numbers Authority

IC	integrated circuit
ICANN	Internet Corporation for Assigned Names and Numbers
ICC	International Chamber of Commerce
ICPEN	International Consumer Protection and Enforcement Network
ICT	Information Communication Technology
IFR	International Federation of Robotics
IGA	Inter-Governmental Agreement
IGO	Intergovernmental Organization
IIA	Internet Industry Association
ILO	International Labour Organization
INN	International Non-Proprietary Names
IOT	Internet of Things
IP	Intellectual Property
IPP	Information Privacy Principles
IPR	Intellectual Property Rights
ISO	International Standards Organization
ISP	Internet Service Provider
ITU	International Telecommunications Union
JPEG	Joint Photographic Experts Group
LAN	Local Area Network
LBS	Location-Based Services
LCIA	London Court of International Arbitration
m-Commerce	mobile Commerce
ML	Machine Learning
MMS	Multi-media Messaging Service
NADRAC	National Alternative Dispute Resolution Advisory Council
NBN	National Broadband Network
NCC	National Credit Code (US)
NCCP	National Consumer Credit Protection Act 2009 (Cth)
NDB	Notifiable Data Breaches
NDES	National Digital Economy Strategy
NEAC	National Electronic Authentication Council
NECS	National e-Conveyancing System
NFC	Near Field Communication
NICTA	National ICT Australia Ltd
NIST	National Institute of Standards and Technology (US)
NOIE	National Office for the Information Economy
NPP	National Privacy Principles
NSW	New South Wales

List of Abbreviations

NT	Northern Territory
NTCRS	National Television and Computer Recycling Scheme
OAIC	Office of the Australian Information Commissioner
ODR	Online Dispute Resolution
OECD	Organisation for Economic Co-operation and Development
OEM	Original Equipment Manufacturer
OGIT	Office of Government Information Technology
OSD	Open Source Definition
OSI	Open Source Initiative
OTC	Overseas Telecommunications Commission
P2P	Peer-to-Peer
PaaS	Platform as a Service
PACE	Platform for Accelerating the Circular Economy
PCEHR	Personally Controlled Electronic Health Records Act 2012 (Cth)
PCS	Producer Compliance Scheme
PDA	Personal Digital Assistant
PEFO	Pre-election Economic and Fiscal Outlook
PGP	Pretty Good Privacy
PIN	Personal Identification Number
PKAF	Public Key Authority Framework
PKI	Public Key Infrastructure
PKT	Public Key Technology
PMG	Postmaster General's Department
POS	Point of Sale
PSTN	Public Switched Telephone Network
RA	Registration Authority
RAA	Registrar Accreditation Agreement
RBA	Reserve Bank of Australia
RFI	Request for Information
RFID	Radio Frequency Identification
RFP	Request for Proposals
RFT	Request for Tender
SA	South Australia
SaaS	Software as a Service
SANS	System Administration, Audit, Networking and Security Institute
SAR	Special Administrative Regions (Peoples Republic of China)
SCAG	Standing Committee of Attorneys-General

SCPA	Semiconductor Chip Protection Act 1984 (US)
SEATS	Stock Exchange Automated Trading System
SEC	Securities and Exchange Commission (US)
SET	Secure Electronic Transaction
SHTTP	Secure Hypertext Transfer Protocol
SME	Small to Medium Enterprises
SMTP	Simple Mail Transport Protocol
SMS	Short Message Service
SOE	Statement of expectations
SOS	Settlement Online System
SSL	Secure Socket Layer
S	Solving the e-Waste Problem
SVC	Stored-Value Cards
TAF	Telecommunications Access Forum
TCPIP	Transmission Control Protocol Internet Protocol
TCPSS	Telecommunications (Consumer Protection and Services Standards) Act 1999 (Cth)
Telecom	Australian Telecommunications Commission
TIAA	Telecommunications (Interception and Access) Act 1979 (Cth)
TIO	Telecommunications Industry Ombudsman
TLD	Top Level Domain
TLS	Transport Layer Security
TMT	Technology, media and telecommunication
TOLA	Telecommunications and Other Legislation Amendment (Assistance and Access) Act 2018 (Cth)
TPA	Trade Practices Act 1974 (Cth)
TPM	Technological Protection Measures
TRIPS	Trade Related aspects of Intellectual Property Rights
UCC	Uniform Commercial Code (US)
UCCC	Uniform Consumer Credit Code (US)
UDHR	Universal Declaration of Human Rights
UDRP	Uniform Domain Name Dispute Resolution Policy
UNCITRAL	UN Commission on International Trade Law
UNIDO	United Nations Industrial Development Organization
UNITAR	United Nations Institute for Training and Research
UNU	United Nations University
URL	universal resource locator
USD	US Dollar
USO	Universal Service Obligation

List of Abbreviations

USPTO	United States Patent and Trademark Office
VA	Validation Authority
VGI	Volunteered Geographic Information
VOIP	Voice Over Internet Protocol
VPN	Virtual Private Networks
VR	Virtual Reality
WA	Western Australia
WBCSD	World Business Council for Sustainable Development
WCT	WIPO Copyright Treaty
Web 3.0	Semantic or Intelligent Web
WEEE	Waste Electronic and Electrical Equipment
WHO	World Health Organization
WIPO	World Intellectual Property Organization
WPPT	WIPO Performances and Phonograms Treaty
WTO	World Trade Organization
WWW	World Wide Web

Preface

This volume is divided into ten parts with each addressing specific topics as outlined in the Kluwer series on Law and Business. In the Introduction to this work, readers are provided with some background about Australia in terms of its geography, cultural composition and political systems. This discussion is followed by a brief outline of the population, the economy and social and cultural values of Australians. Cyber law terminology and concepts are introduced to ensure that there is a consistency of use and understanding. This leads to a discussion of Australia's competitive position and challenges in the knowledge and information economy and more particularly the state of the economy vis-à-vis its participation in the digital economy. A discussion of e-government follows in line with the government's role in promoting e-commerce and business through policy initiatives and how infrastructure challenges are being met. The achievements here are examined through the prism of international comparisons.

Part I introduces the regulation of the Information Communication and Telecommunications (ICT) and the market. This introduction is important because the ICT sector is pivotal in any examination of cyber law in the country. The background to the legislation is pertinent to understanding the industry structure and the various regulatory entities contained therein. Importantly, access regulation is examined as part of the policy initiatives around competition and consumer protection. The telecommunication market is discussed here within the umbrella of the regulation of consumer protection by way of service obligations and service guarantees. Recourse to the telecommunication industry ombudsman, reforms to the competition regime and consumer safeguards are explained here. Sharp business practices and unethical behaviour have contributed to a lack of consumer confidence in the online environment and the final section of this part deals with the important topics of jurisdiction, conflict of laws and dispute resolution in e-commerce.

Part II explores property rights in the ICT sector. The application of copyright in ICT as part of intellectual property rights protection in Australia is emblematic because of the very nature of the application. Topics in intellectual property in an information age become very important because the greatest assets are intangible and reside in the virtual world. Cyber law as a discipline addresses such issues where intellectual property is prevalent. This part explores the laws governing copyright, trademarks, patents, trade secrets, moral rights, geographical indications and other genres of intellectual property rights. More particularly, chapters are devoted to the legal protection of computer software and databases, circuit layouts, commercial dealings and infringements. Atypical developments, such as the copyleft movement with no rights reserved, business methods and systems and geographic information patents are discussed alongside domain name registration. How to deal with disputes, infringements, defences and remedies are discussed.

Part III examines ICT contracts using the common law of contract and legislation. This part begins with an introduction to the principles and elements of contract law and analogizes these topics to an online virtual world where there may be no written documents per se. Contract issues in e-commerce are related to various forms emanating from the technology such as hardware contracts, software contracts, turnkey contracts and software distribution agreements. Of importance here is the distinction between employees versus independent contractors in personnel contracts. Also, computer service bureau contracts can encompass both the provision of services as well as of physical equipment and machinery. Government contracts are given a separate treatment because of its unique nature and where the procurement process is quite different from those in the commercial world. The complexities of procurement, government outsourcing generate different kinds of liabilities where losses are incurred. Other collateral issues are also discussed including liability and ownership of property, the responsibilities of agents and the legal standing of minors, consumer protection and remedies.

Part IV deals with the legal status of electronic transactions. Ideally this topic should have featured earlier in this volume because most of cyber law proceeds from such transactions. However, it is placed here since there was a prior need to discuss the ICT sector generally and to ensure that the placement at this point permits international comparisons with similar cyber law volumes for other jurisdictions in this series. In the Australian context the Electronic Transaction Act permits obligations to be met by providing documents in electronic form. Records may also be kept in digital form. This development has profound implications for business and government and their record-keeping. A chapter on cryptography, certification and security tools provide the scaffold for public key infrastructures to be built so that digital certificates, e-procurement and e-tendering may take place. These trust mechanisms permit e-commerce on a secure basis and confidence in the electronic payment systems. Utmost in these discussions are consumer protection regimes especially those governing the quality of goods and services, consumer credit, voluntary codes of practice and the work towards international standards for consumer protection in cyberspace. With the borderless international cyberspace that e-commerce entails the general principles of jurisdiction in an ICT context is reviewed including venue, choice of law, conflict of law, rules of evidence and dispute resolution.

Part V considers areas of non-contractual liability. Civil obligations refer to 'duties' of responsible adults in a civil society. One set of obligations derives from those legally binding 'promises' that we make and must keep, that is, contract law. However, a second set of civil obligations is found in the law of tort. At the heart of tort law is the doctrine of negligence. Tort law examines those circumstances where a duty arises to act reasonably and where a failure to exercise due care will result in liability for any injury that has been done to either persons or property. A third set of civil obligations arises from an emerging doctrine of unjust enrichment.

This part also explores non-contractual liability in network operations, service providers and product liability. The exploration includes understanding the nature and categories of tort, statutory duties, liability for the negligent provision of information as well as product safety laws.

Part VI focuses on the protection of privacy. In the world of e-commerce or government there are many social issues and parts of society that are impacted by and the result of the use of technology. One of the most important issues for consumers is the protection of privacy. At the same time, this is a critical issue for business because until consumers are confident that their privacy will be protected in an e-business environment, they will refrain from its use. This part sketches the various legal avenues available to protect one's privacy under Commonwealth, State and Territory legislation and related laws. This discussion is important as there is no common law right to privacy save those provided for under trespass and related property rights. The significance of Freedom of Information legislation demonstrates that governments, the largest collector of personal information, have acted in an appropriate way with the data. A focus on privacy in telecommunications is featured in this part because of the very nature of cyber law. Criminal laws, industry codes and specific applications are examined here as well.

Part VII deals with cybercrime and law enforcement. Computer-related crime covers the area of e-business crime. Legal developments and cybercrime are introduced before a discussion of the substantial and procedural law in Australia. Consumers quite rightly are afraid to provide their credit card and other personal information over the Internet because an unauthorized person may get access to that information and use it to commit fraud or engage in other criminal conduct. The common mischiefs and specific cybercrimes are discussed here including cyber-stalking, cyber-bullying, online gambling, obscenity and pornography and anti-vilification and anti-terrorism laws. As with other aspects of cyberspace law, criminal laws may have extra-territorial reach and transcend geographical boundaries. Cyberspace may be extremely difficult to police since the crime may cross several borders and may be very difficult to detect. This part also reflects upon the difficulty of balancing public and private interests in regulating technology to maximize the benefits and minimize any harmful impacts, which technology might bring. The need for international cooperation, the collaboration between industry and law enforcement authorities as well as preventative private action against cybercrime is foremost when reflecting upon international developments.

Part VIII is a response of cyber law to environmental issues and the goals of product stewardship and environmental protection. E-waste management and product stewardship are both global and national concerns as are the local initiatives that have developed. The efforts to reduce e-waste in Australia, New Zealand and other jurisdictions are compared and the role of environmental legislation assessed. Governance and the regulatory framework for environmental law provide the structure for e-waste management for now and into the future.

Part IX briefly outlines developments in technology insofar as it relates to cyber law. Three technologies are examined in detail – geographic information systems, Web 2.0 environments and cloud computing and robotics. With geographic information systems as a technological development, standard legal theory and analysis is applied so that the context of the technology is thoroughly discussed. The law of contract, contracts for service and contracts of service, property rights and the protection thereof, privacy issues and the nature of location based services, liability and risks provide the framework for the discussion. Robotics and artificial intelligence is explored together given the potential impacts these may have on society and on the development of cyber law in this space. The policy framework and strategy will need to provide a coherent structure that both develops this new area of technology as well as the cyber law discipline to achieve the collective advantages and minimization of the risks to society and consumer safety.

Part X concludes by bringing all preceding parts together and discusses how cyber law may mitigate the various risks and strategies involved with these new technologies and the need for a framework of information governance and policy statements.

General Introduction

Chapter 1. General Background of the Country

§1. Geography

1. Australia is the lowest, flattest and, apart from Antarctica, the driest of the continents. Australia comprises a land area of almost 7.7 million square kilometres (sq. km).[1] This land mass makes Australia the sixth largest land area of all countries in the world exceeded only by Brazil, China, the United States of America, Canada, and Russia.

2. Australia is an island continent situated in the Southern Hemisphere between the Indian Ocean and the South Pacific. Except for the coastal areas, much of Australia is dry and arid. Australia's nearest neighbours are Papua New Guinea and Indonesia to the north, New Zealand to the southeast and the Melanesian and Polynesian Islands to the east.

3. In a jurisdictional and economic sense, Australia extends well beyond the mainland continent and Tasmania, including about 12,000 islands. While most of these islands are small, the United Nations Convention on the Law of the Sea allows Australian jurisdiction over large tracts of the ocean and seafloor that surround them. Australia also administers a portion of Antarctica, the Australian Antarctic Territory.

§2. Cultural Composition

4. Although recent migrants are more likely to be from Asia, a majority of Australians continue to be of Anglo-Saxon origin, and the dominant culture, language, manners and customs remain similar to those found in other Anglo-Saxon countries such as England, Canada and the United States. Recent migrants who have acquired permanent Australian resident status were born overseas comprise about 8% of Australia's population aged 15 years and over. The United Kingdom (14%) and India (13%) provided the highest number of recent migrants, followed by China (excluding Special Administrative Regions (SAR) and Taiwan) with 10%.[2] Australia in the

1. ABS 2012 1301.0 – Year Book Australia, 2012.
2. *Ibid.* ABS 2012 1301.0 – Year Book Australia, 2012.

twenty-first century is a multicultural country that is home to significant numbers of migrants from many countries, including Italy, Greece, China and Vietnam.

5. There were estimated to be about 800,000 Aboriginal and Torres Strait Islander people in Australia as of 2019, accounting for 3.3% of the total population.[3] Most of these Indigenous Australians live in non-remote areas (79.8%), and the indigenous population is much younger than the non-indigenous population. The median age was 21.8 years for Indigenous and 37.6 years for non-indigenous.

6. Indigenous Australians experience widespread socioeconomic disadvantage and health inequality. Factors like discrimination and racism, violence, alcohol and drug use and high psychological distress have a negative impact on their social and emotional well-being. Poor social and emotional well-being, in turn, can affect employment, income, living conditions and opportunities. The struggle for recognition and a rightful share of Australia's considerable wealth continues in the new century.

§3. Political System

I. The Constitution and System of Government

7. Australia has a federal system of government within which there are four divisions: Commonwealth, state, territory and local.[4]

8. The formal powers of the Commonwealth Parliament are constitutionally limited to areas of national importance such as trade and commerce, taxation, postal services, foreign relations, defence, immigration, naturalization, quarantine, currency and coinage, weights and measures, copyright, patents and trademarks.[5]

9. However, High Court decisions, Commonwealth-state agreements and use by the Commonwealth of the constitutional power to make grants to the states and territories, have seen the Commonwealth gain influence to other matters including industrial relations, financial regulation, companies and securities, health and welfare and education.

10. All powers not specifically granted by the Constitution to the Commonwealth government are reserved to the states.

---

3. *See* Australian Institute of Health and Welfare (2019) *Australia's Welfare in brief'*, Cat. No. AUS227, Canberra: AIHW, p. 60.
4. Australian Parliament House, Parliamentary Library 2011, *Parliamentary Handbook of the Commonwealth of Australia* (32nd ed., Canberra).
5. *Commonwealth of Australia Constitution Act* 1900 (Imp) 63 and 64 Vic, c 12 (Imp).

11. If there is an inconsistency between state and commonwealth law, the commonwealth legislation prevails.[6]

12. More than half of Parliament's time is taken up with the consideration of proposed legislation. Between 150 and 250 Bills are passed each year, and most are non-contentious, either being 'machinery' legislation necessary for the orderly processes of government, or Bills that propose alterations to existing legislation. Most of the Bills are government Bills; legislation sponsored by private members is rare.

13. The Australian nation was created by the federation of the six British self-governing colonies of New South Wales (NSW), Tasmania, Queensland, Western Australia, Victoria and South Australia (SA). Under the constitutional arrangements that came into existence in 1901, significant powers were retained by these states. State administrative responsibilities include education, police, public health, public transport, agriculture, roads, community services, corrective services, mineral resources, emergency services, ports and the oversight of local government.

14. The state governments derive from the former British Colonies established by British Act of Parliament. However, today, all Australian states have their own constitutions and complete political independence from Britain. All states, except Queensland, have a bicameral legislature with an upper house serving some type of review function. Queensland employs a unicameral parliament.

15. The Northern Territory (NT) and the Australian Capital Territory (ACT) came under the control of the Commonwealth Government in 1911. The NT (since 1978) and the ACT (since 1989) are self-governing territories with powers almost matching those of the states.

16. The Australian political system is one of democratically elected governments – general elections must be held at least once every three years. The governmental framework in Australia draws on features from both the British parliamentary system and the American checks and balances system. Australia is a constitutional monarchy with allegiance to the Queen who maintains a representative at Commonwealth and state levels. By virtue of the Australia Act 1986 (Cth), however, Australia terminated all British control over the former colonies, which would in any way be inconsistent with Australian sovereignty. There is much debate about whether Australia should become a republic and have a president.

17. The government is formed by the majority party in the lower house of Parliament, the leader of which serves as Prime Minister assisted by a cabinet comprised of other members of Parliament drawn from both the House of Representatives (lower house) and Senate (upper house). Membership in the House of Representatives representing geographic regions based upon proportion of population (totalling 150 members) while the Senate is comprised of an equal number of senators (ten) from each state and two from each of the Territories.

---

6. Australian Constitution, s. 92.

18. Since WWII the balance of political power has shifted markedly in favour of the federal government. This is especially so since 1942, when the Commonwealth government began collecting income tax revenue that was then re-apportioned to the states on an agreed formula. The Commonwealth government, supported by the Australian High Court, has also used its 'external affairs' powers to commit Australia to various treaty obligations, which have enabled the Commonwealth government in turn to override any inconsistent state laws.[7]

II. Judicial Power

19. The highest court in Australia is the High Court, which consists of seven justices, though it is unusual for the court to sit en banc.[8] The High Court hears appeals from the state Supreme Courts and is the final Court of Appeal in the Australian legal system. It also acts as the guardian and interpreter of the Australian Constitution. The High Court has original jurisdiction in matters such as indictable Commonwealth offences.

20. Also, on the federal level is the Family Court of Australia, which governs marriage disputes as per the Family Law Act 1975 (Cth).

21. The Federal Court of Australia was created by the Federal Court of Australia Act 1976 (Cth) and began to exercise its jurisdiction on 1 February 1977. The Federal Court of Australia has original jurisdiction in other federal matters, such as industrial law, patents, trademarks, bankruptcy and antitrust. The Federal Court sits in all capital cities as well as other locations from time to time throughout Australia.

22. The Federal Court's original jurisdiction is conferred by over 150 statutes of the Parliament. The Federal Court also has a broad range of appellate jurisdiction.

23. The Federal Court shares first instance jurisdiction with the Supreme Courts of the States and Territories in the area of intellectual property (hereinafter IP) (copyright, patents, trademarks, designs and circuit layouts).[9]

24. Appeal from the Federal Court is to the Full Court of the Federal Court and possibly to the High Court. Each of the States and Territories has its own court system that is comprised of various administrative tribunals, inferior courts, a court of general jurisdiction and a Court of Appeal.

---

7. *See, e.g., Commonwealth of Australia v. State of Tasmania* (1983) 158 CLR 1, in which the Commonwealth Government relied on its obligations pursuant to a world heritage area designation to block the construction of a dam.
8. Until 1986 it was possible to have an appeal from a state Supreme Court to the Privy Council in England. This avenue of appeal ended with the passage of the *Australia Act* 1986 (Cth).
9. http://www.fedcourt.gov.au/about/jurisdiction.

III. Political Parties

25. Australian parliaments have been dominated by the tightly controlled parties since the early twentieth century. Strong party discipline and party unity has made political attitudes more predictable and tended to narrow the parliamentary debate.

26. Australia today has two major political parties: The Labor Party, which on most matters is further to the political left than the more conservative Liberal-National Party coalition, which ruled Australia from the 1950s through the 1970s, and again during much of the past decade. During the 1980s, the Labor Party was in the majority, led for most of that time by Robert Hawke and by Paul Keating. From 1996–2007 Australia was led by the Liberal-National party coalition under the leadership of John Howard. Kevin Rudd was elected prime minister in 2007 and replaced in June 2010 by Julia Guillard, who became Australia's twenty-seventh prime minister and the first woman to win that position. In June 2013, Mr Rudd's party returned him to the leadership and he once again became Prime Minister. The 2013 election saw the return to government of the Liberal-National Party Coalition and the election of Tony Abbott as Australia's Prime Minister, subsequently deposed by Malcolm Turnbull in 2015 and then replaced by Scott Morrison in 2018.

27. Other political parties attract significant support but in small numbers. The Democratic Party for a time had controlled the balance of power in the Federal Senate by agreeing to cast its votes with either Labor or Liberal in order to give them a majority. The Country National Party represents agricultural interests and usually forms a coalition with the conservative Liberal party. In the 2016 Federal Elections for the 45th Parliament of Australia the Greens, the Nick Xenophon Team, Katter's Australian Party, and independents Wilkie and McGowan won a seat each. For the first time since federation, the post-election opposition won more seats than the post-election government in the two most populous states, NSW and Victoria.

§4. Population

28. Though occupying a land mass as large as the size of the continental United States, much of Australia is a sparsely populated desert. Most of the population of approximately 22.4 million live on the fertile coastal regions, and approximately half of the population resides in the seven capital cities. Of these capital cities, Sydney has approximately 4.6 million people, Melbourne 4.2 million, Brisbane 2.1 million, Perth 1.8 million and Adelaide 1.2 million people. Ironically, despite its large land mass and small population, Australia has a population density that makes it one of the most urbanized countries in the world. At the time of writing, Australia's unemployment rate was 5.1% in November 2018.[10]

10. Australian Bureau of Statistics (2018) 6202.0 – Labour Force, Australia (November 2018), at https://www.abs.gov.au/ausstats/abs@.nsf/mf/6202.0.

§5. ECONOMY

29. Australia is a developed country and rich in natural resources. Farming and mining continue to be major exports along with a rapidly growing service industry and minor manufacturing.

30. According to the Heritage Economic Freedom Index, Australia ranks third of all countries behind Hong Kong (first) and Singapore (second). Inflation rate has been low (1.8%) and Australia attracts approximately AUD 60 billion a year in direct foreign investment.[11] Over the twenty years the Index has been in existence, Australia has been among the top ten in terms of overall improvement – a testament to its long-term commitment and achievements in economic reform.[12]

31. Australia's leading farm products are cattle, wheat and wool, followed by dairy products. Australia's major sources of economic activity include: agriculture (including forestry and fishing), mining and quarrying, manufacturing, tourism, and education and financial services (including insurance, real estate and business).[13]

32. Australia is the world's largest exporter of wool and a major exporter of sugar, beef and wheat, rice, eggs, cotton, potatoes and vegetables. Major mining exports are bauxite, industrial diamonds, lead, copper, gold, iron ore, manganese, silver, aluminium, zinc, and nickel.

33. Major service industries include: financial services, tourism, transport, communication, and education.

34. Manufacturing exports include: cars, processed foods, clothing, shoes, and household appliances.

35. Australia also has a significant fishing industry, exporting lobsters, abalone, oysters, prawns, scallops, salmon, and tuna.

36. Australia's major two-way trading partners are China followed by Japan. Approximately 70% of Australia's trade is conducted with Asia-Pacific Economic Cooperation (APEC) nation members.[14]

---

11. http://www.heritage.org/index/country/australia.
12. http://www.heritage.org/index/.
13. Economy Watch: available at www.economywatch.com/world_economy/australia/?page=full.
14. Department of Foreign Affairs and Trade: Composition of Trade Australia. https://dfat.gov.au/about-us/publications/Documents/cot-2018.pdf.

37. Australia has been an active player in the G-20 and internationally through its participation in World Trade Organization (WTO) and other international organizations.[15] In addition it has multiple bilateral and other free trade agreements with other countries.[16]

38. As an advanced economy, Australia has also been among the leading countries in its promotion of both e-government and e-commerce. It consequently has introduced and continues to work on providing the necessary legal infrastructure to promote these developments. This infrastructure includes the general promotion of e-government with cognate legislation.

§6. Social and Cultural Values

39. Australia has a mixed free enterprise economy and it has significantly deregulated some industries, such as banking and aviation. Like many Western democracies, Australia has increasingly moved to a view of government as a guide for general policy, as opposed to a primary deliverer of services. This has led to significant outsourcing of traditional government activities to the private sector and to a blurring of public and private sector economic activity.

40. The social and cultural values that shape and form the foundation of Australia's legal system are found in the traditional freedoms of a free enterprise economy. These include private ownership of property and the right to make a profit from it, freedom of contract, commerce and industry to engage in any pursuit one chooses, freedom of association, whereby one is free to join with others in a commercial venture and freedom of labour, whereby one is free to contract to work in any position as mutually agreed between employer and employee.

41. Australia's cultural values are increasingly shaped by a global economy, as trade barriers have come down, and Australian businesses have operated on an international scale. Economic and social values have also been impacted by Australia's rapid uptake of information technology, such as the Internet. The growth of e-commerce has further accelerated Australia's more global outlook and presents significant challenges to existing commercial laws, which are premised in a world of paper commerce.

15. J.R. Wiseman, *Global Nation: Australia? Australia and the Politics of Globalization* (Cambridge University Press 1998).
16. T. Ciro, B. Maacitelli & S. Muthaly, *Australia and the Global Economy* (Connor Court Pub. 2009).

Chapter 2. The Information Communication Technology (ICT) Infrastructure

§1. Cyber Law Concepts

42. The following section presents brief definitions of key concepts from law, economics, technology, innovation theory, and marketing that will be used throughout this work.

43. E-commerce. In its broadest sense, e-commerce is any type of business transaction or interaction in which one conducts the business or trade electronically. In general, the 'e' in front of any additional activity done off-line refers to the same activity done in an electronic environment. Thus, we speak of e-government, e-conveyancing and e-democracy. Sometimes abbreviations denote relationships such as B2C (business-to-consumer); B2B (business-to-business), G2C (government-to-consumer), C2G (consumer-to-government); G2B (government-to-business).[17]

44. Peer-to-Peer (P2P) *computing. 'Peer-to-peer' computing* is where the end user's computer becomes the storage device which can be accessed by others.[18] Peer-to-peer computing has grown rapidly with people sharing music and videos through such software as BitTorrent, Gnutella and Limewire, and Bearshare. Each of these terms reflects profound changes in the way that society operates and the distribution of political, economic and other power within society.

45. Digital Constitutionalism refers to how the Internet/Web has altered the balance of power. Constitutional Law is study of division of power. The boundaries of information law and rights in digital architecture raise important issues of digital constitutionalism. There is great debate about the extent to which the Internet encourages the growth of greater democracy.[19]

*46. Free (*Libre*) and Open Source Software (FOSS).* Until the early 1970s software was often provided free and users were given both the machine readable or executable code that runs on the computer as well as the source code, the human readable code that provides the programming instructions. Since the 1970s, however, companies began releasing only the machine code, but not the sourceware.[20] Eric Raymond has labelled this the 'Cathedral' model, that is, software designed and

17. http://www.investopedia.com/terms/e/ecommerce.asp.
18. Milojecic et al., Peer-to-Peer Computing (2002) at http://www.cs.ucsb.edu/~almeroth/classes/F02.276/papers/p2p.pdf and Kisembe, P., *Future of Peer-to-Peer Technology with the rise of Cloud Computing*, 8(2–3) Intl J Peer to Peer Networks (August 2017) at http://airccse.org/ijp2p/papers/8317ijp2p04.pdf.
19. W. Yuan, *E- democracy @China: Does it Work?* 3 Chinese J. Commun. 488–503 (2010), doi:10.1080/17544750.2010.516581.
20. J. Lu, *Chinese Culture and Software Copyright,* 11 New Media & Soc. 1372–1393 (2009). doi:10.1177/1461444809341262.

controlled by a small elite.[21] In contrast to this is the 'FOSS' model which Raymond said was more like a 'Bazaar', open to the public with many individual contributors and much fewer restrictions. The Open Source model has been championed especially by Richard Stallman who founded the GNU Project which involved free distribution of software which can track the contributions of each person with the provision that each contributor must make the source code available or open to all under the same terms (known as the GNU General Public Licence (GNU GPL)).[22]

47. This FOSS movement has also led to new models of e-commerce on the Internet and new ways to commercialize open source architectures, including models utilizing P2P interactions and relying on social media and sale of advertising. Facebook, YELP, and Google are examples of these new models. These models increase revenues by making advertising more valuable. In response, traditional players such as Apple have further evolved their models, for example by the introduction of iTunes.

48. The *Internet* refers to the distributed international network of computers that has revolutionized the way we create and use information. As such it has changed almost all aspects of our lives.

49. M-Commerce (Mobile Commerce) refers to the rapidly growing use of mobile devices, especially phones, to conduct business over wireless devices and technologies.[23] Examples include payment systems over one's mobile phone, and push notification by retailers of various sales to mobile devices.

50. Cloud Computing. Although the term 'cloud computing' is recent, the idea of sharing by various businesses a remote and centralized computing facility has been around since the mid-1960s. In a broader sense, cloud computing today refers to a paradigm shift from computing systems that are on-site to a utility model in which shared and scalable technology infrastructure, software applications and business processes are provided over the Internet for a fee. In a cloud environment, servers, operation systems, application software, development, upgrade, maintenance, security, backup, disaster recovery and other business functions no longer reside inside the business or government IT department. Instead, they are delivered via the Internet in the cloud.[24]

---

21. E. Raymond, *The Cathedral and the Bazaar* (2000), http://www.catb.org/~esr/writings/cathedral-bazaar/cathedral-bazaar/index.html.
22. N. Wardrip-Fruin, Noah and N. Montfort, *The GNU Manifesto*, The New Media Reader 545–550 (MIT 2003).
23. Gus Ortega-Montiel, *m-Commerce: Mobile Transactions in Australia* (2014), at https://www.acma.gov.au/publications/2014-06/report/snapshot-m-commerce-mobile-transactions-australia.
24. E. Clark & I. Sims, *Flying into the Hurricane: Law, Policy and Practice Implications of Cloud Computing*, 1 Intl. J. Tech. L. Policy 135–151 (2012).

51. World Wide Web 1.0, 2.0, 3.0, Semantic Web. The *Word Wide Web (Web 1.0)* (WWW) is understood to have occupied the period between 1994 and 2003. Whereas the Internet is the actual physical infrastructure the WWW refers to the data and information shared online. This was the dominant model from the beginning of the Internet to about 2003.[25]

52. Web 2.0 (2004 to present) refers to the development of the WWW as an interactive, collaborative medium as opposed to the passive storage of information models that characterized its earlier uses. This new model, enabled and supported by new software applications such as java script, involved such interactions as: user participation, dispersion of information, the user as a contributor, rich user experience and free classification of information by the user of that information. These new characteristics provide a much 'richer user experience' than earlier models.[26] Examples include social media such as wikis, blogs, Twitter, and Facebook.

53. Semantic or Intelligent Web (Web 3.0). This future version of the Web is one that involves 'intelligent machines' that can perform machine reasoning, and learning that enables it to infer meaning. [27] The underlying technology architecture can enable more meaningful interaction because it enables 'understanding' of and 'makes connections' between pieces of data.[28] A useful way to think about the various iterations of the web is to think of Web 1.0 as (Read-Only); Web 2.0 as (Read-Write) and Web 3.0 as (Read-Write-Execute).[29] The Semantic web is more likely to be open source, widely distributed, available anywhere and using natural language.

54. Convergence and the Internet of Things (IOT). Convergence has several meanings and contexts. One meaning is the convergence of technologies that assume multiple functions that used to be carried out by separate devices. For example, the Wii is a games console, a web browser and a social networking tool. Mobile phones are digital cameras, camcorders, voice recorders, text machines, game stations and phones.

---

25. http://www.labnol.org/internet/web-3-concepts-explained/8908/.
26. D. Breakenridge, *PR 2.0: New Media, New Tools, New Audiences* (1st ed., FT Press 2008); A McAfee, *Enterprise 2.0: The Dawn of Emergent Collaboration*, 47 MIT Sloan Mgt. Rev. 21–28 (2006).
27. http://www.labnol.org/internet/web-3-concepts-explained/8908/.
28. http://www.macmillandictionary.com/buzzword/entries/web3.html.
29. The term was coined by Tim Berners-Lee, the inventor of the WWW and director of the World Wide Web Consortium ('W3C'), which oversees the development of proposed Semantic Web standards. He defines the Semantic Web as 'a web of data that can be processed directly and indirectly by machines'.

55. However, media convergence involves far greater change than a technology shift. Indeed, it changes the relationships between users, genres, industries and markets. It changes the flow of media, who uses what, how they use it and the relationships among the various community of users, communication media and content producers. In short, convergence changes and challenges existing economic, social, political and legal paradigms.[30]

56. A related concept to convergence is the IOT which refers to the growing connectivity between our various devices.[31] Connected devices can communicate with consumers, transmit data back to companies, and compile data for third parties such as researchers, health care providers, or even other consumers, who can measure how their product usage compares with that of their neighbours. The devices can provide important benefits to consumers: they can handle tasks on a consumer's behalf, improve efficiency, and enable consumers to control elements of their home or work environment from a distance. At the same time, the data collection and sharing that smart devices and greater connectivity enable pose privacy, security and other risks.

57. The *'Embedded' Internet* is a term that refers to the reality that the Internet is no longer something external to us but has become embedded into our daily lives.[32] For example, Facebook with many active users, often devoting hours of their daily lives, to interacting on their site. The Facebook community is larger than most countries in the world. New technology giving rise to new forms of business, government and even personal relationships has meant that almost every area of law has been impacted. However, as these developments become mainstreamed and the Information Age matures, it is predicted that the boundaries between Internet Law as a separate subject will gradually disappear.

58. *Virtual Worlds and New Forms of Property.* As the Internet becomes more pervasive in all aspects of life, whole new 'virtual' dimensions have arisen, for example Second Life, which have challenged traditional notions of 'property' and given rise to separate identities and the world of avatars.[33]

59. *Knowledge or Information Economy.* While much debate continues amongst social scientists about whether we have transitioned from an industrial to an information age (The Fourth Industrial Revolution), there can be little doubt that almost everything we do in our twenty-first century society is intimately connected with information creation, retrieval, processing or management to the point where we might even say that today we 'live and breathe' information in an information environment. Our relationship to knowledge is a paramount consideration and has led

30. H. Jenkins, *Convergence Culture: Where Old and New Media Collide* (New York University Press 2006). H. Rheingold, *Smart Mobs: The Next Social Revolution* (Perseus 2000).
31. *See* Atzori et al., *The Internet of Things. A Survey* (2010), at https://www.cs.mun.ca/courses/cs6910/IoT-Survey-Atzori-2010.pdf.
32. *From Mobile to Embedded Internet*: ww.iith.ac.in/~tbr/teaching/presentations/15.pdf.
33. http://secondlife.com/. In ICT, an avatar is the graphical representation of a user or a user's alter ego or character. An icon or figure representing a person in a computer game or on the Internet.

people to talk in terms of an information or knowledge economy. The emphasis is on informational activities and an information industry.[34]

60. Innovation, Disruption and Market Life Cycles. The features of the Internet have stimulated user-led innovation and production of digital content in what has been termed the 'democratizing of innovation'.[35] End users of games and other forms of digital content themselves become producers in order to customize the product or for the purpose of redistribution and enhancement. The terms 'produser' to refer to these producer-consumers and 'produsage' to describe the process of creative reuse.[36]

61. The initial impact of innovation can be dramatic and highly and immediately disruptive.[37] In other areas, real change may come later. For example, ten years after Internet one need only look at impact on newspapers, battles over digital rights and legal system straining to come to grip with the new realities of an Internet Age. In this new Age, there will be profound disruptions in the values, beliefs and practices related to our private lives (protecting privacy, controlling data), in public life (e.g., the need to promote competition, fight terrorism) and our new and rapidly changing information lives, that is, how we use and relate to information.[38]

62. The reality is that there are only twenty-four hours a day and fewer than that in hours awake. Throughout the history of media, a new media takes away customer time from older media and older media dramatically declines. TV, for example, replaced radio, 8-Track cartridges and then compact discs (CD) replaced vinyl records. iTunes now prevails over CDs. Most recently, apps have replaced iTunes – and it took only five years! Revenues from apps were up over AUD 36 billion from last year and rising rapidly.[39] According to data compiled by Intel, 47,000 apps are downloaded every minute![40]

§2. Australia's Competitive Position and Challenges in the Knowledge and Information Economy

63. In this globalized world, Australia has its advantages and disadvantages. Advantages include a well-educated population with a high take-up rate of new

34. J.*H. Boyett & J.T. Boyett, The Guru Guide to the Knowledge Economy. John Wiley& Sons. And Tapscott, Donald. 1996. The Digital Economy.* McGraw-Hill.
35. Eric von Hippel, Democratizing Innovation, http://mitpress.mit.edu/books/democratizing-innovation.
36. Axel Bruns, *Blogs, Wikipedia, Second Life and Beyond: From Production to Produsage* (Peter Lang 2008).
37. Larry Downes & Paul Nunes, *Big Bang Disruption*, Harv. Bus. Rev. (2013), http://hbr.org/2013/03/big-bang-disruption/.
38. *Ibid.*
39. Horace Dediu, *Apps Overtook Music in Less than Five Years – All of Big Media is Next*, at https://qz.com/140507/apps-overtook-music-in-less-than-five-years-all-of-big-media-is-next/.
40. What's Happening on China Internet in One Minute; Top 20 Downloaded Android Social Apps in China.

technology, a solid base of scientific, engineering, and technical expertise and an improved regulatory framework. Australia is also advantaged because of its multicultural society and depth of cultural awareness. This multicultural talent enables Australia to develop and sustain international and global cross-cultural networks upon which tomorrow's business will be based.

64. The disadvantages include distance from major markets, small and aging population, lack of venture capital, under-funded research and education, small size of Australian firms, existence of few head offices of international companies, over-dependence on mining and agriculture, and threats of a significant brain drain of Australia's best and brightest to Europe, America, and elsewhere. The National Strategic Framework for the Information Economy report in December 1998 listed comparative advantages for Australia, a picture which is largely the same today.[41]

65. While Australia has its competitive advantages, challenges remain. According to the Business Council of Australia and others, those challenges include several key reforms, including the need, among others to invest in infrastructure; sustain and even grow its population; implement the Australian National Broadband Network (NBN); repair federal finances, engage in regulatory (financial system, taxation and labour) reforms; reduce the amount of regulatory red tape; and, design laws and regulatory systems that better facilitate the growth of start-ups and sustainable development.[42]

§3. Current State of the Australian Economy

66. Australia was one of the few countries not to go into a recession following the global financial crisis between mid-2007 and early 2009. Government surpluses were expended during this period and Australia begins the second decade of the twenty-first century with significant debts.

67. Since the 2016 Pre-Election Economic and Fiscal Outlook (PEFO) the underlying cash deficit of AUD 37.1 billion (2.2% of Gross Domestic Product (GDP)) is expected in 2016–2017, and improving to a deficit of AUD 5.9 billion (0.3% of GDP) in 2019–2020 as shown in Table 1.[43]

---

41. *See* NOIE 1988, *A Strategic Framework for the Information Economy – Identifying Priorities for Action, National Office for the Information Economy* (December 1998), at www.noie.gov.au/nationalstrategy/index.html.
42. Australian Business Council, *Action Plan for Enduring Prosperity* (2013), at http://www.acbc.com.au/.
43. PEFO 2016, https://treasury.gov.au/publication/pre-election-economic-and-fiscal-outlook-2016.

*Table 1 Major Economic Parameters**

	Outcomes	*Forecasts*			*Projections*	
	2014–2015 (%)	*2015–2016 (%)*	*2016–2017 (%)*	*2017–2018 (%)*	*2018–2019 (%)*	*2019–2020 (%)*
Real GDP	2	2.5	2.5	3.0	3.0	3.0
Employment	1.5	2.0	1.75	1.75	1.25	1.5
Unemployment rate	6.1	5.75	5.5	5.5	5.5	5.5
Consumer price index	1.5	1.25	2.0	2.25	2.5	2.5
Wage price index	2.3	2.25	2.5	2.75	3.25	3.5
Nominal GDP	1.6	2.5	4.25	5.0	5.0	5.0

Source: ABS cat. No. 5206.0, 6202.0, 6345.0, 6401.0

*Year average growth unless otherwise stated. From 2014–2015 to 2017–2018, employment and the wage price index are through the year growth to the June quarter. The unemployment rate is the rate for the June quarter. The consumer price index is through the year growth to the June quarter.

68. Australia's real GDP is expected to grow by 2.75% in 2018–2019 and this growth is expected to strengthen to 3% in 2019–2020.[44] The growth outlook is forecast to support continuing employment growth and keeping unemployment rates low. Economic growth is broadly based indicating a transition away from mining investments. Household consumption, non-mining business investment are expected to support GDP growth over the forecast period. Mining and services exports are expected to support GDP growth.

69. Employment growth is expected to be strong *albeit* slightly slower. The unemployment rate is forecast to fall to 5.5% in the June quarter of 2017 from 5.75% in the June quarter of 2016.

§4. AUSTRALIA'S DIGITAL ECONOMY

70. Key indicators of business use of IT include: Internet access; the use of broadband; web presence; social media presence; and Internet commerce (i.e., the placing and receiving of orders via the Internet) (*see below* Table 2).[45]

71. For the first time, over half of businesses in the Retail trade industry (59%) had a web presence, while 56% had a social media presence.

44. MYEFO 2018–2019 at https://www.budget.gov.au/2018-19/content/myefo/index.html.
45. *See* ABS 2018 *8166.0 – Summary of IT Use and Innovation in Australian Business*, 2016–2017.

72. More than a third of businesses reported having received orders via the Internet (37%), with income obtained from these orders totalling an estimated AUD 394 billion. The scope of Internet income estimates includes both B2B and B2C orders and as such is not adjusted to include only the value-added component of a sale.[46]

Table 2 Business Use of Information Technology, Selected Indicators(a) 2014–2015 to 2016–2017

		2014–2015	*2015–2016*	*2016–2017*
Estimated number of businesses(b)	000	776	799	831
Businesses with(c):				
Internet access	%	94.8	95.3	95.4
web presence	%	48.6	50.1	51.1
social media presence	%	34.0	38.2	40.4
Businesses with Internet access(c):				
broadband as main connection	%	99.2	99.3	99.4
Businesses that:				
placed orders via the Internet	%	55.7	57.0	59.3
received orders via the Internet	%	33.8	36.8	37.1
Internet income(d)	AUD (b)	285.5	321.4	394.3

Notes:

(a) Proportions are of all businesses in each output category.

(b) Business counts are provided for contextual information only.

(c) As at the end of the reference period, 30 June.

(d) ABS uses the Organization for Economic Co-operation and Development (OECD)[47] narrow definition of e-commerce transactions when collecting data on Internet orders and Internet income. Internet income is defined as income resulting from goods and services ordered over the Internet where the commitment to purchase is via the Internet.

73. While 95.4% of Australian businesses had Internet access about half (51.1%) had an online presence in 2016–2017.

74. When it comes to online orders, the proportion of businesses that placed orders online increased from 55.7% in 2014–2015 to 59.3% in 2016–2017. However, there is a noticeable gap between those businesses placing orders online and

46. Further data relating to the proportion of income from Internet orders received, *see* ABS 2018, *Selected Characteristics of Australian Business* (cat. no. 8167.0).
47. *See* OECD http://www.keepeek.com/Digital-Asset-Management/oecd/science-and-technology/oecd-guide-to-measuring-the-information-society-2011_9789264113541-en.

those accepting orders online. There was very little movement when it came to the latter, with 37.1% in 2016–2017 compared to 33.8% in 2014–2015 of Australian businesses accepting orders online.

75. Despite the stagnation in the share of businesses that accepted orders online, the income earned from online orders has grown significantly. In total, AUD 285.5 billion was earned by Australian businesses through online orders in 2014–2015 which increased to AUD 394.3 billion in 2016–2017, an increase of 38.1% over the period.

§5. Participation of Australians in the Digital Economy

I. Internet Activity

76. Internet subscribers. There were 14.7 million Internet subscribers in Australia at the end of June 2018.[48] This is an increase of 3.6% from the end of December 2017.

77. Fibre connections grew by 69.8% between 2017 and 2018 reaching 3.6 million subscribers.

78. Data downloads. The total volume of data downloaded in the three months ended 30 June 2018 was 3.8 million Terabytes (or 3.8 Exabytes). This is a 7.0% increase in data downloads when compared with the three months ended 31 December 2017 and a 28.1% increase compared with the three months ended June 2017.

79. Data downloaded via fixed line broadband (3.7 million Terabytes) accounted for 96.8% of all Internet downloads in the three months ended 30 June 2018.

80. Mobile handset subscribers. As at 30 June 2018, there were approximately 27.0 million mobile handset subscribers in Australia. This is an increase of 1.1% since December 2017.

81. The volume of data downloaded via mobile handsets for the three months ended 30 June 2018 was 246,765 Terabytes. This was a 21.5% increase in data downloads via mobile handsets when compared with the three months ended 30 December 2017 and a 40.9% increase in downloads compared to the three months ended 30 June 2017.

48. ABS 2018 8153.0 – Internet Activity, Australia, June 2018.

II. Household Use of IT

82. The proportion of households with access to the Internet at home has been steadily climbing since 2004–2005 but remained constant between 2014–2015 and 2016–2017 at 86%.[49]

83. For households with children aged under 15 years, 97% had access to the Internet compared with 82% of households without children under 15.

84. Households located in major cities were more likely to have Internet access at home (88%) than those in remote or very remote parts of Australia (77%).

85. *Devices to access Internet at home.* Desktop or laptop computers are used by 91% of connected households. Similarly, mobile or smart phones are also used by 91% of connected households.

86. Tablets were the next most popular type of device used by 66% of households to connect to the internet. Internet connected TVs had the largest increase in usage by households, from 27% in 2014–2015 to 42% in 2016–2017. Internet connected music or video player devices showed a drop in usage from 26% in 2014–2015 to 19% in 2016–2017.

87. *Child protection online indicators.* In 2016–2017, 14% of connected households with children aged 5–14 stated a child had been exposed to inappropriate material and 5% of these households stated a child aged 5–14 had been subject to cyber-bullying.

88. *Internet users and cyber security indicators.* In 2016–2017, 5% of Internet users stated they had experienced abuse of personal information and 9% of Internet users stated they had experienced damage or loss caused by a virus or other computer infection.

89. *Internet access by persons.* In 2016–17, 87% of people were Internet users (persons aged 15 years and over who accessed the Internet in the last three months). People aged 15 to 17 years were the highest proportion of Internet users (98%) compared with the older age group (65 years and over) which had the lowest proportion of Internet users (55%).

90. The three most popular online activities were entertainment, social networking and banking (all 80%). The proportion of internet users accessing the Internet for health services or health research has increased from 22% of Internet users in 2014–2015 to 46% in 2016–2017.

---

49. ABS 2018 8146.0 – Household Use of Information Technology, Australia, 2016–2017.

§6. Emerging Markets and Potential Growth of Australia's Digital Economy

91. Australia has been a leading country both in e-government and in its moves toward an information economy. Government in Australia, like its counterparts in the United States,[50] United Kingdom,[51] Canada,[52] and elsewhere, has sought to transform itself into e-government while at the same time promoting e-business generally.

92. As the world economy recovers from the global financial crisis and as a direct result of significant investment by the Australian government in digital infrastructure, it is a safe prediction that the Australian information economy will continue to grow in all areas: B2C, B2B, and e-government. As demonstrated by Australia's Internet usage statistics quoted above, the size and importance of e-commerce and e-government activity will become increasingly substantial. The efficiencies brought about by e-commerce are expected to produce changed employment patterns. Some areas will grow; others will contract. Demand is likely to be strongest in the areas related to tourism, education, and associated activities. While all States and Territories are winners in terms of efficiency gains, there will be some major adjustments required for those regions relying on traditional export activities.

93. Looking to the future, Australia's presence in a rapidly growing Asian region looks promising. Julian Linklaters Report[53] predicts the exponential growth in broadband connections in emerging markets to grow from 1.3 to 3.7 billion in five years creating substantial opportunities for Australian telecommunications equipment providers, developers and content providers. For example, the report shows that most opportunities in content and applications will come in the form of mobile financial services, which are expected to grow to 876 million users by 2017 generating a market value of almost AUD 30 billion.

94. Cloud ICT services spend by customers in emerging markets was AUD 2.2 billion in 2012 and is set to grow to AUD 10.4 billion by 2017.[54] Cloud ICT – whether Infrastructure as a service, software as a service (SaaS) or platform as a service (PaaS) – will open up new markets for the Australian ICT industry.

---

50. http://firstgov.gov/.
51. www.ukonline.gov.uk.
52. www.gc.ca/. Canada is reputed to be one of the world's leaders in e-government, particularly in the procurement of goods and services. Canada's system, called MERX, provides potential suppliers around the world with a subscriber-based e-tendering service.
53. Julian Linklaters, *Generation Next: 5 Pathways to TMT Growth in Emerging Markets* (2013), at www.tmtgenerationnext.com.
54. *Ibid.*

95. Mobile health is set to generate around AUD 8.8 billion of annual revenues for technology, media and telecommunications (TMT) providers in emerging markets by 2017, as governments use broadband infrastructure to improve health outcomes and maximize healthcare resources. The deployment of mobile health services is becoming a standard component of healthcare delivery.[55]

96. Finally, m-Commerce will continue to grow. In 2014, smartphone adoption in emerging markets will explode.[56] The total number of mobile subscriptions, however, will exceed 7 billion by 2014, according to the International Telecommunications Union (ITU).

55. *See also Deloitte, Technology, Media & Telecommunications (TMT) Predictions* 2019, at https://www2.deloitte.com/au/en/pages/technology-media-and-telecommunications/articles/tmt-predictions.html.
56. Christopher Mims, *In 2014 the next Billion Will Access the Mobile Internet – at $20 a Handset* (6 Jan. 2014), at http://qz.com/163621/in-2014-the-next-billion-will-access-the-mobile-internet-at-20-a-handset/.

Chapter 3. ICT Market and e-Government

§1. Definition of E-Government

97. While there is no uniform or generally accepted definition of it, e-Government can be conceived as the 'e-business of the state'. The UN Global E-government Readiness Report 2004 defined e-government as 'the use of ICT and its application by governments for the provision of information and basic public services to people'.[57] This is justifiable by the fact that both e-government and e-business use the same infrastructure, hardware and sometimes also software. E-Government is the application of ICT to transform the efficiency, effectiveness, transparency and accountability of informational and transactional exchanges within government, between governments and government agencies at federal, state and local levels, citizens and businesses; and to empower citizens through access and use of information and knowledge.

§2. Law and E-Government

98. Legal Infrastructure: One of the essentials for the achievement of a leading Information Economy is the establishment of a legal infrastructure that provides the guidance and certainty required for domestic and foreign businesses to invest in that growth.[58] Australia has realized that the Information Economy will not eventuate unless the legal infrastructure is in place to promote and support it. The legal infrastructure required to support this new architecture and government initiatives in e-commerce law includes the provision of ICT infrastructure; regulations governing content; domain names; protection of intellectual property rights (IPR); electronic signatures and public key encryption; electronic procurement; Convention recognizing electronic form of contracts in B2B international trade; consumer protection and responsive criminal and civil law; protection of privacy; online dispute resolution (ODR); and border protection.

99. If law is to be relevant to, and keep up with, this new e-government environment, it is also important to see law as part of a wider system with many parts that must converge if e-government is to succeed.[59]

100. E-government should also be considered within the larger context of the country's innovation system. This is because the infrastructure provided by e-government is a major factor in the promotion of innovation.

---

57. United Nations, *Global E-government Readiness Report: Towards Access for Opportunity*, Geneva: Department of Economic and Social Affairs & Division for Public Administration and Development Management, UN Publication, 1–182 (2004).
58. J. Ramsfield, *The Law as Architecture* (West-Thomson 2000); Bela Banathy, *Designing Social Systems in a Changing World* (Plenum Press 1996).
59. S.C. Bhatnagar, *E-government: From Vision to Implementation: A Practical Guide with Case Studies* (Sage Publications 2002); and Irani, Zahir & Peter Lov, *Evaluating Information Systems* (Routledge 2013).

§3. GOVERNMENT'S ROLE IN PROMOTING E-BUSINESS

101. The Australian government in support of its *Digital Economy Australia* has established several agencies responsible for various elements of e-commerce.[60] These include the following agencies:

102. *Department of Communications* as the lead Australian Government agency working to support all Australians to realize the full potential of the digital economy. Previously called the Department of Broadband, Communications and the Digital Economy (DBCDE) has since changed its name to the Department of Communications.

103. *Australian Communications and Media Authority (ACMA)* is responsible for the regulation of broadcasting, radio communications, telecommunications and online content. This is in addition to responsibilities on monitoring information on the Internet, radio and TV, phones and licences for consumers and industry.

104. *Australian Government Information Management Office (AGIMO)* at the Department of Finance works across government to maintain Australia's position as a leader in the productive application of information and communications technologies to government administration, information and services.

105. *National ICT Australia Ltd. (NICTA)* is an important part of Australia's innovation system and seeks to generate new opportunities for Australian industry.

106. The *Office of the Privacy Commissioner* has been integrated into the Office of the Australian Information Commissioner (OAIC).

107. The *Australian Competition and Consumer Commission* (ACCC) provides useful guidelines for consumers in relation to Internet commerce. It has also made it clear that competition rules will govern an e-commerce environment, just as it does traditional business contexts.

108. *IP Australia* is the Australian Government agency that administers IP rights and legislation relating to patents, trademarks, designs and plant breeder's rights.[61]

109. The *Consumer Affairs Division of Treasury* is proactive in e-commerce and produced a new code, Building Consumer Sovereignty in E-commerce: A Best Practice Model for Business.

110. *Australian Customs and Border Protection Service* is a critical Commonwealth department for efficient competition in a global economy.[62]

---

60. https://consult.industry.gov.au/portfolio-policy-and-innovation-strategy/the-digital-economy/.
61. http://www.ipaustralia.gov.au/.
62. http://www.customs.gov.au/.

111. State Governments and Grant Assistance. Each of the State and Territory governments also offer a range of services and provide information to assist both businesses and consumers in relation to e-commerce. For example, the Victorian Government e-Business site,[63] Business Victoria[64] which provide information about how to start a business, building a website, social media, grants, risk management, government tenders.

112. The government also offers grant assistance through such programmes such as Startup Smart (business grants)[65] at the Australian Business Financing Centre.[66] Australian entrepreneurs have received funding and assistance from various government agencies and funded government programmes.

63. http://www.vic.gov.au/business-industry/business-practice-management/e-business.html.
64. https://www.business.vic.gov.au/.
65. http://www.startupsmart.com.au/.
66. http://www.australiangovernmentgrants.org/articles.php?indlist=online.

Chapter 4. Australian E-Government Initiatives

§1. Introduction

113. Australia is recognized as one of the leading countries in the move to an Information Economy, and the Australian Government has played a pivotal role in this transformation. This commentary outlines some of the key issues confronting Australia as it moves toward its policy goal of achieving e-government. Many of the underlying issues in the transformation to e-government are the same for most governments.

114. Governments provide the necessary infrastructure conditions to promote a knowledge or information economy. Governments can promote e-business but it is for government itself to be exemplary in its adoption and deployment of new technologies and electronic media. The government is the largest interactive force in the lives of business and consumers. There is growing pressure for governments to move online. E-government is seen as a key factor in increasing the overall competitiveness of the economy.

§2. Government Policy Framework

115. Government promotion of e-commerce was accelerated by the Investing for Growth policy statement on 8 December 1997, which outlined government intent and initiatives to enable Australian business to add to and benefit from the global information age.[67] In 1997, the Commonwealth government established the National Office for the Information Economy (NOIE) to develop, coordinate, and oversee broad policy relating to establishing the regulatory, legal, and physical infrastructure environment for online activities and facilitating e-commerce. On 8 April 2004, the AGIMO replaced NOIE.

116. The Government's e-commerce strategy was originally set out in A Strategic Framework for the Information Economy – Identifying Priorities for Action in January 1999.[68] The framework recognized that it is essential that effective approaches to consumer protection be developed as part of the Government's overall strategy for the Information Economy. This will ensure that work in the area of B2C e-commerce is compatible with that taking place in other areas, including B2B e-commerce and the provision of government services online.

117. The e-commerce policy framework identified ten priorities, including the need to develop a legal and regulatory framework to facilitate e-commerce to encourage more consumers and businesses to conduct more of their business online.

---

67. Commonwealth of Australia, *Investing for Growth. The Howard Government's Plan for Australian Industry* (1997), Canberra, at www.disr.gov.au/growth/.
68. A Strategic Framework for the Information Economy – Identifying Priorities for Action, National Office for the Information Economy, December 1998, www.noie.gov.au/nationalstrategy/index.html.

The Strategic Framework also recognized the need for Australia to influence the emerging international rules and conventions for e-commerce.

118. Since September 2009 significant regulatory reform to introduce more competition and promote greater consumer protection in the Australian telecommunications sector. The majority of the submissions received in response to the National Broadband Network: Regulatory Reform for Twenty-First Century Broadband Discussion Paper released by the government on 7 April 2009 has been supportive.

119. The Government, in its policy statement of 26 August 2009, Australia's Digital Economy: Future, announced initiatives such as the *Digital Education Revolution* to build digital media literacy among school children; *Enterprise Connect* for business advisory services to small to medium enterprises (SMEs) to help increase their productivity; *Small Business Online* that promotes the benefits of the digital economy to Australian SMEs, helping them take advantage of e-business opportunities and expand their online presence; *Government Innovation* that establishes an independent Government 2.0 Taskforce to advise on a range of issues that relate to the emerging agenda of online engagement; *Smart Technology* to demonstrate the ability of technology to make existing energy infrastructure smarter with an investment in the National Energy Efficiency Initiative;[69] and, the development of an Information Policy which promotes 'open government', the free flow of information and about how government handles and uses the information that it holds (public sector information).[70]

120. Over the last several years, Australia has been rated among the top countries in e-readiness by the Economist Intelligence Unit, the business arm of the Economist group. In a report for 2002, Australia slipped from second to sixth overall. The comparison is based upon IT infrastructure, good overall business environment, uptake of the Internet by consumers, and a stable economic and political climate. Also considered are telephone penetration, online security, and IP protection.[71]

§3. Infrastructure Challenges

121. NBN. The Government has approved the establishment of a new company to build and operate a new superfast NBN.[72] This new superfast NBN, built in partnership with the private sector, will be one of the largest nation-building infrastructure projects in Australian history.

122. This new NBN will:

---

69. www.dbcde.gov.au/digital_economy/future_directions_of_the_digital_economy/australias_digital_economy_future_directions/final_report.
70. http://www.oaic.gov.au/information-policy/about-information-policy.
71. AAP, *Our E-Readiness Slips: Report*, *Canberra Times* 15 (25 Jul. 2002).
72. https://www.communications.gov.au/what-we-do/internet/national-broadband-network.

- connect 90% of all Australian homes, schools, and workplaces with broadband services with speeds up to 100 megabits per second, 100 times faster than those currently used by many households and businesses;
- connect all other premises in Australia with next generation wireless and satellite technologies that will deliver broadband speeds of 12 megabits per second; and
- directly support up to 25,000 local jobs every year, on average, over the eight-year life of the project.

123. Unfortunately, the NBN is behind schedule and over-budget. It is presently being reviewed by the recently elected Liberal-Coalition government. The rollout of Australia's NBN was seriously over-budget and behind schedule under the previous Labor Government. The government in 2016 has taken its time in both reappraising the underlying business model on which the broadband is based with a view to substantially reducing the costs. This review is part of a broader review of the telecommunications industry. While this review is being undertaken there are serious regulatory, financial and practical problems to be overcome. Most prominent of these is how to find a cost-effective way to reach remote and rural areas.

124. International Cooperation: Australia has also been a participant in the OECD and International fora dealing with e-commerce issues. For example, Australia has been an active participant in the World Intellectual Property Organization's (WIPO) programme on e-commerce and domain names, including implementation of standards consistent with the WIPO Copyright Treaty (WCT), the WIPO Performance and Phonograms Treaty (WPPT), and the WIPO programme on the Database Treaty and Broadcasting Treaty. Australia has also been active, for example, in other initiatives:

- APEC coordination of e-commerce blueprint, Telecommunications working group.
- United Nations Commission on International Trade Law (UNCITRAL) working group on e-commerce.
- OECD, World Customs Organizations.
- Bilateral e-commerce agreements with the United States, Singapore, Hong Kong, and others, for example, joint statements on E-commerce Canada (February 2000) and China (September 1999).

§4. Australian E-Government in a Global Context

125. The United Nations Public Administration Network conducts a bi-annual e-Government survey first begun in 2001. A part of this survey report includes a section on e-government readiness. This survey provides data on the comparison between countries of the world based on two criteria – the state of e-government readiness and the extent of e-participation of its citizens. A summary index of e-government readiness is based on an assessment of websites for telecommunication infrastructure and resource endowment. This is labelled the e-Government Development Index (EGDI) and shows some interesting patterns.

126. As Australia rolled out its NBN and made progress on other 'Government 2.0' initiatives, it improved significantly in subsequent rankings. In the 2014 UN E-Government survey Australia moved up to second only behind South Korea which has held the top e government ranking since 2010. The UN Report particularly praised Australia's e-government portal: australia.gov.au. noting that: 'The portal offers an extensive list of e-services and forms, both at the federal and local levels, as well as connections to national, local and regional government websites.'[73]

127. According to this index in 2016 the UK was ranked first (EGDI 0.9193) with Australia ranked second (0.9143) followed by the Republic of Korea, Singapore, Finland, Sweden, Netherlands, New Zealand, Denmark and France.[74] E-participation refers to the quality of government information online, ability to organize public consultations online and ability to involve citizens directly in decisions. In both measures Australia ranked second in the world – an achievement marking the progress that has been made in updating public services to keep pace with digital demand.[75]

128. The rankings demonstrate continued leadership and focus on e-government innovation. As well the higher rankings attained by the top fifteen to twenty countries reflect the relative levels of economic, social and political developments in the countries concerned. More importantly, there appears a high correlation between investments in telecommunications, human capital and the provision of government online services.

I. Australia E-Government Leadership

129. Australia's ongoing commitment to remaining a leader in e-government is shown by its Australian Department of Finance launch of an interactive system called GovShare for all Australian Public Service (APS) agencies. Later, as a project of the government's Digital Transformation Agency (DTA), this system will enable agencies to share documents, spreadsheets, find contacts and discuss problems through an online forum. Australia is striving for a whole-of-government open source cloud-based content management system. However, as of 1 December 2017, GovShare has been decommissioned with the DTA assuming responsibilities of the system.[76] The Australian Government National Digital Economy Strategy (NDES)

73. http://unpan3.un.org/egovkb/Reports/UN-E-Government-Survey-2014.
74. https://publicadministration.un.org/egovkb/en-us/Reports/UN-E-Government-Survey-2016.
75. *See also* C. Garner, *Can Australia lead the world in e-government?*, The Canberra Times Public Sector Informant (3 Oct. 2016), and http://www.canberratimes.com.au/national/public-service/can-australia-lead-the-world-in-e-government-20160927-grpkkg.html.
76. As announced on the website https://data.gov.au/organisations/org-dga-cd574697-6734-4443-b350-9cf9eae427a2.

(2011) sets out the vision for realizing the benefits of the NBN and positioning Australia as a leading digital economy by 2020.[77] AGIMO has been tasked in achieving the stated goal of improved online government service delivery and engagement by 2020 where four out of five Australians will choose to engage with the government through the internet or other type of online services.

130. The government launched the Digital Economy Strategy in 2018, following an open conversation with governments, businesses and the community.[78] To ensure sustainability the strategy will evolve over time. The strategy sets out how the government, the private sector and community can work together to build competitive strengths and build new ones; develop world-leading digital business capability for globally engaged, innovative, high-growth businesses of all sizes; drive a culture and mindset that supports lifelong learning; a global outlook and to help respond positively to change; and, address the 'digital divide' in skills and confidence to help all Australians to succeed in a digital economy.

131. *Advancing Australia as a Digital Economy* (2013) is an update of the 2011 NDES and lays out the next steps towards delivering the vision for the year 2020.[79] The strategic update provides an overview of individual initiatives and outlines new initiatives that represent the progress being made by the Australian Government to embrace the digital future. Initiatives include Digital First, a commitment for government to offer its services digitally.

132. The Department of Industry, Innovation and Science in 2017 started *The Digital Economy: Opening Up the Conversation*, which is the start of the dialogue with all Australians where the government sought ideas to help develop the strategy. The responses helped identify the key issues, challenges and opportunities, and the way forward.[80]

133. The myGov is a secure way to access government services online with one login and one password.[81] The advent of digital and mobile technology has made many government services available online and this trend is continuing. The myGov service has around 2 million registered members and is accessed by over 150,000 users each week.[82] A further 2 million members are anticipated to register with the

77. Anne Steward AGIMO, The Australian Government releases the National Digital Economy Strategy (2011) at https://www.industry.gov.au/data-and-publications/australias-tech-future.
78. https://industry.gov.au/innovation/Digital-Economy/Pages/default.aspx.
79. Australian Government Department of Broadband, Communications and the Digital Economy 2013 *Advancing Australia as a Digital Economy: An Update to the National Digital Economy Strategy* (*see* Index of Initiatives in the Executive Summary, p. x) and also ICT Reports Advancing Australia as a Digital Economy – DBCDE June 2013 at http://ict-industry-reports.com.au/advancing-australia-as-a-digital-economy/.
80. Australian Government Department of Industry, Innovation and Science, *The Digital Economy: Opening Up the Conversation* (2017), at https://www.industry.gov.au/sites/default/files/isa_submission_to_digital-economy-opening-up-the-conversation.pdf.
81. About myGov at https://my.gov.au/mygov/content/html/about.html.
82. *Ibid.*

service further expanding to link with State, Territory and local government services. In 2012, 50% of services provided by the Department of Human Services were conducted online.

134. An example of the need for digital delivery of government services is that the Australian Taxation Office (ATO) is required by legislation to send over 10 million notices of assessment in hard copy. It needs to send a further 17 million letters each year on activity statement material. The Commonwealth Government's commitment is to ensure every government interaction that occurs more than 50,000 times per year can be undertaken online from 2017. The aim is also to make all government correspondence available digitally from 2017.

135. The Australian Government National Commission of Audit has recommended that the Government should adopt a transformative strategy to become digital by default for all transactions.[83] The strategy should specify an explicit savings target to drive change. It should act decisively to remove legislative barriers to digital transactions. Further it should set concrete milestones, including switching from an 'opt-in' arrangement for myGov to a default 'opt-out'.

136. Since 2016 the Australian Government has expanded its digital agenda so that Australians can access improved government services online.[84] The DTA will implement wide-scale change in digital capability across government departments, benefiting the public and other users of government services.

A. *National e-Conveyancing*

137. One of the most significant e-government projects was the National E-conveyancing Office to develop a national online conveyancing system. The National E-conveyancing System (NECS) was created by Australian State and Territory governments in 2005. This is an important development because it marks Australia as a world leader in e-conveyancing and because property transactions are one of the most significant and pervasive commercial activities engaged in by almost all Australians at some time in their lives.[85]

138. A National E-conveyancing Council (ARNECC) was established in 2011 to ensure a consistent national approach in the regulation of NEC.[86] This Council was formed under the Inter-Governmental Agreement (IGA) for an E-conveyancing

83. Australian Government, National Commission of Audit (2014) at http://www.ncoa.gov.au/report/phase-one/part-b/10-6-e-government.html.
84. Prime Minister and Cabinet, *Transforming the Commonwealth's Digital Agenda* (14 Oct. 2016), at https://ministers.pmc.gov.au/taylor/2016/transforming-commonwealths-digital-agenda.
85. To further accelerate the NECS, the New South Wales, Queensland and Victorian Governments established the National e-Conveyancing Development Ltd (NECDL). Effective 3 Mar. 2014 the NECDL changed its name to Property Exchange Australia Ltd (PEXA). https://www.pexa.com.au/.
86. Information on ARNECC activities and the legal framework to support the NEC is found at http://www.arnecc.gov.au.

National Law for the purposes of co-ordinating a national approach among the States and Territories in the regulation of an electronic environment for completing conveyancing transactions. ARNECC membership comprises the Land Titles Registrars from each Australian state and territory or nominee.

139. The Strategic Statement issued by ARNECC in May 2014 sets out the purpose, focus and priorities for the benefit of participants in the conveyancing industry throughout Australia. The focus is on developing, implementing and nurturing a safe, reliable, national and sustainable electronic environment for completing conveyancing transactions.

B. Developments in e-Health Records

140. Since 1 July 2012 Australians have been able to choose to register for their own personally controlled electronic health (e-Health) record.[87] An e-Health record gives an electronic summary of a person's health information. Healthcare providers may add to the records following protocols with their access controls. E-Health records include information such as medical history and treatment, diagnoses, medications and allergies. Any person may control their own e-Health record including a choice in restricting health care provider organizations in terms of access and what information may be included.

141. The legislative framework for the government's e-Health record system are provided by the Personally Controlled Electronic Health Records Act 2012 (PCEHR Act) and the PCEHR Rules 2011 and Personally Controlled Electronic Health Records Regulation 2012.[88] The Act, Rules and Regulations limit when and how health information in an e-Health record may be collected, used and disclosed. The unauthorized collection and use or disclosure of an e-Health record information is a contravention of the Act and an interference with personal privacy.

142. The e-Health Record System Operator is the Secretary of the Department of Health and Ageing (DOHA). The System Operator works with a range of agencies and organizations to deliver the e-Health record system. Among others are the OAIC that regulates the handling of personal information under the e-Health record system by individuals, Australian Government agencies, private sector organizations and some state and territory agencies. OAIC investigates complaints about the mishandling of health information and conducts its 'own motion investigations'.[89]

---

87. Department of Health and Ageing *Personally Controlled Electronic Health Record System Operator, Annual Report 2012-2014* (Canberra: DOHA).
88. http://www.comlaw.gov.au/Series/C2012A00063 (PCEHR Act), http://www.comlaw.gov.au/Series/F2012L011703 (PCEHR Rules), and http://www.comlaw.gov.au/Series/F2012L01399 (PCEHR Regulations).
89. https://www.oaic.gov.au/privacy/health-information/my-health-record/.

§5. CONCLUSIONS

143. E-government is not a destination but an ongoing journey. One of the major strengths of e-government in Australia has been its recognition of the importance of developing a legal infrastructure to support business and government as they move toward an information economy. A second major strength has been the intense interaction between public and private sectors in working together to find e-business solutions and to develop the necessary infrastructure in which all levels of business and government can operate in this new environment.

Part I. Regulation of ICT Market

Chapter 1. Introduction and Background

§1. Geography and Market

144. The regulation of ICT in Australia is underpinned by the regulation of telecommunications. In recognition of the effects of technological convergence, the Australian government is moving to bring the regulation of telecommunications and broadcasting closer together through measures such as the amalgamation of the respective regulatory agencies.

145. Telecommunications regulation in Australia has been shaped by the realities of the communications infrastructure, its history and markets, the vast land mass but small and very unevenly distributed population, and small market depth.

146. Australia has a population of over 23 million and an area of over 7.5 million km. Australia is one of the most urbanized countries in the world with almost 64% of its population living in its five largest cities, which, along with most of the remaining population, is clustered predominantly along the coastal fringe, primarily in the east and southeast of the country. Half the continent contains 0.3% of the population, and 84% of the population occupies only 1% of the continent.[90]

147. While the vast bulk of the population lives in the cities, the rural constituencies historically have exercised a significant influence on Australia's policies. Since Federation (1901) the Commonwealth government has been responsible for the regulation of telecommunications under the Constitution. The policy imperative is that there be universal and affordable access to the voice network and untimed local calls.[91] Such access has required delivery of services be made within and between Australia's three largest cities, namely Sydney, Melbourne and Brisbane as well as to the sparsely populated regional and remote areas beyond Australia's 'East Coast spine', on relatively comparable terms. The challenge is further accentuated by such features of Australia's topography as mountains, severe temperature gradients, flooding, cyclones, and termites. For most of the twentieth century, the vehicle chosen to deliver this universal affordable service is the provision of services by

---

90. *See* ABS Australia Yearbook 2012 Catalogue 1301.0 at http://www.abs.gov.au/ausstats/abs@.nsf/Lookup/1301.0Main+Features782012.
91. *Post and Telegraph Act* 1901 (Cth).

government through a statutorily created monopoly carrier whose operations involved the use of cross-subsidies and protection against competition.

§2. Background to the Legislation

148. For the first half of the twentieth century, the Commonwealth Government assumed responsibility for communications.[92] In 1975, domestic telecommunication functions were moved from the Postmaster General's Department (PMG) to the statutory body known as Australian Telecommunications Commission (Telecom). Telecom was given the exclusive right to install, maintain, and operate domestic telecommunications infrastructure and attach lines or equipment to the telecommunications system. The Overseas Telecommunications Commission (OTC), established in 1946, retained its functions in relation to overseas telecommunications. In 1985, a national satellite telecommunications system was established, operated by AUSSAT Pty Ltd, a company jointly owned by Telecom and the Commonwealth Government.[93]

149. From 1975 to 1991 administrative and legislative changes occurred in the provision of telecommunications services in Australia and their regulation, and the first steps were taken to move to competition in the provision of telecommunications. This was largely in response to the growth of private networks by commercial organizations, the increase in demand for communications services as the economy became more service-based, and a concern that Telecom's regulatory functions represented a conflict of interest inconsistent with the Government's position on trade practices reform.[94]

150. In 1989, the Commonwealth established an independent regulator, AUSTEL,[95] and provided for limited competition in some areas where Telecom retained its monopoly over basic telephony to cross subsidize uniform tariff charges and service provision in regional and remote Australia.[96]

151. The Telecommunications Act 1991 (Cth) established a regime under which a limited monopoly was granted to two carriers, Telecom[97] and Optus Communications.[98] Additionally, the Telecommunications Act 1991 (Cth) affected changes in the lead-up to the government's declared intention to open telecommunications to

92. *Post and Telegraph Act* 1901 (Cth), *Wireless Telegraphy Act* 1905 (Cth) and *Overseas Telecommunications Commission Act* 1946 (Cth).
93. H. Raiche, *The Policy Context*, in *Australian Telecommunications Regulation* 3 (Alasdair Grant ed., UNSW Press 2004).
94. *Ibid.* at 5.
95. *Telecommunications Act* 1989 (Cth).
96. Raiche *supra.*
97. Which after its merger with OTC (or AOTC as it then was) in 1992 was renamed TELSTRA in 1995.
98. Following a tender process to determine the Australia's 'second carrier', Optus's majority shareholders were, at the time, UK Cable and Wireless and US RBOT.

full competition by 1997. These changes included the broadening of competition to the Public Switched Telephone Network (PSTN) and the broadening of AUSTEL's powers to deal with interconnection, competition, and consumer protection issues.[99]

152. The Telecommunications Act 1997 (Cth) established the Australian Communication and Media Authority (ACMA) and sought to open the field to full competition with the aim of creating an internationally competitive industry. This included the establishment of an access scheme that sought to give all Australians equitable access to standard telecommunications services. The Telecommunications Act 1997 (Cth) also sought to promote, wherever possible, self-regulation of the industry and contained consumer provisions including customer service guarantees (CSGs), emergency call services and untimed local calls, and confidentiality of information routed through the network.

153. The ACMA is a statutory authority within the Federal Government portfolio of Communications.

154. The ACMA is Australia's regulator for:

- broadcasting;
- the Internet;
- radiocommunications; and
- telecommunications.

155. It was formed in July 2005 when the Australian Communications Authority (ACA) merged with the Australian Broadcasting Authority (ABA).

156. The ACMA licenses Australia's telecommunications carriers and regulates fixed-line and mobile telecommunications.

157. The ACMA's responsibilities include:

- supporting the development of codes of practice for the industry and monitoring compliance;
- monitoring the performance of carriage service providers (CSPs);
- setting and enforcing industry and technical standards, and monitoring industry performance;
- numbering;
- advising consumers on their rights and safeguards; and
- managing the delivery of services to people with a communication impairment.

158. The Telecommunications Act 1997 (Cth) was supported by telecommunications-specific amendments to the Competition and Consumer Act 2010 (Cth) (CCA) and later by enactment of telecommunications-specific consumer protection legislation.

---

99. Raiche *supra.*

159. The principal legislations regulating telecommunications includes:

– the Telecommunications Act 1997 (Cth);
– Parts XIB and XIC of the CCA;
– the Telecommunications (Consumer Protection and Services Standards) Act 1999 (Cth) (TCPSS); and
– Broadcasting Services Act 1992 (Cth) (Schedules 5 and 7).

160. In September 2009, the Minister for Communications, Broadband and the Digital Economy announced extensive reforms to the legislation regulating telecommunications. The legislative reforms followed extensive public consultation through the publication of the 'National Broadband Network: Regulatory Reform for the Twenty-first Century Broadband' discussion paper released in April 2009. The thrust of the reforms focused on the structural separation of Telstra.

Chapter 2. Industry Structure and Regulatory Entities

§1. Service Providers and Network Units

161. The Telecommunications Act 1997 (Cth) establishes a system for regulating telecommunications. The objects of the Act are as follows:

- The main object of this Act, when read together with Parts XIB and XIC of the CCA, is to provide a regulatory framework that promotes:
  - the long-term interests of end users of carriage services or of services provided by means of carriage services; and
  - the efficiency and international competitiveness of the Australian telecommunications industry; and
  - the availability of accessible and affordable carriage services that enhance the welfare of Australians.
- The other objects of this Act, when read together with Parts XIB and XIC of the CCA are:
  - to ensure that standard telephone services and payphones are:
    - reasonably accessible to all people in Australia on an equitable basis, wherever they reside or carry on business; and
    - are supplied as efficiently and economically as practicable; and
    - are supplied at performance standards that reasonably meet the social, industrial and commercial needs of the Australian community;
  - to promote the supply of diverse and innovative carriage services and content services;
  - to promote the development of an Australian telecommunications industry that is efficient, competitive and responsive to the needs of the Australian community;
  - to promote the effective participation by all sectors of the Australian telecommunications industry in markets (whether in Australia or elsewhere);
  - to promote:
    - the development of the technical capabilities and skills of the Australian telecommunications industry; and
    - the development of the valueadding and exportoriented activities of the Australian telecommunications industry; and
    - research and development that contributes to the growth of the Australian telecommunications industry; and
- to promote the equitable distribution of benefits from improvements in the efficiency and effectiveness of:
  - the provision of telecommunications networks and facilities; and
  - the supply of carriage services;
- to provide appropriate community safeguards in relation to telecommunications activities and to regulate adequately participants in sections of the Australian telecommunications industry;

- to promote the placement of lines underground, and taking into account economic and technical issues, where placing such lines underground is supported by the affected community;
- to promote responsible practices in relation to the sending of commercial electronic messages;
- to promote responsible practices in relation to the making of telemarketing calls; and
- to promote responsible practices in relation to the sending of marketing faxes.

162. A synoptic view of the Telecommunications Act 1997 is given in the Figure 1.

Figure 1 Synopsis of the Telecommunications Act 1997 (Cth)

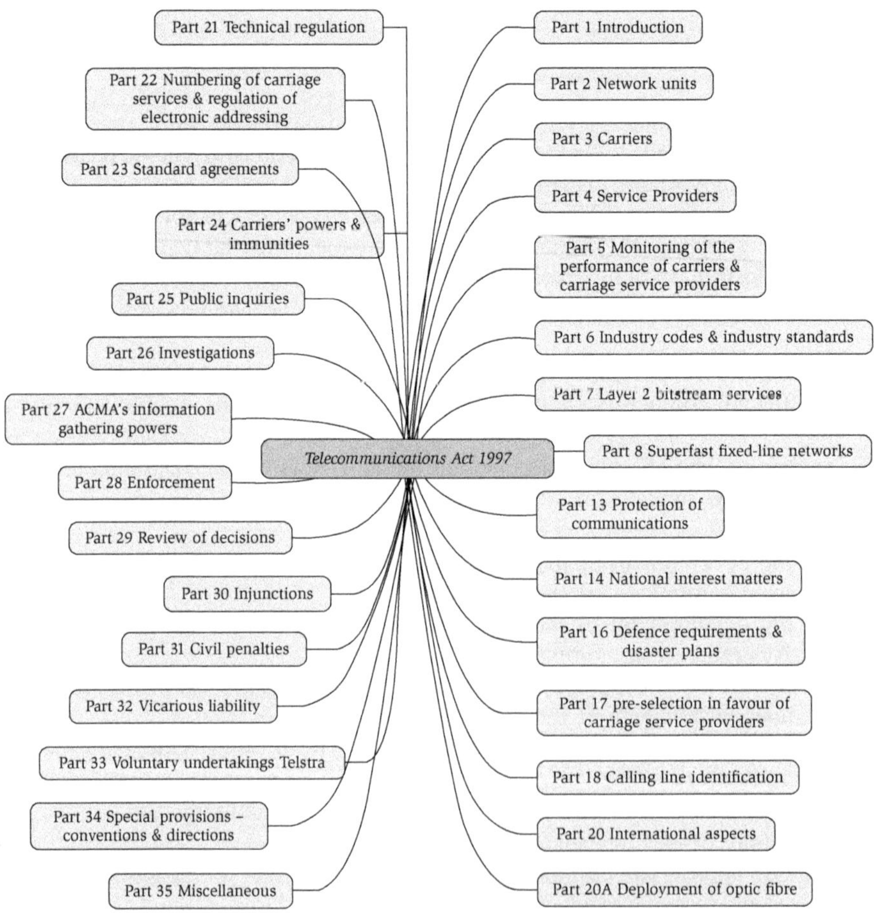

163. Regulatory Policy. The Parliament intends that telecommunications be regulated in a manner that:

- promotes the greatest practicable use of industry self-regulation; and
- does not impose undue financial and administrative burdens on participants in the Australian telecommunications industry; but does not compromise the effectiveness of regulation in achieving the objects mentioned above.

164. The main entities regulated by the Telecommunications Act 1997 (Cth) are carriers and service providers.

165. A *carrier* is the holder of a carrier licence granted under the Telecommunications Act 1997 (Cth). The owner of a *network unit* that is used to supply carriage services to the public must hold a carrier licence unless responsibility for the unit is transferred from the owner to a carrier and exemption applies (section 41).

166. There are four types of network unit:

(1) a single line link connecting distinct places in Australia, where the line link meets certain minimum distance requirements;
(2) multiple line links connecting distinct places in Australia, where the line links meet certain minimum distance requirements;
(3) a designated radiocommunications facility; and
(4) a facility specified in a Ministerial determination.

167. There are two types of service providers:

(1) a CSP; and
(2) a content service provider.

168. A *CSP* is a person who supplies, or proposes to supply, certain carriage services. A *CSP* is a person who supplies, or proposes to supply, certain content services. Service providers must comply with the service provider rules.

Chapter 3. Access Regulation: Part XIC CCA

§1. Introduction

169. Part XIC of the CCA (as shown in Figure 2) sets out the Telecommunications Access Regulations. This Part outlines the nature of declared services and the standard access obligations expected from telecommunications providers. In identifying a declared service, the distinction is made between those provided by the NBN corporation and those that are not part of the NBN.

170. A carriage service, or a related service, supplied, or capable of being supplied, by a carrier (other than an NBN corporation) or a CSP (other than an NBN corporation) is a declared service if: (1) the Commission has declared the service to be a declared service; or (2) the service is supplied by the carrier or CSP, and a special access undertaking given by the carrier or CSP is in operation in relation to the service (section 152AL). Similarly, a carriage service, or a related service, supplied, or capable of being supplied, by an NBN corporation is a *declared service* if: (1) the Commission has declared the service to be a *declared service*; or the NBN corporation has formulated a standard form of access agreement that relates to access to the service; or (3) the service is supplied by the NBN corporation, and a special access undertaking given by the NBN corporation is in operation in relation to the service.

Figure 2 CCA Parts XIB & XIC

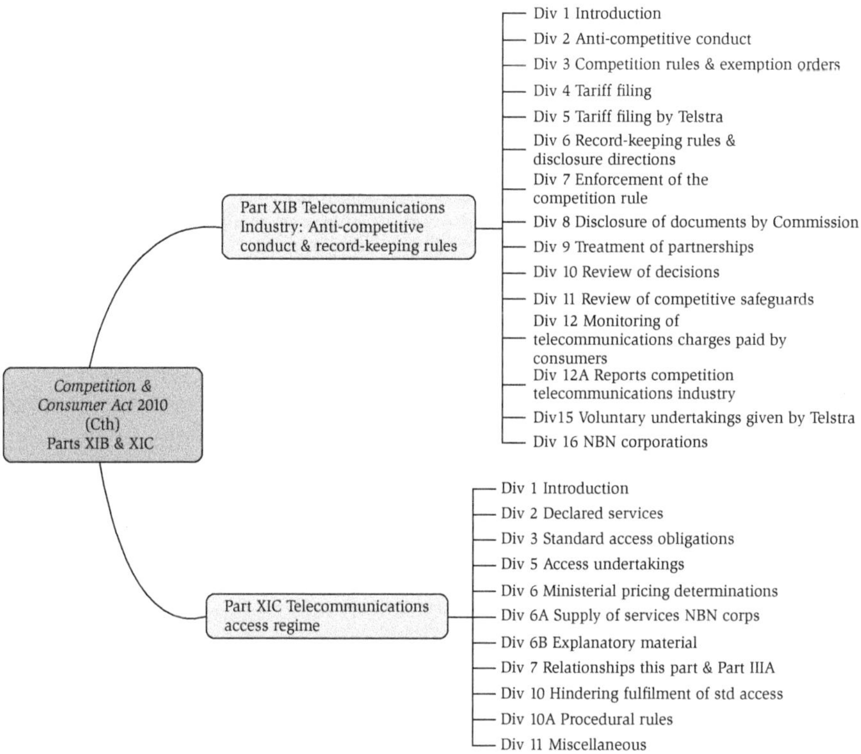

171. All carriers and CSPs who provide declared services are required to comply with *standard access obligations* (category A section 152AR and category B section 152AXB) in relation to those services. The *standard access obligations* facilitate the provision of access to declared services by service providers so that service providers can provide carriage services and/or content services.

172. These obligations are subject to agreement:

- The terms and conditions on which carriers and CSPs are required to comply with the *standard access obligations* are subject to agreement.
- If agreement cannot be reached, but the carrier or CSP has given an *access undertaking*, the terms and conditions are as set out in the access undertaking.
- If agreement cannot be reached, no access undertaking is in operation, but the Commission has made binding rules of conduct, the terms and conditions are as specified in the binding rules of conduct.
- If agreement cannot be reached, no access undertaking is in operation, and no binding rules of conduct have been made, the terms and conditions are as specified in an access determination made by the Commission.

– A carrier, CSP or related body must not prevent or hinder the fulfilment of a standard access obligation.

§2. Object

173. The object of section 152AB of the telecommunications access regime is to promote the long-term interests of end users of carriage services or of services provided by means of carriage services. To determine whether a particular thing promotes the long-term interests of end users of either of the following services (the listed services – carriage services or services supplied by means of carriage services) regard must be had to the extent to which the thing is likely to result in the achievement of the following objectives:

- the objective of promoting competition in markets for listed services;
- the objective of achieving anytoany connectivity in relation to carriage services that involve communication between end users;
- the objective of encouraging the economically efficient use of, and the economically efficient investment in:
  - the infrastructure by which listed services are supplied; and
  - any other infrastructure by which listed services are, or are likely to become, capable of being supplied.

174. Section 152AE of the Act extends to each eligible Territory (within the meaning of the Telecommunications Act 1997 (Cth)) and applies to external Territories.

175. Part XIC of the CCA contains specific provisions relating to the Government-owned company, the NBN, and its role in the ICT industry. An important feature of the telecommunications industry is that competitors must make use of each other's networks. This is because communications services generally require 'any-to-any' connectivity – the capacity of any end user of the service to contact any other end user, regardless of the identity of the suppliers or the network to which they are connected.

176. Part XIC of the CCA establishes an industry-specific regime for regulating access to carriage services and provides the core access arrangements for the telecommunications industry. Arrangements relating to carrier access to certain facilities and network information are contained in Part IIIA of the CCA.

177. The industry-specific nature of this regime reflects the policy imperatives of:

- promoting any-to-any connectivity;
- promoting diversity and competition in the supply of carriage services, content services, and other services supplied by means of carriage services; and

- ensuring access to carriage services is established on reasonable terms and conditions and includes necessary ancillary services such as interconnection, billing information, and access to conditional access customer equipment (such as set-top boxes used in the supply of pay television).

178. The features of the regime have been shaped by other principles being:

- to identify those services for which a genuine access issue exists;
- to give industry the necessary tools and incentives to develop industry-based solutions to access issues;
- to promote reliance on commercial resolution of issues as far as possible;
- to provide easy administrative solutions where genuine access disputes exist and which cannot be resolved by industry consensus or commercial means; and
- to provide commercial certainty while minimizing direct regulatory imposts and also providing sufficient flexibility to deal with access issues in this rapidly converging industry.

§3. Service Declaration

179. A key element of the scheme is the concept of declared services. 'Access obligations' only arise following the declaration of a service. A service may be declared (section 152AL) by the ACCC in two ways.

180. First, the Telecommunications Access Forum (TAF) may recommend that the ACCC declare a service. The second avenue for service declaration is by ACCC public inquiry. The procedures for public inquiries are detailed in Part 25 of the Telecommunications Act 1997 (Cth).

§4. TAF

181. The ACCC can designate a body or association to be the TAF (section 152AI). The TAF has two principal functions under the regime: (1) the recommendation of the declaration of services; and, (2) the submission of a draft access code for approval by the ACCC (the only body which can do so). A TAF must have membership open to all carriers and CSPs, be capable of making recommendations regarding the declaration of services, the preparation of draft access codes, and have a written constitution.

Chapter 4. Regulation of Anti-competitive Conduct: Part XIB CCA

§1. Introduction

182. Part XIB of the CCA sets up the Regulation of Anti-competitive Conduct and Record-keeping Rules.[100] This Part sets up a special regime for regulating anti-competitive conduct in the telecommunications industry.

183. The circumstances in which carriers and CSPs are said to *engage in anti-competitive conduct* are stated in section 151AK as follows:

- A carrier or CSP must not engage in anti-competitive conduct. This rule is called the *competition rule.*
- The Commission may issue a notice stating that a specified carrier or CSP has engaged, or is engaging, in anti-competitive conduct. The notice is called a *Part A competition notice.*
- Proceedings for the enforcement of the competition rule (other than proceedings for injunctive relief) must not be instituted unless the alleged conduct is of a kind dealt with in a Part A competition notice that was in force at the time when the alleged conduct occurred.

184. In addition to the access regime, under Part XIC, the ACCC administers:

- legislation regulating anti-competitive conduct in telecommunications markets (Part XIB of the CCA); and
- legislation regulating international telecommunications operators[101] engaging in 'unacceptable conduct' (the use of market power or of any legal rights or legal status, or engaging in any other conduct, in a manner that is, or is likely to be, contrary to Australia's national interest – Division 3 of Part 20 of the Telecommunications Act 1997 (Cth).[102]

185. This regime applies in addition to Part IV of the CCA, which contains the general anti-competitive conduct provisions. A key element of the regulation of anti-competitive conduct in telecommunications markets is the competition notice regime. This is a regime which facilitates the ACCC's quick response to anti-competitive conduct.

---

100. For a comprehensive treatment of the scheme as it was originally implemented, *see* Commonwealth of Australia, *Anticompetitive Conduct in Telecommunications Markets: An Information Paper* (August 1999).
101. International telecommunications are operators that provide carriage services from overseas that may originate, terminate, or pass through Australia, the supply of goods or services for use in connection with the provision of such carriage services, or the installation, maintenance, operation, or provision of access to a telecommunications network or facility where the network or facility is used to provide such a carriage service: s. 367(6) of the *Telecommunications Act* 1997 (Cth).
102. Section 367(1) of the *Telecommunications Act* 1997 (Cth).

186. Under Part XIB, the ACCC can issue competition notices (Part A and Part B competition notices and injunctions) and advisory notices.

§2. THE CCA

187. Part XIB of the CCA contains the statutory law regulating the telecommunications industry. This Part of the Act specifically provides the regulations preventing anti-competitive conduct within the industry and the requirements for record-keeping rules aimed at the telecommunications 'carriers' and 'CSPs'.

§3. THE COMPETITION NOTICE REGIME

188. The key concepts of the competition notice regime contained in Part XIB are: (1) the competition rule; (2) anti-competitive conduct; (3) competition notices; (4) advisory notices, and (5) exemption orders.

189. Part XIB contains the competition rule, which provides that carriers and CSPs must not engage in anti-competitive conduct.

190. Anti-competitive conduct is defined under section 151AJ of the CCA. That section sets out the two circumstances under which a carrier or a CSP will engage in anti-competitive conduct for the purposes of Part XIB. Those two circumstances are:

(1) taking advantage of a substantial degree of power in a telecommunications market by a carrier or CSP with the effect or likely effect of substantially lessening competition in that or any other telecommunications market; or
(2) takes advantage of that power in that or any other market, and engages in other conduct on one or more occasions, with the combined effect, or likely combined effect, of substantially lessening competition in that or any other telecommunications market.

191. Part A competition notices allow the ACCC to quickly respond to conduct it considers is in contravention of the competition rule and foreshadow court action against the conduct, thereby warning the recipient that the ACCC considers that the recipient should cease the conduct.

192. Part B competition notices enable the ACCC to give particulars of conduct or a defined kind of conduct under a Part A notice, enabling the ACCC to provide the detailed, particularized information required for prima facie evidence purposes for use in its own court action or court actions mounted by third parties.

193. The ACCC may vary or revoke an advisory notice.[103] If it does, it must give the carrier or CSP concerned written notice of the variation or revocation. The notice will cease to be in force if the Part A competition notice ceases to be in force.

194. A carrier or CSP proposing to engage in conduct which may breach the competition rule may apply to the ACCC for an exemption order. Subdivision B of Division 3 of Part XIB of the CCA sets out the circumstances under which a carrier or CSP may be granted an *exemption order*. The ACCC may grant an exemption order where it is satisfied that:

- the resultant public benefit outweighs any public detriment of lessened competition; or
- the conduct will not breach the competition rule.

§4. The Telecommunications Market

195. The competition rule applies only to carriers or CSPs.[104] As noted previously, a 'carrier' means a person who holds a carrier licence issued under the Telecommunications Act 1997 (Cth), and a CSP is a person who supplies to the public certain communications services (as defined in Part 4 Division 3 of the Act).

196. To be anti-competitive for the purposes of Part XIB the conduct must be by a person possessing a substantial degree of power in a 'telecommunications market'. The carrier or CSP must take advantage of the market power with the effect, or likely effect, of substantially lessening competition in that or any other telecommunications market or engage in conduct in a telecommunications market in contravention of sections 151 AJ(2) and (3).

197. A *telecommunications market* is defined in section 151AF of the CCA to mean a market in which any of the following goods or services are supplied or acquired:

- carriage services;
- goods or services for use in connection with a carriage service;
- access to facilities; and
- content services.

198. 'Carriage service' and 'facility' are defined under section 151AB of the CCA as having the same meaning as in the Telecommunications Act 1997 (Cth).

103. Section 151AQB(5), CCA.
104. Section 151AK, CCA.

199. Under the Telecommunications Act 1997 (Cth), 'carriage service' is defined to mean 'a service for carrying communications by means of guided or unguided electromagnetic energy'.[105]

200. 'Communication' is broadly defined in the Telecommunications Act 1997 (Cth) to include communications between people and/or things and includes speech, music, data, text, visual images, signals, or any other form or combination of forms.[106] A service is a 'carriage service' therefore where the service consists of 'carrying' communications by means of electromagnetic energy.

201. 'Carrying' communications (as opposed to initiating or modifying that communication) is defined in the Telecommunications Act 1997 (Cth) to include transmission, switching, or receipt of that communication. The ACCC takes the view that both the natural meaning of the word 'carry' and the apparent legislative intent behind the inclusive definition suggest that the content being carried must be reproduced for the recipient in a form substantially unchanged from that provided to the carrier by the originator.

202. In the ACCC's view, products which could be supplied or acquired in markets, being 'telecommunications markets', may include:

- carriage services (including all forms of voice and data telephony and services such as video carriage, whether on fixed or mobile networks);
- value-added services (intelligent network services) which are for use in connection with a carriage service such as call manipulation (e.g., diversion, call waiting), the use of calling line identification (CLI), or message services (e.g., voice mail, paging);
- the supply of physical components of telecommunications networks used by carriers or CSPs in the provision of carriage services (ranging from handsets through to network components such as switching systems or transmission technologies) and associated services such as development, installation, maintenance, and repair of those components;
- information and related services used in connection with carriage services (e.g., 'help desk' consultancy services, directory assistance services, account management services, or customer billing information);
- other rights (services) used as inputs for creating, offering, or accessing a carriage service (including rights relating to assets such as spectrum or IPR such as patents);
- any bundled or tied package where one component of that package is a carriage service, a good or service for use in connection with a carriage service, or access to facilities; or
- any goods or services whose 'use', have some nexus with an underlying carriage service (such as where those goods or services are accessible only through the use of a carriage service).

105. Section 7, CCA.
106. *Ibid.*

203. Market definition is fundamental to the evaluation of any anti-competitive conduct under section 151AJ(2), as with other provisions in Part IV of the CCA.

204. Market definition provides the basis on which to assess:

- the telecommunications market in which a carrier or CSP does or does not have market power; and
- whether in that market or another market there has been, or will be, a 'substantial lessening of competition'.

205. Under Part XIB, a carrier or CSP can be in contravention of the competition rule under section 151AJ(2) only if it has a 'substantial degree of power' in a telecommunications market. Section 46 of the CCA also deals with market power in other industries. Substantial market power has been taken to mean that the degree of power is more than trivial or minimal and that it is real and of substance.[107]

206. Part XIB of the CCA aims to facilitate vigorous competition in the telecommunications industry by preventing members of the industry with a substantial degree of power in a telecommunications market from engaging in anti-competitive conduct. Carriers and CSPs with substantial market power should not be able to take advantage of that market power to stifle competition.[108]

207. The CCA makes illegal, agreements, arrangements, or understandings to fix the prices at which goods or services are bought or sold.[109] If two or more carriers or CSPs are observed to vary their prices by the same amount and at the same time, this may indicate that they are acting in collusion in breach of the CCA. Nevertheless, in a strongly competitive market where the cross-elasticity of demand for the services of each supplier is very high, individual service providers cannot afford to allow their prices to differ significantly from those set by their competitors.

107. *Mark Lyons Pty Ltd v. Bursill Sports Gear Pty Ltd* (1987) 75 ALR 581, 591–592 per Wilcox J.
108. Trade Practices Amendment (Telecommunications) Bill 1996, Explanatory Memorandum, 6.
109. Section 45A, CCA.

Chapter 5. Regulation of Consumer Protection in Telecommunications Sector

§1. Introduction

208. The interests of consumers of telecommunications services are protected by legislative provisions, either directly or indirectly. The areas of greatest importance are as follows:

- Universal Service Obligation.
- CSG.
- Confidentiality provisions.
- Telecommunications Ombudsman.
- Equipment standards.
- Billing.
- Content regulation.

Figure 3 The TCPSS

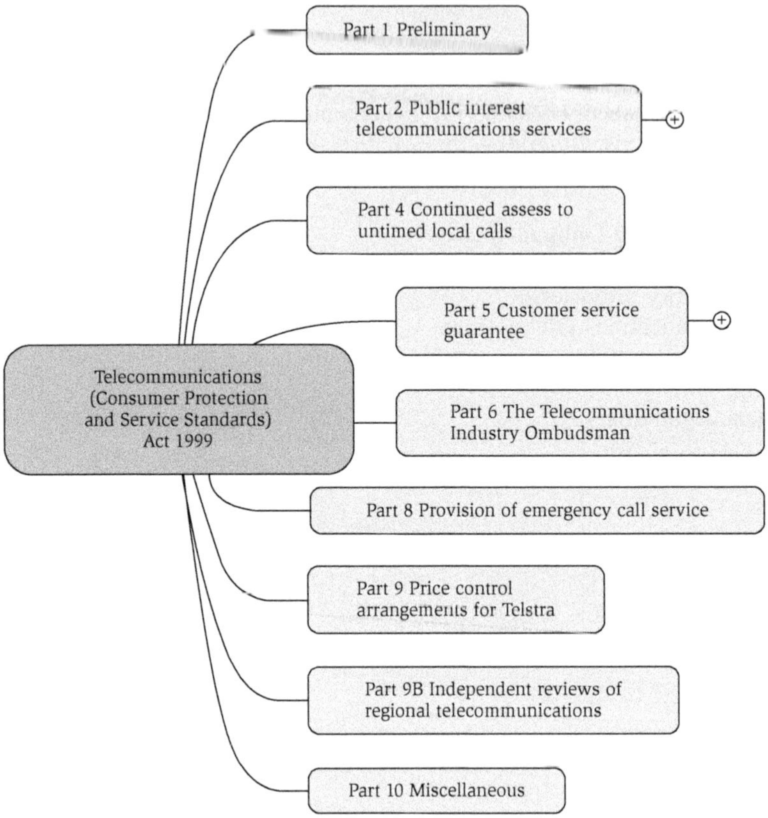

209. Predominantly, these provisions are found in the TCPSS, as well as codes and standards made under the Telecommunications Act 1997 (Cth). They are discussed in this chapter except equipment and content regulation, which are outside the scope of this part. A synoptic view of the TCPSS is given in Figure 3.

§2. Universal Service Obligation

210. The universal service obligation (USO) is the obligation placed on USP to ensure that standard telephone services, pay phones, and prescribed carriage services are reasonably accessible to all Australians on an equitable basis, in whatever part of Australia the reside in or in which they carry on business – Part 2 Public interest telecommunication services.

211. Telstra is currently the sole universal service provider (USP), but additional USP may be declared in the future. As the USP, Telstra is obliged to have a policy statement and marketing plan approved by ACMA. The policy statement and marketing plan outline how Telstra proposes to meet its obligations as USP, including its obligations to those with a disability, those with special needs, and eligible priority customers.

212. A central object of the USO regime is that the losses arising in the course of fulfilling the USO are to be shared among carriers. The Minister may expand the funding base to include CSPs but has not done so to date.

213. A separate obligation related to the USO is the digital data service obligation (DDSO). The DDSO is the obligation placed on a digital data service provider to ensure that digital data services are accessible to all people in Australia on an equitable basis, wherever they reside or carry on business. The DDSO consists of two obligations – the general DDSO for people in general digital data service areas (approximately 96% of the population) and the special DDSO for people in special digital data service areas (approximately 4% of the population, usually living or working at a distance of more than 4.5 km from their local telephone exchange). A special and general digital data service provider is obliged to have in place a special and a general digital data service plan that sets out how it will fulfil its obligations as the digital data service provider within each area.

214. Telstra, as the primary USP, must offer service to all customers in the contestable Universal Service Areas, but other carriers may be approved by ACMA as competing USP for those areas.

§3. CSG

215. The CSG is designed to encourage service improvement and prevent poor service. Telecommunications companies are required to meet minimum performance requirements for specified services and compensate customers when they fail to meet these requirements.

216. The CSG Standard covers the supply of standard telephone services, including voice-grade services used to connect to the Internet or for a facsimile machine. Enhanced call-handling features that require activation by a phone company are also covered, including call waiting, call forwarding, call-barring, caller number ID, and calling number display (CND) blocking. These services are commonly referred to as CSG services.

217. Phone companies must meet maximum time frames for:

– connection of a CSG service;
– repair of a fault or service difficulty; and
– attending appointments with customers.

218. The CSG only applies where a phone company offers a CSG service at a customer's location. It does not apply to:

- mobile phone services;
- Internet services;
- customer equipment, such as the telephone handset;
- disconnection of services; or
- pre-selection (change of phone company or 'churn') delays.

219. The CSG does not apply to customers with more than five phone lines.

§4. Telecommunications Industry Ombudsman

220. Part 6 of the TCPSS provides that carriers and eligible CSPs must enter the scheme which provides for an ombudsman the Telecommunications Industry Ombudsman (TIO) to investigate, make determinations in relation to, and give directions relating to complaints about carriage services by the end users of those services.[110]

221. The TCPSS provides for the TIO to:

- issue an evidentiary certificate stating that a CSP has contravened a CSG performance standard and setting out particulars of the contravention;
- investigate complaints about breaches of performance standards under the CSG; and
- investigate complaints about the application of Mass Service Disruption Notices under the CSG.

222. Part 6 of the TCPSS provides that:

- the TIO may (with consent) have powers and functions conferred on him or her by industry codes or standards;
- the ACMA must be satisfied that the TIO has been consulted about the development of an industry code before it registers the code; and
- the ACMA must consult with the TIO before it mandates an industry standard.

223. Clause 3.1 of the Constitution of the TIO states that its functions are:

- to investigate, make determinations relating to, and give directions relating to, complaints about carriage services by end users of those services;
- to exercise any functions conferred on the TIO by an industry code or industry standard in relation to any member of the TIO Limited including in the case of

110. Section 128(4), CCA.

an industry code where the member has undertaken to comply with it or, if the code has been registered by ACMA, has been directed by ACMA to comply with the Code;
- to exercise any other functions conferred on the TIO under any legislation, including for example, the power to issue a written certificate stating that a specified CSP has contravened a CSG standard set by the ACMA and setting out particulars of the contravention, or the power to approve guidelines for the interception of telecommunications by a carrier; and
- to investigate, make determinations relating to, and give directions relating to, certain complaints by owners or occupiers of land in respect of which a carrier has exercised its statutory powers.

224. Clause 7.1 of the TIO's Constitution outlines other powers and responsibilities of the TIO that include:

- liaison with other industry bodies, ACMA, the ACCC and other relevant government authorities developing working procedures with these bodies where appropriate;
- developing procedures for the fair, just, economical, informal and expeditious handling of complaints;
- at the TIO's discretion, making general observations about the operation of the TIO scheme in any public forum;
- acting as an conduit to the public for the receipt and referral of complaints; and
- keeping data on complaints or requests for information, both for reporting purposes and to identify the sources of practices giving rise to similar complaints.

§5. Broadcasting Services

225. The final pillar of the regulation of the ICT Market is in the Broadcasting Services Act 1992 (Cth).[111] Under section 1 of the Act national broadcasters who operate a transmitter are subject to restrictions regarding the services that may be transmitted in digital mode using the transmitter. Owners and operators of broadcasting transmission towers must give digital broadcasters and datacasters access to the towers for the purposes of installing or maintaining digital transmitters. Applications to the AAT for review of a decision regarding access may be made by the person seeking access, or by the owner or operator of the facility to which access is sought.

226. Schedule 5 Online Services and Schedule 7 Content Services are most pertinent in this discussion insofar as consumer protection are concerned.

111. https://www.legislation.gov.au/Details/C2018C00375.

227. Schedule 5 sets up a system for regulating certain aspects of the Internet industry. If the Commissioner is satisfied that Internet content hosted outside Australia is prohibited content or potential prohibited content, the Commissioner considers that the content is of a sufficiently serious nature to warrant referral to a law enforcement agency must (1) notify the content to an Australian police force; and, (2) notify the content to ISP so that the providers can deal with the content in accordance with procedures specified in an industry code or industry standard (e.g., procedures for the filtering, by technical means, of such content). Section 8 of the Act defines the Internet Service Provider (ISP) as persons who supply or proposes to supply an Internet carriage service to the public.

228. Part 5 on Industry Codes and Standards provides that bodies and associations that represent the ISP section of the Internet industry may develop industry codes. Compliance with an industry code is voluntary unless directed by the Commissioner that a participant in the Internet industry comply with the code. The Commissioner has a reserve power to make an industry standard if there are no industry codes or if an industry code is deficient. Finally, the Commissioner may make online provider determinations regulating ISP. Compliance with industry standards is mandatory.

229. Part 6 gives online provider rules. Section 85 states that a Federal Court may order a person to cease supplying Internet carriage services.

230. Part 8 relates to the protection from civil and criminal proceedings. Section 88 provides for the protection from civil proceedings for ISP:

- Civil proceedings do not lie against an ISP in respect of anything done by the provider in compliance with:
  - a code registered under Part 5 of this Schedule; or
  - a standard determined under Part 5 of this Schedule;

  insofar as the code or standard deals with procedures referred to in the Schedule.

- Civil proceedings do not lie against an ISP in respect of anything done by the provider in compliance with clause 48.

231. Section 90 states that it is the intention of the Parliament that this Schedule is not to apply to the exclusion of a law of a State or Territory to the extent to which that law is capable of operating concurrently with this Schedule.

232. Schedule 7 on Content Services relates to complaints to the Commissioner about prohibited content or potential prohibited content, in relation to certain services (Figure 4). The Commissioner may take the following action to deal with prohibited content or potential prohibited content:

- in the case of a hosting service – issue a take-down notice;
- in the case of a live content service – issue a service-cessation notice; and

– in the case of a links service – issue a link-deletion notice.

233. Schedule 8 Online Content Services provides for ACMA to make online content service provider rules about gambling promotional content provided on an online content service in conjunction with live coverage of a sporting event. The ACMA may exempt an online content service, or an online content service provider, from the online content service provider rules. If an online content service provider contravenes the online content service provider rules, the provider may become liable to pay a civil penalty. The ACMA may give a remedial direction to an online content service provider if the provider contravenes the online content service provider rules.

Figure 4 Broadcasting Services Act 1992 (Cth) Schedules 5 and 7

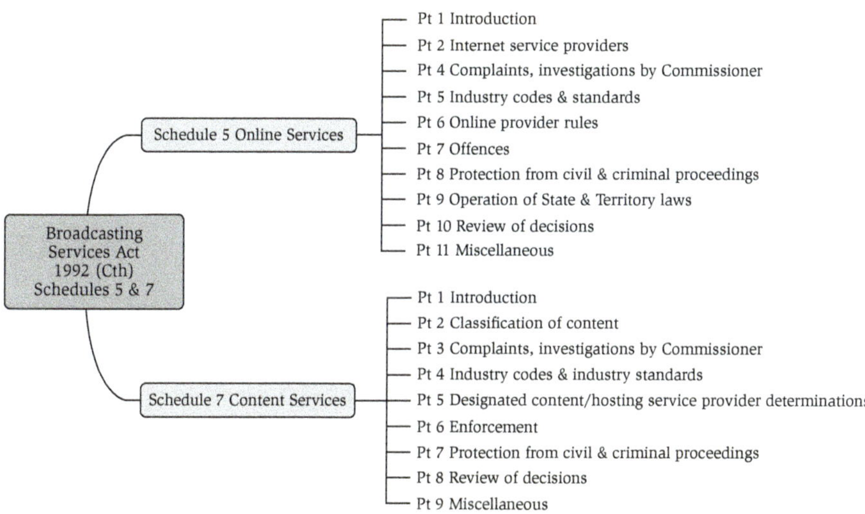

Chapter 6. Telecommunications Reforms

§1. Introduction

234. On 15 September 2009 the Minister for Communications, Broadband and the Digital Economy announced extensive reforms to the legislation regulating the telecommunications. Those reforms have now been implemented.

235. According to the Minister's announcement, the reforms were principally aimed at:

- addressing Telstra's high level of integration to promote greater competition and consumer benefits;
- streamlining and simplifying the competition regime to provide more certain and quicker outcomes for telecommunications companies; and
- strengthening consumer safeguards to ensure services standards are maintained at a high level.

§2. Structural Separation of Telstra

236. The first element of the package relates to the structural separation of Telstra. It was the Government's view that Telstra was one of the most highly integrated telecommunications companies in the world across the fixed-line copper, cable, and mobile platforms.

237. The NBN which was established by the Commonwealth government on 7 April 2009 was the first step in the implementation of the above reform. NBN is wholly owned by the Commonwealth of Australia as a Government Business Enterprise (GBE), incorporated under the Corporations Act 2001 (Cth) and operated in accordance with the Public Governance, Performance and Accountability Act 2013 (Cth).

238. This initiative by the government created a wholesale entity to provide all retail telecommunication companies with access to the network. NBN is to design, build and operate Australia's wholesale broadband access network and underpinned by a purpose to connect Australia and bridge the digital divide. This meant that Telstra still had its own copper and fibre network and the NBN was creating its own fibre network. On 23 June 2010, Telstra entered into a contract with the government's NBN to transfer its existing network for AUD 11 billion. In effect the vertical separation of Telstra will be complete when the contract has been finalized.

239. Since establishment, the Government has presented NBN's mandate through a Statement of Expectations (SoE) which is supplemented from time to time by policy directives and correspondence. NBN's current objectives are set out in the 24 August 2016 SoE.[112]

§3. Reforms to the Competition Regime

240. The Minister's announcement also stated that the proposed legislation would streamline the arrangements in Part XIC of the TPA and this has now been achieved by a new Part XIC of the CCA, as discussed above. The new law allows parties to access regulated services so that:

- the ACCC will determine terms and conditions for a three- to five-year period, following consultation with industry;
- the ACCC determines the principles to apply for longer periods; and
- the ACCC makes binding rules of conduct to immediately address problems with the supply of regulated wholesale services.

241. The legislation to reform the arrangements in Part XIB have been enacted and now form part of the CCA so that the ACCC can address breaches of competition law and conduct damaging to the market.[113] Part XIB complements the anti-competition provisions contained in Part IV of the CCA which has a generic application to all businesses including the telecommunications industry.

242. The ACCC is not required to consult with a party before issuing a competition notice, a process previously prone to delay and obstruction.

243. The legislation also makes it clear that the competition notice regime applies to content services – such as subscription television services – delivered by carriers and CSPs.

§4. Consumer Safeguards

244. The legislation strengthens the USO by enabling the Minister to specify the standards, terms and conditions of services, connection and repair periods, and reliability requirements of the standard telephone service. Telstra is required to meet new minimum performance benchmarks. Failure by Telstra to meet the requirements will expose Telstra to a civil penalty of up to AUD 10 million.

---

112. https://www.nbnco.com.au/content/dam/nbnco2/2018/documents/Policies/soe-shareholder-minister-letter.pdf.
113. *Telecommunications Legislation Amendment (Competition and Consumer Safeguards) Act* 2010 (Cth).

245. The legislation also includes more stringent rules on the removal of pay phones and new provisions to allow people concerned about a pay phone removal to apply to the ACMA to direct Telstra not to remove a pay phone.

246. The legislation provides for new minimum performance benchmarks to require telephone companies to meet or exceed the CSG time periods for a certain proportion of cases. Failure to comply will result in civil penalties or on-the-spot fines.

247. The legislation also provides the ACMA with increased powers to issue infringement notices (on-the-spot) fines instead of commencing procedures in court.

248. The Minister also announced that the Government would exempt carriers with a revenue less than AUD 25 million per annum from paying an annual carrier licence charge and reporting to the ACMA, as costs of compliance are often considerably higher than their monetary contribution.

Part II. IPR in the ICT Sector

Chapter 1. IPR in ICT

§1. Introduction

I. IPR

249. IP refers to the property of the mind or intellect and is any intangible 'thing'. IP can be an invention, original design or the practical application of a good idea. IP law protects the rights in these creative and inventive endeavours of inventors and developers and gives them certain exclusive economic rights for a limited time to profit from these creative works or inventions.

250. However, this claim to property rights will also depend on particular circumstances and relationships because employers may have prior claims, as do independent contractors. An employer is the first owner of IPR in a work created by a person in pursuance of their employment under a contract of service. Similarly, IPR in certain commissioned works vests in the commissioning party. Partners to an invention may also jointly claim ownership to the IP.

251. Ownership of IPR is the legal recognition and reward that one receives for creative effort. The legal position in initial ownership of IP is that it can be modified by agreement either expressly or by implication from conduct. Ownership apart, the law also enables the community-at-large to access the products of IP. Note that the protection is for 'rights' rather than physical property and therefore IP is a form of intangible property.

252. In the US copyright exists for a public good; namely to permit and advance 'the sciences and useful arts'. Therefore, the purpose of copyright law has never been intended to reward creators, rather, it was viewed as a means to an end and not an end in itself. But at the same time, it also suggests that there is no closing down of access to ideas, information and creativity.

253. IP thus is the generic name that encompasses a bundle of rights, which protect innovation and reputation. It includes the regimes of copyright, patents, trademarks, designs, circuit layouts, plant breeder's rights, confidential information (or trade secrets), and a miscellany of others such as moral rights and sui generis (one of a kind) rights. While each of these genres applies to different aspects of innovation or reputation, specific legislation protects each of these forms of IP. In general, the framework for these pieces of legislation are largely based on a country's obligations under international treaties which it may have signed or acceded to.

254. In the ICT context it may be noted that IP is omnipresent because the ICT professional is engaged in all kinds of inventive, creative, original endeavour. The Geographic Information professional may also be involved in the compilation of data to build databases. The data may be expressed in graphic and textual form in order to communicate ideas. All these activities and delivery methods should be deemed valuable enough for the ICT professional to seek some form of protection from loss, theft, and inadvertent slippage into the public arena. But, at the same time the geographic information professional needs to be mindful of avoiding any infringement of the rights of others and the consequent liability that might arise from such infringements.

255. Especially with IPR, the boundaries separating what may be in the public domain and who owns what can be 'fuzzy' and the boundaries easily transgressed. The potential for infringement is further exacerbated in the digital environment given the ease with which information and data may be sent over the Internet with easy replication and the production of derivative works. A practical difficulty is in tracing the lineage of the data or the author of the work. The need to be able to trace lineage could arise for one of a number of reasons such as either to give attribution to the work, to seek permission, or to sheet home liability for damage that may have been caused from errors emanating from the data.

256. Various Australian government publications and reviews return to the theme that IP is crucial to the promotion of innovation.[114] Innovation is integral to the competitiveness of organizations and nations, and innovation drives economic growth. The conferring of enforceable rights on those who produce creative intellectual output gives the incentive for people to engage in these endeavours and IP protection offers rewards for the investment of time and effort.

257. There is the continuing debate as to how to cope with the changes brought about by information technology to the copyright regime. One view suggests that copyright law must be strengthened by extension and tightening in the form of a 'big stick' transmission right that should be protected. An opposing view argues that copyright law is dead in the online environment and that there must be other ways to protect rights, and to fulfil obligations and responsibilities. To date, it appears that a middle ground is gaining ascendancy given that the law has been forced to deal with technological change both by reference to precedent as well as by activism on

---

114. *See* Copyright Convergence Group 1994, *Highways to Change*, Canberra: AGPS, Department of Industry, Science and Resources 1999, *Shaping Australia's Future. Innovation Framework Paper*, Canberra: AGPS and Australia House of Representatives Standing Committee on Legal and Constitutional Affairs 1999, *Advisory Report on the Copyright Amendment (Digital Agenda) Bill 1999*, Canberra: Australian Parliament House.

the part of owners and users of copyright material. Despite its imperfections the IP regime appears to be working and adapting to the new environment. But, the continuing task is to create laws that can be flexible, adaptive and innovative in this new environment and to make clear whom the beneficiaries such reforms should serve.

258. In the electronic environment two dilemmas are readily apparent – one is the concept of the 'form of expression' and the other is that of 'browsing'. The quandary in the first is that copyright owners seemingly have been disadvantaged with the advent of photocopying and the various exceptions under copyright law. Now however, it may be possible to use technology to track and charge every 'use' of the work online such as a 'pay-wall', no matter how small a part of the work that is 'used'. In the second dilemma, it used to be the case that on buying a book a purchaser had unlimited access to it for reading, reflection, review and critique, and other scholarly activities. However, in the electronic environment it may be possible that any browsing may be monitored, and fees may have to be paid to a collecting agency on a pay-per-view basis.[115]

259. The copyright world of the 16th C printer's monopoly with its Royal Prerogatives and Charters empowered by the Statute of Anne of 1709 that gave copyright owners protection, has been radically transformed by the digital era of 'bits and bytes' and instantaneous, perfect copies. Since the first formulations of copyright protection much has been asked of the original ideals of copyright in particular and IP in general. There is persistent and intense pressure to look for new forms of protection and to reward and yet safeguard the public interest in the free flow of information. Ironically while the electronic world is borderless, IPR attain international recognition founded on domestic laws.

§2. IPR Protection in Australia

260. The framework facilitating the protection of IPR in Australia is by common law, equity and statute. At common law the protection of IPR in goods and services is found in goodwill or commercial reputation attached to a name, mark or trade dress (get-up). In equity, trade secrets and confidential information is protected by the equitable action of breach of confidence. An underlying objective of such protection is to foster innovation, the creation and design of new technology, and new methods of doing business. Through legislation, the degree of protection is variable for ICT products and services, the most relevant being copyright, database protection, patents, trade secrets and trademarks, and business methods. Other kinds

115. In Australia, the Copyright Agency Ltd. (CAL) is the collecting society for both 'authors' and publishers and whose function is the collection of payments of use of copyright material as well as the distribution to members. Similarly, in the US the Copyright Clearance Centre Inc. (CCC) performs the same functions (*see* http://www.copyright.com). The US *Copyright Act* created the Copyright Royalty Tribunal, an independent agency appointed by the President to set royalty rates and distribute royalties for compulsory licences.

of protection of peripheral importance to ICT include moral rights, geographical indications, photographs and fonts. A brief summary of IPR protection is given below.[116]

I. Copyright

261. The Copyright Act 1968 (Cth) protects the rights of authors and creators in their 'works' of original creative effort. Such rights include the right to reproduce the work and to make copies and the right to present it to the public. Copyright is a type of property based on a person's creative skill and labour. The basis of this right is to prevent others copying the work without authorization, in the original form in which the creator has expressed the idea or information. In Australia, there are no formalities other than affixing the copyright notice and symbol – the letter c enclosed in a circle thus © and the name of the creator and date.

262. In Australia, copyright is free and automatically safeguards original works of art, literature, music, films, broadcasts, and computer programs from copying and certain other uses. Copyright exists as a bundle of economic rights pertaining to what one may do with the original work and other copyright material. Copyright subsists in an article, for example in a book and whilst the creator may have ownership of the copyright, the book is owned by the person who purchased it.

II. Databases and Compilations

263. 263 Copyright can and does subsist in compilations of facts as found in directories and databases. In a work that records facts whether it be an encyclopaedia, a map, a directory, a catalogue, a database or some other factual compilation there is neither copyright in the facts nor in each individual fact so presented. The author or creator however may have copyright in the form in which the facts are presented if there has been an intellectual effort in the selection or arrangement of the facts. Copyright may also subsist if the author or creator has done the work or incurred expenses in gathering the facts. The Copyright Amendment (Digital Agenda) Act 2000 (Cth) is designed to fulfil obligations under the Internet Treaties namely for the protection of computer programs and databases.

III. Patents

264. The Patents Act 1990 (Cth) protects rights of inventors in their inventions provided certain threshold requirements have been satisfied such as novelty, inventiveness, utility and non-obviousness. A patent grants monopoly rights to inventors

116. IP Australia, *What is Intellectual Property?* (2004), athttps://www.ipaustralia.gov.au/understanding-ip and Attorney General's Department (AGD), *A Short Guide to Copyright* (2003), at http://www.law.gov.au/.

of new inventions. The monopoly is for a limited period of twenty years for the inventor to exploit the invention. Patent registration in Australia is usually filed with a patent office such as IPAustralia. Any disclosure of the invention before the patent application is filed will prevent registration. Where disclosure about the invention is necessary such as to employees, business partners, or advisers, it must be done on a confidential basis and a written confidentiality agreement. Artistic creations, mathematical models, plans, schemes or other purely mental processes cannot be patented.

IV. Business Methods and Systems

265. US patent law permits the patenting of inventions that could not currently be patented in Australia or the UK One example is that of patents for business methods and systems. In the US methods of doing business may now be patented just like any other patent. Rather than an inventive product the subject matter relates to a new, useful, and non-obvious way of doing business. There is no general definition of a business method patent. An instance is the US Patent and Trademark Office's (USPTO) grant to Amazon.com for a so-called one-click patent as a business method patent.[117] This patent is for a system and method for placing an order to purchase an item via the Internet.

V. Designs

266. The Designs Act 2003 (Cth) protects rights in relation to the appearance of an article so long as its features are novel or original. This Act increases the threshold of distinctiveness required to obtain enforceable design registration and which may make it easier to prove infringements of registered designs. To be registered, the design must be *new* – not known or previously used, and *original* – that is, the design has never been applied to the product although it may have been applied to another type of product. Registration of a design may subsist for up to 16 years. Some designs may also qualify for protection under copyright.

VI. Trade Marks™

267. The Trade Marks Act 1995 (Cth) protects the marks used by traders in relation to their goods and services to indicate the origin or trade connection of those goods and services. A registered trade mark is one for which protection is granted to a letter, word, phrase, sound, smell, shape, logo, picture, manner of packaging, or a combination of these. The trade mark shown as ™ is used by traders on their goods and services to indicate their origin and to distinguish such goods and services from those of other traders. Initial registration is for 10 years with possibility

117. US Patent No. 5,960,411 issued on 28 Sept. 1999.

of further renewals. Trade mark law is jurisdiction oriented more so than either copyright or patent law. The duration of the patent and trade mark registration and protection also varies by jurisdiction.

VII. Moral Rights

268. The Copyright Amendment (Moral Rights) Act 2000 (Cth) recognizes the moral rights of creators and authors in their works even if they may have assigned their copyrights to someone else. Moral rights are a separate category of right apart from 'economic' rights normally associated with copyright. Here the rights protect the creator's honour and reputation and can prevent changes to a work.

VIII. Geographical Indications

269. Geographical Indications protection identifies a good as originating at a locale. Geographical indications are the identification of a country or region where the quality, reputation or other characteristic of a product is essentially attributable to that geographic region, for example, *Champagne, Bordeaux* and *Cognac* readily identify regions in France that produce these wines and spirits. There are exceptions to protection, however, where the geographical indications become generic so that the names used refer to the 'process' or the grape variety, for example, Dijon mustard, Shiraz wine.

IX. Protection of Other IPR

A. *Trade Secrets and Confidential Information*

270. Trade secrets and confidential information are protected by an action in equity for the breach of confidence. This protection may be achieved by a confidentiality agreement with employees to stop them from revealing trade secrets or proprietary knowledge during and after their employment. The common law action of passing-off or an action for misleading or deceptive conduct protects the business reputation and goodwill in unregistered trademarks or trade names.

B. *Photographs*

271. Photographs are protected by copyright the moment they are taken and the right to protection is automatic and free. The length of time a photograph is protected depends on when the photograph was taken and when it was first made available to the public. With celebrities and well-known personalities, they may have a right to control their name or likeness is used.

C. Fonts

272. Fonts as in typography for print and other works are capable of special copyright protection. Copyright may be found to exist in fonts per se as artistic works and hence its unauthorized use can be an infringement of someone's rights. Thus, fonts may be licensed to others for their use. Such artistic works may also be capable of protection as a trade mark under the appropriate legislation.

273. The summary table below on the basic features and characteristics of IPR gives a comparison of the basic features of the different mechanisms for protecting IP in Australia, the types of works protected, duration and formalities (Table 3).

§3. IPR International Environment

I. IPR Conventions, Agreements and Treaties

274. The rationales for protection of IPR spring from international conventions, agreements and treaties. Domestic copyright and IPR legislation in most countries is strongly influenced by a country's participation in, and signatory to, international agreements. The first and still most important is the Berne Convention 1998. Then there are those administered by the WIPO, based in Geneva, a specialized agency of the United Nations, and the requirements of the Agreement on Trade Related Aspects of Intellectual Property Rights (TRIPS) emanating from the WTO Agreement of January 1995.

275. There is also the WCT and the WPPT adopted by the WIPO Diplomatic Conference on 20 December 1996. Both these 'Internet Treaties' update the Berne Convention, the Rome Convention and the TRIPS Agreement, and came into force in 2002.[118] To date Australia has not signed either treaty. Member countries comply with the Treaties or face the prospect of losing membership and thus protection of IP materials in other countries. In cases of blatant infringement of copyright, trade sanctions may follow.

118. Details of these conventions, agreements and treaties may be found at http://www.wipo.org/about-wipo/en/index.html.

Table 3 Summary of the Basic Features and Characteristics of IPR Protection in Australia

Right	*Types of Property / Interests Protected*	*Information Technology Examples*	*Duration*	*Formalities*
Copyright	(a) original literary, dramatic, musical or artistic works (b) sound recordings, films, broadcasts, or cable programs (c) typographical arrangement of published editions	Code and scripts for automating data processing Codes to generate databases from computer output	Generally, life of the creator plus fifty years after death. *TRIPS life of author plus fifty years after death.*	None. Automatic upon the work being 'created' and put into a tangible medium.
Digital Agenda Database Right	Computer programs with technical protection mechanisms Databases	Encryption, digital watermarks Data bases that are sui generis (of its own kind)	As with copyright *TRIPS fifty years.* Sui generis right runs for fifteen years. *TRIPS fifty years*	None. None
Patents (a) Standard patent	New inventions including industrial processes	New type of printer design, computer casing, new method of making computer chips	Twenty years from date of patent registration. *TRIPS twenty years.*	Application to IP Australia to be registered
(b) Innovation patent (previously petty patent)	All other types of invention that do not satisfy a standard patent application		Eight years from date patent is sealed	Application to IP Australia to be registered
Business method and systems	Automated mapping systems, contour following devices, software mapping solutions that dynamically produce map locations and maps	Computer system to identify local resources, interactive automated mapping system	Up to twenty years from first registration.	Application IP Australia to be registered

Right	*Types of Property / Interests Protected*	*Information Technology Examples*	*Duration*	*Formalities*
Designs (a) Registered Designs	'New' designs, being features of shape, configuration, pattern or ornament applied to an article and having 'eye' appeal	Aesthetically pleasing designs including typographical fonts and masthead designs for brochures and advertising material	Up to a maximum of sixteen years from creation but initially for a period of twelve months. *TRIPS ten years.*	Registration by application to the IP Australia
(b) Design Right	'Original' designs, being any aspect of shape or configuration of the whole or part of an article. Applies to functional and aesthetic designs excluding spare parts and surface decoration.	CD cases, templates for drawing map symbols	Up to a maximum of sixteen years from creation or ten years from first use in public	None. Automatic as with copyright
Registered Trade Mark™	A mark – device, brand, label, name, signature – used to indicate a connection in a course of trade between the goods or service and the owner of the mark.	ESRI, MapInfo, MapQuest, GeoMedia, Trimble	Initially for ten years but renewable in ten-year periods indefinitely. *TRIPS seven years and renewal indefinitely*	Applications for registration to the IP Australia
Moral	Any creative work of the intellect that qualifies for copyright protection	ESRI legend information design used in Arc/Info, ArcView	Life of author plus fifty years after death other than film which ceases on the death of maker.	None
Geographical Indications	Identification of a region where the quality, reputation or other characteristic of a product is essentially attributable to that geographic region	*Coonawarra, Claire Valley, Margaret River*	Indefinite so long as reputation is maintained with continued use. *TRIPS as with trademarks.*	Approved by Geographical Indications Committee on set criteria

Right	*Types of Property / Interests Protected*	*Information Technology Examples*	*Duration*	*Formalities*
Trade secrets and confidential information	Almost anything of a confidential nature	Idea for a new program code or invention (prior to patent registration), customer lists, business methods.	Until such time that the subject matter falls into the public domain.	Depends on confidentiality agreements with employees, partners, and other parties.
Passing-off	Trade names, product 'get-up' and styles	Software names or acronyms that are unregistered as trademarks but around which it has acquired a reputation associated with goodwill.	Indefinite so long as the name, get-up or style is associated with reputation, for example, by continued use.	None
Circuit Layouts	Topography pattern or arrangement of layers in IC chips in eligible layout (EL)	New design of IC	Ten years initially at creation to a maximum of twenty years. *TRIPS ten years.*	None
Plant Breeder's Rights	New variety as distinct, uniform and stable and is clearly distinguishable from any other variety	Geographical indications and geographic regions	Up to twenty-five years for trees or vines and twenty years for other species	Registration with IP Australia

Note: The standard duration of protection under the TRIPS is given in italics in the 'Duration' column.

276. Overview of IPR Treaties:

- Berne Convention for the Protection of Literary and Artistic Works 1998;
- Rome Convention for the Protection of Performers, Producers of Phonograms and Broadcasting Organizations 1961;
- TRIPS 1995;
- The Internet Treaties WCT and WPPT.

§4. COPYRIGHT © AND ICT

277. Copyright is the exclusive right given to a creator to reproduce, publish, perform, broadcast and adapt a work. In Australia the Copyright Act 1968 (Cth) and the Copyright Amendment Act 1984 (Cth) applies. Copyright does not exist apart from the Act and vests in the creator as soon as the work is created even though it may be unpublished. There is no registration requirement in Australia.[119] A royalty is a monetary consideration received by the owner of a copyright in a work from a person for a licence to make copies of that work.

278. Copyright impinges on nearly every aspect of ICT. ICT systems applied to any data will involve a system of hardware, software and reiterative procedures that are designed to support the capture, management, manipulation, analysis, modelling and display of spatially referenced data.

279. Copyright is primarily concerned with the prevention of unauthorized copying. It is a right to prevent the unauthorized reproduction by a third party of the form in which a person has chosen to express ideas.[120] Paradoxically copyright law developed out of a right to copy, hence, copyright. In the Middle Ages, the owner of a manuscript was understood to have possessed a right to grant permission to others to copy it, a right that could be exploited for profit. The closest analogy being religious monasteries that charged a fee for permission to copy one of their books.[121]

280. Copyright protects 'works' grouped by category such as: literary, dramatic, musical, artistic, and 'subject matter other than works', such as film, sound recording, television and sound broadcasts, and published editions. Each category attracts certain exclusive rights to the copyright owner provided three main requirements are met. The first is that the author is a 'qualified person' such as an Australian citizen or resident. The second is that the work must be 'original' and is the product of an author's skill and labour. Finally, the work must be reduced to a 'material form' such as writing.

281. A grant of copyright lasts the life of an author plus fifty years after the death of the author. An unpublished work enjoys perpetual protection; however, publication 'triggers' the start of the time limitation of fifty years. Affixing the copyright symbol, ©, is not relevant but may be valuable in proving ownership and date of creation especially when a dispute arises.

---

119. In the US, Taiwan, and Canada registration has ceased to be a prerequisite for the subsistence of copyright although it can be a necessary condition of suing for infringement and/or recovery of damages. In Japan, the registration provision remains.

120. S. Ricketson *The use of copyright works in electronic databases*, *Law Inst. J.* 480–482 (1989).

121. *See* M. Rose, *Authors and Owners: The Invention of Copyright* 9 (Cambridge, MA: Harvard University Press 1993).

282. Exclusive rights in 'literary works' granted under section 31(1) of the Copyright Act 1968 (Cth). Such rights can also be sold or transferred to another person. An agreement of the assignment of copyright in ICT must be in writing.[122]

283. A 'fair dealing' or 'fair use' clause permits users to copy limited amounts of a work for one's personal research or study purposes. The permitted use here is in terms of the type of use rather than the amount used that is determinative. It is a technical violation of copyright to reverse engineer (or de-compile) someone else's computer program.

284. Section 10(1) of the Copyright Act 1968 (Cth) defines 'literary work' to include a table or compilation, expressed in words, figures or symbols whether in a visible form or otherwise and includes a computer program or compilation of computer programs. This section recognizes the importance of IT and its manifestations.

285. Any single work may have separate copyright interests in terms of separate 'owners' and different duration of copyright protection, because of the different commencement dates for the various copyrights embedded in the work. Thus, a video recording will incorporate a script, music and rights to making a film in which each interest may belong to a different person with different types of copyright protection involved lasting for different lengths of time.

I. ICT Data on the Internet

286. Given the architecture of the Internet, one of the major concerns therefore is the protection of IPR. As a data producer, for instance, the concern is the prevention of copyright infringement. In general, most materials published on the Internet is protected by copyright unless otherwise denied. The concept of fair use / fair dealing simply says that if someone obtains a copyrighted product legally then that person may legitimately use such copies for personal purposes. However, when that person redistributes the material, then copyright is infringed. This is despite the information being value-added and augmented, or even given away free by the latter user.

287. While it is nearly impossible to prevent illegal copying using technology, there have been attempts to ensure the origins of material are maintained. On maps and images, one could use watermarks (sometimes called 'fingerprinting') inserted unobtrusively and invisible to the naked eye, to discourage users from breaking the law. Alternatively, one could introduce 'copyright traps' in the form of including false but insignificant features such as misspelling names, inserting (or omitting) cul-de-sacs in streets, encoding messages or random colours into the bits that constitute a raster image which will be preserved even if the image is altered in anyway.

---

122. *Copyright Act* 1968 (Cth) s. 196(3).

288. If data were distributed for viewing only then the data could be degraded sufficiently to make it useful for viewing only but not much else. Alternatively, a raster map in GIF or JPEG format[123] may look nice but would be of little use without the extensive metadata on the projection used to generate the pixel coordinates. Vector maps may be drawn with false coordinates using map centimetres instead of real-world meters which would look alright on a computer screen but will not be positionally correct on a mapping system. All these technological features are meant to provide an audit trail of evidentiary material if litigation were to take place and proof of ownership were to be required by the courts.

289. The term digital rights management (DRM) describes a technology for identifying, trading, protecting, monitoring and tracking all forms of rights usages over both tangible and intangible information assets including management of right holder relationships. Geospatial DRM manages all rights, not only the rights applicable to permissions over digital geographic data.

290. However, given that some users are so intent in using the information, the strategy adopted should be one that simply facilitates the use of the data and information. This may be achieved via reseller licences, and by selling rights to alter and/or redistribute the data and maps, with appropriate restrictions, acknowledgments and price to be paid. The licensing process can be as simple as that described by Brinson et al. (2001).[124]

---

123. Graphics interchange format (GIF) a common raster graphics data format to display images. Raster data in this format is compressed for simple graphics with up to 256 colours. Joint Photographic Experts Group (JPEG) is an industry committee that develops standards for digital photographs. This acronym is commonly used for raster data formats and the data files are compressed to optimize the true-colour images of photographs and remote sensing images. However, this format is 'lossy' in that a small amount of data is lost in the compressing process giving a lower quality image than the original.

124. J.D. Brinson, B. Dara-Abrams, D. Dara-Abrams, J. Masek, R. McDunn & B. White, *Analyzing E-Commerce & Internet Law* 428–429 (Upper Saddle River, NJ: Prentice Hall 2001).

Chapter 2. Legal Protection of Computer Software

291. A computer program is deemed to be a 'literary work' under section 10 Copyright Act 1968 (Cth) in which case the programmer is the owner of copyright in the computer program. Computer software is IP and is also protected by patent law. Copyright protection is automatic when recorded in tangible form. However, copyright extends only to expressions of an idea but not to the ideas, procedures, methods of operation or mathematical concepts. Patent law, on the other hand, bestows an exclusive grant to an invention which may be a product or process for a new way of doing things or offers a novel technical solution to a problem. Copyright is formality free in any country party to the Berne Convention for the Protection of Literary and Artistic Works. Patents are granted after an examination process by a government agency. The law relating to the patentability of software is not harmonized internationally.[125] In 1970s the WIPO was driving at special kind of (sui generis) protection for computer programs but failed to get international support.

292. The threshold to protect computer software is relatively low. This is because in developing software technical requirements of the programming code mandate that there is only one way to achieve a certain result as a fact, then that software is rendered uncopyrightable. Copyright protects the whole program so long as it represents creativity. [126]

293. In the computer program context, the author may be one of the following persons: the programmer, the person who conceived the idea which was implemented by the programmer, the operator of the computer on which the program runs, or the person who commissioned the work produced by the computer.[127] In other words, the author is a 'natural' person.

294. Copyright provides the right holder an exclusive right to copy the work and to make it available to anyone. However, copyright does not extend to the usage of the work, for example, one may read a book without permission. To install and run a program there is a need to make copies and the permission is granted by way of a licence. The exhaustive rights to copyright extend only to the first sell and reselling a legal copy does not infringe copyright even though reselling software requires new copies.

---

125. https://www.wipo.int/copyright/en/activities/software.html.
126. Most software can be divided into several levels including a user interface, application programming interfaces (APIs), algorithms and data structures. (1) *Level One: User Interface.* This involves how the user interacts with the program. (2) *Level Two: API.* This involves how the software is used by another program. The API may be protected by two areas of law – copyright and trade secrets. (3) *Level Three: Algorithms and Data Structures.* This includes the substantive features of the software. This level may be protected by trade secret law. Stephen Bullock, *Is There Legal Protection for Software?* (2017), at https://www.legalteamusa.net/is-there-legal-protection-for-software/.
127. *See* Ricketson (1984) *supra* at 442 and the English position in *Express Newspapers Inc. Plc. V. Liverpool Daily Post and Echo Plc.* (1986) 5 IPR 193 which distinguishes between 'works' generated by a computer and 'works' produced with the aid of a computer.

295. De-compilation (sometimes referred to as 'reverse engineering') of the computer software is permissible if only to obtain the information necessary to achieve the interoperability of an independently created computer program. However, the rules require that there is an existing right to use the program, that the information is not readily available elsewhere and that the information may not be used for other purposes.

296. Trademarks as brands are preferable for marketing computer programs. Trademark protects brands, like the name of the program, a logo, or a graphic symbol and distinguishes a program from competing programs. However, trademarks do not protect the program itself and neither does it prevent the unauthorized copying of the program code. Especially in mass markets, brands can be very valuable, it is easy and relatively inexpensive to register a trademark. But, trademarks need to be defended through a registration process.

297. Embedded software is normally found in programs that control devices other than the usual computer. These programs have been written for a specific piece of hardware. The embedded software may be copyrightable like any software and as part of hardware may be easier to patent than inventions in stand-alone software.

298. The ecosystem for smart phone applications (apps) including those of Apple, Google Android, Microsoft Windows have their own rules, guidelines and technical constraints, which may limit copyrightability. Standards in the mobile telecommunications industry may also set constraints. This is because certain functionality is required to be implemented in a standard way to make it interoperable with other systems, leaving little room for creativity. Generally, smart phone applications are copyrightable and patentable like any computer program with their own licensing policies

299. For example, Facebook apps with SaaS sitting on top of the Facebook platform suggests limited applicability for IPR protection. To comply with the technical environment, the platform necessarily constraints the functionality and implementation of the app. But apps are copyrightable as with any computer program.[128]

128. Stephen Bullock (2017) *supra.*

Chapter 3. Legal Protection of Databases

§1. Electronic Databases

300. When data are reduced to digital form, one of the first attributes that can become blurred by data processing is the control over the ownership of IPR. With digital products it may be as impersonal as pressing a button to transfer the data electronically. Similarly, the copyright notice on a digital copy may easily be deleted with the press of a key. While digital data may be handed over in a diskette one is unable to examine the article or to preview its contents as one could do with a book or printed document. However, one may add new data to the dataset.

301. The dilemma is one of tracing 'paternity' and ownership of the digital data. This is where a metadata layer becomes useful not only to describe what is being done, but also by whom, and at what stage. The product could be one where there may be multiple copyright owners and a 'new' copyright work will conceivably be the whole of the work.

302. In terms of maps and electronic databases it is said that the originality requirement is 'low' under Australian copyright law with little or no scope for a cartographer to create a fully 'original' result. This may be because geographic information systems (GIS) aim for accuracy and standardization in order to make the database more accessible.[129] The information in the database makes it valuable and the arrangement, selection and formats gives the work originality. Significantly, it has been noted with some irony that the more comprehensive a database the less scope is there to lay a claim to copyright protection based on originality. This is because in a comprehensive database, there may be nothing left to 'select'[130] and thus satisfy the requirements of the Copyright Act 1968 (Cth).

303. Electronically stored databases may be no different from non-electronic databases (e.g., printed paper copies of data) and therefore should raise no new copyright issues. Non-original databases do not quality for copyright protection because there may be no originality in the selection and arrangement.[131]

---

129. P. Eldred, *Geographic information systems and copyright: Are we on the right road*, WALIS News (March 1995), pp. 13–18 at 14.

130. *See* D.S. Karjala, 'Copyright in electronic maps', *Proceedings of the Conference on Law and Information Policy for Spatial Databases,* Tempe AZ, October, NCGIA & Center for the Study of Law, Science and Technology, Arizona State University College of Law (1994), at http://www.spatial.maine.edu.tempe/karjala.html. And in 35 *Jurimetrics J.* 395-415 (1995).

131. P. Lindsay, *Copyright Protection of Electronic Databases*, 4(1) *Journal of Law and Information Science* 287–292 (1993).

I. Authorship of a Database or Compilation

304. Databases generated from remote sensing satellite data raise considerable doubt as to whether the data in its raw form is a 'work' and merits copyright protection. The decision whether raw data and databases qualify for copyright protection will depend on an assessment of the degree of originality, the arrangement of the data and the skill in constructing the database. Uncertainty also arises as to who the 'author' of the resulting work is, if indeed there is a human 'author' at all. It seems likely that Australian courts would find some person as the author even though this issue was not addressed in a recent database case.[132]

305. The question of the 'authorship' of a compilation is complicated by technological developments. Intelligent computer software adds further information to a database whereby a compilation may be assembled by a 'robot' computer (bot). There is doubt whether the original compiler of the database still retains a claim to copyright. The original compiler logically cannot claim copyright in the information added by either a bot or another user.[133]

II. Database Rights in Derivative Works

306. In constructing a database, distinctions must be made between those that are 'constructed' and those that are 'acquired' from other sources as well as a combination of both.[134] In constructed databases the developer has complete control over the content and form of compilation of the database. The copyright issues may be determined in terms of 'what' is copyrightable and who owns such rights. For acquired databases use and control may be purchased or obtained through a licence agreement.

307. Contractual agreements may need to ensure those specific rights and obligations concerning the use, distribution and ownership of the data are preserved. The difficulty here is whether copyright protection will subsist in favour of both the developer and the data provider. A further complication arises when attempting to apportion the compensation that may be due either to one or both parties. Equity suggests that the compensation should be settled in terms of the contributions of each party to the whole. The European Union (EU) Directive on the Legal Protection of Databases has addressed the issues of database rights and such protection at length.[135]

---

132. *Telstra Corporation Ltd v. Desktop Marketing Systems Pty Ltd* (2001) 51 IPR 257.
133. J.T. Cross, *Protecting Computer Databases under the United States Copyright Laws: Implications of the Feist Decision*, in *Computers and Law* 113–127 at 115 (I. Carr & K. Williams eds, London: Intellect Books 1994).
134. *See* Milrad (1994) for a further discussion of the legal issues of the respective rights of ownership, use and distribution of different kinds of databases.
135. EU Directive 96/9/EC.

III. Revisions

308. Electronic databases are subject to constant revisions and updates. One view is that each revised and updated version should be entitled to a separate copyright protection. The problem occurs when someone other than the owner makes minor changes to an existing database. It is suggested that the person making changes may not claim copyright in the amended version. Indeed, that person may have infringed copyright in the absence of permission to use and to amend the data.

IV. Compilations and 'Sweat of the Brow'

309. In assessing whether a work attracts copyright protection the test of originality holds that the author has expended a minimal degree of skill, judgement and labour to achieve a result and that the work has not been copied from elsewhere. This concept of originality is most difficult to apply in relation to factual compilations in the form of a geographic database since copyright protection may not subsist in raw factual data.

310. The selection of facts, its inclusion or exclusion and its arrangement and presentation may be crucial in deciding whether copyright protection is available. In ICT there is doubt whether computer-produced data can claim copyright protection, whether such data are original and if so, who is the author? Also collated information in the form of an electronic database has become subject to interpretation. This is because the Australian Copyright Act 1968 (Cth) section 10(1) makes it clear that compilations of information will be protected as a 'literary work' only if a court is satisfied that the compilation represents a suitable degree of originality. Subject to these provisos, an electronically stored database will be entitled to the same amount of protection under the Copyright Act 1968 (Cth) as a conventional database in hardcopy form.

311. Facts, as such, are not protected under copyright law.[136] The principle that facts per se are not copyrightable is reflected in various statutes in the UK and US.[137] However, courts in various Commonwealth jurisdictions have found ways to protect factual compilations within copyright law. Protecting such compilations serve important social policy objectives such as the dissemination of public information and promoting an open democratic government where the citizenry are constitutionally entitled to know what their governments are doing.

312. Cross (1994) provides an interesting analysis and commentary on the central issue of copyright protection in compilations and the kinds of protection that

136. J.T. Cross, *supra* at 113.

137. In the UK s. 35 of the *Copyright Act* 1911 and s. 48(1) of the *Copyright Act* 1956 include 'compilation' under the scope of protected subject matter. In the US § 103 *Copyright Act* 1976 Pub. L. No. 94-553 *as amended* by the *Berne Convention Implementation Act* of 1988 Pub. L. No. 100-568 *currently codified* at 17 USC. §§ 101-810 allows copyright protection to extend to compilations of information but only to the new material contributed by the author of the compilation.

are available to different types of electronic databases.[138] The arguments for and against the protection of databases spring from *Feist Publications v. Rural Telephone Service Company*.[139] This analysis may be contrasted by the Australian case of *Desktop Marketing Systems Pty Ltd v. Telstra Corporation Ltd*.[140]

313. Facts are not copyrightable because the author has not created them.[141] However, a compiler of a database may obtain copyright protection for the selection and arrangement of the facts in an original and creative way. It is easy to identify the point at which the database takes on sufficient structure, coherence and order to qualify the database as an original work. Much of the effort in a database is expended in collecting and transforming the data into a computer. Its real value depends on the amount and quality of information it contains.

314. Significant differences in approaches have been taken to give protection to compilations and database around the world. Even within the US there is continual debate on the impact of the *Feist* decision. On the one hand, there are fears of an unbridled 'free-rider' problem where there may be those who will take the fruits of a compiler's efforts without having to pay for it.[142] On the other hand, there are those who take the view that the decision in *Feist* is making a return to sound copyright principles because the reduction of copyright protection lessens the possibilities of putting monopoly power over information in select hands.[143]

315. In *Desktop Marketing Systems Pty. Ltd. V. Telstra Corporation Ltd.*[144] decided in the Federal Court in Australia suggests that under Australian law only a low threshold of originality is required, and copyright protection is available for the effort of gathering and listing of data. This decision appears out of step with international approaches for the protection of databases. As well certain assumptions regarding authorship have been made which may open the way for future challenges. In *Feist*, the decision emphasized originality in the sense of requiring a minimum degree of creativity in selection and arrangement of the data in a database.

316. The Australian approach in Telstra is enigmatic for several reasons. First, it ignores the basic principles of copyright law because it protects the information and facts in a work rather than the form of expression of that work. Second, the decision prevents 'second comers' from building on the ideas and the creation of value added or derivative products. Finally, the decision may have the effect of potentially conflicting with Australian competition laws where the database owner could choose to refuse to licence the copyright in the compilation or charges prohibitive

138. J.T. Cross, *supra*, 113–127.
139. 111 SC 1282, 113 L. Ed. 2d 358 (1991).
140. [2002] *FACFC 112.*
141. *See Feist* 111 S. Ct.; 113 L.Ed. 2d. at 370 per O'Connor J.
142. J.C. Ginsburg, *'No "sweat"?' Copyright and other protection of works of information after* Feist v Rural Telephone, 92 Columbia. L. Rev. 338 (1992).
143. J. Litman, *Copyright and Information Policy*, 55 Law & Contemporary Problem 185 (1992).
144. *[2002] FACFC 112.*

licence fees.[145] While section 46 of the Trade Practices Act 1974 (Cth) (TPA) deals with the misuse of market power and anti-competitive practices section 31(1)(a), the Copyright Act 1968 (Cth) bestows exclusive rights to reproduce and adapt a work on the copyright owner.

317. Several alternative solutions to the impasse have been suggested such as contract law in addition to the use of technological protection measures (TPM). The tort of unfair competition was proposed but rejected by the High Court in *Moorgate Tobacco Co Ltd v. Philip Morris Ltd (No. 2).*[146] Compulsory licensing and sui generis rights have also been given as alternatives. Compulsory licensing, also known as statutory licensing, use of the data is permissible but users have to pay a royalty to the copyright owner. This is thought to be administratively cumbersome and there is no agreement as to what the 'correct rate' of charging might be. While this solution may partially solve the 'free rider' problem, access to socially significant data is available to the general public for data collected with taxpayer funds.[147]

318. In Australia, legislative intervention may be required to review of copyright protection of databases and compilations. The present path shows that copyright laws are going in the direction of virtually granting a monopoly in mere information, patently out of step with the rest of the world.

V. Maps as Factual Compilations and Mere Representations

319. Wolf has described why courts, erroneously, have treated maps like 'directories' just as in the white pages listing in *Feist.*[148] Arguably, the source of such errors in interpretation may be traced to an over-dependence on the 'sweat of the brow' theory as a substitute for originality as in *Telstra*. More importantly, it reflects the confusion between maps as factual compilations and maps as a pictorial representation of reality. (*See* discussion on GIS below in Part IX.)

145. *See* C. Lee, *High Court Hangs up on Issue of Copyright and Compilations*, 16(4) Australian Intellectual Property Law Bulletin 45–60 (August 2003).
146. (1984) 156 CLR 414; 3 IPR 545.
147. *See* S. Givoni, *Pushing the Boundaries of Copyright: Protection of Databases*, 15(8) Australian Intellectual Property Bulletin 113–118 (January 2003).
148. D.B. Wolf, *Is There Copyright Protection for Maps after Feist?*, 39 J. Copyright Society 224 (1992); and D.B. Wolf, *New Landscape in the Copyright Protection for Maps:* Mason v Montgomery Data Inc., 1(4) GIS Law 14–17 (1993).

A. 'Thin' Copyright Protection

320. The term *thin copyright* has been coined especially for map products.[149] Thin copyright provides protection against the 'grosser forms' of copying and encourages the adding of value either through verification or revision or through improvements in presentation.[150]

321. In other words, a veneer of copyright protection is afforded to, say an electronic database which is made up of various elements including compilations that are 'normally' not copyrightable and those 'creative' elements which are copyrightable. When assembled together the new work may attract copyright as it is ostensibly a newly created original work. Thus, while there may appear to be infringements of copyright works, the new work has value-added to the original by way of revision, updating and improvements in presentation. The infringement of copyright is thinly veiled and explains the term 'thin' copyright.

322. More generally, it appears that many national copyright laws provide protection for databases irrespective of whether they contain protected works or not. However, most also require that the databases be characterized by some minimum level of originality or intellectual creation by reason of its selection and arrangement. Different levels of originality and creativity between jurisdictions introduce uncertainty for database producers as to whether the database will qualify for copyright protection. Thus, some countries provide special protection to those works that lack the minimum level of originality to safeguard the investment in producing the database.

323. Nordic countries, for example, have adopted a common provision which states that 'Catalogues, tables and similar productions in which a great number of items of information have been compiled, as well as programs, may not be reproduced without the consent of the producer until ten years have elapsed from the year in which the production was published.'[151]

324. In Japan, similar provisions apply when an amendment to the Copyright Act in 1985 makes specific reference to 'data base works'.[152] Data base is defined as 'an aggregate of information such as articles, numerals or diagrams, which is systematically constructed so that such information can be searched for with the aid of

---

149. Karjala 1994 *supra.*

150. R.A. Gorman, *The* Feist *Case: Reflections on a Path-Breaking Copyright Decision*, 18 Rutgers Computer & Tech LJ 731 (1992).

151. *Copyright in Literature and Artistic Works*, Act No. 158 of 31 May 1961 (Denmark), Art. 49; *Copyright in Literature and Artistic Works*, Law No. 404 of 8 Jul. 1961 (Finland), Art. 49; *Property Rights in Literary, Scientific or Artistic Works*, No. 2 of 12 May 1961 (Norway), Art. 43; and *Copyright in Literary and Artistic Works*, Law No. 729 of 30 Dec. 1961 (Sweden), Art. 49.

152. *Copyright Act* 1970 (Japan) Law No. 48 of 1970, Art. 12.

a computer'. These are protected as independent works 'where, by reason of the selection or systematic construction of information contained therein, [they] constitute intellectual creations'.[153]

325. From the above discussion, the emergent unresolved issues seem to be the special protection accorded to database producers to authorize exclusive reproduction, in whatever manner or form; limitations to this right in respect of literary and artistic works including the database; and the minimum protection the database. These unresolved issues remain contentious as they may fall outside the scope of international copyright conventions and the principle of national treatment. And the special protection might dilute copyright protection where it might otherwise be applicable.

§2. European Union Database Directive

326. As everywhere else, the pressing issues concerning databases include duration of protection, authorship, ownership, and protection of non-original databases and rights to unfair extraction. The European Union Directive on the Legal Protection of Databases applies to 'a collection of independent works, data or other material arranged in a systematic or methodical way and individually accessible by electronic or other means'.[154] The Directive does not apply to computer programs as this is given protection in a separate EU Software Directive of 1991.[155] The Database Directive introduces a unique two-tier protection scheme for electronic and non-electronic databases. First, Member States will provide protection of databases through copyright as intellectual creations. Second, the Database Directive introduces sui generis database right that prevents the unauthorized extraction or re-utilization of contents of a database.

I. Sui Generis: Database Right

327. A *database right* protects the 'sweat of the brow' of a database producer who has made a substantial investment in either obtaining, verifying or presenting the contents of a database (Article 7 section 1). The scope of the database right extends to 'preventing the extraction and/or re-utilization of the whole or a substantial part of the database evaluated qualitatively and/or quantitatively of the contents of a database'. There are limited statutory exceptions (Article 9) such that there are no special privileges for journalists, quotation rights, library privileges or the reuse of government information.

153. Law for Partial Amendments to the Copyright Law of 23 May 1986 (Japan), Art. 2(1) (xter).
154. 96/9/EC (OJ L7, 27 Mar. 1996).
155. European Union Council Directive 1991 Legal Protection of Computer Programs 91/250/EEC OJ L 122/42 of 17 May 1991.

§3. CONCLUSIONS

328. Databases represent great investment of time, skill and capital to put together. If the prevailing view were not to offer copyright protection for databases, then economics would dictate the size, scope and scale of the production of such databases by either public or private enterprise. On the other hand, if there were copyright protection for databases whether by the special or usual kind then private enterprise may perceive this to be a lucrative new market niché ripe for exploitation. The issue of copyright in databases thus distils to questions of access and monopoly rights, economics and policy. The ascendancy of one over the other may delineate the boundaries of protection for creators of electronic databases. Little or no protection will give insufficient incentives to develop and maintain databases. Too much protection may stifle research, development and learning and at the same time encourage the negative aspects of monopoly power as well as civil disobedience.

329. An important implication for ICT industry is that data providers should be alert to the opportunities for licensing arising from database rights while data users should be careful in avoiding violating either the copyright or database right of owners of databases. Such owners should also be vigilant to unauthorized use especially if the database is online and to label databases with clear notices to show that it is protected by a database right. Developers of databases should also keep a record of work they undertake in building the resource including time and money spent on its maintenance and the dates when databases are significantly updated. This latter is important if a new database right is to apply and a new period of protection to begin.

Chapter 4. Legal Protection of Circuit Layouts

§1. Introduction

330. The origins of the Australian scheme for protection of circuit layouts is understood within the context of US developments. Because of the inadequate protection accorded computer chip designs by trade secret, copyright, and patent law, the American Congress passed the US Semiconductor Chip Protection Act 1984 (SCPA) to provide a completely new form of IP protection not for the semiconductor chips themselves, but for their most easily copied part, the circuit layout designs or 'mask works'.[156] The US Congress sought to induce other nations to enact similar protections by including a reciprocity section in the law that provided, in part, that the US would provide IP protection for chips made in other countries only if those other countries would enact or make 'good faith efforts and reasonable progress' toward establishing a legal regime that would provide protection substantially similar to that provided by the SCPA. Australia and most other advanced industrial nations applied for and received interim protected status. By so doing, Australia committed itself to providing adequate reciprocal IP protection to semiconductor chip design layouts.

331. A second impetus for passage of the Australian Circuit Layouts Act 1989 (Cth) (CLA) is the Treaty on Intellectual Property in Respect of Integrated Circuits (the 'IPIC Treaty'). Australia participated in the negotiation of this treaty under the auspices of the WIPO in 1989. The treaty committed its signers to passing legislation to protect semiconductor chip designs.

332. Negotiation over IP rights protection was also part of the Uruguay Round of the General Agreement on Tariffs and Trade (GATT) negotiations and resulted in the TRIPS, WIPO, 26 May 1989 (which became effective on 1 January 1995). Australia and 120 other nations have adopted the Uruguay Round results, including TRIPS. Under TRIPS the minimum standards its signers are to meet is mandated and they may provide greater protection for IPR if they so choose. Among the TRIPS agreement many provisions is a section dealing specifically with semiconductor chip design layout protection. Essentially, TRIPS bound its signers to enact the protective legislation that the IPIC Treaty had called for, with some changes demanded by the US and Japan. Thus, Australia's anticipated obligations under TRIPS provided a third stimulus to passage of the CLA. Australia's law protecting circuit layouts draws heavily from earlier versions of such laws passed in the US,[157] UK,[158] Europe[159] and Japan.[160]

---

156. US 17 USC. ss 901–914.
157. Although the *Circuits Layouts Act* 1989 (Cth) is patterned primarily upon the US *Semiconductor Chip Protection Act* 1984, it contains at least four important differences. First, its definition of an 'IC' in s. 5 is broader than the US definition of a 'semiconductor chip product', s. 901(a)(1), most particularly in that it protects IC formed on any material whereas the SCPA law is more restrictive. Second, the SCPA contains no creativity requirement for protection, s. 902(b), but the CLA does in

333. A semiconductor chip is a tiny electronic integrated circuit (IC). It is called a semiconductor because it is neither fully conducting nor fully non-conducting; rather, it can be fabricated to partially conduct electricity in ways selected by its designers. It is called an IC because the electrical circuit is integrated with the semiconductor material, usually silicon. The chip contains a series of electronic gates and other electrical components organized in a three-dimensional structure fabricated from the silicon base. Engineers design the circuit layout (topography) of the chip's electric circuits. The layouts are roughly analogous to an architect's plans for a house.

§2. Background: Circuit Layout Protection

334. The *CLA* provides a sui generis form of IP protection for circuit layouts. The Act's passage was a product of diplomacy emanating from negotiations for Free Trade Agreements with various countries. The CLA commenced on 1 October 1990. This legislation provides that owners of circuit layout designs are not required to register them to be granted rights. Under the same principles as underlie copyright law, circuit layout rights automatically protect original layout designs for IC and computer chips. A synoptic view of the main divisions of the CLA is shown below Figure 5.

335. The owner of an original circuit layout has exclusive rights to: (1) copy the layout in a material form; (2) make IC from the layout; and (3) exploit it commercially in Australia.[161]

336. From the first commercial exploitation, which must occur within ten years of creation of the layout, or ten years from when it was first made, exclusive rights continue for a period of ten years, with the result that the maximum possible protection period is twenty years from the year of making an EL.

s. 11. Third, the SCPA contains a registration requirement, s. 908, which has no comparable provision in the CLA. Finally, the CLA contains a broad innocent infringement defence in s. 20, whereas the SCPA requires even innocent infringers to pay a reasonable royalty, s. 907(a)(2).

158. UK Semiconductor Products (Protection of Topography) Regulations 1987 (SI 1987 No. 1497), later replaced by Design Right (Semiconductor Topographies) Regulations 1989 (SI 1989 No. 1497).

159. In the EU to encourage Member States to qualify under the reciprocity provision of the US SCPA, the Council of the EEC issued Directive 87/54/EED, OJ No. L 24, 27 Jan. 1987, p. 3.

160. Japan enacted on 31 May 1985 the 'Act Concerning the Circuit Layout of a Semiconductor Integrated Circuit'. The law took effect on 1 Jan. 1986.

161. https://www.ipaustralia.gov.au/understanding-ip/getting-started-ip/types-of-ip.

Figure 5 A Synoptic View of the CLA

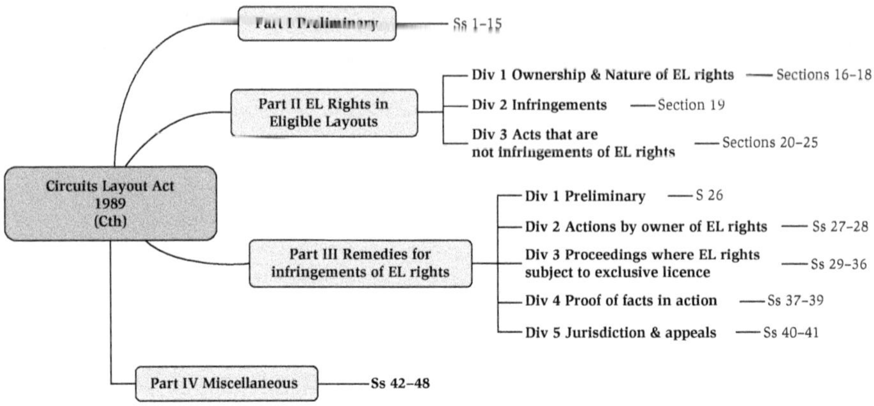

§3. Relationship with Other Areas of IP

337. It can cost tens of millions of dollars and take several years to research and develop a new generation semiconductor chip, yet that same chip can be disassembled, its essential design or layout photographed, and a perfect copy fabricated for a tiny fraction of that cost and in just a few months. Today, however, many believe that changes in technology and fabrication techniques have made circuit layout design piracy much less feasible than it once was, rendering sui generis legal protection less necessary than had originally been thought.

338. This alleged ease of 'reverse engineering' neutralizes the protection chip designs might otherwise be provided by trade secret law. Patent law does not provide satisfactory protection because chip designs are developed more by 'sweat of the brow' effort than by the inventiveness that is the sine qua non of patent protection. Copyright law provides inadequate protection for computer chips because of the fundamental rule that copyright law does not protect useful or utilitarian articles standing alone.

339. Therefore, traditional forms of IP protection are not adequate to protect designers of semiconductor chips. Although the CLA draws heavily from copyright law concepts and somewhat less from patent law principles and some aspects of IC may be entitled to protection under these regimes, the CLA provides a unique form of IP protection for circuit layouts.

340. The interrelationship with other areas of IP has meant that enactment of the CLA has required consequential amendments to the Copyright Act 1968 (Cth) section 10(1), the Designs Act 1906 (Cth) sections 4(1), 6, and the TPA section 51(3).[162]

162. *See generally* Halsbury's Laws of Australia, Designs (Vol. 15) para. [240-3610].

341. Note that the Australian copyright legislation explicitly precludes the possibility that certain aspects of IC may also be protected under copyright or patent law. The definition of 'artistic work' under the Copyright Act 1968 (Cth) section 10(1), expressly excludes 'circuit layout'. Thus, the design drawing of a circuit layout, the photolithographic mask and a photograph of a layer could not be considered as forms of 'artistic work' under Copyright legislation. However, the layout data (e.g., a written logic statement as opposed to the physical form of the logic device itself) incorporated in an IC may be a 'literary work' as it is 'written' and in 'material form' and given that the definition of 'material form' under the Copyright Act includes any form of notation or code whether or not the recording is visible. As a literary work, the IC would arguably be protected should it be infringed if copied by a design drawing, photolithographic mask or layout data or an IC in the same form.

342. Object code, which may be stored electro-physically as a pattern of electronic circuitry, is protected as a result of amendments to the Copyright Act in 1986, section 10(1) definition of a computer program. Thus, the logic instructions inherent in an IC could constitute a computer program and be protected under Copyright Law.[163]

§4. Protection under the CLA

I. Criteria for Protection

343. The criteria for protection of circuit layouts to confer monopoly rights include originality section 11, eligible persons section 5, eligible foreign country section 14, commercial exploitation section 8, and EL section 5.

II. Nature of Protection

344. The Act presumes that the maker of an EL is the first owner of the layout's EL rights in section 16(1).[164]

345. During the period of protection, the owner of EL rights is accorded three exclusive rights:

(1) to copy the layout, directly or indirectly, in material form, section 17(a).
(2) to make an IC in accordance with the layout or a copy of it, section 17(b).
(3) to commercially exploit the layout (and copies of it and IC made in accordance with the layout or copies of it) in Australia, section 17(c).

---

163. *See Autodesk v. Dyason* (1992) 173 CLR 330. *See also* A. Christie, *Integrated Circuits and Their Contents: International Protection* Ch. 13 (Law Book Company 1995).
164. *Circuits Layouts Act* 1989 (Cth) s. 16(1).

III. Length of Protection

346. The Act protects EL rights for between ten and twenty years, with the period granted depending on the circumstances.

§5. Commercial Dealings

I. Assignment and Licence of EL Rights

347. EL rights are personal property and as such may be assigned or licensed, section 45(1).

II. Prospective Ownership

348. The Act makes various provisions for prospective ownership of future EL rights, including that if a person who would be the owner of prospective EL rights upon their coming into existence assigns those rights (wholly or partially) via a signed writing to another (the 'assignee'), then when the rights come into existence they vest in the assignee or his or her successor in title, section 44(1).

III. Advantages of Marking

349. EL rights are entitled to protection whether or not marking occurs. However, evidentiary advantages arise from such marking should infringement litigation occur. Specifically, the Act provides that if at the time an EL (or a copy of it or an IC made in accordance with it or an article into which such a circuit has been incorporated) was first imported or distributed by way of trade, the layout (or the copy, the circuit or a package containing it, or the article) bore a prescribed label or mark, such label or mark constitutes prima facie evidence that any person dealing at or after that time with the layout (or copy or IC) has been notified of the subsistence of EL rights in the layout, section 44(2).

IV. First Sale Doctrine and Parallel Importation of Integrated Circuits

350. The protection provided to the owner of EL rights is not to disrupt normal commerce by impeding the proper availability of IC used in machinery and consumer appliances, section 24.

351. Although the owner of the EL rights can still prevent the copying of the circuit layouts, it cannot control the importation or distribution of the legitimately acquired chips. Thus, section 24(1) has the effect, *inter alia*, of ensuring that there is no prohibition on parallel importing of IC made in accordance with an EL.

V. Parallel Importation of Software

352. The second portion of the Act that seeks to ensure proper commercial availability of products incorporating properly acquired chips are rules dealing with the importation of integrated chips embedded with copyrighted software, section 24. This provision involves the interplay of the CLA with the Copyright Act 1968 (Cth) and addresses the situation where an IC contains a copy or an adaptation of a copyrighted computer program.

353. Section 37 of the Copyright Act 1968 (Cth) provides that it is copyright infringement to import a copyrighted article into Australia if the importer knows or should know that the making of the article would, if it were made in Australia by the importer, constitute an infringement. Section 38 provides that a copyright is infringed by the selling, leasing, or exhibiting of an item in Australia if the importer knew or should have known that the article, if it had been made in Australia by the importer, would have constituted a copyright infringement.[165]

354. Thus, parallel importing of computer programs is permitted by the CLA if those programs are stored in IC, whether those circuits are contained in kitchen appliances or computer game circuit boards, creating a limited exception to Copyright Act's 1968 (Cth) provisions. This exception is required in order to accomplish the CLA's purposes, which did not include prohibition of importation of legitimately manufactured circuits.[166]

355. Relevantly, the Australian Government sought to clarify matters through introduction of the Copyright Amendment (Parallel Importation) Act 2003 (Cth) which made some provisions for parallel importing, primarily affecting the *grey market*, which had appeared to fill the void left by the confused situation discussed above.

§6. ACTS OF INFRINGEMENT

I. Elements of Infringement

356. An EL right is infringed by a person who during the protection period and not having a licence from the owner (a) copies or authorizes the copying of the layout in a material form[167] (b) makes or authorizes the making of an IC in accordance

165. Although these restrictions on parallel importation have been heavily criticized, as in the 1992 Report of the Price Surveillance Authority on its Inquiry into Prices of Computer Software finding that retail computer software prices in Australia are on average 49% higher than in the US, the April 1995 report of the Copyright Law Review Committee recommended their retention.
166. Therefore, under current law parallel importation of IC is treated differently than parallel importation of computer programs. And this fact creates a difference in treatment of parallel importation of computer programs depending on whether they are stored in an IC or not.
167. 'Material form' is defined in s. 5 as 'any form of storage (whether visible or not) from which the layout, or a substantial part of it, can be reproduced'.

with the layout, or (c) commercially exploits, or authorizes the commercial exploitation of the layout in Australia 'if the person knows or ought reasonably to know, that he or she is not licensed by the owner of that right to do so', section 19. The first two types of infringement are known as 'primary' or 'direct' infringement; the commercial exploitation type of infringement is a 'secondary' or 'indirect' infringement.[168]

357. Infringement can occur without copying or making or commercially exploiting the entire EL. The CLA specifies that any reference to doing any act in connection with a layout includes doing that act with a 'substantial part' of the layout, section 13(a). However, any similarity in circuit layout designs that is necessitated by the technological requirements of the product should not be actionable.

§7. Defences

I. General

358. Part II Division 2 section 19 of the CLA specifies activities which are 'not infringements of EL rights'.

II. Statutory Defences

359. Innocent Commercial Exploitation. Generally, knowledge of the existence of another's EL rights is not required for infringement of the Act, section 21(1). However, the CLA provides a defence for innocent commercial exploitation, sections 20–25. These include copying for private use, copying for teaching or research purposes, evaluation or analysis, permitted use under licence, for purposes of defence or security.

360. The CLA is silent on the issue of which party bears the burden of proof in relation to a reverse engineering defence. However, the general rule adopted by Australian courts is that the burden of proof lies on the party asserting such a defence.[169] The CLA further allows the creation and commercial exploitation of a new, original circuit layout or IC based on the reverse engineering evaluation and analysis of another's layout. However, this new layout or IC created by such reverse engineering must itself be original.[170]

168. *Nintendo Co. Ltd. v. Centronics Systems Pty* [1994] 121 ALR 577.
169. This was applied by the court at first instance in *Nintendo v. Centronics Systems* (1991) 23 IPR 119, at 132.
170. Originality is defined in s. 5 of the Act, under 'eligible layout'. *See Nintendo Co. Ltd. v. Centronics Systems Pty* [1994] 121 ALR 577 in which the defendant produced a scaled-down version of the plaintiff's layout. It was held that this involved no evaluation or analysis and no intellectual or unique design work and was therefore not 'original'. It was therefore not exempted from infringement.

III. Common Law Defences

361. For circuit layouts, it may be argued that the idea/expression in underlying copyright defence found in copyright law, is ineligible for protection.[171] However, the form that comprises the layout is protected by the CLA. Applying the idea/expression principle in this way, it may be a defence that the alleged layout in question copies only the function, but not the form, of the protected layout and is therefore not an infringement.[172]

§8. Remedies for Infringements

I. Who May Bring an Action

362. The CLA limits the rights to bring an action to the owner of EL rights and the exclusive licensee of the owner, Part III sections 27–30. A non-exclusive licensee cannot sue for an infringement.

II. Available Remedies

363. The CLA specifies various remedies for infringements of EL Rights. The court may 'grant an injunction (subject to such terms, if any, as the court thinks fit) and either damages or an account of profits', section 27(2). In assessing damages, the court considers the flagrancy of the infringement; any benefit accruing to the defendant because of the infringement and all other relevant matters, section 27(3). Having considered all these factors, the court may award 'such additional damages as it considers appropriate in the circumstances', section 27(4). In an action in which the owner and exclusive licensee's interests are involved, the court in assessing damages must consider 'any pecuniary remedy already awarded to the other party', section 33.

364. In cases of innocent infringement, the plaintiff is not entitled to damages, 'but is entitled to an account of profits in respect of the infringement, whether any other relief is granted or not', section 35.

III. Groundless Threats of Legal Proceedings

365. Under the CLA where a person, including the owner of EL rights, uses 'circulars, advertisements or otherwise, threatens a person with an action or proceeding

---

171. *See* A. Christie, *Integrated Circuits and Their Components: International Protection* 131–135 (North Ryde, NSW: The Law Book Company Limited 1995).

172. Because the 'literary' distinctiveness inherent in a circuit layout is low, practitioners searching for copyright parallels in this area should compare alleged infringements of such items as compilations and directories.

in respect of an infringement of EL rights, the person threatened may bring an action for a declaration to the effect that the threat is unjustifiable, an injunction to stop the threat, and may recover any damages sustained, against the person making the threats unless that person can show that there was an infringement of the EL rights of the person making the threat', section 28.

§9. Procedural Matters

I. Limitation of Actions

366. The CLA specifies that an action must be brought within six years from the date when the infringement took place, Part III, Division 2, section 28.

II. Proof of Facts

367. The CLA creates some evidentiary presumptions. 'EL rights will be presumed to subsist in the circuit layout to which the action relates if the defendant does not put in issue the question of whether those rights subsist in the layout' and where EL rights subsist in the layout, the plaintiff claiming to be owner will be presumed to be the owner if the defendant does not put in issue the question of ownership, Part III Division 4 section 37.

III. Jurisdiction and Appeals

368. The CLA confers jurisdiction on the Federal Court of Australia with respect to actions in relation to infringements of EL rights under the Act, section 47. The CLA further provides that jurisdiction, when exercised by the Supreme Court of a State or Territory, shall be exercised by a single judge of the Court. An appeal in relation to a matter under the CLA and from a decision of a court of a State or Territory lies: '(a) to the Federal Court of Australia; or (b) by special leave of the High Court, to the High Court', section 41.

Chapter 5. Other IPR in ICT

§1. Moral Rights

369. The moral rights regime was introduced in Rome (1928) and was contained in the Paris Revision (1971) of the Berne Convention. The revision gives protection of moral rights such as the right to paternity and right to integrity and it would be up to member countries to impose either civil or criminal sanctions. Australia as a Convention signatory is bound by the principle of national treatment, which means it recognizes moral rights and is now part of the Copyright Act 1968 (Cth) as amended in 2000.[173] National treatment means that works are protected in countries of the Convention on a reciprocal basis, foreign nationals are to be treated the same as citizens.

370. In 1988 the UK introduced specific legislation for the protection of non-economic rights of creators for the first time.[174] The US Copyright Act does not recognize moral rights and few court decisions can be said to have helped establish any recognized moral rights. IP lawyers have argued that US legal practice has provided many attributes of moral rights despite not having amended the legislation to make such rights explicit. Case law is said to adequately protect such rights under the rubric of related legal regimes such as defamation, privacy and unfair competition. Thus, while the US signed the Berne Convention in 1991 and in so doing recognized the moral rights that protect a creation, such rights have not been explicitly established by legislation in the US.[175] The US has never adhered to recognizing moral rights mainly because of a lack of such a tradition.[176]

371. In the ICT industries generally there does not appear to be a moral rights regime per se but rather one that is interpreted as a national treatment issue. Thus, the ownership of foreign copyright by virtue of international conventions, agreements, and treaties may bring with it moral rights if the work is to be published in a jurisdiction which recognizes such rights. The author's rights to attribution and acknowledgment, the right to integrity of the work to be published unaltered and the inalienable rights of the author, may be preserved under such circumstances.

372. Defences to infringement include those that have been undertaken in good faith or where the author had given genuine consent or where an exception applies.

173. *Copyright Amendment (Moral Rights) Act* 2000 (Cth).
174. *Copyright Designs and Patents Act* 1988 (UK) ss 77–89.
175. A.W. Branscomb, *Who Owns Information? From Privacy to Public Access* 86 (New York: Basic Books 1994).
176. In a limited way one may read moral rights as having appeared in a statute. The US *Visual Artists Rights Act* 17 USC §106A provides protection for moral rights for works of fine art only – prints, drawings and some types of photographs.

I. Moral Rights

373. Copyright protects only a limited class of acts such as copying and publishing for a limited time. However, another set of rights, recognized by Australia, Europe and the Berne Convention – *droit moral* – protects the integrity of a creator's work in terms of reputation and honour.[177] Moral rights are not transferable and remain with the author and heirs for fifty years from the year of the author's death. Moral rights include a:

- right to attribution, that is, the right to claim authorship of a work;
- right not to have authorship of a work falsely attributed; and
- right to integrity, that is, the right to object to any distortion, mutilation or other modifications which might be prejudicial to the artist's honour or reputation.

374. Under traditional copyright protection, the right to control publication has economic implications because an author may be permitted to take a benefit on the price every time the work is sold subsequent to its initial disposal. *Droit moral,* however, introduces a non-economic component to copyright protection and may be exercised by individuals and co-authors. Moral rights subsist in literary, dramatic, musical and artistic works and films but not sound recordings, broadcasts or published editions.

II. Sui Generis Rights

375. In the light of the limited protection provided to databases and compilations of fact under copyright law, there have been suggestions that a law should be created for a sui generis right in databases, independent of copyright law and other common and statutory law.

376. The electronic age has brought about the ready appropriability of information borne on or near the face of widely distributed products.[178] In manufacturing economies, trade secrecy laws provide significant lead times for firms to recoup investments. In information economies trade secrecy protection offers little because of the greater amount of know-how that is borne on the face of an information product. Thus, in order to address the needs of emergent information economies there is

---

177. Members of the EU and eastern European countries recognize a *droit de suite* right that allows creators to benefit from resale of their work. This is an optional right for member countries of the Berne Convention. It operates only in those countries that choose to recognize such rights (Ricketson 1984, *supra* at 380, 432–434). It is doubtful if such a right is being contemplated either in Commonwealth jurisdictions or in the US. *See generally* P. Groves, *Moral Rights*, in *Copyright and Designs Law. A Question of Balance. The Copyright, Designs and Patents Act, 1988* Ch. 6 114–135 (London: Graham & Tratman 1991).

178. Know-how borne 'on the face' of software products refers to the information and knowledge revealed in using the program or in the user manuals. 'Near the face' refers to the underlying program that may be revealed through de-compilation of publicly distributed object code.

an urgency for a new legal regime that will provide, artificially at least, a lead time that is functionally equivalent to that under trade secret law.

377. Sui generis rights may provide a middle position for information products that either cannot fit into any of the established IP regimes or where the negative aspects under current IP law provide little or no protection. The difficulties in applying copyright principles to electronic databases need not be rehearsed, suffice to say that the weight of legal opinion suggests that it is time to try and find novel solutions for new products that accompany information systems.

§2. Business Methods and Geographic Information Patents

I. Business Methods

378. While business methods have become patentable in Australia it may be noted that such patents may need to be closely monitored.[179] The concerns are whether business methods patents encourage innovation and whether patents have been granted to truly novel ideas. Furthermore, much of the controversy surrounding such patents is a consequence of 'the relative inexperience' of patent offices around the world in this new field of patenting.

379. A business method patent is like any other patent except that the subject matter happens to relate in some way to a method of doing business. There is generally no definition of a business pattern save by way of an example. The Amazon.com 'One-Click' patent, often cited as a classic example, is directed to a system and method for placing an order to purchase an item via the Internet.[180] The methodology involved is one where information associated with one user is pre-stored by a website. When that user orders items from the website, with only one click of a mouse – clicking a link associated with the item – the user may order that item without having to do much else.

380. A search of the US Patent Office (USPTO) website for business method patents will show that many different types of such patents have been issued, some of undue scope.[181] Rappa (2002) has summarized the various kinds of business models and the variety of ways these types of patents that may be categorized and implemented.[182]

179. *See* Australian Advisory Council on Intellectual Property (AACIP), *Report on a Review of the Patenting of Business Systems* (2004), at http://www.acip.gov.au/library/bsreport.pdf.

180. US Patent No. 5,960,411 issued 28 Sept. 1999.

181. http://www.uspto.gov/patft/index/html for access to the USPTO's searchable databases.

182. These include various models: *brokerage* with brokers as market makers, *advertising* as an extension to the traditional media broadcast model, *infomediary* or information intermediaries, *merchant* for wholesalers and retailers of goods and services, *manufacturer* where buyers are contacted directly and the distribution channel compressed, *affiliate* in which purchase opportunities arise wherever people may be surfing on the net, *community* based on user loyalty, *subscription* where

381. Most other countries are taking a more cautious approach compared to the expansiveness of the US approach. Many are working towards the international harmonization of IP law and the globalization of commerce. For example, the Patent Offices of US, Japan and EU have met on several occasions and report a 'consensus' opinion consisting of two propositions. (1) 'A technical aspect is necessary for a computer-implemented business method to be eligible for patenting', and (2) 'to merely automate a known human transaction process using well-known automation techniques is not patentable'.[183]

382. The position of the European Patent Office (EPO) is given in the Convention on the Grant of European Patents, known as the European Patent Convention (EPC). The EPO will grant a European patent for new inventions that involve an inventive step and is susceptible to industrial application (EPC Article 52(1)).

II. Geographic Information Patents

383. While patenting has traditionally been for the protection of new manufactured goods increasingly patents have been sought and obtained for use in the ICT and geographic information industries. A search of the USPTO's online database for 'Geographic Information System' and 'GIS' reveals that there were over 105 'hits' that satisfied the Boolean search parameters. The abstracts of selected geographic Information type patents reveal an interesting mix. Some patents are from the related field of computing such as database design. Most are in the areas of image processing, global positioning systems (GPS) navigation and routing, vector and raster based geographic data, map-based directory systems, three-dimensional interactive image and terrain modelling systems, and methods for mapping and conveying product location. There is one patent in particular which is currently of great interest and dismay to the geographic information industry at large.

384. It appears that the day of the patent in the ICT and geographic information sector has now unavoidably arrived and that every sensible organization in the sector should be patenting their inventions and improvements.[184] But patent law is territorial and as such there is a need to file patents in many jurisdictions to ensure its global enforcement. While lodging patents can be an expensive exercise it would have to be weighed up against the potential revenue streams it might generate. Forum shopping suggests that the US market would be a lucrative one not only because of its size but also because of its 'expansive' patent laws that also permit

users are charged a fee to subscribe to a service and *utility* a metered service pay-as-you-go approach. *See* M. Rappa, *Managing the Digital Enterprise* (2002), at http://www.digital-enterprise.org/models/models.html.

183. *See* Report on Comparative Study Carried Out Under Trilateral Project B3B, 14–16 Jun. 2002 at http://www.european-patent-office.org/tws/front_page.pdf.

184. J. Radcliffe, *Death of Copyright – Long Live Patents*, 2003 Cambridge Conference, Ordnance Survey, Southampton, UK Paper 4D.2B (2003).

the patenting of business methods and systems. The marriage of ICT and business methods would offer organizations that create and patent significant breakthroughs a market niche and market dominance.

§3. The Digital Agenda

385. The 'Digital Agenda' is a broad term that is used to describe the implementation of the 1996 WCT (Article 11) and WPPT (Article 18) that focuses predominantly on the protection of copyright content in the digital networked environment. The Copyright Amendment (Digital Agenda) Act 2000 (Cth) which came into operation on 4 March 2001 and the US Digital Millennium Copyright Act 1998 (DMCA) are of a similar genre. Both enactments and similar ones in other jurisdictions provide legal protection and legal remedies against circumventing TPM used by copyright owners to protect their work from piracy.[185] These enactments have implications for the ICT industry and those involved in the development and implementation of online technologies or those who work with other digital media.

386. The definition of a 'work' under Australia's Copyright Act 1968 (Cth) is much enlarged including computer programs and code, digital movies and pictures, e-mails, compilations and a wide variety of different works incorporated in multimedia presentation. Web-based ICT products – interactive maps, dynamic map queries, databases – would thus be caught under this Act. The amendments to the Act extend the traditional protection of copyright laws to original electronic and digital works. Similar to the DMCA in the US a balance between the increased rights of copyright owners and the public interest in access to information has created a series of exceptions to new owner rights. A majority of these are an extension to existing rights in the digital environment.

387. Under the Copyright Act 1968 (Cth) the severity of the penalty depends on the type of infringement and whether the offender is an individual or a company. A new technology-neutral right of communication is provided to enable communications over the Internet. The legislation also introduces prohibitions against the development and sale of copyright-circumvention tools which could be physical (a hardware key or dongle) or non-physical (such as software tools). It is also an infringement of copyright to remove DRM information or to deal with material that do not have DRM information.

388. Even with the adoption of the DRM model, while it may not stop all forms of piracy, such as 'insider' copying of master files, the system can prevent the illegal and unauthorized uses of digital content. In addition, it may be possible to track every use of the content such as how many times it is used, when it is used and so on which may bring with it grave privacy implications.

---

185. Section 116A (Australia) and s. 1201 (US) respectively. *See also Copyright, Design and Patents Act* 1988 (UK) s. 297A, and *Copyright Act* 1994 (NZ) s. 226(2)(a).

§4. Atypical Developments and Other Legal Issues

I. The 'Copyleft' Movement and No Rights Reserved

389. Given the impracticalities of policing and enforcing IPR in the ICT industry, there has grown up a movement under the rubric of FOSS. FOSS makes available its source code free for public use and encourages users to debug, change the source code and redistribute the derivative software. 'Free' in this sense is the freedom to use the software program for any purpose, to study how it works and adapt it to one's own needs, to redistribute copies and to improve and share it with the community. It does not mean that the price is zero, since FOSS can be traded in the market. Users are encouraged to think 'free speech' not 'free lunch'.[186] The idea of 'free' software is not new given that during the 1960s and 1970s when most people were using mainframe computers, source code was freely accessible and taken for granted.

390. In the US, AT&T's Bell Labs led the way in developing the UNIX operating system and associated language 'C' that could run on different and varied hardware. Under terms of a regulated monopoly deal with the US Department of Justice, AT&T could not sell UNIX for profit and so it distributed source code to universities and others to improve the software and fix bugs. The thinking of the day was that software was given away free as a hook to encourage people to buy proprietary hardware.

391. The logic of free software broke down in the late 1960s when the US Department of Justice filed a massive antitrust suit against IBM forcing it to 'unbundle' its systems and to sell its software separately. IBM sold mainframes with operating systems that did not distribute source code. In fact buyers had to sign non-disclosure agreements simply to get executable copies.[187] These decisions marked the birth of the modern commercial software industry and by 1975 the start of the widespread use of Microsoft software. The arrival of the personal computer in the early 1980s also made software extraordinarily valuable. This is where FOSS came into its own and reinvented itself in the mid-80s.

392. To replace traditional copyright, the Free Software Foundation (FSF) developed a standard copyright agreement, the GNU Public Licence (GPL) often called 'copyleft'.[188] The central idea of the GPL is to prevent cooperatively developed open/free software source code from being turned into proprietary and restrictively copyrighted software. The GPL states that users are permitted to run the program, copy the program, modify the program through its source code, and distribute modified versions to others. What programmers may not do is add restrictions to the program. This is the 'viral' clause of GPL since source code that has

186. Free Software Foundation (FSF), *The free software definition* (1996), at http://www.fsf.org/philosophy/free-sw.html.
187. R.T. DeLamarter, *Big Blue: IBM's Use and Abuse of Power* (New York: Dood, Mead 1986).
188. *See* GNU GPL http://www.gnu.org/licenses/gpl.html.

been 'copylefted' is to be released using GPL as well. The rapid spread of the Internet in the early 1990s accelerated FOSS activity with the development of the GNU/Linux PC operating system. The official GNU/Linux version 1.0 operating system was released in 1994 and became a credible competitor to Microsoft in the PC operating system market.

393. In the 1990s there was also an alternative institution for 'free' software – the Open Source Initiative (OSI) as a response to the decision by Netscape to publicise the source code for its WWW browser. OSI requires entities distributing FOSS to satisfy the Open Source Definition (OSD) in its copyright statement.[189] While copyleft GPL requires any redistribution of GPL software to be released only under GPL, the OSD allows redistribution under the same terms, but does not require it. OSD source code must be distributed with the software or otherwise made available for no more than the cost of distribution. Anyone may redistribute the software for free, without owing royalties or licensing fees to the author. Anyone may modify the software or derive other software from it and then distribute the modified software under the same terms. OSI removes the viral impact of the GPL. Towards the end of the 1990s the FOSS process had proved its viability not only in building complex software packages that could compete with proprietary products in other market segments.

394. In the new millennium, the Creative Commons project was given worldwide impetus with the release of Lessig's book The Future of Ideas.[190] The Creative Commons is an organization based at and sponsored by Stanford University, offers a number of licences designed to allow the broader use of copyright material. The licence allows the licensee to use copyright matter subject to one or all of the following conditions: attribution, non-commercial distribution, no derivative works – verbatim copies only, and share and share alike. The Creative Commons is also engaged in the international commons (iCommons) project to post and translate their licence to other legal jurisdictions.[191]

395. The Creative Commons has since released its new computer-readable copyright licence designed for artists, writers and programmers who want to give the public access to their works.[192] The Founders Copyright licence, in the form of code that can be added to a digital work, allows authors to specify exactly how other people can use the work and lets those details show up in a search engine. The Creative Commons is dedicated to expanding the number of works of any nature in the public domain. Under the terms of the Founders Copyright between the Creative Commons and a contributor, a contract will guarantee that the relevant creative work will enter the public domain after fourteen years. During the first fourteen

189. http://www.opensource.org/osd.html and http://www.opensource.org/docs/definition.php for more details.
190. L. Lessig, *The Future of Ideas. The Fate of the Commons in a Connected World* (New York: Random House 2001).
191. For an example of an organization using the Creative Commons licence, *see* the Public Library of Science site at http://www.plos.org.
192. http://www.creativecommons.org/projects/founderscopyright.

years the creator will enjoy all the rights that conventional copyright protection permits. In version 1.0 of the Licensing Project Creative Commons will help build licences that tell others about works that are free for copying and other uses – but on certain conditions.[193]

II. Addenda to FOSS

396. There is little doubt that access to IT is a means of enabling and hastening economic development of poor countries. In doing so, it will help developing countries leapfrog developmental stages of IT implementation. FOSS will assist such countries from depending on a few software suppliers who are often located elsewhere. In addition, the sharing of software applications across the public sector in these countries will reduce duplication of licence expenses on proprietary software. The introduction of a diversity of software reduces the possibility of failures caused by viruses that tend to attack a software monoculture. Moreover, FOSS may help avoid the use of expensive proprietary software and closed data formats.

397. FOSS is not an alternative to the IPR regime. Rather FOSS requests users to respect the IP of the software's author(s) as outlined in the GPL or OSD licence. Governments are expected to provide the legal protection and remedies when this is necessary and deserved. Moreover, the restrictive IP licensing regime may provide no encouragement for ICT development in developing countries. Ironically the increasingly stringent enforcement of IPR demanded by proprietary software producers may further encourage and hasten the switch to FOSS. With free access to source code there is empowerment as well as simple price advantage. One example is the FOSSFA initiative for Africa where the Action Plan for 2003–2005 proposes three distinct approaches a government might take in formulating its FOSS policy.[194] A neutral approach ensures a choice is supported and discrimination against FOSS is eliminated. The enabling approach sees policies geared towards creation of the capacity to use FOSS. The aggressive approach is one where governments actively encourage the development of FOSS through both legislation and policy.[195]

193. There is also a variant to the Creative Commons licence developed by Open Content. The Open Publication Licence lets anyone freely see, modify, and redistribute the content. Changes or additions must be marked as such, and anyone who releases a modified version must describe where to find the original work. The author retains copyright and can prohibit redistribution. *See* http://www.opencontent.org/openpub/.

194. The text for the FOSSFA statement is at http://www.prepcom.net/wsis/1046170300.

195. *See* FOSSFA Action Plan 2003–2005 at http://www.fossfa.org/resources.html.

III. Geographical Indications

398. Geographical Indications are place names and words associated with a place that are used to identify the origin and quality, reputation or other characteristics of products for example, 'Tequila', 'Champagne', 'Basmati' rice, or 'Parmagiano Reggiano' cheese. Article 22 of the TRIPS Agreement defines a standard level of protection, that is, geographical indications must be protected in order to avoid misleading the public and to prevent unfair competition. Article 23 provides a higher or enhanced level of protection for geographical indications for wines and spirits.

399. There are some countries that want to extend this list to a wider range of products including food and handicrafts. Among the allowable exceptions to the agreement are when a name has become a common or generic term for example 'cheddar' now refers to a type of cheese not necessarily made in Cheddar in the UK Also, when a term has already been registered as a trade mark, for example in Italy, 'Parma' is a type of ham from the region of the city of Parma, but in Canada it is a registered trade mark for ham made by a Canadian company. To date since the Doha mandate of 1997 and the Cancún Ministerial Conference of 2003 member countries of the WTO have been working towards creating a multilateral register for wines and spirits; and extending the higher level of protection beyond wines and spirits.[196]

400. In Australia the Australian Wine and Brandy Corporation Act 1980 (Cth) (AWBC) was amended in 1992 to comply with Article 23 of the TRIPS Agreement and Article 6 of the EU on Trade in Wine Agreement.[197] There appears sufficient protection conferred by domestic law to ensure that the public would not be misled or for there to be unfair market competition.[198]

401. The geospatial industry can and does play an important role in determining geographical indications. Prior to 1992 and the TRIPS Agreement there was no legal mechanism for defining Australian wine regions. States were carved into zones and then regions within zones with possible sub-regions on arbitrary and populist grounds. With amendments to the AWBC, criteria were put in place to clearly define regions and zones. Other than minimum requirements of growers, hectarages and output per annum there were other geographical factors in the criteria. The geographical elements include the geology, soil types, temperature, harvest dates, use of water, State and Local government planning Acts, history of grape growing, and documentary proof that the region is known and recognized to the outside world.

---

196. http://www.wto.org/english/tratop_e/trips_e/gi_e.htm.

197. *See* C. Cheung, *Feta Cheese – Geographic Indication or Generic Term?*, 16(9) Intellectual Property Law Bulletin 133–135 (2004). *See also* M. Blakeney & M. Kretschmer, *Intellectual Property and Geographical Indications: A Legal and Economic Analysis* (London: Edward Elgar Publishing 2004).

198. For example, the *Trade Marks Act* 1955 (Cth); *Trade Practices Act* 1974 (Cth); common law tort of passing-off, labelling legislation in *Commerce in Trade Description Act* 1905 (Cth); and State and Territorial food legislation.

402. Geologists have determined that many of the best wines in Australia come from vines grown in soils on top of limestone, the so-called terroir of a region. Evidence from radiometric maps show how geophysical tools can be used to locate better-drained soils. For example, air borne remote sensing radiometric tools measure natural radioactivity of potassium, uranium and thorium. In addition, soil types and soil profiles including soil chemistry all play important parts in determining the quality of the grape harvest.[199]

IV. Photographs

403. While the topic of photographs might appear to be peripheral to the interests of ICT professionals, the unique, dynamic and multimedia possibilities of the Internet to store, present and deliver information have created a whole new methodology of both fair use/dealing and what constitutes copyright infringement. Photographs in general are protected under relevant copyright legislation worldwide, whether in print form or on the Internet. The difficulty is to decide what constitutes fair use.

404. In the US, for example, the case of *Kelly v. Arriba Soft Corporation*[200] revolved around the use of 'thumbnail' pictures. The issue before the court was one of what constituted fair use. The court held that where the thumbnail could be enlarged to a higher resolution, then the copying is not excused as fair use but an infringement of the exclusive right to display the pictures for which there is copyright protection. The case held that 'in-line linking' or 'framing' constituted a copyright infringement where market harm is caused. In-line linking refers to the importation of an image from another site and to display this as if it were part of the importing website. Framing refers to one where a website displaces another website in a captured window or frame.

405. There are several implications for the Geographic Information industry. First, aerial photographs and Landsat images are now obtainable from various Internet sites where an index may be shown to customers to assist in the ordering process. Such resellers must ensure that users are unable to download the photographs and images to but to force them to purchase these products. Second, photographs and images may be no different from maps displayed on Internet sites. In the case of maps, it is important that all the marginal IPR references are preserved on the map. This is because it may be possible to capture such maps in a frame and a screen-shot taken of the display that may then be printed. To do so is to violate fair use and the rights of the copyright holder. Also, copyright owners have an exclusive right to display and publish works and a licence or permission is required before

199. C. Pain & J. Nightingale, *Geology proves fruitful for viticulture*, AusGeo News 63 (October/November 2001), p. 3. *See also* D. Farmer, *The Red Soils of Coonawarra, Part of a Unique* terroir, 7(6) *The Australian and New Zealand Wine Industry Journal* (December 2002), and at http://www.winetitles.com.au.

200. 280 F.3d 934 (9th Cir. 2002).

anyone else may do the same with the material. Furthermore, in-line linking and framing may infringe IPR. A web designer may be able to divide a web page into distinct frames, permitting some regions to remain constant on a page while other frames contain content that is reloaded as necessary as the user navigates through the site. A web design may incorporate contents of a third-party website into one frame and surround this with content contained in the local server. The Scottish Court of Session case of *Shetland Times Ltd. v. Wills*[201] illustrates how easily copyright infringement can occur on the net.[202]

V. Fonts

406. In Australia, a newspaper masthead comprising Chinese calligraphic characters is an 'artistic work' capable of copyright protection as well as being a trade mark capable of protection under the Trade Marks Act 1995 (Cth). In *Australian Chinese Newspapers Pty. Ltd. v. Melbourne Chinese Press* (2003) 58 IRR 1 the court was satisfied that the requisite level of thinking had gone into the creation of the whole work including the masthead and therefore was an original artwork capable of copyright protection. The art and the creation of the characters were sufficiently expressive and the artist had exhibited a sufficient degree of thinking in producing the work.[203]

407. A claim of copyright in computer-aided typography fonts in a brochure has also been argued. *Lott v. JBW & Friends Pty. Ltd.* [2000] SASC 3 is an appeal to the Supreme Court of SA from a decision in the Magistrates Court where copyright was found to exist and to have been infringed. The respondents had stated that they were commissioned to produce a brochure Opera in the Outback. There was a dispute over unpaid fees as well the respondents had sought damages for 20 occasions of infringement of copyright.

408. The Supreme Court of SA found that the respondents had designed the graphic bar; that they owned the copyright in it; and that the Director of the Company that had commissioned the design and authorized the publication of the graphic bar in advertisements was personally liable for the breach of copyright. Additional damages were awarded for the flagrancy of the infringements even though it was argued that there was an implied licence and a customary arrangement to use commissioned designs for additional advertisements. The Court found the agreement was unambiguous and the licence was limited only to the use of the graphic bar on the brochure.

---

201. (1996) 37 IPR 71; and [1997] SCLR 160.

202. *See* earlier reference to deep linking and the *Ticketmaster Corporation v. Microsoft Corporation* No. 97-3055 DDP (CD Cal. 12 Apr. 1997).

203. C. Pappas, *Can Copyright Subsist in Chinese Characters?*, 16(9) Intellectual Property Law Bulletin 150 (February/March 2004).

409. For the ICT industry, fonts used on maps have been carefully chosen to provide effect and contrast. The size, shape, colour and weight of the font used can illuminate and bring out important features. Many of the fonts used in the industry are invariably those which are either in the public domain or those used under licence from major corporations such as Monotype Corporation, International Typeface, and Agfa Monotype. The design and artwork that accompany the fonts on maps may have a degree of creativity, originality and artistic merit that together are capable of protection under copyright laws. More importantly, the person commissioning the work may claim copyright ownership unless there is an assignment of those rights, as in the case of bespoke computer software discussed previously where the programmer retains copyright.[204] A summary of the various means of protecting IPR is given diagrammatically in Figure 6.

Figure 6 Protecting IPR: A Summary

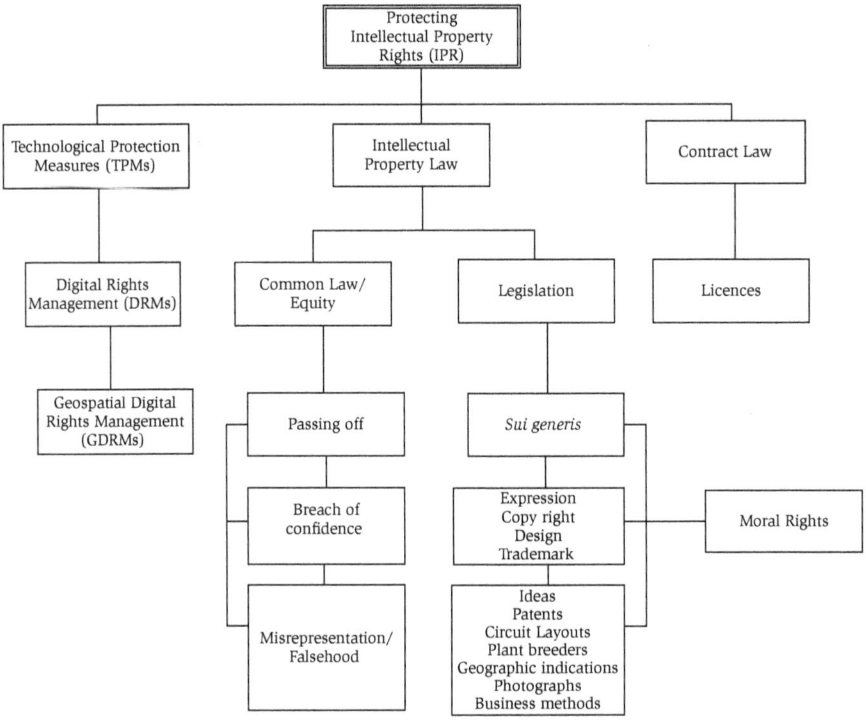

204. G. Cho, *Geographic Information Systems and the Law* 67–68 (Chichester: John Wiley & Sons, 1998).

Chapter 6. Business Names and Internet Domain Name Registration

§1. Registration of Business Names

410. Alongside the design attributed to an enterprise, the business name is probably the most visible and therefore valuable trading tool available to it. In Australia a business name is protected by the States and Territories through application of Business Names Acts which are substantially identical. These aim at protecting the business from another trader using the same name, and the interests of the public by requiring persons who do business in a name other than their own to register their names, addresses and nature of the business carried on. The issues are critical in the impersonal electronic environment in which Internet business is done. Another important factor is that business name legislation also gives limited protection against the tort or civil wrong of passing-off by denying registration for names which are identical or substantially similar to a previously registered name. Registering a business name does not in itself give you any exclusive rights over the use of that name – only a trademark can give provide that kind of protection.

411. Unfortunately, the existence of limitations imposed by a lack of effective cross-jurisdictional cooperation between registering authorities limits the effectiveness of the scheme. Under the Corporations Law 2001 (Cth) section 374 requires a company must be registered under a chosen name which must be used in all company transactions, at the same time citing a unique Australian Company Number (ACN) and Australian Business Name (ABN) allocated by the Australian Securities and Investments Commission (ASIC).[205]

412. In practice, however, the system of business name regulation through legislation suffered from serious drawbacks. The various State and Territory acts allowing registration did not confer any proprietary rights over a business name. This was no defence to deliberate attempts by pirate firms seeking to masquerade as other firms by using substantially similar or even identical trading names within a jurisdiction.

413. All business name registrations are now managed by the ASIC. All business names registered under State and Territory registers have now been transferred to ASIC's national business names register.[206]

414. The business name registered and used by a firm will frequently be the product name by which the firm is known to the public and on which its trading success rests. In such a circumstance, its protection is of the utmost importance, and for a firm to effectively protect a business name, the best course might well be to eschew reliance on business name registration as protection and to register the name

205. Section 374 *Corporations Law* 2001 (Cth).
206. www.search.asic.gov.au/gns001.html.

as a trademark under the Trade Marks Act 1995 (Cth). Alternatively, where a rival is detected attempting to use the name, the firm might wish to become proactive and utilize some remedy such as the TPS section 52 in proving that by using another's business name the offending party has engaged in conduct which is misleading or deceptive.[207]

415. The Australian Consumer Law 2010 (Cth) (ACL) may well prove to be the best option against the practice of cybersquatting (the practice of masquerading a business in which it has no expertise). Section 18 of that Act prohibits misleading or deceptive conduct, and it also prohibits misrepresentations as to affiliations, approvals and endorsements. It is a breach of the ACL to represent that your company or products have a commercial connection with another company or its products if no such connection exists.

§2. Domain Names

I. Definition

416. Every computer connected to the Internet and every web page is allocated a number under the Internet protocol. This number or address enables computers connected to the Internet to locate each other. Each address consists of twelve digits separated by full stops (.) into four groups of three numerals, for example, 123.456.789.876.

417. A domain name is also termed a uniform resource locator (URL). Because numbers are difficult to remember, a system of names was developed to represent the numbers. People can more easily remember Amazon.com than the URL number behind it. URL's are structured into four or more segments. First, the transfer protocol is stated (http or ftp). Second, a network sector is given (e.g., www for the World Wide Web), third a domain name is used. This domain name is divided into a unique segment (e.g., the trade name of a business); a generic portion (the Top Level Domain (TLD) which indicates the type of entry owning the domain name (e.g., government body, commercial entity, educational institution). Finally, the country code, for example, '.au' for Australia. All four segments can be seen in the domain name of the University of Canberra: www.canberra.edu.au.

418. Domain names under generic Top-Level Domain Names (gTLDs) may be registered with one of more than two thousand ICANN-accredited registrars, or their resellers. Registrars are accredited by the Internet Corporation for Assigned Names and Numbers (ICANN) organization and certified by the registries to sell domain names. They are bound by the Registrar Accreditation Agreement (RAA) with the ICANN organization, and by their agreements with the registries. Resellers are organizations affiliated with or are under contract with registrars to sell domain names and other services offered by the registrar such as web hosting or e-mail

207. Section 52 *Corporations Law* 2001 (Cth).

mailboxes. Resellers are bound by their agreements with the registrars whose services they sell and are not accredited by ICANN organization. The registrars remain responsible and accountable for all domain names sold by their resellers. ICANN organization maintains a list of current ICANN-accredited registrars on its web site.[208]

419. Domain name registrations under country code Top-Level Domain Names (ccTLDs) can be made through the ccTLD operators.[209]

II. Typology of Domains

420. Originally there were seven gTLD that described the type of organization involved. These included:

(1) '.com' for commercial corporations.
(2) '.org' for various organizations that do not fit other categories.
(3) '.net' for organizations involved in Internet operations.
(4) '.edu' for educational institutions, like the University of Canberra.
(4) '.gov' for government departments and other entities, example, act.gov.
(5) '.mil' for military and defence entities.
(6) '.int' for international organizations.

421. The ICANN has added seven more gTLDs:

(1) '.biz' for businesses.
(2) '.info' for unrestricted general use.
(3) '.pro' for professional firms like doctors and lawyers:
(4) '.name' for individuals.
(5) '.museum' for museums.
(6) '.coop' for cooperatives.
(7) '.aero' for air transport industries.[210]

422. There is ccTLD which adds a country designation following the categories of domains listed previously. In the case of Australia, the ccTLD is '.au'.

423. In 2005, ICANN's Generic Names Supporting Organization (GNSO), which is the main policy-making body for gTLD, began a policy development process to consider the introduction of new gTLDs, based on the results of trial rounds conducted in 2000 and 2003. Although no new action has been taken at the time of writing, significant expansion of gTLD offerings are expected after 2014.

---

208. https://www.icann.org/registrar-reports/accredited-list.html.
209. https://www.icann.org/resources/pages/register-domain-name-2017-06-20-en.
210. The US has been lobbying for a specialized 'Kids domain that would provide an online safe-haven for children'. *See* http://www.newsbytes.com/news/01/167478.html.

III. Administration of Domain Names

424. ICANN was established in 1998. It is a private non-profit corporation that runs the domain system via a memorandum of understanding with the US Department of Commerce.[211] It came up for renewal in September 2002. The ICANN website links to the various registrars' registration website.[212]

425. Domain name registration in Australia started with the Internet Assigned Numbers Authority (IANA) which was the predecessor to ICANN. IANA granted responsibility for the 'au' ccTLD to Mr Elz in Australia in 1986 when the domain name system was first introduced into Australia. Mr Elz persuaded the University of Melbourne and other research bodies to become involved in the Internet in its pre-commercial form.

426. In 1996, Mr Elz signed a five-year licence with the University of Melbourne's commercial unit, Melbourne IT, to register second level '.com.au' domains. Since that time eleven second level domains have been established under the '.au' ccTLD. These include: asn.au, com.au, conf.au, csiro.au, edu.au, gov.au, id.au, info.au, net.au, org.au and oz.au

427. In 1999 the Australian non-profit company, auDomain Administration Limited (auDA), was established and endorsed by the Australian government as the body that should manage the 'au' ccTLD. Elz sub-delegated to auDA his management authority over the second level 'com.au' which comprises about 85% of all domain names. In July 2000, auDA entered into a controversial agreement with Melbourne IT not to register '.com.au' domains until after Melbourne IT's rights to register domain names via Mr Elz's authority expired in Oct 2001.

428. In May 2001, auDA approached ICANN, asking that the management of the entire 'au' ccTLD domains be formally re-delegated to auDA. An agreement to this effect was signed in October 2001.

429. In November 2001, auDA assumed technical and administrative control over the entire.au domain space. This was a major step to the introduction of a new system of 'au' ccTLD management that allows for competition in the provision of domain name services. Under the new system, AusRegistry Pty Ltd has been awarded the tender to provide registry services for the 'com.au', 'net.au', 'asn.au', 'id.au', and 'org.au' domains.

430. AuDA has also developed a Uniform Domain Name Dispute Resolution Policy (UDRP) implemented in relation to the 'au' ccTLD. It has also developed a

211. https://www.icann.org/registrar-reports/accreditation-qualified-list.html. This page links to the various registrars' registration website. For information on the various geographic domains, *see* www.iana.org/cctld.html. The ICANN website is at www.icann.org/registrars/accredited-list.htm.
212. For information on the various geographic domains, *see* https://www.iana.org/domains/root.

Code of Practice governing Domain Name Suppliers.[213] Finally, auDA has also undertakes a consumer protection role and regularly issues consumer briefings and warnings regarding domain name issues.[214]

431. AuDA operates under Commonwealth telecommunications legislation that reflects the federal government's powers under the Australian Constitution in relation to communication.

432. AuDA has progressively developed new policies and introduced competition for the delivery of domain-related services domain registration. It is not a government-owned corporation and is not established by specific Commonwealth legislation. However, its powers and responsibilities are delineated by federal law such as by the Telecommunications Legislation Amendment Act 2000 (Cth), which amended the Telecommunications Act 1997 (Cth) and the Australian Communications Authority Act 1997 (Cth) regarding responsibilities of the ACA (now ACMA) and ACCC in relation to electronic addressing.

433. The new '.au' registry ushered in a lighter regulatory regime. Companies can now have more than one Australian 'com.au' name and can register names according to trademarks.[215]

§3. Registration in Australia

434. An emerging issue is registration of domain names in other than the English language. While 75% of domain names are registered in English, yet only 5% of the world speaks English, and change is inevitable, and there has been considerable press coverage about cybersquatting in relation to English business names, driving many businesses to look at other languages. US company Verisign's subsidiary, Network Solutions and other companies have started registration services for language domains in sixty different languages.[216] Until recently, the only languages available were English, Chinese, Korean and Japanese. The Chinese Internet Network Information Centre (CINIC), has protested at this monopoly by US companies and sought to take control of Chinese registries. Singapore based I-DNS (www.i-dns.com) is yet another player in the Asian domain name market. Finally, with its multicultural background, Australian businesses are active in multilingual e-commerce. In fact, some firms are already using call centres placed in Melbourne, for example, because so many native speakers from diverse languages are available there.

---

213. http://www.auda.org.au/.
214. For a list of auDA policies, *see* http://www.auda.org.au/policy/.
215. N. Lindsay, *Looser Domain Name System Takes Over*, Australian Financial Review 45 (1 Jul. 2002).
216. www.nsi.com.

435. In mid-2014, AuDA announced a review of its Policy Rules and Guidelines for Community Geographic Domain Names (CGDN).

436. The auDA adopted a policy on the issuing of domain names in the Open Second Level Domain Names (2LD) category, with a set of general policies underscored by specific criteria regarding eligibility.

I. Unassignable Licence

437. Upon the issuance of a domain name, it becomes unassignable. The licence agreement used in Australia provides that the licence via a domain name does not confer any legal rights to the name. Nor does it provide any immunity regarding an objection from another party about either the registration or the use of the domain name. The licence is revocable either upon the decision of a domain name dispute resolution panel or a court order.[217]

§4. Domain Name Dispute Resolution Procedure

438. Under ICANN rules, all Domain name registrars must follow the UDRP. Under the policy, most types of trademark-based domain name disputes must be resolved by agreement, court action, or arbitration before a registrar will cancel, suspend, or transfer a domain name. Disputes alleged to arise from abusive registrations of domain names (e.g., cybersquatting) may be addressed by expedited administrative proceedings that the holder of trademark rights initiates by filing a complaint with an approved dispute resolution service provider.

439. To invoke the policy, a trademark owner should either (a) file a complaint in a court of proper jurisdiction against the domain name holder (or where appropriate an in rem action concerning the domain name), or (b) in cases of abusive registration, submit a complaint to an approved dispute resolution service provider.

I. Australian Domain Name Dispute Resolution Procedures

440. Many ccTLDs, including Australia, have chosen to use the UDRP as a starting point and then modify it to suit the local context. For example, in the.uk registry, they have decided to use a mediation procedure as a first step before escalation to formal arbitration. However, given there are almost 200 different countries involved in Domain Name registration, it would be desirable if all domain name disputes adopted the same procedure.

---

217. http://www.auda.org.au/pdf/auda-2003-01.pdf.

II. Domain Name Versus Trade Mark

441. The fact that a company has incorporated under a name does not automatically give it rights to get a domain name registered under that name. Thc fact that a business has been using a name does not necessarily give it a right to obtain a domain name registration for that name. Someone else may have already registered that name as a domain name or may be using that name as a trademark, either of which may preclude anyone else from registration of that domain name

442. In contrast to a domain name, which creates no IPR, a trademark is a recognized IPR and it will normally prevail over a domain name which offends the trademark protection.

443. Companies naturally seek to register domain names that incorporate their key trademarks. However, if two companies have virtually identical trademarks, but relating to different classes of goods or services, the domain name rights will normally go to the first entity to register. For this reason, it is important to register early.

444. There has not occurred in Australia the same level of cybersquatting experienced in the US. This is because the registration process (a) has required the domain name holder to have a legitimate business interest in acquiring that name; and (b) the registration process itself checks the registration application against the trademark database to look for prior registrations of the name.

III. Critique of the UDRP Cybersquatting

445. It is important to realize that while the domain name dispute resolution procedures have the advantage of speed and low cost, there are also disadvantages. Under the UDRP and procedures modelled upon it there is no discovery available as in normal commercial arbitration. In contrast to the full range of awards available through litigation and even arbitration, UDRP awards are limited to either: (a) cancellation or de-registration of the offending domain name; or (b) transfer of the domain name to the legally entitled owner. The URDP procedure does not permit the resolution of other issues and is not appropriate for the resolution of complex legal issues. There can be no award of damages or other relief. Finally, in contrast to the privacy and finality of an arbitral award, parties may appeal an UDRP decision in the courts, but this has seldom been done. Because decisions are not binding, plaintiffs may in fact pursue litigation and the URDP avenues of redress at the same time.[218]

218. UDRP decisions are listed on the ICANN website: http://www.icann.org/udrp.

§5. REFORM

I. Australian Reforms

446. The auDA's advisory panels have released several reports and reviews for public consultation and reforms to the .au domain space. Another presented a model for introducing competition into the domain name services.

447. Among its recommendations auDA has resolved that the following reforms be adopted and implemented:[219]

- No restriction be placed on the number of domain names a single entity may hold.
- au domain names continue to be licensed only to Australian entities.
- Applicants must declare a bona fide intention to use the domain name.
- There continues to be a connection between the domain name licence holder and the domain name, though this need not be the company name or trading name.
- Existing prohibition on registering generic and geographic domain names should continue.
- A limited number of second level domain names be introduced such as the new gTLDs.
- A new dispute resolution policy be developed that largely adopts the ICANN UDRP as applied to Australian conditions.

II. Reform of ICANN

448. Over the years the role and future of ICANN has been the subject of much debate.[220] Among the suggested reforms for ICANN greater accountability and to give other governments greater say through the Government Advisory committee.

449. An important issue is that ICANN defines and enforces IP rules regarding rights in domain names, which inevitably has a highly significant impact on the ability of Internet users to access information and therefore, the meaningful exercise of the right to freedom of expression.

450. Over the years, however, several concerns have been raised about ICANN's legitimacy in taking policy decisions in certain areas due to its corporate governance arrangements, in particular:[221]

- the lack of independence from the US government as regards the IANA function;

---

219. https://www.auda.org.au/assets/Policies/auDA-Policy-Review-Panel-Interim-Report-15-May-2015.pdf.
220. *See, e.g.,* white paper by the US National Telecommunications and Information Agency of the Department of Commerce: http://www.ntia.doc.gov.
221. http://www.article19.org/resources.php/resource/37494/en/icann-reform:-recommendations#sthash.MQQMsJrt.dpuf.

- the lack of representation of developing countries within ICANN;
- the disproportionate influence of the Government Advisory Committee (GAC);
- the lack of accountability of the Board;
- an indication that support for ICANN and its role is not universal is evident.[222]

451. Another problem with new domain names is that they are open to two types of abusers such as:

(1) the squatters, who have no legitimate interests; and
(2) those who have limited rights in one area and want generic positioning unavailable under Trademark law.

452. At the request of the Australian Government, WIPO has undertaken a Second Domain Name Process dealing with disputes about geographic indications and terms, International Non-proprietary Names (INN), names of international intergovernmental organizations (IGO), personal names and trade names. As part of this process, WIPO considered protection of geo-political terms (e.g., Europe) and geo-ethnic terms (e.g., Aborigine). In 2006 ICANN informed the Secretariat that while it had not been possible to achieve consensus among ICANN's constituencies concerning the recommendations of the Second WIPO Internet Domain Name Process, that progress might be possible with the protection of names and acronyms of IGO. Subsequently, ICANN in 2007 recommended that new gTLD agreements may provide for protection of the names and acronyms of IGOs at the second level through a Dispute Resolution Procedure (separate from the UDRP) incorporated in new gTLD contracts. To date such policy remains under consideration for implementation.[223]

453. Another suggested reform is the extension of the UDRP to handle generic drug and government names. No doubt the popular domain name dispute resolution service offered by WIPO will gradually be extended to cover new domain areas such as government organizations, generic names for pharmaceutical substances and international organizations.[224]

454. In July 2013, the US Department of Commerce Internet Policy Task Force issued the Copyright Policy, Creati*vity, and Innovation in the Digital Economy* (the Green Paper), which examined the major copyright issues, such as digital performance rights, technology protection measures and mass digitization projects, and

---

222. A group calling itself the 'People for Internet Responsibility' issued an open letter in March 2012, 'Overcoming ICANN: forging Better Paths for the Internet' describing ICANN a 'failed experiment' and recommending the immediate transfer of Internet-related function performed by ICANN to another non-profit organization. *See* http://www.pfir.org/statements/icann.
223. http://www.wipo.int/amc/en/processes/process2/.
224. *See* 'The Recognition of rights and the Use of Names in the Internet Domain Name System: Report of the Second WIPO Internet Domain Name Process', http://wipo2.wipo.int.

their relation to the Internet economy. The Green Paper proposed steps that should be taken legislatively, as well as voluntarily via private sector initiatives, to fully utilize the Internet economy while adequately protecting privacy and copyright rights.[225]

225. http://www.uspto.gov/news/publications/copyrightgreenpaper.pdf.

Chapter 7. IPR: Infringements, Defences and Remedies

§1. Infringements

455. In Australia, the Copyright Act 1968 (Cth) provides that it is an infringement of copyright to do any of the acts exclusively reserved for the copyright owner without the copyright owner's permission. The Act also covers the importation of works into Australia for sale where the making of such works would have constituted an infringement. Moreover, to 'authorize' infringements is also proscribed. In practice such statutory provisions have been difficult to enforce not only because of the way the law is framed but also because such difficulties are directly attributable to the technology involved. With the convergence of IT there is a gradual a move away from physical media towards electronic digital media. Nationally and internationally copyright law protects the bulk of IPR with little need for registration. Trademark and patent protection requires country by country registration. However, in the case of trans-border flow of physical as well as electronic data and materials the enforcement of IP law has become problematic.

456. Fair dealing and fair use of copyright protected materials are limited to private, non-commercial or educational uses. Once one begins to deal commercially with the work, fair dealing or fair use may no longer apply and copyright may be infringed. However, it is not an infringement of the reproduction right to use the work in a way that does not produce copies of that work. This means that the work must be used as a 'whole' and unchanged; the user must acknowledge the original source of the work and the user may read or orally convey the contents of a work to another.

I. Territorial Copyright and Parallel Importation

457. Sections 37 and 102 of the Copyright Act 1968 (Cth) entitle owners of copyright to prevent others importing into Australia articles such as books, records, computer software which contain copyright material. Sometimes referred to as a 'territorial copyright', it applies to all articles with or without the consent of the owner of the copyright in the country of manufacture.

458. Where the imported article is manufactured with the consent of the copyright owner it is sometimes referred to as 'parallel importation' or 'grey marketing. Sections 38 and 103 of the Copyright Act 1968 (Cth) make it an infringement of copyright by selling unauthorized imports or dealing commercially with them.

459. One reason for these sections of the Act is that the articles would be 'devalued' if such work were imported. But, consumers of books, music and computer software have criticized this reasoning because it artificially supports a higher price for the product. Also, some articles are unavailable in Australia because the copyright owners have failed to import these articles.[226] New provisions for the importation of books have come into force since 1991.[227]

460. Section 37 of the Copyright Act 1968 (Cth) prevents parallel importing. This permits publishers to carve up national monopolies and manipulate prices making the market uncompetitive and with undesirable consequences. There is a view that parallel importing should not be maintained in the face of the irrelevance of national boundaries for works distributed through the Internet.[228,229]

II. Substantiality Requirements

461. Section 14(1) of the Copyright Act 1968 (Cth) provides that an infringement will be made out where a copy or reproduction relates to the whole work or a substantial part of it. However, the Act gives no guidance as to how the word 'substantial' is to be tested or applied. Case law suggest that it need not be a large part, but it must be an important or vital part in relation to the whole work. The test therefore is a question of fact and degree having regard to the circumstances of each case. It is the quality of what is taken in relation to the work as a whole and not the quantity that is abstracted.[230]

462. Reproducing facts without copying the expression or arrangement of facts will not be considered a reproduction of a substantial part of the work. In the context of databases there is often great difficulty in separating facts from expression of facts as demonstrated with the EU Database Directive arguments presented previously. This is because in such cases it is not simply the arrangement or the expression of the facts but rather the computer program, the so-called database management system (DBMS), which organizes and searches the database that is important. When the material form in which the copyright exists is different from the form the infringing work is embodied in, it may not be possible simply to look for visual or literal similarities in the arrangement to test whether the two works are substantially the same.[231]

---

226. *See Interstate Parcel Express Co. Ltd. V. Time-Life International (Nederlands) BV and Anor* (1977) 15 ALR 353; and *Bayley & Co. v. Boccacio Pty. Ltd. and Ors.* (1986) 8 IPR 297.
227. *Copyright Act* 1968 (Cth) ss 44A and 112A.
228. R. Appel, *Copyright in a digital age. Chaos in the debate*, ANU Reporter (13 Dec. 1995), p. 7.
229. There are no such parallel importation restrictions either in the US or in Japan, P. Knight & J. FitzSimons, *The Legal Environment of Computing* 48 (Sydney: Addison-Wesley Pub. Coy. 1990). In the UK and Hong Kong, copies made by licensees are restricted by the terms of their licences to territories outside the country into which the product is being imported, *Copyright, Designs and Patent Act* 1988 (UK).
230. P.G. Leonard & P.A. Spender, *Intellectual property protection of databases*, 9 Information Services & Use 33–43 (1989).
231. *See* B. Gaze, *Copyright Protection of Computer Programs* 142–165 and 181–194 (Sydney: Federation Press 1989).

463. Databases also pose other types of copyright problems. One problem relates to whether products of databases acknowledge the copyright existing in works that are selectively being put into a computer or its memory. The legal position is that if the data are not protected by copyright there is no legal obstacle to it being inserted into a database. But where the work is subject to copyright, the possibility of breach of copyright will depend on the size and scope of the use made of the data in totality or each datum of the database. To copy the whole database would obviously infringe copyright. Infringement will not arise if only key words or abstracts are drawn from the previous work since this merely amounts to the taking of ideas that are not protected.

III. Reproduction in Material Form

464. The phrase 'reproduction in material form' is particularly difficult to apply to electronic databases. This is because the work may be stored 'internally' in the computer as well as stored 'externally' on some storage media or device. The problem arises where a work is stored on a database without having been previously embodied in some other material form. The issue is whether a hardcopy of this database is a 'reproduction of the work' and is in a similar form prior to its storage on the database.

465. Alternatively, there is considerable doubt at the time the work is keyed directly into the computer database whether the printed copy or any other form of electronic storage or display device is an objectively similar 'reproduction' of the original work.[232] Thus, documents originating (or created) in digital form present considerable difficulties because it is more problematic in determining what constitutes a 'work', and indeed a 'page' of that work.

§2. Defences to Infringement

466. There are three types of defences to copyright infringement. In the first place, public interest may allow certain kinds of infringement of copyright. This view holds that the public interest may outweigh private economic gains.

467. In the second instance there may be a defence if a creator can demonstrate independent creation. Copyright protection, unlike other IPR, is not absolute and is concerned with preventing someone taking improper advantage of someone else's work. An improper advantage is the copying of someone else's work. Unauthorized copying is one important component of 'improper conduct'. In order to evidence copying the question of access to pre-existing works may be determinative of the

232. Ricketson (1989), *supra*, p. 480; and S. Ricketson, *Copyrights and Databases*, in *Essays on Computer Law* 67–98 (G. Hughes ed., Melbourne: Longman Cheshire 1990).

issue. Where there has been access to pre-existing works a case of substantial reproduction may be made out in contrast to a claim of no access, in which case a court could infer the existence of a defence of independent creation.[233]

468. A final defence to infringement is where copyright laws allow copyright to be overridden in cases of fair dealing / fair use. Here the balance between monopoly rights and a public's unfettered access is tipped in favour of the latter to allow for scholarly research, study, critique and news reporting.[234] The concept of 'fair dealing' as such is not defined and the difficulty for doing so has been recognized. It is a matter of degree so that the user of the work does not derive an unfair competitive advantage.[235] One qualification to this defence is the requirement of due acknowledgment of the work extracted. Giving the name of the author and title of the work may be deemed to be acknowledgment.

469. In the UK, in terms of news reporting *Beloff v. Pressdram Ltd.*[236] established a limitation on the use of this defence on public interest grounds in so far as the publishing of a leaked private confidential memorandum was concerned. However, in the case of *Commonwealth of Australia v. John Fairfax & Sons Ltd.*[237] the Australian High Court was more lenient in accepting the availability of the defence to copyright infringement where some public interest in the publication of the confidential Department of Defence document could be established.

§3. Remedies

470. In Australia the remedies available to an infringement of copyright are formidable including restraints by injunction, the award of damages, and an account of profits. Criminal offences attach to illegal importation of copyright works and there are seizure and forfeiture provisions as well. In Australia, the 'infringing copies' are deemed to belong to the copyright owner. Interlocutory injunctions forbid the continuance of an allegedly infringing activity pending a full hearing of the defence. Such injunctions may be obtained on short notice so long as the plaintiff acts quickly, that a court is satisfied that a prima facie case exists and that on the balance of convenience, a defendant is not seriously and disproportionately prejudiced by the injunction. The plaintiff also undertakes to provide compensation if the defence ultimately succeeds. All injunctions are discretionary and may not be awarded if damages will adequately compensate the plaintiff.[238] A plaintiff is entitled to damages sufficient to compensate for the loss suffered. Exemplary damages are available for flagrant infringements of copyright as are conversion damages where the infringing copies are deemed to be the property of the copyright owner.

---

233. Compare *Bradbury v. CBS* 287 F. 2d. 478 (1961) with *Sutton Vane v. Famous Players Film Ltd.* (1923-28) MacG. Cop. Cases 6.
234. *See* ss 40, 41, 42 *Copyright Act* 1968 (Cth).
235. Lord Denning M.R. at 1027 in *Hubbard v. Vosper* [1972] 1 All ER 1023.
236. [1973] 1 All ER 241.
237. [1981] 32 ALR 485.
238. *Copyright Amendment Act* 1992 (Cth) ss 115 and 116.

471. Alternatively, a plaintiff may elect to claim an order equivalent to profits made through infringement. This is a discretionary equitable remedy and will not be awarded unless damages are an inadequate compensation. Under the Copyright Act 1968 (Cth) criminal offences attach to the importation of infringing copies of works for commercial purposes. The penalties are severe and can be very effective since a person with a criminal record would have difficulty in successfully tendering for government contracts or obtaining entry visas to other countries. The Customs & Excise Legislation Amendment Act 1988 (Cth) has also amended seizure and forfeiture provisions. The powers of the Australian Customs Service (ACS) have been increased in relation to investigation of the importation of goods. Infringing items may be seized and forfeited to the Commonwealth. The remedies awarded are always at the court's discretion.

Chapter 8. Summary

472. Arguably, in the electronic age, it appears that copyright offers the widest and most appropriate means of protecting the expression of ideas contained in maps, compilations, electronic databases and GIS in general. It is very much a live debate in legal and academic circles as to what and how much protection copyright can offer ICT and all its accoutrements in a globalized world where not only is infringement difficult to detect but nearly impossible to do so in an electronic world. What laws and therefore what jurisdiction become important questions.

473. There is a view that if we are to have laws to govern IPR we should strive to articulate a generic version of rights, obligations, and prohibitions. This is opposed to passing laws confined to fact situations, that is, to pass laws to cure a fact that is the cause of a problem.[239] However, in some instances this ideal might not be possible. ICT products and services, for instance, does not fit neatly into any of the specific categories of 'works' whether literary, dramatic, musical or artistic, but is the product of human creativity. Unlike other protected works, ICT products and the databases accompanying these are open to copying and unauthorized use the loss of authorship in the data in perhaps a single iteration.

474. The law is still not settled in protecting computer programs, much less ICT or GIS systems of any kind. As observed previously it is impossible to use an information system without making a copy of it first. This is radically different from traditional protected works where such copying is unnecessary. The display of data on a computer screen may constitute a reproduction in material form, as well as a 'public performance', albeit ephemeral since the display may be switched off. A print of the data stored in the computer may infringe copyright and if this were part of an electronic network, the network manager may be in breach for authorizing an 'infringement'. The dynamic nature of a database with frequent updates may make it impossible to determine when protection for the data begins.

475. There is a clever and succinct adage about copyright that states that 'what is worth copying is prima facie worth protecting'.[240] With respect the information age will make this rule of thumb and copyright an anachronism. Computer-based information storage and retrieval systems now challenge copyright law by offering new and creative ways of disseminating ideas. Whereas in a previous age copyright was concerned with copying – books, music on audiotapes, paper products by photocopiers, film by videotape – ICT is threatening to make copyright law obsolete. The new technology is part of a long line of copying methods and there is a fundamental change in that what is being copied – information in its purest form. Information has now been liberated from a physical object and floats, as it were, in cyberspace. ICT is now posing a greater challenge to a legal system that is expected

239. P. Broekhuyse, *Copyrights and wrongs: Lawyer's view of the net*, The Australian IT, The Australian, 55 (25 Jul. 2000).

240. Per J. Peterson, *University of London Press Ltd v. University Tutorial Press Ltd* [1916] 2 Ch 601.

to protect it. Laws take time to change since rapid changes per se may be counter-productive. Here practitioners and users of Geographic Information are expected to contribute to changes in the law rather than to leave it in the hands of manufacturers and software developers who may look to protect their own self-interest.

476. At present, IP in general, and copyright specifically, provides 'thin' protection to information systems, computer programs and databases. It may take some time for the law to adapt to the rapid changes brought about by IT. How quickly these changes will come about will depend on how much impact it has on society at large and the seriousness of such impacts on the socio-political economy. Previously there has been a balancing of interests between an author's rights and the dissemination of knowledge. Today, it seems that the balance is in restricting ICT and the dissemination of knowledge for society. But in striving to achieve such a balance 'care must be taken not to impede the development and use of data processing tools by unduly restrictive or complex legislation'.[241]

477. It may be that licences and agreements may become the definer of boundaries of permitted uses instead of copyright law or an industry-market standard. The importance of contract law cannot be underestimated since under licensing conditions both parties may benefit overall. On the one hand, the copyright holder may be able to achieve revenue maximization using a variety of licences for time limitations on use, limited distributions to licences at lower prices for groups of users (say non-commercial) and unlimited uses for a higher price. The enforcement thus focuses on pursuing infringements of the licence terms, a breach of contract. Users of the technology could benefit because of lower prices, easier access to the data, improved variety of content, and more certainty with the law. The issues that remain then are whether users will be willing to adopt such new distribution methods and how law makers can ensure that user rights are preserved and kept in balance with those of the vendors of IT products. '… [T]he role of copyright law may in time decline in both the protection of IP at hand and in providing fair access to that IP.'[242]

478. In the information age Walter Wriston has observed that the world economy operates on a 24 x 7 'information standard time'.[243] Commercial, financial and other data are disseminated continuously to millions of computer terminals worldwide. Such data are the grist of commercial, political and social decision-making and such decisions in turn become part of the data stream that informs the world. For the world to keep up with this information standard time there is a degree of certainty of protection of IP of data and information in terms of what is being protected, how it is being protected and for how long protection subsists. In addition, such protection must exist within an international legal system that is not only understood by

241. J.C. Risset, *Problems Arising from the use of Electronic Computers for the Creation of Works* (1979), UNESCO/WIPO doc. GTO/3 1979, Paris and Geneva: UNESCO, WIPO.

242. A. Segkar, *The Declining Relevance of Copyright Law – How Contract May Become the Key*, 6(10) Internet Law Bulletin 121–125 at 122 (2004).

243. *See* W.B. Wriston, *Twilight of Sovereignty: How the Information Revolution Is Transforming our World* (New York: Scribner 1992); and Branscomb 1994, *supra* at 151.

all but also one that has international recognition and therefore mutually enforceable across jurisdictions by way of national treatment. To achieve this ideal would mean that all the 'leakages' to copyright have been staunched and civil disobedience by way of pirating, copying and other infringement would have been eradicated and the creators of original products justly rewarded for their efforts.

Part III. Contract Law and ICT

Chapter 1. Introduction

479. Information and communication technology (ICT) contracts is narrowly defined to encompass only those types of contracts that one could make with the 'click' of a mouse online in an e-business environment. ICT contracts encompasses all types of agreements and contracts that relate to ICT. The question that may be asked is whether electronic contracts are recognized by the law.

480. In 2000 the UNCITRAL finalized the Model Law on Electronic Signatures adopted on 5 July 2001.[244] A Working Group on E-commerce examined the possibility of developing a convention that dealt with electronic documents of title and electronic contracting. This examination resulted in the United Nations Convention on the Use of Electronic Communications in International Contracts (CUECIC) adopted by the General Assembly on 23 November 2005.[245] The CUECIC updates the Model Law on E-commerce 1996. The Convention enhances the legal certainty where electronic communications are used by private parties engaged in international e-commerce. The CUECIC also eliminates legal obstacles to the use of modern means of communication in contract formation.

481. The Convention addresses issues such as the location of parties, time of contract formation, the distinction between offers and invitations to make offers, time and place of offer and acceptance, automated transactions, and the information to be made available to parties. In general, the Convention reflects the approach of Australian contract law previously discussed under the Electronic Transactions Act 1999 (Cth) (ETA).[246] The principles of functional equivalence and technology neutrality are maintained. The UN CUECIC was signed by eighteen countries including Australia.

---

244. UNCITRAL (2001) *Model Law on Electronic Signatures, available at:* http://www.uncitral.org/uncitral/en/uncitral_texts/electronic_commerce/2001Model_signatures.html.
245. UNCITRAL UN Doc A/60/515 (23 Nov. 2005) at http://www.uncitral.org/uncitral/en/uncitral_texts/electronic_commerce/2005Convention.html.
246. For details of the draft Convention, *see* AGD (2008), *Australia's accession to the UN Convention on the Use of Electronic Communications in International Contracts 2005: Proposed amendments to Australia's electronic transactions law – Consultation paper* (November), at https://www.ag.gov.au/RightsAndProtections/ECommerce/Pages/UNConventionElectronictransactionsininternationalcontracts.aspx.

482. The Australian Commonwealth Attorney General released the Copyright Law Reform Committee's (CLRC) report on Copyright and Contract. The final report of the Committee dated 30 April 2002, follows a year-long inquiry into the relationship between copyright and contract law. The report examines the ways contracts are being used in the digital environment to set the terms and conditions of access to, and use of, copyright material. The report looks at the effect contracts have on copyright as set out in the Copyright Act 1968 (Cth) and, particularly the exceptions to the exclusive rights of copyright owners.

§1. Principles of Contract Law

483. Contracts are the most common legal institution in everyday life. We enter into contracts in various ways, sometimes in a formal way by signing documents and having it witnessed and sealed and sometimes in informal ways without documents but with shaking of hands and on a 'gentleman's agreement'.

484. A first function of a contract is to signify an agreement that becomes operative when two parties intend it to be binding, that is, committed to the agreement. That agreement may be one in which one party will do something in return for which the other party will do something else – a 'meeting of the mind'. There has been an offer made, and that offer has been accepted. Therefore, we have a simple contract.

485. A second function of a contract is that it defines the respective roles of the parties and the terms by which the parties agree to be bound. It is more likely that this second role is in written form rather than expressed orally, that it has been arrived at after lengthy discussion and negotiation between the parties or that both agree to the carefully prepared terms presented by one of the parties. The presumption here is that the bargaining positions of the parties are on the same terms not only of economic strength, but also of experience in these types of negotiations.[247]

486. As contracts can take different forms, it is very important to understand the various terms used in the preceding brief discussions. As both sides strive for 'certainty' as well as covering as many contingencies as possible, and especially in online environments, contracts should be comprehensive and unambiguous to avoid causing any difficulty in interpretation.

247. *See generally* N.C. Seddon & M.P. Ellinghaus, *Cheshire and Fifoot's Law of Contract* (7th Australian ed., Butterworths 1997). *See also* D. McBurnie & E. Levinson, *Contract: Sales of Goods over the Internet. E-Commerce: The Implications for the Law Series* (The Law Book Co. 2001).

§2. Elements of a Contract

487. A contract is a legally enforceable agreement. Most rules of contract law in Australia derive from the common law, although there are different statutory provisions in each of the States covering various aspects. There is no one form of contract since it may be oral, written, a mixture between oral and written, or a series of documents linked together by a master agreement. The test of whether there is a contract between the parties depends on the actions of the parties, including what they have said and what they have written. Australia adopts an objective test in relation to contract formation.

488. In an electronic context, contracts may be formed by an exchange of e-mail, through a page on the website, at an online auction, or through an online portal. Thus, at common law there will be a binding contract and an intention to create legal relations if the following elements are present: (a) an *offer* which is *accepted*; (b) *valuable consideration* for the promises given; and, (c) *consensus* as to the subject and all major aspects of the contract.

I. Offer and Acceptance

489. For a contract to come into being, there must be a firm 'offer' by one party that is 'accepted' in its precise terms by another. There is very little that may be required to constitute offer and acceptance. *Carlill v. Carbolic Smoke Ball Co.* [1893] 1 QB 256 illustrates some of these points. This case also shows how a contract may be concluded at 'arm's length' since there was no face-to-face contact, unlike most bargains made in the marketplace between two traders. This is especially apposite in an online context where the two parties may not have met face-to-face but through the media of the Internet.

490. To determine whether there was a contract, the courts would look to see if these were mere negotiations and an 'invitation to treat'. The 'invitation to treat' is simply a legal term to mean an invitation for another party to offer to provide goods or services. Thus, in an online context, the invitation to treat may be posted electronically on a website, an electronic mailing list, or sent by e-mail to a specific recipient. But to avoid the possibility that the invitation may constitute a unilateral contract, that is, a contract taken up by a customer without reference to the offeror, websites now customarily include disclaimers indicating that statements made are not offers or unilateral contracts but are mere invitations to treat.[248]

491. In the context of the Internet, the offeror may wish to incorporate standard terms and conditions into a contract by including these on the web page. Thus, in order that these standard terms and conditions form part of the contract, the offeror must put these to the offeree so that they have a reasonable opportunity to read them.

---

248. *See* M. Chissick & A. Kelman, *Electronic Commerce: Law and Practice* (Sweet & Maxwell Ltd 1999).

To minimize legal risks, it is prudent to set out all the terms and conditions in full and up front in such a manner that the offeree cannot avoid seeing them. While this might appear annoying, some reflection should be given to balancing the risks against the certainty of concluding the contract for the business.

492. Potential liabilities may also be minimized by using disclaimers or exclusions. The effectiveness of these disclaimers is underpinned by contract law in the sense that information and services will only be provided if the person reading it agrees to the disclaimer. In general, such disclaimers or exclusions must be brought to the attention of a user and accepted by the user (e.g., by clicking the I Agree icon) in order to be enforceable.

493. Furthermore, terms and conditions of a website may place limits on those users of the website. These depend on several factors including the geographical area, the purpose, or their contribution to the site. However, the terms and conditions of a website may not exclude or restrict all liability arising from the operation or functioning of the website in all circumstances.

494. The design of the website is thus critical. When a purchaser presses the 'place order' button, a page incorporating the terms should appear automatically. The purchaser must then be made to click on a 'submit offer on these terms' button to send the order to the seller. Hence, on the assumption that the display of information on the website is an invitation to treat, the website visitor makes an offer (offeror) in relation to the good or service displayed, and the seller (offeree) communicates acceptance of that offer to the offeror on the website. Contract law will generally regard that a contract has formed. The jurisdiction of the website visitor is the place where the communication of the acceptance was received. It follows that if the offeree uses another method to communicate acceptance, for example, by posting a letter, the place where the letter was received is where the contract is formed.

495. In ICT, a request for tender (RFT) is a classic example of an invitation to treat. While not a contract in itself, the negotiations and agreements that follow an RFT may go toward the formation of a contract. As a result, the RFT may give rise to an identification of potential suppliers of goods or services that might be required by a government department and to a special kind of a contract arising from the RFT.

496. Similarly, websites and electronic mailing lists can be seen as advertisements and shop fronts that display goods and prices and give customers an opportunity to look at their goods before purchase. Such activities are then simply invitations to treat rather than offers. So is the example of an auctioneer's call for bids on an online auction site. This is a first step toward an offer and eventual purchase.

497. One issue that is emerging is the question of whether machines can accept offers. In the so-called ticket cases, in *Thornton v. Shoe Lane Parking* [1971] 1 All

ER 686, the court held that a car park machine had made an offer which was accepted when the customer put money into the slot in the machine.

498. In a US jurisdiction, in *State Farm Mutual Auto Ins. Co. v. Brockhurst*, 453 F.2d 533 (10th Cir. 1972), it was held that a computer could form a contract for the renewal of an insurance policy as the computer operated via instructions in a program written by the insurance company. Thus, if online businesses are bound by contracts 'accepted' by their computers, such businesses are also bound if, for example, a computer were to behave in a peculiar way because of a hardware fault. Computers are also incapable of accepting contracts in which the customer may have altered some of its terms. Online business contracts, therefore, are often inflexible, and terms cannot be added or deleted by customers. Any such variations would thus require a face-to-face discussion, negating the very essence of engaging in online business.

499. Sometimes computers may be programmed to carry out transactions automatically. For example, electronic agents might be used:

- to initiate or respond to electronic messages without review by a human;
- as an online shopping agent programmed to surf the Internet and make purchases; or,
- as an inventory control system programmed to place orders when stocks reach set levels, for example, in electronic data interchange (EDI) systems.

500. The legal status of electronic agents is untested. However, if an electronic agent has been programmed to respond to certain criteria and circumstances, then by extension such acts are by, and with a person's authority to implement their intentions and, therefore, can make and accept contractual offers on their behalf. The proviso is that such contracts are unexceptional and without the need to modify terms and conditions.

501. Article 4.1(a) of the CUECIC defines electronic communication broadly as 'any statement, declaration, demand, notice or request, including an offer and the acceptance of an offer, that the parties are required to make or choose to make in connection with the formation or performance of a contract'. Other issues addressed by the CUECIC include:

- The use of electronic communications to make invitations to treat.
- The determination of a party's location in the electronic environment.
- The time and place of dispatch and receipt of electronic communications.
- Use of automated message systems for contract formation.
- The criteria to be used for establishing functional equivalence between electronic communications and paper documents, as well as between electronic authentication methods and handwritten signatures.

502. In May 2010 the Standing Committee of Attorneys-General (SCAG) and Attorneys-General resolved to adopt nationally consistent amendments to their respective e-commerce laws to enable Australia to fully accede to the CUECIC.[249] As a result the Electronic Transactions Amendment Act 2011 (Cth) contains provisions addressing the issues raised by the CUECIC including (1) Invitations to treat in the electronic context; (2) The rules on electronic signatures; (3) Use of automated message systems in e-contracting; (4) Determination of the location of parties; (5) Default rules for the time and place of dispatch and receipt of electronic communications; and, (6) Keystroke errors that have unintended consequences for contract formation.[250]

503. Other issues about acceptance of a contract in online environments include the question of jurisdiction and where the contract is formed and whether the postal rule is applicable in such environments. In the case of a 'click-wrap' contract one may ask whether acceptance of the contract formed in the country where customer clicks the 'I accept' icon or where the server for the website is located or when the acceptance is communicated to the suppliers in their country of location. Common law principles suggest that a contract will be formed when acceptance is in fact communicated to the offeror – the receipt rule.

504. Courts have examined whether the postal rule is applicable to other methods of communication such as telex and facsimile documents. *Entores Ltd. v. Miles Far East Co.* [1955] 2 QB 327 suggests that the postal acceptance rule will not apply to methods of communication which are 'virtually instantaneous' – phone, fax, and telex, but not by telegram. Thus, whether the communication is instantaneous will be a significant factor in determining whether the postal acceptance rule will apply, but this is not decisive because no test case has been mounted with 'click-wrap' agreements.

505. Among private custom now in common use is the fax-then-mail procedure designed to ensure a paper record of an agreement. However, such a procedure invites a different legal problem. A party seeking to resile from the agreement communicated by fax could argue that the fax was not the final communication and that the deal was open until the original paper was mailed. In such a case, the parties may need to clarify which is the operative communication. Arguably, the postal acceptance rule may apply to an e-mail message and an acceptance effective once the e-mail was sent. The jurisdiction of the contract in that case will be that of the offeree. It has been argued that the rule should not apply to e-mail acceptance because this would place an unfair burden on offerors.[251] Moreover, the sender of an e-mail would know if a message has been received via error messages received or automatic responses to message receipts. At the same time, an e-mail message

249. AGD (2008), *Australia's accession to the UN Convention on the Use of Electronic Communications in International Contracts 2005: Proposed amendments to Australia's electronic transactions law – Consultation paper* (November), at https://www.ag.gov.au/RightsAndProtections/ECommerce/Pages/UNConventionElectronictransactionsininternationalcontracts.aspx.

250. https://www.legislation.gov.au/Details/C2011A00033.

251. S. Downing & J. Harrington, *The Postal Rule in Electronic Commerce: A Re-Consideration*, 5 Commun. L. 43, at 44 (2000).

may become lost or garbled in transmission, and this may again place greater burdens on the offeror than may be warranted if the postal acceptance rule were to be applied to acceptances by electronic means.

506. Australia adopted the 1996 UNCITRAL Model Law on Electronic Commerce, which was intended to remove legal barriers to the use of electronic communications and provides 'functional equivalents' to the use of paper-based documents.[252] The Model Law provides a set of internationally acceptable rules that may be used to overcome some of the main obstacles when conducting legal transactions in cyberspace. Thus, in Australia, electronic transmissions are no longer an issue as it has been addressed in the ETA insofar as e-business with government agencies are concerned.

507. In Europe, the introduction of the EC Directive on the Protection of Consumers with respect to Distance Contracts permits Internet consumers to be entitled to a seven-day cooling-off period for contracts made at a distance. A similar non-compulsory provision exists in the Australian Direct Marketing Association (ADMA) Code of Practice (2006).[253] The ADMA Code of Practice was developed to set standards of conduct for direct marketers, minimize the risk of breaching legislation, promote a culture of best practice, serve as a benchmark in settling disputes and increase business and consumer confidence in doing business with ADMA members who are bound to the provisions of the Code. Where there is any conflict or inconsistency between the Code and any Commonwealth, State or Territory legislation or regulation, that legislation or regulation shall prevail to the extent of the conflict or inconsistency. ADMA Members must comply with all Commonwealth, State or Territory legislation relating to business and direct marketing practices.

II. Valuable Consideration

508. Valuable consideration is merely something given in return for a promise, the price for a promise indicating that something more than mere good intentions is involved. In law, valuable consideration may consist either in some right, interest, profit, or benefit accruing to one party or some forbearance, detriment, loss, or responsibility given, suffered, or undertaken by the other.[254]

509. A mere promise to do something is not enforceable unless it is given in return for consideration. The consideration or price need not be something tangible such as money; it may just be a mere promise in return.

252. *See* United Nations, *UNCITRAL Model Law on Electronic Commerce with Guide to Enactment* (1996), at http://www.uncitral.org/uncitral/en/uncitral_texts/electronic_commerce/1996Model.html.
253. http://www.adma.com.au/assets/Uploads/Comply-Documents/ADMA-Code-of-Practice3.pdf.
254. *Currie v. Misa* (1875) L.R. 10 Ex. 162 *per* Lush J.

510. A consideration is 'executed' when the promise is made in return for the performance of an act, that is, some value toward the promise has already been given. In contrast, past consideration at law is no consideration at all because any contract based upon consideration that is past will not be enforceable. This is because the promisor has already done the act or given consideration or is obliged to do it anyway. Thus, a person seeking to enforce a contract must be able to prove that the act along with the promise of the other party together constitutes a single transaction.

511. In online situations, valuable consideration could simply be the giving of a credit card number even though no funds are transferred. This may occur when such numbers are sought as 'security' to further the purposes of the negotiations. A problem that may arise is when erroneous or stolen credit card numbers are used, and it is here that the offeror and credit card provider assumes the burdens of the risks of non-payment for goods and services rendered.

III. Consensus

512. The central question is to what extent has there been agreement or consensus between the parties. Ergo, if there are outstanding issues to which there is no agreement, and which is considered essential, then it will be extremely unlikely that there can be a legally enforceable contract.

513. It may be suggested that in an online contract, silence may amount to acceptance despite the general rule to the contrary. To protect oneself, sellers should generally set out their terms and conditions clearly on the website, and it is assumed that the seller will accept his or her own terms and conditions and will accept any order placed by customers. Because of such risks, it may be prudent for sellers to specify the means by which they will accept offers made by customers. Equally, mere inaction cannot constitute acceptance. Thus, the statement 'if I do not hear from you, I assume that you agreed to this contract' is an ineffectual statement and unenforceable at law.

§3. Requirements for a Written Document

514. Sometimes agreements cannot be enforced unless in writing. For example, the sale of a house or land must be in writing. Such a requirement may be traced back to the English Statute of Frauds of 1677, where leases of land acquired the force of leases only when put in writing and signed by the parties or their agents.[255] Though largely superseded by legislation such as the Sale of Goods Act in England

255. Statute of Frauds 1677, ss 4, 17 rendered unenforceable ('no action shall be brought') a range of contracts unless the agreement or some note or memorandum of it was in writing and signed by the party to be charged or by the authorized agent (Hocker, PJ& Heffey, *PG Contract, Commentary and Materials* 9 (7th ed., Law Book Company 1994)).

and Australia,[256] the requirement of a written document persists in the relevant legislation for assigning or licensing copyright, patent, trademark, and designs. Many credit transactions and dealings in intangible rights are subject to legislation requiring writing, mainly to protect those who may be adversely affected.

515. Formal requirements may be satisfied in an electronic environment with the use of digital signatures. Section 9 of the ETA and corresponding State and Territory legislation such as that in NSW and Victoria expressly provide that writing in electronic form will satisfy legislative requirements. The Act also provides for recognizing electronic signatures – section 10.

516. Oral contracts may be entered into and are bound by the 'parole' evidence rule. This is a rule of evidence that prohibits any party to a written contract from adducing evidence to contradict, vary, add to, or subtract from its terms. The parole evidence rule is, however, no more than a general rule to which there are numerous exceptions. Clearly, this rule is inapplicable in an electronic environment that has yet to develop voice recognition technology to a level of sophistication where it is being used extensively in business negotiations and for contract formation purposes.

§4. Terms of a Contract

517. The terms of a contract are designed to give efficacy to the intention of the parties. The *terms of any contract* can be viewed as either being express or implied. The former is relatively easier to deal with since they are the ones that the parties have discussed and decided to include in the contract. *Implied terms* may be a bit more intractable as these could be imposed by relevant legislation.

I. Express Terms

518. Under English law, where there is a written contract and on what appears whole and complete on its face, a court will presume that the words contain the entire contract and are not to be varied by any oral terms. Therefore, where a contract is partly written and partly oral, there will be a difficult job of deciding what parts of the oral statements are to be included in the contract. In such a case, courts will then rely on the intentions of the parties. However, where the oral agreement is reduced to writing, then the written agreement constitutes the whole contract. Written terms will generally be preferred in construing a contract.

519. Especially in e-commerce, there has emerged a trend in contract formation where one party requires its customers to download terms and conditions from a website and then to accept these by signing a hard copy and returning it to the other

256. *Sale of Goods Act* 1893 and 1923 (UK); *Sale of Goods Act* 1895 (SA); 1895 (WA); 1896 (Tas); 1896 (Qld); 1923 (NSW); 1954 (ACT); 1972 (NT).

party by post. This act creates a higher degree of certainty in the transactions, for not only is there notice made of such terms, but also the agreement to specific terms of the contract. This will avoid misinterpreting representations made either in writing or in negotiations.

520. It is very important to be aware of the difference between a term of a contract and a mere representation. For example, in the purchase of a computer system, a buyer relied on the promises of a salesperson that the system could do certain things. When the system was found to have been unable to perform such things, there may be no requirement in the contract that it did so.[257] To form part of the contract, both parties must have intended that the statements of the salesperson formed part of the contract. Thus, in electronic contracts where no signed documents are made between parties, the terms and conditions may yet be incorporated into a contract provided that reasonable notice of the terms is provided to either party.

521. Two further issues are of material importance. The first issue is the timing and placement of the statement. Any representation made during early negotiations but not repeated later is unlikely to form part of the contract. Likewise, a representation made after the formation of the contract will unlikely form part of the contract. Thus, customers should be made aware of relevant documents or web pages containing contractual terms and conditions; otherwise, these may not be part of the contract so formed. Should such terms and conditions go unread, then when a dispute arises courts would examine the transaction and ask where a reasonable person would expect to find such terms in the document.

522. In addition, there is the question of whether the notice on the web page, for example, would objectively be expected to contain contractual terms. It is obvious that in commercial websites a reasonable person would easily discover such terms and conditions. A magistrate judge of the US District Court for the District of Massachusetts has held that the forum selection clause in a click-wrap agreement between an ISP and a subscriber was enforceable. This is an example of how forum selection clauses in 'click-wrap' contracts have received favourable treatment in the courts.[258]

523. A second issue concerns the skill and expertise of the person making the statement. Where the person making the representation is placed in a position to know the truth of the statement, a court will be more willing to infer an intention that the statement forms part of the contract. This is especially important in the sale of information technology and its products, where technical specifications can be accurately given rather than simply a general statement as to the reliability of the system.

257. *Christopher Hill Ltd v. Ashington Piggeries Ltd* [1969] AC 441.
258. *Hughes v. McMenamon*, D. Mass., Civil Action No. 2001-10981-RBC, 28 May 2002, reported in *Electronic Commerce and Law Report* 7, no. 23 (2002): 568.

524. Furthermore, in an online context, the terms to a contract may be particularly difficult especially where a website may offer to supply goods and services, but its terms are found on a different part of the website or in an obscure hypertext link. There is no certain way to ensure that the customer has accessed these terms, let alone read them, and therefore, the question arises as to whether the offer and terms have been adequately communicated to the offeree. As a result of the legal implications of this issue, customers are forced to go through a set of screens and click the 'I Agree' button before proceeding to the next stage. This 'click-wrap' technique provides an effective way of ensuring that terms and conditions of the proposed contract have been communicated to the customers.

525. In *Hotmail Corp. v. van Money Pie Inc.* 1998 WL 388389, 47 USPQ 2d 1020 (BNA) (ND Cal. 16 April 1998), it was held that a 'click-wrap' was a valid means of acceptance. However, there have been cases where visitors to a website could be 'deep-linked' into the pages of a different website and hence overlook reading the terms and conditions associated with that different website's offerings. Thus, in *Ticketmaster Corp. v. Tickets.com Inc.* 54 USPQ 2d (BNA) (1344 US D. Cal. 27 March 2000), a court concluded that a contract had not been created between the plaintiff and defendant simply because the plaintiff had displayed terms and conditions at the bottom of its website. The US Court of Appeals for the Second Circuit has ruled that the downloading of software did not constitute a manifestation of adequate assent to make an arbitration clause enforceable where the text was located behind a link off the bottom of the download screen. In this case, the terms were behind a link that could only be seen by scrolling down on a web page. A 'reasonably prudent' user would not have learned of the existence of the terms before responding to an invitation to download free software.[259]

II. Implied Terms

526. Implied terms are those which are not agreed to by the parties explicitly at the time of agreement, but which the courts and legislators have decided to import on behalf of the parties. Thus, in the sale of a computer system, the implied terms would be that the seller is the lawful owner of the system, that it is sold according to a description and corresponds to that description, that the system is fit for a particular purpose and is sold as such, and that it is of a merchantable quality. In this way, the law attempts to give commercial efficacy to business transactions.

527. It has been shown that implied terms may arise in several ways, including industry practice, terms implied by the courts, and implication by statute.[260] Especially in the ICT industry, there are certain accepted practices and usages that are

259. *Specht v. Netscape Communications Corp.*, 2d Cir., Docket Nos 01-7860(L), 01-7870(CON), and 01-7872(CON), 1 Oct. 2002, reported in *Electronic Commerce & Law Report* 7, no. 39 (2002): 999.

260. P. Knight & J. Fitzsimons, *The Legal Environment of Computing* 124–126 (Sydney: Addison-Wesley Pub. Coy, 1990).

familiar to all in the industry. It is the practice that software development contracts do not assign copyright nor source codes given to users. On a literal interpretation of the contract, the user who is paying for a software package has neither copyright nor usage rights to the program. However, there is always an implied term that the user may have a right to the program along with a duty to keep the source codes confidential. A further implied term may be that the user has no right to sublicense the software to other parties to use the program.

528. The implied terms mentioned in the previous paragraph may be considered contentious statements especially as it relates to 'bespoke' or customized software written to the requirements of a client. Bespoke software, by definition, is supplied pursuant to a direct contract between a programmer and a client.[261] The software may not exist at the time of the contract. Two legal implications arise from these.

529. The first legal issue is that a bespoke contract may vest IPR of the software to the client including copyright, confidentiality, and patent rights. It has been held that if there were no express provision as to ownership, it would be open to a court to imply that notwithstanding the general rule, in equity the copyright belongs to the client. However, in order to reach such a conclusion, there would have to be some evidence that this was the intention of the parties. In *Saphena Computing Ltd v. Allied Collection Agencies Ltd* [1995] FSR 616, a company that commissioned software to be written claimed that it owned the software by reason merely of that fact. The claim was denied by the learned Recorder Staughton L.J. stated that 'the commissioning of a computer program by a person is not of itself sufficient to vest the copyright in that program in that person'. However, in *John Richardson Computers Ltd v. Flanders* [1993] FSR 497 at 516–19, the Court held that the computer program written by independent contractors belonged in equity to the company that commissioned them.

530. The second legal issue arising from bespoke software arises from the nature of the contract. Sometimes the agreement could be either a sale or a hiring of the software. A bespoke software contract could also be one either for services alone, if no materials are transferred, or for work and materials, the major component of which – the provision of services – forms a large part of the whole contract. The terms to be implied from either of these will depend on the circumstances of each case. The provision of services implies that it will comply with the specific requirements or achieve a given result. The provision of materials in the form of software and documentation implies that the software will be reasonably fit for its purpose. In most cases, however, the user may seek to impose express warranties in order to ensure the desired outcomes are achieved.

531. The terms implied by the courts include the fact that in a contract to provide say, programming services, it will be rendered in a careful and 'workmanlike' manner in a safe environment. Another is a force majeure clause that could be

261. G. Smith, *Software Contracts*, in *Computer Law* Ch. 2, 53–80 at 74 (C. Reed ed., 3d ed., Blackstone Press Ltd 1996).

implied where some event occurs which renders the performance of the contract impossible – government prohibition, war, destruction of the subject matter of the contract by an 'act of God' – for which neither party will be held liable.

532. Terms implied by statute merely codify the common law, so that most of these are terms implied in the sale of goods, commercial code, and the special cases related to consumer contracts and consumer protection legislation. Thus, in every contract of sale of goods there is an implied warranty relating to ownership of the goods being sold, fitness of goods for the purpose it is sold, general 'merchantability' of goods, 'quiet possession' of goods, that is, the buyer will get legal ownership of the goods free of any encumbrance, and that the goods conform with the description or sample. Such practices have since been extended to loans, leases or hire of goods, and for the supply of services.

533. In practice, the difficulty with all implied terms is that they are only mentioned when the parties are in dispute and ironically at a time when it will be virtually impossible to agree either as to the existence of the terms or as to their meaning. The broad warning, therefore, is to define as carefully as possible, expressly and in writing, agreement on as many issues as possible and exclude all other terms. It is also important that both parties read carefully all 'boilerplate clauses' (stereotypical clauses) which are usually appended at the end of a contract and which ironically are reproduced in very small type. The courts will construe this first before it proceeds to imply any term into the agreement.

534. In addition to deciding whether a term is expressed or implied, it is also important to establish whether it is a condition or a warranty. A condition is any term (either express or implied) that is of major importance to the contract, while a warranty is a minor term of a contract. The importance of this distinction lies in the fact that a breach of condition entitles the affected party either to reject the contract or reject the contract and sue for damages. The breach of a warranty only confers a right to sue for damages. Ironically, standard boilerplate clauses tend to be the least read and yet the most harmful to parties of a contract, especially when disagreements arise.

535. Definition clauses are very useful in reducing repetition in explanations and clarifications and in defining precisely what is meant. Once a term is defined, it cannot be used to mean something else, and the courts will construe the meanings very strictly. Definitions are introduced the first time a word is used or in a separate 'definitions' section.

536. Warranties and indemnities are usually given by a supplier to limit its liability and ensure one party indemnifies the other for losses as a result of the performance of obligations under the contract.

537. Parties to a contract insert dispute resolution clauses either at the time of contract or at the time of a dispute arising to have disputes resolved by various alternative dispute procedures including arbitration. International arbitration systems include rules such as those of the UNCITRAL, the London Court of International Arbitration (LCIA) Rules and the International Chamber of Commerce (ICC). In addition, there is a mass of local law governing the conduct of arbitration, which sometimes permits the exclusion of reversion to legal remedies.

538. Arbitration clauses in computer contracts should be used with great caution given that it has hidden traps for the unwary. The US District Court for the Northern District of California has ruled that an arbitration clause demanded as a condition of using PayPal Inc.'s electronic payments service unconscionably deprived users of their rights to a fair adjudication of their legal claims. The Court has also questioned whether the user agreement – that was created as an online 'click-wrap' contract – was in fact a valid contract. It faulted the electronic evidence offered by PayPal to prove the existence of the agreement, and it also questioned whether the plaintiffs were bound by modifications to the user agreement that PayPal made subsequent to their initial click-assent to the original deal.[262]

III. Shrink-Wrap and Web-Wrap Terms

539. Software licences were used originally as a means of protecting suppliers when copyright laws did not cover computer software. The supplier 'lent' or gave 'on license' or 'bailed' the goods for the use of the licensee in return for a fee. In recent times, software suppliers introduced licences as a means of reminding buyers of the rules governing copyright as well as to abide by customer protection laws. Thus, 'box-top' licences and 'break-seal' licences purport to bind consumers to a contract when the customer opens the software package and hence signifies acceptance of terms and conditions.

540. The enforceability of ordinary principles of contract law with the advent of mass marketing devices on the Internet has brought in the issue of whether there is appropriate notice of and assent to terms. Especially when inspecting electronic goods, one may need to open the box or break the seal to read the conditions attached to the contract.

541. Shrink-wrap agreements commonly accompany software products in which terms are sealed inside shrink-wrapping and/or appear when software is installed. The terms of these agreements are not accessible until after a product is purchased and opened/installed. The outside of the wrapping may or may not indicate that terms are forthcoming. Where terms are displayed upon installation, the user may also be required to click an 'I Agree' or similar icon before installation can be completed.

542. Click-wrap agreements indicate a party's assent to terms of an agreement offered online by clicking on an 'I Agree' or similar icon.

---

262. *Comb v. PayPal Inc.*, N.D. Cal., No. C-02-1227 JF (PVT), 30 Aug. 2002, in *Electronic Commerce and Law Report* 7, no. 36 (2002): 927.

543. Browse-wrap agreements are used by many websites and deem that the act of browsing the website constitutes acceptance of their terms. While broadly the law of contract holds that terms cannot be incorporated into a contract after acceptance of an offer, the question of incorporation of terms is particularly relevant to shrink-wrap and browse-wrap agreements, where purported terms are not notified until after a product is purchased or until after access to a website has been granted.

544. As Australian courts have yet to consider whether shrink-wrapped terms can be properly incorporated into a contract, the generally accepted position is that these terms may be enforceable because of the so-called ticket cases. In Australia, the purchaser is generally considered to be the offeror, and the vendor the offeree, for the purposes of retail sales. However, the ticket cases have held that a ticket received after payment of a service may represent an offer containing terms that are accepted when the recipient goes ahead with the contract. A term may be incorporated if reasonable notice of the term is given and there is a reasonable opportunity to reject the term, prior to the assumption of binding contractual obligations. The more unusual and/or harsher a term, the greater the effort that must be made to bring it to the attention of the party to be bound.

545. Such developments have given rise to two concerns about mass-market agreements. The first is that the public cannot or will not ordinarily be able to negotiate their own terms. The second is that the standard terms may override exceptions granted in an Act or impose other undesirable restrictions.[263]

546. As previously noted, certain jurisdictions have required that all terms and conditions to the contract be placed outside the package in order to overcome the rule against introducing terms and conditions after a contract has been agreed to. Licence conditions are included to give warranty protection in limiting liability, to control the use of the software, and, under consumer protection laws, the terms under which goods may be returned because of defects. The issue revolves around whether reasonable notice of the terms was provided to the customers prior to or contemporaneously with the formation of the contract. The reliance on shrink-wrap contracts suggests that contracts are formed once the customer opens the package and finds the pre-printed terms and conditions.

547. In the United States, however, such arguments have been rejected by some courts as in *Step-Saver Data Systems Inc. v. Wyse Technology and Software Link Inc.*, 939 F.2d 91 (3rd Cir. 1991); *Arizona Retail Systems Inc. v. Software Link Inc.*, 831 F. Supp. 759 (D Ariz 1993). In those cases, the courts have held that the contracts were formed when the customer negotiated the order for the software over the telephone and that the shrink-wrap contracts contained in the packaging were additional terms to which the customer had not consented to. What is important to note here is that the seller had not informed the customer of the shrink-wrap terms and conditions during the original telephone conversation.

---

263. G. Founds, *Shrink-wrap and Click-wrap Agreements: 2B or Not 2B?* 52 Fed. Commun. L. J. 100 (1999).

548. In recent times, US courts have accepted that contract formation occurs when the pre-packaged terms and conditions are delivered to customers. However, goods that were delivered on a 'accept or return' basis and as such makes a distinction from previous decisions such as in *Hill v. Gateway 2000 Inc.*, 105 F.3d 1147 (7th Cir. 1997); *Brower v. Gateway 2000 Inc.*, 246 AD 2d 246, 37 UCC Rep. Serv. 2d 54 (NY 1998).

549. In *ProCD Inc. v. Zeidenberg*, 86 F.3d 1447 (7th Cir. 1996), the terms of a licence agreement were found not to place an unreasonable burden on the licensee; the shrink-wrap licence was enforceable. Since this landmark decision, courts have tended to enforce shrink-wrap agreements that are 'commercially reasonable' and valid under contract law so long as consumers have the right to reject the terms and receive a refund on opening the product.[264] Also a recent Massachusetts decision shows that some courts are willing to review mass-market licences and the circumstances surrounding their acceptance, in the light of their 'reasonableness' from the consumer's perspective as in the case of *Williams v. AOL Inc.*, 962 Mass. (Superior Court of Civil Action 2001).

550. In B2B transactions where each business may use its own forms and standard contracts, there is a danger that there will be potential conflicts in terms of a contract. In such situations, it is essential that the conflicting terms and conditions be avoided through the development and use of standardized forms that both businesses can use. This is to avoid the classic legal dilemma of the 'battle of the forms'.

§5. Contract Issues in E-Commerce

551. Trading over the Internet often involves contracts with people living in different countries and states. A business website can potentially fall into the trap of becoming legally liable with anyone who has access to it – characterized here as a jurisdictional risk. In practice, this may mean complying with a range of legislation for different states, territories, and countries in relation to a host of issues including taxes payable, compliance with statutory requirements in terms of consumer protection, product liability, and licences and permits needed to trade.

552. In e-commerce, several contract law issues have arisen, and these include:

- *Offer and acceptance and jurisdiction.* To which countries and states the website is targeted is an important consideration as this may determine the governing law of the contract.
- *Intention and online contract terms.* The click through contract should be sufficiently certain and clearly communicated. Each of the parties must be of the 'same mind' about the terms of the contract as well as payment methods.

264. Hale and Dorr Internet Law, *Are* Click through *Agreements Enforceable?*, at www.wilmerhale-.com, e-mail alert on 26 Apr. 2001.

- *Identity, legal capacity, and authority to contract.* Especially in an online environment, there should be technical procedures that verify the age of the party to an online contract to avoid lack of enforceability because of legal incapacity of a party, proof of each party's identity and age, and in using software agents to allow errors to be identified and corrected prior to concluding the contract.
- *Legislation affecting the form and validity of online contracts.* Contract legislation and codes of practice dealing with electronic transactions specifically, consumer protection, international laws and laws of evidence, and computer-generated records when disputes arise need to be addressed to avoid a failure of the contract.

Chapter 2. Hardware Contracts

553. Any contract for the purchase of a computer system usually contains provisions relating to hardware. The specifics of a tailored hardware contract would need to provide specifications of the system being purchased, the amount, payment and delivery and installation of the hardware. There should also be agreement as to ongoing obligations to maintain and service. In the event of any repairs and upgrade of equipment either as remedial work or preventative maintenance is also to be specified.

554. At a basic level in a hardware purchase agreement, the price and equipment to be bought may be specified. The vendor may be required to install the hardware, in which case the user assumes the duty to provide suitable premises. The contract may also provide for partial payments on staged delivery and installation.

555. The practice is for provisions that relate separately to the hardware since legislation in the US has compelled manufacturers to 'unbundle' their systems as was the case of *Control Data Corporation v. IBM*, 3 CLSR 862 (1973). Previously, manufacturers gave only a global price for the complete computer system.

556. Any computer system is capital intensive; thus, making decisions about changes to them can be a major one. Moreover, the changeover from prototype to production system is neither easy nor cheap. Various problems can surface including being sold machines that were never constructed in *US v. Wegematic Corp.*, 360 F.2d 674 (2nd Cir. 1966) or inefficient machines that did not perform up to specifications Public Utilities Commission for *City of Waterloo v. Burroughs Business Machines Ltd.*, 2 O.R. 472 [1973].[265] Any hardware contract must specify both a description as well as prescribe performance according to agreed criteria. Acceptance of the machines should be at the buyer's determination of specified levels of performance, installed on time and according to the contract – and not on what the supplier or manufacturer has certified.

557. Other points to note include questions of compatibility with the purchaser's current computing systems and other peripheral equipment, the margin of spare capacity in the system to allow for future growth, and whether the buyer is tied to the original equipment manufacturer (OEM) or is free to purchase compatible equipment from other manufacturers. In the United States, litigation against retaliatory practices by some manufacturers who refuse to maintain modified equipment has resulted in the prohibition of such practices, as was the case of *Advanced Memory Systems Inc. v. IBM*, 3 CLSR 183 (N.D. Cal.) (1972).

---

265. *See also Investor's Premium Corp. v. Burroughs Corp.* (D. S.C. 1974) 389 F. Supp. 39; *Applications Inc. v. Hewlett Packard Co.* (S.D.N.Y. 1980), 501 F. Supp. 129, *aff'd* (2nd Cir. 1982) 672 F.2d 1076; and *Schatz Distributing Co. Inc. v. Olivetti Corp. of America* (Kan. Ct. App. 1982) 647 P.2d 820.

558. An aspect frequently overlooked is the issue of title. The general law is that risk also passes on delivery. This means that if the goods are accidentally damaged, destroyed, or stolen, the purchaser in possession of them will be responsible. While the supplier may wish to have title to the goods pass as late as possible, the supplier will try to have risk pass as early as possible. The user must take careful note when risk passes and insure against loss from that point.

559. Warranties are appropriate in hardware purchase agreements as these deal with the quality of materials and workmanship of the physical components of the hardware.

560. Below is an illustration of how a State government has devised and implemented a contract proforma for the procurement of ICT equipment. The NSW government introduced in 2018 a new short form ICT contract called the Core& agreement.[266] The aim is to deliver end-to-end commercial lifecycle management that optimizes how the NSW government buys and uses technology.

561. All NSW government agencies are required to use the Procure IT contracting framework when they buy ICT-related goods and services from a supplier. This is mandated by the Procurement Board Direction 2017-02. Suppliers of ICT to NSW government are required to be registered on the ICT services prequalification scheme and part of the prequalification scheme is agreement to the Procure IT framework.

562. The NSW Core& agreement consists of four available solution requirements. These are (1) professional services; (2) As-a-service, namely cloud services; (3) software covering licensed software hosted by the agency with options for maintenance and support; and, (4) hardware that covers a one-off supply of hardware (excluding ongoing ordering of hardware nor an option for hardware leasing).

563. The key terms of the NSW core agreement include IP with all IP retained by the supplier and licensed to the agency with the exception of professional services where IP are owned by the agency unless specified otherwise; privacy and security that is compliant with relevant laws and industry standards; liability with the supplier's liability being capped at two times the agreement value subject to exclusions such as personal injury, property damage or breaches of IP, privacy or confidentiality with no exclusion of liability for consequential loss; and termination of the agreement for breach not remedied within 14 days or termination for convenience subject to paying for disengagement assistance on a time and material basis.

564. NSW Government agencies are not permitted to vary the standard terms and conditions of the Procure IT framework without written approval of the

266. https://www.procurepoint.nsw.gov.au/before-you-supply/ict-contract-templates/core-agreement-low-risk (link is external).

Department of Finance, Services and Innovation. The exception is the case of beneficial variations which clearly improve the agency's contracting position. Examples of beneficial variations are amendments improving or adding to the agency's legal rights by imposing additional obligations to the supplier.

Chapter 3. Software Contracts

565. Bespoke software developed for an application or specially developed or modified for a client's needs should always have a written contract. It is very important to define precisely what is to be delivered by the developer and the cost of development. This can take the form of a fixed price, but precise details must be given of what is to be expected for that price. Misunderstandings and unfounded expectations can result in protracted litigation. Fixed price contracts should also contain mechanisms for determining cost variations to the contract as people change their minds during the process of software development. However, contracts for development not limited by a fixed price should also specify precisely the work to be done, development progress, and agreed variations. The most important feature of software contracts, however, is the specification of the software to be written. If it cannot be adequately specified at the time of the agreement, there should be a mechanism where the specification can be agreed. No software should be written unless it is subject to the specifications signed off by both parties.

566. The common types of information technology contracts for licences, services, software development include:

- Contracts for physical goods and equipment.
- Contracts for the supply of products.
- Contracts for the supply of services including one-time deployment, one-time training, managed services, outsourced services, software maintenance.
- Contracts for the customer development (services) and supply of solutions or applications.

567. Normally, the main terms of a custom contract are: price, statement of work, deliverables, assumptions, responsibilities and estimated schedule.[267]

568. It is to be noted that the term 'software' is not a term of art and can take on different meanings under different circumstances. For present purposes, the term refers to instructions that are given to the computer to perform certain tasks. The term is sometimes used to include software support by way of advice and assistance to the user. Note also that a systems program such as Microsoft Windows Operating System refers only to the program to drive a computer, whereas an applications program such as Word, MYOB, or Access is designed to do specific tasks such as word processing, keeping payroll records, and maintaining databases, respectively, in addition to others. The considerations in any software contract should include the operating system to be supplied, the peripheral devices to be used, computer languages supported, conversion of pre-existing software (McDonell Automation Co., 49 Comp. Gen. 124 (1969)), compatibility with the 'old' computer and a reserve or backup computer (Manufacturing Data Systems Inc., 5 CLSR 723 (1974)), and how to expand the capacity of the system in the future.

---

267. One example of an agency providing such services is found at http://urlm.co.uk/www.softwarecontracts.net.

569. Insofar as application programs are concerned, the buyer has four choices:

(1) develop a computer package in-house;
(2) hire outside programmers to do the work ('custom' or 'bespoke' software);
(3) purchase off the-shelf packages ('canned' software);[268] and
(4) computer programs to be written by a software bureau.

§1. Bespoke Software

570. In ICT it is very important to specify the tasks explicitly, to set timelines for completion of tasks, to establish benchmark tests before final acceptance, and to set out criteria for assessment of damages. These will protect both the supplier and purchaser as the contract provides protection against arbitrary decisions and conflicting interpretations of the specifications.[269] In addition, where software has been developed under contract, it is necessary to specify the provision of documentation.

571. Other aspects to be considered include trial of the system, the financial responsibility for provision of such trials, installation, updating and maintenance, and the question of proprietary rights in the package. Such rights are critical if the buyer wishes to sell this program to others and will therefore need exclusive rights as well as preventing the software bureau disclosing the package to other competitors in the field.

572. The provision of both hardware and software in a contract has also attracted litigation as to whether a service or a good is being provided. It appears that in supplying both hardware and software, the courts have tended to consider these as constituting a sale of goods.

573. In *Toby Constructions Products Pty Ltd v. Computa Bar (Sales) Pty Ltd* [1983] 2 NSWLR 48, a Court held that the sale and installation of hardware and software and the training of the purchaser's staff constituted a sale of goods. The judge stated that the 'system, software included, whilst representing the fruits of much research and work, was in current jargon off-the-shelf, in a sense mass produced'.

574. Similarly, in *Micron Computer Systems Ltd v. Wang (UK) Ltd*, unreported 9 May 1990 (QBD), the Court treated the supply of a computer system as comprising both the hardware and software as a sale of goods.

---

268. Here the program developer retains proprietary interests and supplies only the 'object code' which remains a trade secret. *See Health Micro Data Systems Inc. v. Wisconsin Department of Revenue*, Wisconsin Tax Appeals Comm. No. 87-S-418, 23 May 1989; *Com-Share Inc. v. Computer Complex Inc.*, 3 CLSR 462 (E.D. Mich.) (1971), 338 F. Supp. 1229 (E.D. Mich. 1971).
269. *Terry Thrift Jr. v. Sandra Hubbard et al. EMIS Software Inc.*, US CA 5th Cir. No. 93-8609 February 1995, 44 F.3d 348.

575. *Caslec Industries Pty Ltd v. Windhover Data Systems Pty Ltd* (Federal Court of Australia No. G627/90, 13 August 1992, unreported) is a typical case of a computer installation gone wrong. Caslec was in the electrical contracting business. In 1986, it decided to automate its manual costing and invoicing system. Caslec signed a software licence and maintenance agreement with Windhover in 1988. After installation of the new system, problems were discovered as interim invoices were not generated as planned, double invoices were sent, incorrectly recorded accounts were received and paid, incorrectly 'fatal error' messages were generated, and data was corrupted. Windhover responded that the hardware was at fault and disagreed with the terms of the software agreements. The Court chose to characterize the transaction as a supply of services, not goods. Compared with the agreed price of about AUD 25,000, Caslec was awarded almost AUD 100,000 in damages.

576. Software-related contracts have posed specific difficulties when attempting to distinguish between the supply of goods and/or the provision of services.

577. In Australian jurisdictions the Sale of Goods Act is legislation that governs transactions for the sale of goods. Although the Australian Consumer Law (ACL) as set out in Schedule 2 of the CCA is now primarily used in B2C transactions, the Sale of Goods Act continues to apply in B2B transactions and in some B2C transactions.

578. The Sale of Goods Act 1923 (NSW) applies to transactions where the seller agrees to transfer, or transfers, property in goods to the buyer for a money consideration. So, for the Sale of Goods Act to apply, the following elements must be present: (1) a contract of sale; (2) transfer of property; (3) goods; and (4) money consideration.

579. The contract must be for the purchase of 'goods'. 'Goods' are tangible objects. Under the Act, 'goods' are not: attached to the ground; part of the land; money; intangible property, such as IP; or, contracts for service, such as a contract between an accountant and a business.

580. In some cases, it can be difficult to differentiate contracts for service from contracts for goods. To decide whether a contract is a contract for goods or a contract for service, one needs to consider what the primary substance of the contract is. For example, if one pays an IT professional to write a computer program, the question is: Is one paying for the computer program (which is a good) or is one paying the programmer to write the program (which is a service)? If the program is the assembly of applications and the IT professional is simply assembling it to ensure interoperability of the various sub-programs, the primary substance of the contract is the computer program. However, if the computer program is a bespoke one and the IT professional is exercising a special skill in assembling and writing it, the work may be classified as a contract for service.

581. In the UK the Sale of Goods Act 1979 (UK) relates to goods alone, whereas the Supply of Goods and Services Act 1982 (UK) relates to both goods and services. But, in both these Acts there is an implied condition that the goods will be reasonably fit for the purpose for which they were intended and that they were of 'merchantable quality'. In terms of services, it is implied that they were provided with reasonable skill and care and performed in a timely manner. In both Acts, whether it was a supply of goods or services depends on the particular facts of the case.

582. The context could be entirely different if the government agency that supplies data and information and actively markets the information. Here there is a complete change of responsibilities as the context has shifted for that government agency. Such a shift will affect jurisdictions in which the 'custodianship' regime prevails. In this scenario, the government agency not only has the responsibility of keeping custody of public data and information, but also in its subsequent use either in-house or by external bodies. The data supplied as a sale or a licence to use may carry an implied warranty that the information may be relied upon. In some instances, there will be contractual obligations imposed on the government agency supplying the data. In any event, whether obtaining information through open records laws or through the marketplace, the question of liability must always be addressed.

583. Issues of payment whether subject to a fixed price or progress payments should be addressed in the contract. In addition, issues of IP should be noted carefully and explicitly. For example, copyright will not be assigned from the developer to the client in the absence of an explicit agreement. If copyright is assigned, the client should require delivery of the source code. If copyright is not assigned, then an express licence from the developer to the customer in comprehensive terms is mandatory.

§2. Personnel Contracts: Employee Versus Independent Contractor

584. Many personnel contracts are concerned with the performance of services on a temporal basis. Where only maintenance of the computer system is concerned, there are few contentious issues that can arise. However, where personnel are hired for program development work, then an employer should be more aware of the pitfalls. The service provider may well wish to contract on a temporal basis to avoid being committed to the performance of a specific task. There is also the prospect of a fixed fee and a minimum of risk. However, the customer needs to scrutinize the contract carefully to see exactly what is being promised. Even with the prospect that the customer may terminate the contract, there are other risks such as incomplete software; the lack of documentation, annotation, and source codes; and how easily someone else may complete the task. It may be prudent to tie payments to personnel to the different stages of program development where the nature of the task makes this feasible.

585. Other features of personnel contracts include place of work, number and quality of personnel involved, rates of remuneration, overhead costs, and formula for charging. In this respect, it should be unequivocal the extent to which a customer is to be liable to the service provider's employees where contracts are terminated prematurely.[270]

---

270. *Telecomputing Services Inc.*, 1 CLSR 953 (1968).

Chapter 4. Turnkey Contracts

586. The term turnkey in previous times has been conceived as meaningless. *In Cable (1956) Ltd v. Hutcherson Bros Ltd* [1969] HCA 37; (1969) 123 CLR 143 his Honour Barwick CJ made an observation and statement on 'turnkey':

> Nothing can be made, in my opinion, of the use of the word 'turnkey'. It is not a term of art and, even if it could be taken to mean that the works must be handed over as a going concern, I would not have thought that in the context of these articles the word or expression meant that the builder warranted the efficacy of the works he had agreed to erect.

587. The terms 'package deal' contracts used in the US and the UK description of 'design-and-build' are useful synonyms. The use of such contracts identifies the allocation of risk which is borne by the contractor as well as identifying the issue of what 'substantial completion' means under a turnkey contract. *Alstom Ltd. v. Yokogawa Australia Pty Ltd & Anor (no 7)* [2012] SASC 49 involved a contract for the refurbishment of a coal fired power plant at Port Augusta, SA. This case demonstrates the extreme risk inherent in the turnkey approach. The failure to perform was identified and the contract did not limit the liability of Alstom either expressly or by necessary implication. The case of *Rolls-Royce New Zealand Ltd v. Carter Holt Harvey Ltd* [2004] NZCA 97; [2005] 1 NXLR 324 (23 June 2004) involved the issue of the duty of care owed by the turnkey contractor and a related disclaimer clause.

588. Turnkey or a turnkey project is a type of project that is constructed so that it can be sold to any buyer as a completed product. This is contrasted with build to order, where the constructor builds an item to the buyer's exact specifications, or when an incomplete product is sold with the assumption that the buyer would complete it.

589. A turnkey project is one where the essential design emanates from, or is supplied by, the contractor so that the legal responsibility for the design, suitability and performance of the work after completion rests with the contractor.[271] Hence, a turnkey computer system is a complete computer including hardware, operating system and application(s) designed and sold to satisfy specific business requirements.

590. The term turnkey is also used in ICT industry to describe pre-built computer 'packages' in which everything needed to perform a certain type of task (e.g., audio or video editing) is put together by the supplier and sold as a bundle. This often includes pre-installed software, various types of hardware, and accessories. A website with a ready-made solution is called a turnkey website.

271. https://en.wikipedia.org/wiki/Turnkey.

591. Under Australian law, turnkey contracts are covered under the general common law of contract and under the relevant Commonwealth, State and Territories laws of the sale of goods legislation. These are discussed elsewhere in this book.

Chapter 5. Software Distribution Agreements

592. Computer software is what drives most of ICT. Such software is very portable as well as easily duplicated. The software is of high value, and its portability means that it has relatively low freight, insurance, and storage costs associated with it. The biggest threat to such products is the prevalence of unauthorized copying. Because of these characteristics, vendors of software often require a distribution agreement to protect their property. Software may be distributed in one of two ways. It may be purchased and distributed as a finished application for specific use, or it may be manufactured by the distributor itself.

593. Contracts associated with software distribution are characterized by several features. There is an assumption that there has been granted an express right to reproduce the software such as a general licence. Then there is the assumption that there has been granted an express licence in respect of the supplier's trademarks for reproduction on packaging and express controls on the appearance and quality of packaging and manuals.

594. Suppliers usually do not make huge profits from sales because the profit margins are small. Instead, suppliers tend to rely on royalty arrangements whereby the software is not 'sold' but rather licensed or supplied on some basis. Contracts spelling out royalty payments should be specially constructed because vague expressions such as 'net receipts' or 'gross receipts' and domestic sales versus export sales can all reduce such payments.

595. A further issue to deal with is that of taxation in the country of origin as opposed to that of the supplier's country. In general, great care should be given to the terms of the agreement. All contracts should provide for certain minimum performance obligations and failure to comply to permit early termination. In addition, careful consideration should be given to outlining the distributor's support obligations. Failure to adequately support the software will result in the supplier's loss of reputation. Updates to correct 'bugs', upgrades, and new versions should also be dealt with. A distributor may also need to have some limited access to part or all of the source codes for the software to deal with malfunctions in the programs.

596. The OECD has provided a definition for electronic software distribution agreements. Such agreements are used by the owner of a software product to authorize a distributor to provide software online. Distributors must ensure that the end user accepts the terms of the agreement before downloading the software. Distributors should also maintain the software on a secure server and must comply with export laws and restrictions where applicable.[272]

---

272. *See* OECD Glossary of Statistical Terms, Electronic software distribution agreement at https://stats.oecd.org/glossary/detail.asp?ID=4747 derived from the Working Party on the Information Economy (1998) *Measuring Electronic Commerce: International Trade in Software* report available at http://www.oecd.org/dataoecd/32/52/2094340.pdf.

Chapter 6. Maintenance Contracts

597. Sometimes it is desired that a software maintenance contract be kept separate from the licence agreement for the supply of equipment but that these be executed together. The commencement of a software maintenance contract is usually at the end of any warranty period in the licence agreement, although there may be no good reason for this as software warranties and software maintenance are different in nature.

598. Maintenance usually covers both the fixing of errors in the software and the provision of enhancements. Defining the maintenance to be provided will depend on the software package and should be carefully negotiated so that both the description of the services and appropriateness of the service are accurate to avoid unexpected time and material charges. A dilemma is whether to stick with older versions of software that work or to adopt new releases, especially where charges are involved. It seems reasonable to expect that the user be provided with a certain amount of time to make changeovers by permitting one or two intervening releases before the maintenance provider may advise of its intention not to continue maintenance. Other issues in a maintenance agreement include the non-inclusion of source code to licensees (as an industry practice), expenses incurred in providing maintenance, the right for any party to suspend services such as non-payment or unsatisfactory performance, and whether in a periodic contract it may be desirable to include a clause causing the contract to roll over after the initial term expires.

Chapter 7. Facilities Management

599. Facilities management is the process of servicing computers at the service provider's site through to the logistics of maintaining supplies and preventative maintenance of hardware. The advantage of such an arrangement is that the facilities manager may be able to benefit from the economies of scale, and in some cases, convenience where customers may wish to move equipment and its IT personnel off-site. Facilities management encompasses many of the same services as a bureau service, the one difference being in the responsibilities of ensuring that insurance covering the equipment is adequate and risks are minimized. Such equipment may be acquired directly from the manufacturer and installed on the facility manager's site, or it may simply be existing equipment that a customer wants to relocate. Also, the facilities manager needs to be assured that the licensor of the customer's software has given permission for the use of the applications and operating system software on behalf of the customer and to move the software, if necessary, to another site. Thought should also be given to termination provisions and what happens to the equipment at that time. As ICT personnel may also be moved with the equipment, their welfare need also be taken into account.

600. An example of a facilities management services arrangement may be taken from the SA's Department of Planning, Transport and Infrastructure.[273] The Service Level Guidelines spell out the Facilities Management Service Arrangements, the Service Level Guidelines, Fees, Relevant Documents and Guidelines on contractor safety, roles, responsibilities and relationships. Within the Services Arrangements are spelt out the mandated and non-mandated services, reimbursable services that include preventative maintenance, breakdown maintenance, replacement or refurbishment maintenance, minor works, and legal and governance arrangements. The Service Level Guidelines identify the roles and responsibilities of parties and dispute resolution processes.

601. As will be noted from the example described, a greater part of the facilities management agreement is one of contract for service by an independent contractor. Hence, both the common law of contract and Australian legislation on the provision of services will apply.

---

273. https://www.dpti.sa.gov.au/__data/assets/pdf_file/0019/413164/Facilities_Management_Services_Arrangements_-_Service_Level_Guidelines.pdf.

Chapter 8. Network Services

602. Access to Internet services and the network provided by ISPs create special problems. The supplier of such access and the users will naturally be concerned with the continuity of access and the quality of the service provided. These can be dealt with by the contract. However, issues of the potential liability in negligence of a supplier of services, unfair competition, and other emerging issues need to be addressed.

603. Internet services required will depend on geographical location of the user, the supplier as well as the type of broadband connections one has.[274] In considering ISP services attention should be paid to the following items:

- Internet speeds.
- Data requirements.
- Data allowances.
- Choice of an Internet service.
- Internet phone services.
- Choice of an Internet phone service.
- Internet rights and asserting rights.

§1. Computer Service Bureau Contracts

604. Such contracts are usually performed off premises and not subject to the general control of a customer.[275] The customer provides the data and application programs to be run on a bureau's computer system. Sometimes bureaus themselves provide the programs with the customers responsible for the data. The savings in time and cost can be considerable. Such contracts are essentially for the supply of services that in part include the delivery of physical goods. This is an important consideration given that it will determine how the transaction will be taxed under local law. In turn, contract for services will determine whether the sale of goods legislation will apply, including warranties to be implied, incorporation of oral terms, and the exclusion by express provisions.

605. In *Associated Tabulating Services Inc. v. Olympia Life Insurance Corp.*, 414 F.2d. 1306 (5th Cir.) (1969), no contract was drafted, so that it made difficult to assess the question of the duration and termination of the contract.

---

274. *See* advice from the Australian Competition & Consumer Commission (2014) at http://www.accc.gov.au/consumers/internet-phone/internet-services.

275. *See also* a discussion in Commerce Clearing House Inc. (CCH) (1992) *Guide to Computer Law*, 'Computer Hardware and Software as Goods' (CCH para. 7120); 'Hybrid Transactions: Contracts Including System Support Services' (CCH para. 7140); and 'Time-Sharing and Service Bureau Contracts' (CCH para. 7160). *See also generally* M. Calvert, *Technology Contracts. A Handbook for Law and Business in Australia* (Butterworths 1995).

606. As in other types of contracts, parties should find out their mutual responsibilities in the provision of facilities, services, and data and what happens when one party fails to perform. The way premature termination is to be handled and the assessment of liabilities need to be spelled out. In terms of confidentiality and copyright of material, the customer is at greater risk given that the data are processed at a bureau. Application programs should remain confidential to the customer and not be part of the bureau's stock in trade.

Chapter 9. Government Contracts

607. The Australian Government agencies use model contracts for their information technology needs such as the generic SourceIT Model Contracts.[276] The use of these contracts is designed to develop sound commercial agreements efficiently and effectively. The use of these contracts encourages good business practice and minimize the risk of conflict and disagreements between agencies and suppliers. While not removing the need for professional legal advice altogether, model contacts promote greater efficiency and uniformity in the industry.

608. The original suite of SourceIT model contracts were designed to cater for simple procurement of:

- Hardware Acquisition and Maintenance;
- Software Licence and Support – Commercial off-the-shelf (COTS) Software;
- Software Licence only (not covering support) – Commercial off-the-shelf Software; and
- ICT Consultancy Services (SourceIT Plus includes semi to complex ICT contracting).

§1. Simple procurement

609. Simple procurement is conducted in an environment where routines, methods and procedures are well established. It usually involves the purchase of standard services or COTS items where:

- the level of risk is minimal;
- standard terms and conditions are used with minimal or no alteration;
- the goods and/or services do not require any development to be undertaken prior to acceptance;
- value for money considerations are restricted to price, quality, fitness for purpose and compliance with required timeframes and delivery needs;
- payment of the contract price will generally only be made following delivery and acceptance of the supplies and/or services; and
- specialist advice on legal, contractual, technical or financial considerations is not likely to be required.

§2. Semi-complex Procurement

610. The more complex a procurement becomes, the more preparation needs to be carried out, including contracting considerations. Use of previous procurement

276. *See* Department of Finance, *SourceIT Model Contracts* (2018), at https://www.finance.gov.au/policy-guides-procurement/sourceit-model-contracts/.

contracts is a useful starting point and likely being tailored to an agency's requirements. The SourceIT Plus model contract can be used to cater for moderately complex ICT procurement.

§3. Government Outsourcing

611. One of the means by which the Commonwealth government maintains a leading edge in ICT is to outsource its information technology needs. Outsourcing means contracting for services at any scale – small or large, batch processing of data, online service bureau services, systems integration, or facilities management. Rather than perform work in-house, a government agency contracts with a service supplier to perform the work. Sometimes this also means the transfer of technology to the new service supplier who performs that work. In this way, the government agency can concentrate on its core business activities. The goals of outsourcing include the use of better expertise or technology for the same cost and obtaining the same expertise or technology for less cost.

612. Outsourcing contracts are structured to achieve a result – not simply the performance of a service. In addition, the government agency must assess its interests and risks inherent in the process of achieving its goals. Typical among these interests are the transferring of assets, transferring of certain employees, reduction in the costs of achieving the desired results, and a degree of security. Such outsourcing contracts must, therefore, consider the ownership of assets, conflict of interest, nature of the relationship with the parties – partners or mere suppliers, change of suppliers at the end of a contract, clear and full description of the outsourced services desired, remedies for poor performance, price controls, IPR issues, transfer of all existing contracts to or from the supplier, security arrangement, and issues of dispute resolution.

613. The Commonwealth Privacy Commissioner has given advice to government agencies on outsourcing and privacy.[277] This advice includes suggested privacy clauses and general advice concerning privacy when outsourcing. It is also applicable to non-IT contracts where personal information is handled by contractors. The purpose of these clauses is to impose upon a contractor many of the obligations that an agency is subject to under the Privacy Act 1988 (Cth). Important changes to the Privacy Act 1988 commenced on 12 March 2014.[278] The changes include a new set of Australian Privacy Principles (APP) that will regulate the handling of personal information by Australian Government agencies and some businesses.

---

277. *See* Privacy Commissioner (1994), *Advice for Commonwealth Agencies Considering Contracting Out (Outsourcing) Information Technology and Other Functions. See* www.privacy.gov.au/news/p6_4_19.doc.

278. *Privacy Amendment (Enhancing Privacy Protection) Act* 2012 (Cth).

Chapter 10. Damages

614. Damages are compensation or indemnity for loss suffered owing to a tort or breach of contract or breach of some statutory duty committed by some other person. The principle is that the injured party should be put as nearly as possible in the same position, as far as money can do it, as if the injury or loss had not taken place. The amount of damages that will be awarded to a party may differ according to the cause of the action the party relied on. That is, damages that are payable to a successful plaintiff may differ according to whether the action is brought in contract, tort, or pursuant to a statute. Thus, under the law of contract, damages are calculated according to the dollar amount of the contract plus the so-called incidental and consequential damages.

615. Consequential damages, also known as special damages, are damages that can be proven to have occurred because of the failure of one party to meet a contractual obligation. The damage goes beyond the contract itself and into the actions that flow from the failure to perform. The claim giving rise to the damages may affect the estimates associated with a given type of damage, including consequential damages. This is to distinguish between a breach of contract as against a tort claim.

616. The legal theory behind 'consequential damages' is attributed to the nineteenth century English case of *Hadley v. Baxendale* [1843-60] All ER Rep 461 in which a miller contracted for the purchase of a crankshaft for a steam engine at the mill. The party agreeing to produce the part did not deliver for inspection on time and the miller sued to recover not only the direct costs that were incident to the alleged breach, but also to recover the costs and/or losses resulting from the production shutdown because of the failure to timely delivery of the crankshaft. Thus, the *Baxendale* precedent is that 'consequential damages' are recoverable where a contract is breached by a party that knows – or is deemed to know – that ordinary expectancy, reliance, or restitution damages will not suffice to meet damages caused by the breach.

617. Incidental damages include expenses reasonably incurred in the transport of the goods, receipt and custody, any commercially reasonable charges, commissions incurred, and any other reasonable expenses incident to delay or other breach. In *Consolidated Data Terminals v. Applied Digital Data Systems Inc.*, 708 F.2d 385 (9th Cir. 1983), a buyer recovered incidental damages which included all reasonable expenses in inspecting, shipping, handling, and storing the defective computer terminals.

618. In the US, the Uniform Commercial Code (UCC) Article 2-715(1) defines consequential damage as including 'economic loss resulting from the buyer's general or particular needs of which the seller had reason to know at the time of contracting and which could not reasonably have been prevented by cover or otherwise'. So, it is not necessary for the seller to foresee the specific injury or level of harm. The standard is that of the reasonable person in the seller's position.

619. In moving from general to specific damage arising from a breach of contract, there may be, however, two major problems that need to be overcome. The first concerns the assessment of damages for loss resulting from a breach of contract, and the second is when loss is too remote from the breach for recovery to be allowed. Under most circumstances, a plaintiff may seek damages for loss of bargain, damages for reliance upon the promise of the party in breach, or restitution for sums paid under the contract.

620. A court in the US would award damages for loss of profits if it were properly substantiated. In the case of *US v. Wegematic Corp.*, 360 F.2d 674 (2nd Cir. 1966), the plaintiff made a good bargain in contracting with the defendant for the supply of computing equipment at a certain price. However, the defendant could not perform at that price, and the nearest compatible machine was some AUD 180,000 more. This loss of bargain was thus easily quantified as was the loss of anticipated benefits as this was specified as a daily rate in the contract.

621. In the UK the general measure of damage will compensate for the loss of the bargain, although there is more doubt as to whether a plaintiff can recover both for the capital loss and loss of profit as was found in the case of *Cullinane v. British 'Rema' Manufacturing Co. Ltd* [1954] 1 QB 292. However, this has since been criticized. So, providing that depreciation is accounted for, the problem of double recovery will be eliminated.[279]

622. The reliance of one party on another is highlighted in *Applied Data Processing Inc. v. Burroughs Corp.*, 394 F. Supp. 504 (D. Conn. 1975). The plaintiff acted on the defendant's representation that a certain machine gave excellent performance. The plaintiff had spent extra money converting software, training staff, and other labour costs. However, the machine did not perform up to expectations. The problem in assessing damages rested on the construction of the adjective 'consequential'. The defendant while accepting a loss of bargain had occurred nevertheless argued that it should be characterized solely in terms of a loss of value – the difference between the value of the machine promised as against its value as delivered. The plaintiff had relied on the representations made by the defendant. The plaintiff chose to calculate damage by assessing the cost of providing services of the promised quality from a different supplier that amounted to a much larger sum. If the loss were calculated as a loss of profit, it would have been regarded as 'consequential' and hence eliminated by the exclusion clause.

623. Restitution for sums of money paid may or will be awarded where the breach was so fundamental as to justify a buyer rejecting the goods and to recover the price. The common law position is that damage suffered as a result of defective performance of the goods including cost of securing effective performance elsewhere but less any effective benefit from the defective goods may be awarded.

---

279. *See* J.K. MacLeod, *Damages: Reliance or Expectancy Interest*, J. Bus. L. 19 (1970).

624. In *Wausau Paper Mills Co. v. Chas T. Main, Inc., U.S. D.C., Western District, Wisconsin*, No. 91-C-0524-C, 9 April 1992, 789 F. Supp. 968, a provider of design engineering services was given the responsibility to interface, coordinate with, and assist the supplier of a new computer system on a project for a paper mill company. The services company was found to be not liable in tort recovery for economic losses incurred by the plaintiff after the project incurred excess costs and production losses. Wisconsin's economic loss doctrine precluded the recovery because the parties had a contract that included a warranty provision, even though the limitations provision in the contract left the paper mill company without a remedy for damages for any of its breach of contract claims. The damages awarded included lost production, reverse engineering costs, pricing damages for the sale of the cheaper product, and lost customer sales. A similar case is that of *Advanced Micro Devices Inc. v. Intel Corp.*, Arbitration award, 24 February 1992, Palo Alto, CA. (CCH paragraph 60,368).

625. The question of interest on outstanding sums may be extremely important, especially in the context of computer contracts. In the UK, the right to interest is discretionary with the practice being that it is allowable for readily ascertainable sums where a creditor is kept out of money through the fault of the creditor.[280]

626. More generally, the damages payable for breach of contract will be governed by the ordinary rules of 'remoteness of damage' at common law. This is either as a matter of construction of the terms used in an exclusion clause or in substitution for it where it has been held ineffective for one reason or another. This common law rule is from *Hadley v. Baxendale* (1854) 9 Exch. 341. In this case, it was held that the damage must either arise naturally or be such as may reasonably be supposed to have been in the contemplation of the parties at the time of contracting as the provable result of the breach. This is implicit in the general common law rule that the plaintiff must take all reasonable steps to mitigate one's loss. Here everything depends on the court's view of damages that arise naturally, what the parties ought to have contemplated, and a judgment of what was reasonable in the relevant circumstances.

627. In Australia, England and common law countries the concept of remoteness in contract is more expansive and recovery consequently more limited than is the case in tort.[281] In addition, in common law countries, a plaintiff can generally recover for loss of bargain in contract, but not in tort. In the US, damages for the loss of bargain can be recovered in tort, and because the rules dealing with remoteness are no more favourable in contract than in tort, it is generally desirable to use tort.[282] Thus, choice of law in order to frame one's claims is most important if a

280. *Harbutt's Plasticine Ltd v. Wayne Tank & Pump Co. Ltd* [1970] 1 QB 447.
281. *See Koufos v. C. Czarnikow Ltd* (*The Heron II*) [1969] 1 A.C.350.
282. *See Sandy Koplowitz v. Andre Girard*, Fla. D.C.A., 4th District, No. 93-1781, 9 Aug. 1995 (CCH para. 47,310) and compare this with *Advanced Micro Devices, Inc. v. Intel Corp.*, Arbitration Award, 24 Feb. 1992, Palo Alto, CA (CCH para. 60,368).

more favourable result is sought. Damages for the loss of a bargain can be recovered in tort in the US, while the rules governing remoteness are no more certain nor favourable in tort than in contract. Popular opinion suggests that where a tortious cause of action exists, a plaintiff will be well advised to use it. In the US, punitive damages are generally not permitted in a contract action in the US in the absence of an independent tort.[283]

283. *See* Art. 2.14 of the UCC and at CCH para. 8400.

Chapter 11. Collateral Issues

628. Contractual issues discussed previously, however, cannot be taken in isolation. This is because there are interactions between the law of contract and tort, between contract and statutory provisions, and the issue of copyright and ownership after a contract has been fulfilled.

§1. Liability and Ownership of Property

629. In many areas of contract law, statutory provisions have been written to formalize the rules, especially those relating to liability and the assessment of loss or damage. The developments in part arise from consumer protection laws in which the two parties contracting at arm's length are also in unequal bargaining positions. In addition, with most computer software being manufactured in different parts of the world, there is a need to identify the party that will be responsible when things go wrong and when a customer wishes to return the goods for a refund. Given that software is usually distributed as a finished product, there must be an express licence in a supplier's trademark for reproduction on packaging.

630. The placing of trademarks on goods made by a distributor is considered use in trademark law. This is to be distinguished from a distributor of finished goods already marked by the supplier. The interpretation here is that the distributor is merely displaying a mark in relation to a supplier's goods and not attempting to profit from the use of the trademark because of market recognition and reputation. These distinctions become important when the question of liability arises, and customers need to know from whom one should seek redress when there are problems with the product. Because software is easily portable and easily copied, it is unusually attractive to piracy with the result that 'unauthorized' copies may flood the computer market. For pirated copies, distributors and suppliers will deny any liability for those copies not bearing the original authentic trademark or label.[284]

631. The question of ownership, copyright, and patent is an area of both contract law as well as rules governing IP. Most software development contracts do not assign copyright, but only a licence to the end user to use the computer programs. There is an expectation on the part of the customer to have 'rights' to use as well as claims to 'ownership' of the software products because of the contract. *Bartsch v. Avtex Airservices Pty. Ltd.* (1992), 107 ALR 539, 23 IPR 469, illustrates how identifying interests can assist negotiations. Avtex contracted for the development of a computer-assisted flying theory course but failed to obtain ownership of the IP developed. However, normal industry practice seems to suggest that there are no such 'rights' or claims to 'ownership' unless the developer has explicitly 'assigned'

284. One large software manufacturer has even put on a hologram of its logo on all packing of its products. This authenticates the genuine product since the hologram is difficult to copy and expensive to reproduce.

ownership to the customer. In the absence of such an assignment, the customer may only have usage rights to the computer program.

632. Where copyright is assigned, the customer should require the delivery of the source code. If no assignment is made, an express licence in comprehensive terms is thought mandatory and desirable with the source code put in escrow now generally known as source code escrow.[285] This is a mechanism by which the source code of a computer program and all relevant documents are given to an independent third party for safekeeping in the event that the supplier ceases business or is unable to support the software.

633. Some consideration should also be given to software maintenance after delivery of both the computer hardware and software. In the case of a contractor/consultant brought in to develop software programs, the practice seems to be that the contractor is entitled to keep the working documentation with no obligation to deliver the source code. The argument is that the situation is analogous to architects and lawyers who keep and retain documents relating to their clients. However, the contractor may agree to assign these to the customer.

634. From the customer's perspective, the only way the customer can legally require the escrow agent to release materials to the customer is to have a contract with the escrow agent. This can be either a two-party contract between the customer and the escrow agent or a tripartite contract between the owner, escrow agent, and customer. If the only contract that exists is between the owner and the escrow agent, the customer is unlikely to be able to enforce disclosure.

635. A further development is 'Internet escrow' especially where auctions and e-commerce is undertaken. The escrow works by placing money in the control of an independent and licensed third party in order to protect both the buyer and seller in a transaction. When both parties verify that the transaction has been completed according to the terms of their respective agreement, the money is released. If at any point there is a dispute between the parties in the transaction, the process moves into a dispute resolution mode. The outcome of the dispute resolution process will determine what happens to the money in escrow.[286]

§2. Minors and Agents

636. In the electronic environment, it would be remiss not to mention capacity and authorization to enter contracts. The common law presumption is that a person who enters into a contract has full capacity to do so. However, there are a group of

285. 'Escrow' is an old legal term with origins in the law of deeds. A deed is binding upon delivery, so an escrow agent is usually an independent third party who holds a sealed deed and guarantees its delivery to an intended party once certain conditions are met. This is useful in cases where a software developer goes out of business and the customer needs access to the source code to modify and update.

286. *See* Wikipedia http://en.wikipedia.org/wiki/Escrow.

persons who may be barred from entering contracts, such as minors, mentally disabled persons, drunks, and bankrupts. Each of these produce unique issues in the context of contracts concluded online. The offeror has no knowledge of the identity of the customer and will therefore need to explicitly ask for more information and a confirmation that the person has capacity to enter into contracts. The issue of the capacity of minors is therefore of most significance in an e-commerce situation. In addition, the use of debit cards by minors, whether it be their own or those of an adult (but used without permission), can pose further problems.

637. All Australian jurisdictions have statutes that set the age of majority at 18 years.[287] Other jurisdictions may have different age thresholds. Transactions are usually binding on a child only if they can be shown to be for the child's benefit. Where no such benefit exists (e.g., the purchase of a car for which the child could neither possibly complete nor practically use), then the contract is not binding, and the merchant may have to bear the loss from a failure of the minor to comply with the terms of the contract.

638. In the case of agents, common law suggests that where an agent has actual authority to conclude a contract on behalf of a principal, the principal will be bound by the contract formed. However, it may arise that where an agent does not in fact have authority but concludes a contract, the validity of the contract may hinge on other indicia. The absence of ostensible authority will place the agent personally liable to contracts agreed to.

639. On the Internet, businesses would have to overtly ask for such authority before a contract can be said to have been formed. The presumptions of section 128 of the Corporations Act 2001 (Cth) may apply in that persons dealing with a company are entitled to make assumptions that the person is assumed to be an officer or agent of the company they are dealing with. It is thus evident that companies and businesses have developed policies in the use of e-mail and Internet connections that provide its agents and employees with online identifiers and 'clothing' to enter into contracts with the world at large.

§3. Consumer Protection

640. There are other applicable laws that may impinge on contract formation in the Internet environment insofar as consumer protection is concerned. In particular, the principal legislation regulating trade practices in Australia is the *TPA*, repealed

---

287. *See*, for example, *Age of Majority Act* 1974 (ACT); *Minors (Property and Contracts) Act* 1970 (NSW). Legislation in New South Wales, South Australia, and Tasmania provides that a person acting as a guarantor of a minor's contract can be enforced against the guarantor. Minors can also generally be sued on cheques, bills of exchange, or promissory notes. The signature of a minor is valid to draw, issue, or indorse.

and replaced by the CCA especially Part V Schedule 2 that deals with consumer protection and how corporations may engage in certain conduct in trade and commerce.[288]

§4. Remedies

641. In general, remedies may be classed under injunctions of different types that have been used when one party seeks redress but for various reasons may be unable to do so. An *injunction* is a court order by which a party to an action is required to do or refrain from doing something. Injunctions are either restrictive or mandatory. Regarding time, injunctions are either interim or perpetual. Two injunctions of immediacy are Anton Piller orders and Mareva injunctions.

I. Anton Piller Orders

642. An Anton Piller order is a form of an order for discovery and is used where there may be grounds for believing that documents will be destroyed before they can be inspected and disclosed and used in evidence at a court hearing. Such orders are given where there are grave doubts about the credibility of the other party. The order allows a claimant and legal advisers to enter premises of the other party to copy and to remove any documents or property. The order is made *ex parte*, and a contempt of court ensues on non-compliance. The criteria before such an order could be given have been outlined by L.J. Omerod in *Anton Piller KG v. Manufacturing Process Ltd* [1979] 1 All ER 779. The requirements include:

- That there must be an extremely strong prima facie case.
- The damage potential or actual damage must be very serious for the client.
- There must be clear evidence that the respondent possesses incriminatory documents or things and that there is a real possibility that the respondent may destroy these.
- Such an order has been given in an alleged software piracy in the case of *Gates v. Swift* [1981] FSR 57.

II. Mareva Injunction

643. Sometimes a security for claims is sought in order to lay claim on a respondent's assets. Mareva injunctions may be applied for where there is a great danger that a respondent may dispose of assets to defeat any award of the court or arbitrator. Initially such an injunction was developed to deal with foreign litigants who disposed of all their assets overseas in order to avoid execution and the distress of

288. *See also* B. Finch, *Consumer Protection on the Internet*, in *Going Digital 2000: Legal Issues for E-Commerce, Software and the Internet* (A. Fitzgerald et al. eds, Sydney: Prospect Media Pty Ltd 1999).

judgment. The effect of such an injunction is either to restrain a defendant from removing assets from the jurisdiction pending trial or so that an award may be enforced within the jurisdiction of a court. The application is by way of a summons to a judge or a superior court ex parte.[289] At other times, either the courts may get things wrong because of the veracity of the evidence or the misapplication of the correct law and interpretation of cases. A litigant may apply for restitution – a writ by which a defendant, on successful appeal, is restored to all that had been lost by the execution of the judgment which is reversed.

289. *Mareva Compania Naviera v. International Bulk Carriers Ltd* [1980] 1 All ER 213.

Part IV. Electronic Transactions

Chapter 1. Legal Status of Electronic Transactions

§1. Introduction

644. Information technology presents many challenges to traditional notions of law – so much so that a major paradigm shift is needed in many areas. These include rights to privacy, protection against defamation by e-mail, computer crime, electronic data interchange, IP questions, transborder data flow issues, rules of evidence, and use of expert systems. As technology transcends national boundaries and globalization continues, the trend is towards developing uniform international laws. New technology brings with it challenges as well as opportunities. The world of e-commerce poses many interesting legal questions to which government, industry, and the public will look to the legal profession for answers. Government departments, the legal profession, information technology specialists, universities, businesses, and those from other disciplines will have to muster the talent, energy, and drive to participate fully in the public debate and policy-making regarding these issues. In this way, society in general, and Australian e-commerce in particular, will obtain the maximum benefit of such technology while at the same time offering protection when such technology is misused.

645. In general terms, Australia has urged that countries adopt a light touch to the regulation of e-commerce and continues to so advocate. The US has likewise advocated minimal online regulation. In contrast, the EU suggests that there is a need for more intrusive governmental regulation with labour, environmental, and taxation standards incorporated into e-commerce laws.

646. E-commerce and e-business have been major topics of concern for governments, business, and citizens alike. E-commerce is the term used to refer to commercial services on the Internet and includes B2C services, B2B services such as using EDI in the automotive sector, and, e-Markets as deployed in airline booking systems and the financial markets. On the other hand, e-Business is the term used to refer to the commercial operations conducted using e-commerce. In recent times mobile e-commerce (m-Commerce) conducted using a mobile device has become commonplace. A further term is Web 2.0 i-Commerce system – the non-commercial Internet system that uses user-provided content and the so named participatory web.

647. Vast amounts of time and effort are being expended in examining how best to make such transactions efficient, effective, and as a widely accepted means of doing business.[290] The various permutations of the business-to-government (B2G), consumer-to-government (C2G), and government-to-government (G2G) transactions suggest the complexity of the task.

648. Numerous studies and reports of working parties to address some of these issues including:

- the need to establish an efficient and universally accepted payment system that is both secure and protective of privacy;
- the need to resolve the issue of jurisdiction in terms of which law applies to electronic transactions;
- the problem of designing appropriate legal mechanisms to resolve online disputes; and
- policy questions, including the issue of taxation of transactions conducted in cyberspace.[291]

649. This chapter addresses some of the issues in electronic transactions by examining and analysing the Australian government's response to doing public business online. Such a response is by way of new policy and implemented by legislation.

650. An evaluation and analysis of the ETA is undertaken. The UNCITRAL Model Law on Electronic Commerce provides a reference point.[292] This Model Law provides the template for all other electronic transaction legislation globally.

§2. E-Commerce and the Internet

651. As Australia moves from an industrial to an information society, commerce will increasingly take place in an electronic world as opposed to a physical one. Accordingly, no firm today can ignore the issue of e-commerce and e-business. The most obvious development is the growth of business on the Internet where, according to an IBM advert, 'Every month 53,000 new servers connect to the Internet. That's 1.2 servers per minute going online. And the scary part is, this is only the beginning.'[293]

---

290. M. De Zwart, *Electronic Commerce: Promises, Potential and Proposals*, 21(2) UNSW Law Journal 1 (May 2000), http://www.austlii.edu.au/au/journals/UNSWLJ/1998/45.html.

291. Australian Taxation Office (1997) Tax and the Internet, Canberra: AGPS. *See also* D. Bentley, *The ATO, Tax and the Internet: The Emperor's New Clothes?*, 9 Revenue LJ (1999) at http://kirra.austlii.edu.au/au/journals/RevenueLawJl/1999/5.pdf.

292. UNCITRAL Model Law on Electronic Commerce with Guide to Enactment 1996, General Assembly Resolution 51/162 available at http://www.uncitral.org/uncitral/en/uncitral_texts/electronic_commerce/1996Model.html.

293. Internet & E-Commerce: Special Report 1999, *In Search of Planet Profit*, Australian Financial Review (9 Mar. 1999).

652. In Australia about 5% of total sales are undertaken online with an estimated value of AUD 19–24 billion in 2009.[294] Of this, however, about 20–25% of Australian online shopping is on an overseas website (valued between AUD 4–12 billion). Australian retail sales on domestic websites is estimated to be only at 2–3% and may be explained by the relatively small number of retailers participating in e-commerce and the lack of an e-commerce strategy by many large retail chains and department stores. This is beginning to erode profitability. Coupled with the ease of shopping online and the strong Australian dollar many consumers are increasingly purchasing from offshore retailers.

653. According to modelling by Australia Post online shopping in Australia reached 8% of total traditional retail sales at the end of 2017, a 1% rise on the year before. Australians spent AUD 21.3 billion buying goods online, an increase of 18.7%. The online spending growth outstripped traditional retail by 16.2%.[295]

654. Beyond Australia 99.9% of global online spend sits outside of Australia. Online shopping is growing around the world, with the global e-commerce goods market worth USD 1.57 trillion in 2017. That figure is set to increase by a further 19% in 2018 and reach over USD 2 trillion by 2019.[296] The growth of the e-commerce market creates more opportunities for Australian businesses to expand overseas. Today, Australia's top five export markets are China, Japan, Republic of Korea, United States, and India. Collectively, these countries represent 58.4% of our total export market.

655. It must be realized that e-commerce is not just about the Internet. E-commerce involves many other media as well – the use of the telephone, Intranets involving electronic data interchange (EDI), and smart card technology, to name a few. E-commerce in general raises specific legal issues such as consumer protection, privacy, and validity of electronic signatures.

656. As the world of commerce is transformed from a paper-based to a digital one, in Australia, as elsewhere, the law is struggling to keep up. Yet, as a technologically advanced country, it is in the interests of Australian business that the Government moves quickly to establish the legal framework infrastructure that will achieve the appropriate balance between promotion of e-commerce and regulations to satisfy concerns about consumer protection, privacy, and security. Given that

---

294. Anne Fitzgerald, *e-Contracts*, in *Internet and E-Commerce Law, Business and Policy* 740 (B. Fitzgerald et al. eds, Sydney: LawBook Co. 2011). *See also* Frost & Sullivan, *Australian Ecommerce Market 2010 Underdeveloped and Lags US and UK by Three Years* (July 2010), at http://www.frost.com/prod/servlet/press-release.pag?docid=207380860.

295. Australia Post, *e-Commerce: Inside Australian Online Shopping* (2018), at https://auspost.com.au/content/dam/auspost_corp/media/documents/2018-ecommerce-industry-paper-inside-australian-online-shopping.pdf. The data in the report are based on analysis of goods bought online and delivered by Australia Post between January 2016 and December 2017. It also draws on modelled estimates from Australia Post consumer surveys, statistics from the Australian Bureau of Statistics (ABS) and publicly available information.

296. *Ibid.* citing Euromonitor sources.

e-commerce activity is not restricted by physical borders, Australia's laws in this area must also take note of what is happening in other regions of the world and attempt to influence international treaties and agreements in a way that is consistent with the promotion of world trade.

657. In 1998 the Australian government set up an Electronic Commerce Expert Group (ECEG) to report on the need for legislation to support the regulation of e-commerce transactions.[297]

658. In one sense, e-commerce is a new and largely unregulated frontier where digital marketers are free to ride the electronic range in search of fun, adventure, and profit. In another sense, however, e-commerce is heavily regulated. Not only do all the Australian laws (the repealed TPA now replaced by the CCA, and the Privacy Act 1988 (Cth)) applying to paper-based commerce apply to e-commerce, but also so do a number of emerging laws and codes which are designed specifically to deal with the Internet and other forms of new technology.[298] In addition, as e-commerce spreads across national borders, there is a possibility that not only Australian laws, but also the laws of many other countries may be applicable. The problem then is that there may be too many laws that claim jurisdiction and the resultant uncertainty about which laws will govern a particular transaction, plus the uncertainty of how paper-based laws will deal with such new realities such as digital signatures and digital contracts.[299]

659. A further problem is the Government's reliance on private regulation of the Internet and the use of legislation only when private regulation proves unsatisfactory. For lawyers, this means that there is little available in the form of case law or legislation that regulates this space. Instead, lawyers must become familiar with codes and industry standards that are frequently updated and changed.

660. As mentioned previously, cross-border issues also abound. It is often difficult to determine where a content provider may be located. Even when the location is determined, the digital nature of the Internet means that a business can shift locations in a matter of hours. Locating a server is not the same thing as finding the legal identity behind the machine. At the same time, allowing users to sue content providers in the local court of each user means that the content provider can be sued in multiple jurisdictions simultaneously for essentially the same act. Australian law on these issues is unsettled. Australia has looked to the US, where decisions have emanated on the issue of Internet jurisdiction.[300]

297. ECEG, *Electronic Commerce: Building the Legal Framework* (April 1998), https://trove.nla.gov.au/version/46663891.
298. National Advisory Council on Consumer Affairs, *Consumer Protection in Electronic Commerce: Principles and Key Issues* (April 1998), www.dist.gov.au/consumer/eleccomm/princip.html.
299. Electronic Applications, ASIC Policy Proposal Paper, http://download.asic.gov.au/files/ris-electapps.pdf.
300. *See, e.g.*, *Playboy Enterprises Inc. v. Chuckleberry Publishing Inc.* (1999) F. Supp. 1032, where the acceptance of jurisdiction of a US court in relation to a website in Italy was based on the interactive nature of the site; *State of Minnesota v. Granite Gate Resources* (1997) No. C6-95-7227,

§3. THE ETA: BACKGROUND

661. The ETA is based on the recommendations of the ECEG that reported to the Attorney General in March 1998. The Expert Group recommended that the Commonwealth enact legislation based on the UNCITRAL Model Law on Electronic Commerce. The ETA received Royal Assent in December 1999 and commenced by Proclamation on 15 March 2000.[301]

662. The ETA aims to prevent the invalidation of transactions merely because they have been conducted electronically. Until 1 July 2001, the ETA will only apply to those Commonwealth Acts specified in regulations. When the legislation was passed about 278 Commonwealth Acts have been specified in regulations, including the Australian Prudential Regulation Act 1998 (Cth), Banking Act 1959 (Cth), Currency Act 1965 (Cth), Financial Corporations Act, 1974 (Cth), Financial Sector (Shareholdings) Act 1998 (Cth), Privacy Act 1974 (Cth) (section 63 only), TPA (section 170 only), and various superannuation legislation.[302] From 1 July 2001, the ETA applies to all Commonwealth legislation (other than those specifically excluded by the regulations).

663. The Electronic Transactions Regulations 2000 (Cth) list the provisions of 157 federal Acts and Regulations which continue to be exempted from the operation of the ETA.[303] The States and Territories ETA typically exempt a much more narrowly described group of transactions from the scope of the legislation.

664. The ETA is part of the Government's strategic framework for developing the information economy in Australia. The strategic framework reflects Government's commitment to ensuring that all appropriate Government services are available online by 2001.[304] In general, the ETA allows e-commerce to fit into the same legal framework as traditional paper-based transactions. The goal is to ensure that the technological developments brought about by e-commerce can be dealt with within the existing legal system, while allowing business and consumers to determine the most effective technological choice for their purposes.[305]

---

where a company located outside the US used a website to advertise its planned e-gambling site and indicated it would be legally accessible in Minnesota. The Minnesota Court held this to be a breach of the fair-trading laws.

301. The Act, Explanatory Memorandum, and background materials are available from the AGD's e-Commerce home page at https://www.ag.gov.au/RightsAndProtections/ECommerce/Pages/default.aspx.

302. This is sixteen less than originally anticipated. These pieces of legislation have been 'dropped' on advice of the AGD because they contain provisions that will be difficult to be satisfied in an e-commerce environment.

303. For a listing of legislation to which the Act does not apply, *see* https://www.legislation.gov.au/Details/F2011C00367.

304. *See* Australia Department of Communications, Information Technology and the Arts, *Australia's Strategic Framework for the Information Economy 2004-2006* (2004), at https://catalogue.nla.gov.au/Record/3415839.

305. D. Giles, *You've Got Mail ... or Have You?*, 3 Internet L. Bull. 12, 14 (2000).

665. Progressively from 1999 onwards the Commonwealth, States and Territories have all passed legislation mirroring the Commonwealth Act.[306]

666. The Commonwealth is working in collaboration with the States and Territories to develop a national uniform legislative scheme to facilitate the use of electronic transactions. The plan is for each government to enact legislation within their jurisdiction to facilitate the removal of existing legal impediments to e commerce. The key differences between the State and Territory legislations and the ETA are that the State and Territory legislations apply to the interpretation of the common law as well as legislation, does not differentiate between communications with private organizations and communications with government bodies, and does not provide for a staged introduction of the ETA. The State and Territory legislations applies to all State and Territory legislations other than those exempted by regulations and the common law by proclamation.

667. In general, therefore, the ETA is built on three underlying principles, namely:

(1) Functional equivalence, or the guarantee that paper and electronic documents will be on the same legal footing.
(2) Technology neutrality, that is, the law will not discriminate between different forms of technology.
(3) A principled approach to electronic signatures.[307]

668. A graphical representation of the *ETA* is shown as Figure 7.

306. *See Electronic Transactions Act* 2000 (NSW); *Electronic Transactions Act* 2000 (Victoria); *Electronic Transactions Act* 2000 (SA); *Electronic Transactions Act* (Tasmania) 2001; *Electronic Transactions Act* 2001 (Queensland); *Electronic Transactions Act* 2000 (WA); *Electronic Transactions Act* 2000 (Northern Territory); and *Electronic Transactions Act* 2001 (ACT).

307. Consultation Paper released by the Australian Government entitled 'Australia's accession to the UN Convention on the Use of Electronic Communications in International Contracts 2005; Proposed amendments to Australia's electronic transactions laws: Consultation Paper November 2008', Minister's Foreword, p. 2; M. Sneddon, Legislating to Facilitate Electronic Signatures and Records: Exceptions, Standards and the Impact of the Statute Book, 21(2) UNSW Law Journal (1998), http://www.unswlawjournal.unsw.edu.au/article/legislating-to-facilitate-elctronic-signatures-and-records-exceptions-standards-and-the-impact-on-the-statute-book/.

Figure 7 Schematic to the ETA

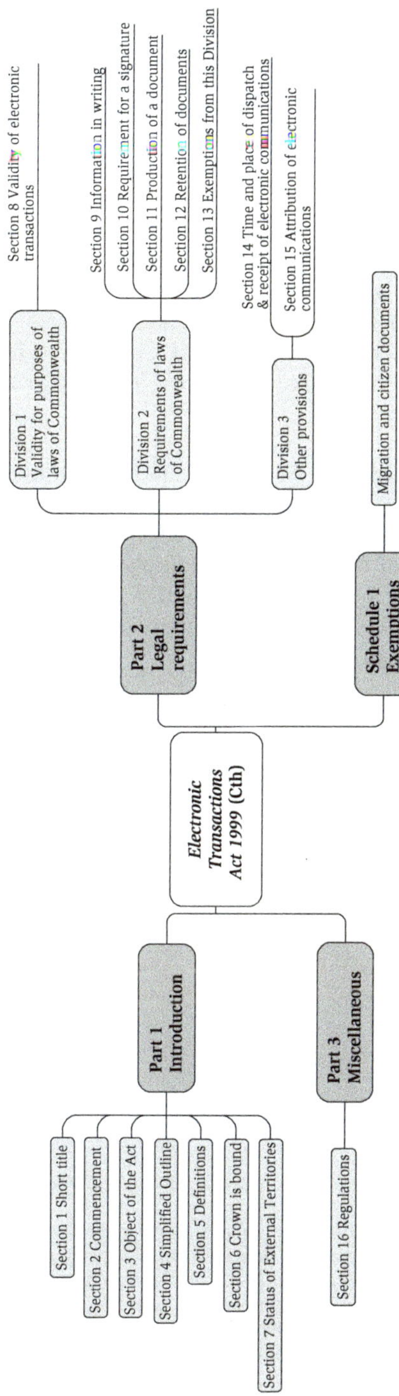

Source: Summarized from details of the legislation at https://www.legislation.gov.au/Details/C2005C00 484.

669. A distinction is made between a digital signature and a digitized signature. A digital signature refers to the use of a cryptic mathematical function and private key verification scheme in order to determine the identity of a person, purported to have made the signature. However, digitized signatures refer to the scanned signature superimposed upon a document such as a letter or contract. For purposes of the ETA there is no difference between electronic and digitized signatures.[308]

670. A person must consent to receiving electronic communications from the Government. Consent can be inferred from a person's conduct. Express consent is not required. The consent provisions, however, do not extend to Commonwealth entities. Herein lies an inconsistency as it would be impossible to fulfil the Government's wish and commitment to delivering all Commonwealth services electronically. Some provisions of the ETA are vague, and it may take a few court challenges to give full meaning to the Act.[309]

671. As the Commonwealth is excluded from the operation of the consent provisions, it must accept all electronic communications. However, the Commonwealth is given certain specific powers. The ability to satisfy a legal requirement electronically is conditional upon a person complying with any information technology (IT) requirement for communication with a Commonwealth agency, including any electronic signature technology that must be used and any action a person must take to verify receipt of information.

672. The ETA also sets out default rules that apply in the absence of any contrary agreement between the parties, regulating what is deemed to be the time and place of dispatch and receipt of electronic communications and the attribution of electronic communications.

673. The ETA also provides that any other laws that deal specifically with the use of electronic communications to satisfy writing, signature, production, or retention requirements will be preserved.[310] The ETA does not override any existing laws that deal specifically with these matters.

---

308. *See* P. Bolam & R. Choi, *Electronic Signatures: When Are They Effective?*, Internet L. Bull. 118–120 (October 2012).
309. For example, the ETA leaves to the courts the decision as to whether the postal acceptance rule would apply to a particular contract; if it does, presumably, the time, place of dispatch, and receipt of communications provisions found in s. 14 of the ETA would come into play and be applied. *See* J. Forder & P. Quick, *Electronic Commerce and the Law* 67–74 (Milton 2001).
310. The Australian Archives has developed three general information papers about how to keep track of incoming and outgoing electronic communications. These papers are available on the Australian Archives website at www.naa.gov.au.

§4. FUTURE DEVELOPMENTS

674. The National Electronic Authentication Council (NEAC) was established to promote the use and development of electronic authentication in Australia. NEAC is supported by a secretariat in the NOIE. However, the NEAC was disbanded in February 2002. The AGIMO within the Department of Finance and Deregulation has taken over the roles formerly undertaken by NEAC. AGIMO's task is to make Australia a leader in the productive application of ICT to government administration, information, and services.

675. The UNCITRAL Model Law on Electronic Signatures was adopted by the UN General Assembly on 5 July 2001.[311] Like the Model Law on E-commerce1996 the principles of functional equivalence and technology neutrality are maintained.

676. The United Nations CUECIC which was adopted by the General Assembly on 23 November 2005.[312] CUECIC updates the Model Law on Electronic Commerce 1996.

677. The aims include enhancing legal certainty and commercial predictability where electronic communications are used by private parties engaging in international e-commerce. The UNCITRAL Model Law on Electronic Signatures attempts to achieve three purposes:

(1) to create a presumption of signature for certain electronic signatures that comply with specified requirements (essentially digital signatures);
(2) to set out the responsibilities of signatories, relying parties and certification service providers; and
(3) to provide rules for the development of cross-recognition frameworks for electronic signatures between different countries.

678. The workability problems stem from the Commonwealth's decision to leave it to the States and Territories to adopt the model legislation. The Commonwealth rejected the option of a comprehensive federal legislation because of worries that such a scheme would be open to constitutional challenge.

§5. A NOTE ON DIGITAL SIGNATURES

679. As originally enacted the ETAs have stated a requirement under a Commonwealth, State or Territory law for a person's signature to be provided was satisfied by an electronic communication that uses a method which identifies the person and indicates their approval of the information communicated.

---

311. UNCITRAL Model Law on Electronic Signatures (2001), at https://uncitral.un.org/en/texts/ecommerce/modellaw/electronic_signatures.
312. UNCITRAL UN Doc A/60/515 (23 Nov. 2005) at http://www.uncitral.org/uncitral/en/uncitral_texts/electronic_commerce/2005Convention.html.

680. However, where specific legislative provisions are enacted setting out the requirements governing signatures in electronic communications the provisions will override the general provisions on signatures in the electronic transaction legislation.

681. An Australian court was prepared to accept the 'typed' name of the sender at the end of an e-mail as the sender's signature in *McGuren v. Simpson* [2004] NSWSC 35 at [22].

682. The issue of whether a resolution of a Board member that had been sent by e-mail was validly received was reviewed in the Victorian Supreme Court. *In Legal Services Board v. Forste*r [2010] VSC 102 the judge held that the Board had consented to the Board member providing their signature by e-mail and it was clear from the e-mail message that the Board member had intended the typed name to represent their signature.

683. In *eBay International AG v. Creative Festival Entertainment Pty Ltd* (2006) 170 FCR 450; [2006] FCA 1768 at [48] Rares J held that a contract was formed when the consumer clicked the 'Send this Order' button on the website.

684. In *Getup Ltd v. Electoral Commissioner* (2010) 268 ALR 797; [2010] FCA 869 Perram J ruled in favour of a political activist group Getup by holding that the requirement to sign the electoral enrolment form was satisfied by a member of the group using a digital pen on a laptop computer and transmitted to the Electoral Commission through the Internet.

685. The case of *Leo v. Paulsen* [2010] QCAT involved the making of an offer of settlement to another party sent by e-mail to the applicant. The Tribunal held that the offer was valid for the purposes of the relevant Queensland Act and was signed in accordance with section 14 of the ETA 2001 (Qld). Similarly, it was possible for a party to submit an objection to a development proposal in electronic form via the City Council's online facility (*Harding v. Brisbane City Council* [2008] QPEC 75).

686. However, digital signatures raise other important issues that have not been addressed by the ETA. In implementing public key infrastructure (PKI) and public key authentication framework (PKAF), the Government has put in place certain principles and standards by which electronic signatures may be used in electronic communications with public agencies.[313] The concern here is the extent to which an individual may be able to have more than one digital persona – individually as a person and corporately as a company or business entity. Next, there is the issue of whether the digital signature is to be used for security and authentication or will its implementation raise privacy concerns.

313. Draft Uniform Rules on Electronic Signatures, UNCITRAL Working Group on Economic Commerce, https://digitallibrary.un.org/record/444617.

687. PKI is an integrated system of non-government certification bodies that have developed means of cross-verification. This system produces authenticity by assuming that each authority wishes to protect and enhance its reputation. This assumption is then tested as each authority checks the security of another authority's system. In this way, one authority often carries the seals of others as a testament of its own reliability. In return, that authority will test and seal numerous others. However, PKI is still in its developmental stages, and most progress has been made by way of industry cooperation rather than by legislative fiat.[314]

688. Digital signatures are perceived to be foolproof. However, the very basis of its integrity depends on how secure is the process by which the e-signature was created. While it is true that even with handwritten signatures forgeries may be perpetrated, as is the vulnerability of other biometric systems, the public needs to be reassured of the security of e-signatures. Authentication of e-signatures is very different from its security. Indeed, the very use of e-signatures in electronic communications with a public agency suggests a loss of anonymity compared to most other transactions between individuals such as in the marketplace, in cash-based transactions, or even in conversations with the person sharing the seat on a bus.

§6. Summary and Conclusions

689. Australia is not alone in this endeavour of the promotion of e-commerce, however.[315] For example, the UK has passed Electronic Communications legislation. In Europe, there is the EU Directive on Electronic Signatures as approved on 30 November 1999 by the EU. In the US, there is the Uniform Electronic Transactions Act 1999 and the Electronic Signatures in Global and National Commerce Act (E-Sign) 2000, and similar electronic transactions legislation exists in Hong Kong, India, Malaysia, and Singapore.[316] The rules are designed to facilitate the increased use of electronic signatures in international business transactions.

---

314. There remain many legal issues that are unresolved, for example, *see* Australian Privacy Commissioner, *Privacy Issues in the Use of Public Key Infrastructure for Individuals*, 2001, available at www.privacy.gov.au/publications/dpki.html.

315. For a detailed review of the e-commerce laws of each of the US states and every country in the world that has passed or is considering such laws as well as links to the Acts, *see* McBride's website at www.mbc.com/ecommerce.html.

316. *Electronic Transactions Ordinance* 2000 (HK SAR); *Information Technology Act* 2000 (India); *Digital Signature Act* 1997 (Malaysia); *Electronic Transactions Act* 1998 (Singapore).

Chapter 2. Cryptography, Certification and Security Tools

§1. Introduction

690. E-commerce is dependent on hardware and software tools as well as administrative and legal infrastructure that provide the appropriate mix of rights and responsibilities. Such ingredients are also necessary to provide both businesses and consumers the appropriate level of trust and certainty of outcome so that businesses and consumers will have confidence in e-commerce transactions. As the transactions are undertaken electronically and hence are 'faceless' interactions, offers and acceptances, payments, and other business require some sort of security technology and procedures.

§2. The PKI

I. Development in Australia

691. In May 1998, the Government released the Gatekeeper Report (Office of Government Information Technology (OGIT) 1998), which outlined a strategy for the development and use of public key technology (PKT), or a generic PKI, for electronic transactions with, between, and within Commonwealth agencies. The Gatekeeper Report recommended the establishment of the Government Public Key Authority (GPKA) for accrediting various companies who comply with approved standards to provide this public key encryption technology.[317] The framework sets out the requirements for organizations to become accredited to issue digital keys and certificates for use in government for PKI-based authentication. The policy requirement under the Gatekeeper PKI Framework states that Australian Government agencies must only use digital keys and certificates issued by a gatekeeper-accredited organization for PKI authentication. Australia Post now joins Baltimore Certificates, eSign Australia Pty. Ltd., the ATO, health eSignature Authority Pty. Ltd., Telstra and others as among those who have achieved Gatekeeper accreditation.

692. The Government is involved in the system as a user through its Project Gatekeeper Strategy. An authority was established to develop an accreditation process for private certification authorities (CAs) to use to gain accreditation as CAs accepted by the Federal government. The Federal government will only deal with PKIs that are part of those CAs. The process is based upon work done internationally, standards developed by Standards Australia, and the ITU, the International Standards Organization (ISO) standards designated X509, and OECD Guidelines on Cryptology.

317. Gatekeeper Public Key Infrastructure framework at https://www.dta.gov.au/our-projects/digital-identity/join-identity-federation/accreditation-and-onboarding/gatekeeper-public-key-infrastructure-framework.

693. PKI must also be seen in the context of the general recognition of electronic transactions and signatures. In Australia, the Commonwealth Government has recognized the legality of electronic signatures under the *ETA*.

II. Definition

694. PKI is a set of hardware, software, people, policies and procedures needed to create, manage, distribute, use, store and revoke digital certificates (DC). In using cryptography, a PKI is an arrangement that binds public keys with respective user identities by means of a CA. The identity of each user within each CA domain is unique. A validation authority (VA) provides this information on behalf of the CA to third parties. The binding of keys is established through a registration and issuance process which may be undertaken by software at a CA or under human supervision. The PKI role that assures this binding is called the registration authority (RA) which ensures that the public key is bound to the individual to which it is assigned in a way that ensures non-repudiation.[318] The intention is to enable users to securely communicate on an insecure public network and to reliably verify the identity of a user via digital signatures. Hence the PKI is a system for the creation, storage, and distribution of DCs which are used to verify that a public key belongs to a certain entity.

695. PKI is built on the four pillars that of authenticity, confidentiality, integrity, and non-repudiation. When an electronic message is received by a user or a system, the identity of the sender needs to be verified (i.e., *authenticated*) in order to determine the identity of the sender. To identify a user, at least one of the following types of information is generally required:

- something you have (e.g., a token);
- something you know (e.g., a personal identification number (PIN)); or
- something you are (e.g., fingerprints or signatures).

696. When a message is sent electronically, both the sender and the receiver want to ensure that the message received is exactly the message transmitted by the sender. A message that has not been altered in any way, either intentionally or unintentionally, is said to have maintained its integrity.

697. The term repudiate means to refuse to accept as having rightful authority or obligation. Well-designed e-commerce systems provide for non-repudiation, which is the provision of irrefutable proof of the origin, receipt and contents of an electronic message.

698. Public key encryption allows digital signatures to be fixed to electronic messages. Such signatures make forgery and repudiation so difficult as to be impractical and provide a means to detect alterations and other tampering.

318. *See* Wikipedia 'Public key infrastructure' http://en.wikipedia.org/wiki/Public-key_infrastructure.

699. PKI may also be combined with biometrics (such as a fingerprint, iris scans, or voice recognition) to protect one's private key. *Biometrics* is a security technique for checking and verifying identities that employs digitally created 'maps' of an individual's physical characteristics such as thumbprints, voice recordings, or iris scans. These are stored by a security system and are later compared when accessed by the individual.

III. Workability of PKI

700. PKI promises much but problems remain. Identified security and policy issues take time, money, and training for the people involved. These problems have led some researchers to be concerned whether PKI as it currently exists will meet the standard required under the ETA that the digital signature be in all circumstances 'as reliable as was appropriate for the purposes for which the information was communicated'.[319] Other problems with PKI include its cost, the fact that businesses with subsidiaries may need multiple certificates, and that public keys are required and must be distributed to all parties. Such conclusions are also mirrored in the US where a recent government report concludes there is a way to go yet before PKI technologies will realize their promise.[320] As to the future, it is likely that PKI will largely be used in B2G contexts such as customs and tax.

§3. Digital Certificates, E-Procurement and E-Tendering

701. Digital Certificates (DC): A partial solution to identity problems is found in the DC issued as part of the Goods and Services Tax (GST). In the GST registration process, the Federal Government issues a DC. Such a certificate purports to prove the identity of any person one would be dealing with over the Internet. The DC is a data file that has been issued by a CA to an individual or organization to identify them to online services. Such a certificate not only enables businesses to identify themselves to government agencies such as the ATO, but also to other business partners. There are other uses for the certificate such as electronic signatures, especially once the scheme is national in scope and used by all. Companies will be able to display their ABN and the new DC on their web pages.[321]

702. The DCs are a device to allow all Australian businesses to conduct secure transactions with the Government. This is a necessary component of the legal and technical infrastructure required for online procurement. Every Australian business with a current ABN can apply for an ABN-DSC (digital signature certificate). Each business will be entitled to one primary ABN-DSC and several secondary ones. The secondary ABN-DSCs are linked to the ABN and may be used for dealings with any

319. *See* Smith, *Public Key Infrastructures: Debunking the Myths*, 3 Internet L. Bull. 122 (2001).
320. *See* US General Accounting Office, *Information Security Advances and Remaining Challenges to Adoption of Public Key Infrastructure Technology* (GAO-01-277), at www.gao.gov.
321. J. Davidson, *Taking Care of Business on the Web*, Australian Financial Review (23 Jul. 1999).

government department. The ABN-DSC is linked to business name and contact details. Thus, anyone in receipt of an ABN-DSC can verify the identity of the sender. The scheme applied initially to Commonwealth agencies only.

703. Electronic procurement (e-procurement). Refers to the automation of any part of the procurement to payment process with e-commerce tools. Among an array of such tools include: electronic catalogues, electronic purchase orders and automated approvals. As the name implies an e-catalogue provides a list of supplier products that is accessible through the Internet. E-catalogues are best sent to end users for retail goods that are described as 'high volume low value' products. Such e-catalogues may be managed in-house, outsourced to a third party or hosted and managed by the supplier.[322]

704. An electronic purchase order is a document that provides both the terms of an order and the purchaser's terms and conditions. Such an order enables electronic communications between buyer and supplier and is most useful for one-off purchases of relatively significant items.

705. Automated approvals translate an organization's delegation and authority rules into an electronic hierarchy for use in approving orders. Such approvals are usually used in an electronic transactional e-procurement financial management system. The use of these tools has been evaluated.[323]

706. The key element to the Australian government's e-procurement strategy is an e-tendering system to procure and purchase goods and services. Mostly regulated by common law principles of contract law and protocols such as the Australian Standard Code of Tendering (AS 4120-1994) and other state specific and industry-specific codes several Australian e-tendering systems are in use. The Commonwealth's AusTender system and the NSW's e-Tendering website are examples.[324]

---

322. See Australian Government, Department of Finance and Administration, Procurement, at http://www.finance.gov.au/procurement/; Department of Finance and Administration (DOFA) (2002) Commonwealth Procurement Guidelines and Best Practice Guidance. Canberra, Australia: DOFA; Australian Government (2019) Commonwealth Procurement Rules, at https://www.finance.gov.au/government/procurement/commonwealth-procurement-rules; and K. Vaidya, A.S.M. Sajeev & G. Callender, Critical Factors that Influence E-procurement Implementation Success in the Public Sector, 6 J. Pub. Procure. 70–99 (2006)..

323. Australian Government, Department of Finance and Administration, AGIMO, *Review of the e-Procurement Demonstration Projects and Case Studies on e-Procurement Implementations* (2005), at: http://www.agimo.gov.au/publications/2005/may/e-procurement_research_reports.

324. *See* the Commonwealth's AusTender site at http://www.tenders.gov.au/federal/index.cfm and NSW's e-Tendering system at http://www.tenders.nsw.gov.au.

§4. E-COMMERCE TRUST MECHANISMS AND SECURITY TOOLS

707. Other well-known electronic tools in use in the business world for security and authentication include secure sockets layer (SSL) and secure electronic transaction (SET) protocols that are used in SETs, for example, sending credit card information over the Internet.

I. SSL

708. SSL protocol is a non-proprietary (open) worldwide standard for authentication, data encryption-decryption, and ensuring privacy for use over a network such as the Internet.

709. SSL is application-independent and allows other security protocols such as Hyper Text Transfer Protocol (HTTP), SET, and Telnet to be used over it. SSL provides a high level of data integrity and security by encrypting the entire data stream and by sending it over a secure channel. SSL has since been superseded by the transport layer security (TLS) protocol. Versions of both SSL and TLS are in widespread use in applications such as web browsing, e-mail, Internet faxing, instant messaging, and voice over Internet protocol (VOIP) telephone services.

II. SET Protocol

710. SET protocol is a non-proprietary (open) industry standard developed jointly by MasterCard and Visa for secure online e-commerce, credit card transactions over a network such as the Internet. Under SET, a buyer provides credit card numbers to the merchant in encoded form. The merchant cannot decode the numbers but can forward these to the card issuer for verification and approval. SET by itself is not a payment system but a set of protocols. SET uses DCs and public key cryptography to allow parties to identify themselves to each other and to exchange information securely.

711. A SET purchase involves three parties – the cardholder, the merchant, and the card issuer (a financial institution). The cardholder shares the order information with the merchant. The merchant shares payment information with the card issuer. A SET dual signature completes the partial sharing of information while allowing all parties to confirm that they are handling the same transaction. The dual signature is an innovation introduced by SET. The purpose is the same as the standard electronic signature – to guarantee authentication and integrity of data. The dual signature links two messages that are intended for two different recipients – cardholder to merchant and merchant to card issuer. The merchant does not need to know the cardholder's credit card number, and the card issuer does not need to know the details of the cardholder's order. The link is needed so that the cardholder can prove that the payment is intended for this order.

712. Key features of SET include the confidentiality of information, the integrity of the data transmitted, cardholder account authentication, and merchant authentication.

III. Virtual Private Networks (VPN)

713. VPN are systems that allow businesses to access their internal networks and computers over the Internet or other public network using encrypted 'tunnels' to ensure that data cannot be accessed without authorization. VPN involve the use of advanced encryption and 'tunnelling' technologies to use the Internet to create a 'virtual' private network that uses the public facility of the Internet.[325]

714. Some government departments in Australia and many businesses with mobile workforces use VPN to create mobile offices where employees can still communicate in a secure environment. Unfortunately, VPN can be expensive to implement and are not suitable for B2C transactions.

IV. Passwords

715. Passwords are the most common form of security protection, but also one of the least secure. The advantages of password protection are that it is easily understood, easy to change, and inexpensive. The disadvantages are that it can be compromised by users, does not authenticate the data being transferred, and can often be transmitted insecurely.

§5. Export of Encryption Technology

716. Australia and the US have signed a joint statement on e-commerce entitled Cooperation on Electronic Commerce covering key policies and principles including private sector leadership, minimal government intervention, neutral taxes, and self-regulation.

717. Over forty governments, including Australia, have signed the Wassenaar Arrangement that allows for exports of encryption technology with up to fifty-six bits for all cryptographic products and sixty-four bits for mass-market software or hardware. Currently, cryptographic items are strictly controlled. However, mass-market software is exempt.[326] The Wassenaar Arrangement was established to contribute to regional and international security and stability. This was aimed to be achieved by promoting transparency and greater responsibility in transfers of conventional arms and other technologies such as computers thus preventing destabilizing accumulations.

---

325. *See* VPN Tunneling discussion at: http://compnetworking.about.com/od/vpn/a/vpn_tunneling.htm.
326. www.wassenaar.org for more details relating to information technology equipment.

Chapter 3. Legal Aspects of Electronic Banking and Payments Systems

§1. Introduction

718. Financial transactions and payments systems in the electronic environment present many new and interesting challenges, not least of which is how to adapt existing methods to new ways of working electronically. At the same time, these also present many financial and legal risks to businesses as well as to consumers, but which in turn gives rise to many new business opportunities to those who can provide assurances in order to create trust in the electronic environment.

719. At the beginning of the Internet age, the banking industry had feared 'disintermediation' of its various functions and franchises. Disintermediation in banking is the idea that as technology makes knowledge about borrowers, access to payments systems, and other financial services more widely available, the banks will no longer be needed as intermediaries. The traditional task of measuring risks and providing valued services based on specialized information and infrastructures possessed by banking institutions is now beginning to disappear. Non-bank financial institutions and financial investors now have the means to measure a borrower's ability to repay. Such institutions could lend directly in place of depositing their funds in low-interest bank accounts. Payment mechanisms can now create and facilitate a wholly decentralized system for monetary transmissions without the need for banks.

720. Interestingly, universal access to information and systems has not resulted in significant disintermediation in finance. Instead, it has given birth to a new group of intermediaries – non-bank institutions that are astute enough to make use of new business tools and electronic technologies and are able to offer value in the marketplace.

721. The Wallis Inquiry (1996) into the financial system in Australia had observed that the Internet would transform banking business for financial institutions and customers alike. With the substantial investment in upgrading telecommunication infrastructure to accommodate wireless and broadband technology as well as the uptake of information technology by most Australians, the scope for electronic banking and payments systems has widened considerably. While it can be expected that penetration of the technology will be deep, the Wallis Inquiry report identified security and reliability as the two key issues requiring immediate resolution.

722. Accessibility to electronic banking services, especially in rural Australia, and the deployment of encryption and authentication technologies make it now possible to conduct full banking activities totally electronically almost anywhere.[327]

I. Need for Third-Party Assurance of Web-Based E-commerce

723. In Australia, transactions over the Internet involving consumers are subject to the same consumer protection legislation as physical transactions. Thus, Australian federal statutes such as the repealed *TPA* and its replacement the CCA, Fair Trading Act 1987 (Cth), Contracts Review Act 1980 (Cth), and the Privacy Act 1988 (Cth) apply to online transactions just as they do to traditional forms.

II. Electronic Financial Transactions and Payments Systems

724. Various types of electronic financial transaction payments systems are discussed in conjunction with the different emerging legal issues. While contractual issues are foremost with electronic financial transaction, other forms of electronic payments methods such as digital cash and cheques pose other legal challenges such as liability for tortious acts including crime, theft, and issues of privacy and personal data as well as financial regulations infringements.

725. A 'payments system' refers to arrangements which allow consumers, businesses and other organizations to transfer funds usually held in an account at a financial institution to one another. These include payment instruments such as cash, cards, cheques and electronic funds transfers which customers use to make the payments. The payments system is usually an unseen arrangement that ensures funds move from accounts at one financial institution to another.

726. Electronic money includes both chip card-based and digital stored-value systems that function as a medium of exchange but differs in two very important respects from 'cash' – notes and coins issued by a central bank. Electronic money is not legal tender that is accepted for the payment of debts; it is an obligation of a private company rather than of the central bank. In addition, electronic money products are traceable to the payer. In contrast to cash where the payer is anonymous.

727. Electronic financial transaction and forms of 'cybermoney' are a type of electronic contracting that is well established and for which a legal regime has crystallized. Electronic financial transaction means any transfer of funds other than by cheque, draft, or similar paper instrument that is initiated through an electronic terminal, telephone, computer, magnetic tape or electronic media to order, instruct, or authorize a financial institution to debit or credit an account. The term also includes

327. https://www.aph.gov.au/About_Parliament/Parliamentary_Departments/Parliamentary_Library/pubs/rp/RP9697/97rp16.

point-of-sale (POS) transfers, automated teller machine (ATM) transactions, direct deposits or withdrawals of fund, and transfers initiated by telephone or tapping an electronic medium.

728. Other generic terms are used to describe the transfer of funds, whether physical or virtual. Thus, we may have e-cash where a digitally encoded 'coin' is withdrawn from a bank over the Internet, saved on a user's hard disk, and then sent to others in payment for goods and services.

729. Smart cards and stored-value cards (SVCs) are essentially electronic cash in which an embedded microprocessor is used to pay for goods and services, operating in much the way as telephone cards commonly used worldwide.

730. Smart card trials that have been conducted elsewhere include Quick Link, a reloadable card which has been in operation in Newcastle, NSW, since 1995. Transcard is also a reloadable card using contactless technology initially designed and deployed for public transport ticketing purposes. VisaCash is both a disposable and reloadable card launched in the Queensland Gold Coast for use by visitors and residents alike. In addition, there is the MasterCard Cash card, a reloadable card which was trialled in Canberra in 1996. The idea of reloadable cards hinges not only on the reuseability of the physical card, but also in helping users budget their expenditures to the limit of the value stored on their cards to a lower maximum value, compared to debit and credit cards, where much higher maximum limits are made available.

731. As background, until 2012 the Australian Electronic Funds Transfer Code of Conduct set out the procedures governing the relationship between users and providers of electronic financial transactions.[328] The operation of the code is monitored by the Treasury and the ACCC. The Australian Payments System Council has assumed responsibility for ensuring that financial institutions comply with the revised code of 1998.

732. The EFT Code provides protection to customers by governing unauthorized electronic financial transaction transactions, an electronic financial transaction transaction error, liability for electronic financial transaction losses, and against whom claims may be made. It applies to transactions that are initiated by a customer through an electronic terminal by the combined use of an electronic financial transaction card or a PIN. Issuers and subscribers of the Code must comply with the APP of the amended Privacy Act 1988 (Cth) that applies to public sector agencies and bodies and the Privacy Amendment (Private Sector) Act 2000 (Cth) – the act governing private sector enterprises.

733. The ASIC (2008) published an amended version of the Electronic Funds Transfer Code of Conduct. A proposal to introduce a PIN@POS for credit card

328. *See* EFT Code available at https://asic.gov.au/regulatory-resources/financial-services/epayments-code/.

transactions has also been introduced. The proposal involves consumers being given the option to use a PIN rather than a manual signature for credit card transactions.[329] The PIN@POS initiative further expands the coverage of the Code.

734. It is to be noted that credit card transactions authorized by a manual signature are excluded by the EFT Code. This is because under the EFT Code a manual signature authorization is not an 'access method'.

735. The EFT Code currently applies only to transactions initiated by an individual using an electronic terminal, an EFT card, and a PIN. While some smart card transactions require a PIN to complete, most will not.

736. Internet banking is outside the scope of the Code, unless it involves the use of a smart card and PIN, and the Code will not apply to digital cash transactions or BPAY transactions.

737. A new and expanded EFT Code was launched by the ASIC in April 2001 and amended again in 2008. The expanded EFT Code became binding on Code subscribers in April 2002. The main objective for the expansion of the EFT Code is to create a technology-neutral Code covering all forms of consumer EFT, such as Internet banking and stored-valued smart cards. As technological advances have not been covered by the existing EFT Code, the new Code has been greatly expanded.

738. Under the new EFT Code, Part A covers the rules and procedures governing the relationship between users and account institutions in EFTs involving electronic access to accounts. Part B encompasses rules for consumer stored-value facilities and stored-value transactions, while Part C deals with rules for privacy, electronic communication between EFT Code subscribers and users, and Code administration and review.

739. The new EFT Code makes changes to stored-value facilities and privacy and provides an expanded definition of electronic financial transaction. To help prevent major losses through fraud, the new EFT Code also includes provisions dealing with daily transaction and other periodic limits on accounts. There is a flexible approach to technological developments such that the EFT Code includes a right to apply to the ASIC to modify parts of the Code where it is deemed necessary to do so.

740. Electronic financial transactions are now regulated by the e-Payments Code which is a voluntary code of practice which is administered by the ASIC.[330] The Code sets out the obligations of businesses to consumers, consumer rights and

329. www.fido.gov.au/fido/fido.nsf/byheadline/Electronic+Funds+Transfer+%28EFT%29+Code-+of+Conduct.

330. The e-Payments Code is found at https://asic.gov.au/regulatory-resources/financial-services/epayments-code/.

responsibilities and what to do in the event of a complaint or dispute, most commonly, unauthorized transactions. The Code covers ATM transactions, EFTPOS purchases, purchasing goods by credit card either online or by phone, mobile phone or Internet banking, telephone banking and transactions using stored-value facilities (such as debit cards).

741. The e-Payments Code has commenced. Organizations have been progressing transitioning from the old EFT Code to meet the deadline of 20 March 2013. Such organizations include all banks, credit unions and building societies that currently subscribe to the EFT Code together with non-banking subscribers.

742. The e-Payments Code has an important role in regulating consumer electronic payment transactions, including ATM, EFTPOS and credit card transactions, online payments, internet and mobile banking, and BPAY in Australia. It complements other regulatory requirements and obligations under the Corporations Act 2001 (Cth) and the National Consumer Credit Protection Act 2009 (Cth) (NCCP). ASIC administers the e-Payments Code, including monitoring compliance and conducting regular reviews.

743. The Internet Industry Association (IIA) Code of Practice aims to establish confidence in and encourage the use of the Internet. This Code contains provisions relating to the fair handling of information, privacy and confidentiality, dispute resolution, and content classification.

744. In general, other industry codes of conduct and codes of practice will apply where that industry is subject to an industry code of practice. Thus, where a banking service is delivered over the Internet to an individual, it is a 'banking service' according to the definition of that term in the Code of Banking Practice. This implies that the dispute resolution, notification, and information provisions of the Code will apply to that Internet banking service.

745. ASIC approves codes as set out in Regulations Guide RG 183 in accordance with section 1101A of the Corporations Act 2001 (Cth). This is a statutory power to approve voluntary industry codes of conduct. However, ASIC does not have to power to mandate industry codes. Industry must decide in the first instance whether to develop a code, and then whether to have that code approved by ASIC. RG 183 describes key features of an effective code regime that may apply to the financial services industry. In certain circumstances a breach of a code is a breach of a contract with a financial institution. This gives the consumer a right to take legal action for breach of contract.

746. A charge card, also known as a debit card, is one which does not charge interest but which requires the monthly account generated by the subject transaction to be settled in full on receipt. A credit card, on the other hand, enables the cardholder to defer full payment of the principal debt from one month to the next on payment of a minimum percentage of the outstanding balance, generally covering the interest charge, government duties, and part of the principal debt.

747. Credit cards normally involve three or sometimes four parties: the cardholder, merchant, and financial institution (includes the merchant's financial institution as well as the cardholder's). Thus, within the three-party system, there are three sides, but four contracts:

(1) the agreement between the issuer and the cardholder;
(2) the merchant agreement between the merchant and the merchant's financial institution or organization with which the merchant is affiliated;
(3) a sales agreement, that is, a purchase between the cardholder and the merchant; and
(4) a reimbursement agreement between the merchant's financial institution and the cardholder's financial institution via a clearinghouse.

748. There are various areas where contractual obligations need to be carried out by the parties at various stages of a transaction. Merchants have numerous undertakings such as to honour all valid cards, to use reasonable care to detect forged signatures, to permit financial institutions to debit a merchant's account with all relevant charges, and to allow financial agencies to inspect books of accounts and records relating to card transactions. The cardholder's liabilities and rights also have been spelled out in a Consumer Credit Code as well as rights to sue under the CCA, the Sales of Goods Act, and at common law in contract or tort.

749. Credit cards are a popular payments method of e-commerce purchases. Previous methods of using credit cards for Internet purchases involved sending card details by fax or e-mail to the Internet merchant. This practice raised fears of credit card fraud, including credit card details being intercepted over the Internet by unauthorized parties and the impersonal nature of Internet transactions making it difficult to validate online authenticity of customers and merchants.

750. Concerns about credit card fraud led to the development of techniques to safeguard the viability of using credit cards as an Internet payment method. The inclusion of SSL in the latest Web browsers enhances this capability. SSL allows the encryption of credit card numbers and provides protection from tampering.

751. A stored-value smart card is a plastic card that contains a microprocessor chip that can store more information than existing magnetic stripe cards. It can also perform simple computing operations. The smart card is generally inserted into a terminal where the card touches a read-write mechanism that allows information to be passed to and from the card and the terminal.

752. Smart cards, which store digital data, have a wide range of uses, including medical applications, personal organization, and so on.[331] Smart cards can be used as a credit card, a debit card to execute account transfers, or as something more

331. S. Newman & G. Sutter, *Electronic Payments – The Smart Card: Smart Cards, E-payments & Law – Part I*, 18 *Computer Law & Security Report* 235 (2002); Privacy Committee of New South Wales, *Smart Cards: Big Brother's Little Helpers* (Sydney: NSW Parliament 1995).

secure than the magnetic stripe card. Where a smart card functions as a stored-value card, it has been called an electronic purse or an e-wallet. As mentioned previously, to promote the use of smart card technology, the industry has developed a Smart Card Code of Conduct. This Code provides minimum standards, which among other things provides for a system of dispute resolution; requires that cardholders be issued with clearly expressed terms and conditions of use; mandates that this information be distinguished from marketing promotions and be provided prior to use by the consumer; provides information about fees, access, notice procedures, and cardholder's rights; and provides protection to the cardholder in the case of fraudulent or negligent conduct of card subscriber employees or agents.

753. Most common smart card applications are credit cards, electronic cash, computer security systems, wireless communication, loyalty systems, banking, satellite television and identification. A smart card reader attached to a personal computer may be used to authenticate a user. Web browsers can also use smart card technology to supplement the SSL for improved security of Internet transactions.[332]

754. The Department of Finance and Deregulation, through the AGIMO has developed a National Smartcard Framework for smart cards. This Framework provides mechanisms that evidence identity and service requirements by specifying minimum requirements for applications and infrastructure interoperability. This Framework has been developed in consultation with Australian Government agencies, state and territory governments and industry.[333]

755. Two main types of smart cards are in use – contact smart cards and contactless smart cards. Information in a contact smart card may be read if a card is inserted directly into a card reader. With contactless smart cards, low frequency radio waves communicate with readers, hence they can be read from a short distance away. In technical terms the technology is about 'Near Field Communication' (NFC) chips that are used for very short-range radio transmissions. A pair of NFC transmitters can communicate at a maximum of just a few centimetres and some need to be 'tapped' for a transaction to be concluded. The Mastercard 'Pay Pass' credit card is one such example. NFC is also used in mobile phones for payments in conjunction with an electronic wallet and for setting up connections between Bluetooth devices.[334]

III. Areas Needing Assurance

756. There are many insurmountable problems and issues to be grappled with including areas where assurance is sorely needed. These include:

332. *See* ALRC discussion on smart cards at http://www.alrc.gov.au/publications/9.%20Overview%3A%20Impact%20of%20Developing%20Technology%20on%20Privacy/smart-cards.
333. Australian Government Information Management Office, *Australian Government Smartcard Framework* (2008), at http://www.agimo.gov.au/infrastructure/smart_cards.
334. An explanation of some technical details may be found at http://www.pcadvisor.co.uk/how-to/mobile-phone/3472879/what-is-nfc-how-nfc-works-what-it-does/#ixzz2wSgsgthW.

- Business practices: Issues relating to billing and payment policies, shipping policies, refund policies, tax collection policy, and consumer protection.
- Transaction processing integrity: What systems are in place to ensure information is handled properly; how does the company ensure it does not lose orders; and controls on accurate posting.
- Privacy of data: Does the firm have a privacy policy? Is it adequate? Is it disclosed? Can customers verify data and change it or delete it? Is compliance monitored?

757. Billing practices address day-to-day operations and likely raise more evidentiary issues than any other legal theory. On the other hand, transaction processing integrity will infuse business confidence and trust so that customers have the necessary assurances. The absence of such integrity may lead to tortious liability and failure of contract. Public policy requirements now impose strict guidelines on protecting consumers and their privacy. While codes of practice for privacy are extant the amendments to the Privacy Act 1988 (Cth) in 2000 make it compulsory for all private sector organizations to adhere to standards for handling information.[335]

758. Important changes to the Privacy Act 1988 commenced on 12 March 2014.[336] The changes include a new set of APP that will regulate the handling of personal information by Australian Government agencies and some businesses. The APP replace both the Information Privacy Principles (IPP) that applied to Australian Government agencies and the National Privacy Principles (NPP) that applied to some private sector organizations. The APP cover the collection, use, disclosure and storage of personal information. They allow individuals to access their personal information and have it corrected if it is incorrect. There are also separate APP that deal with the use and disclosure of personal information for the purpose of direct marketing (APP 7), cross-border disclosure of personal information (APP 8) and the adoption, use and disclosure of government related identifiers (APP 9).[337]

§2. Electronic Payments Systems (EPS)

I. Internet Banking

759. Internet banking in various forms is growing rapidly in Australia.[338] The changeover to Internet banking may be traced to changing consumer behaviour

---

335. *Privacy (Private Sector) Amendment Act* 2000 (Cth).
336. *Privacy Amendment (Enhancing Privacy Protection) Act* 2012 (Cth).
337. *See* the Privacy Chapter *infra* and Australian Privacy Principles at https://www.oaic.gov.au/privacy/australian-privacy-principles/.
338. *See* M. Talukder, A. Quazi, and M. Sathye, *Mobile Phone Banking Usage Behaviour: An Australian Perspective*, 8(4) Australasian Accounting, Business and Finance Journal 83–104 (2014). doi:10.14453/aabfj.v8i4.6M.

coupled with individuality, mobility, independence of time and place, and flexibility. Financial transactions can now be undertaken by anyone with banks and financial institutions (non-banks). Financial service companies using the Internet have discovered a new distribution channel. Complex financial products may be offered at lower cost without compromising in quality to a larger number of customers. Such customers are neither bound by geography nor by time of day or night given the 24/7 cyberworld of the twenty-first century.

760. Internet banking is accompanied by its attendant risks and hence the need for basic protocols including customer authentication, coding of private data using cryptography, and the use of digital signatures to obtain legal bindings to contracts. As a result, the familiar HTTP (hypertext transfer protocol) has been extended to SHTTP (secure) as well as HTTPs to ensure safe transmission. Other protocols to ensure security include home banking communication interface (HBCI), SET, and SSL software technology discussed earlier. As will be noted, the solutions are both hardware- and software-based, and any customer will need access to these in the first instance.

761. Currently, there are several ways businesses accept payments by electronic means. The differences in payment acceptance are only in their detail as discussed below.

II. Electronic Payments Systems (EPS)

762. Many financial institutions are offering their customers the ability to pay their bills electronically by instructing their financier institutions to debit an account that the customer holds with that financier and pay an amount to a third party through the telephone or the Internet.

763. An example of an EPS is the BPAY scheme, a form of remote or virtual banking, in use in Australia since November 1997. Customers of financial institutions participating in the BPAY scheme can pay funds to other participants in the BPAY scheme, using a telephone or, in some cases, Internet banking facilities. The BPAY scheme is an EPS, allowing customers (individuals and businesses) to instruct their financial institutions to pay amounts of money to nominated people or institutions (called billers). BPAY's advantage is that it allows a payer to pay bills of varying amounts to participating billers at any time.

764. Developments in the world of virtual cash suggest the use of cryptocurrencies. A cryptocurrency is a digital or virtual medium of exchange that uses encrypted software to maintain a secure and transparent network for transactions controlled collectively by those using the network. The market for such payment instruments includes e-cash, NetCash, Milli-cent and lately bitcoin and others such as litecoin, dogecoin, Ethereum, ripple, megacoin, kitthcoin, lottocoin, duboons, hobonickles, nanotoken and philosopher stones.[339]

III. Digital Cash (DC)

765. Digital cash is an electronic method of payment on the Internet.[340] A DC issuer will issue a digital coin message signed or encrypted with its private key, with the secret key known only to the issuer. That message will contain the identity of the issuer, its Internet address, the amount of the coin, its serial number, and an expiry date. In addition, the issuer maintains records to ensure the coin cannot be spent twice – an e-banking problem addressed by block chain technology.[341] St. George Bank was Australia's first bank to issue digital coins. Since 1997, the Deutsche Bank in cooperation with the Dutch firm DigiCash has offered electronic cash in the form of prepaid cards.[342]

766. The digital cash technology, launched by Digicash in 2017, is digitally 'minted' as electronically signed financial instruments such as coins and banknotes.[343] Digicash can be held on smartphones, computers or storage media. Just like cash, online users can transfer financial instruments between each other via free, instant transactions. The encryption technology used means that the electronic financial instruments can securely circulate over public communication networks, without the risk of theft or counterfeiting

767. E-cash is anonymous digital money whose validity is checked online by the corresponding financial institution. The system was developed by DigiCash and has been offered by Mark Twain Bank, St. Louis since 1995. Similarly, Deutsche Bank AG, Frankfurt (Main) has offered e-cash to its customers since October 1997.[344] E-cash security is achieved by using an asymmetric cryptographic algorithm. Account access may be protected additionally by using personal passwords.

---

339. *See* Stephen Hutcheon, *Cracking the Cryptic World of Virtual Cash*, Sydney Morning Herald, 9 (8–9 Feb. 2014).
340. https://www.cs.bham.ac.uk/~mdr/teaching/modules06/netsec/lectures/DigitalCash.html.
341. A block chain is a digital database containing information (such as records of financial transactions) that can be simultaneously used and shared within a large decentralized, publicly accessible network. It also refers to the technology used to create such a database. *See* Wikipedia https://en.wikipedia.org/wiki/Blockchain.
342. *See* Christopher Kuner, *The Bundesbank and Electronic Cash*, Journal of Internet Banking and Commerce at http://www.icommercecentral.com/open-access/the-bundesbank-and-electronic-cash.php?aid=38790&view=mobile.
343. https://cmcrc.com/better-than-blockchain-digital-financial-instruments/.
344. https://www.chaum.com/ecash/.

768. NetCash was developed at the University of Southern California.[345] An important goal of the project was to use existing accounting systems and procedures of most financial institutions in order to reduce setup and investments costs. This method is based on a decentralized approach requiring the cooperation of all participating financial institutions and a reduced level of anonymity.

769. NetCash coins have a face value and a serial number, an address of the issuing server, and an expiry date. In NetCash, coins from a currency server are encoded with a public key and then sent to the dealer. The anonymity of the customer may be guaranteed by using a new session key for each message. The dealer transfers coins received immediately to the dealer's currency server. From the currency server, the dealer may either receive new coins or a corresponding value may be credited to the dealer's account. Final clearing is done by the currency servers. The serial numbers of all coins that are not sent back and not yet expired are stored on the currency server in order to avoid double spending. This means reduced anonymity.

770. The Milli-cent micropayment technology was developed by Digital Equipment Corporation (DEC) to manage small payments.[346] A customer buys a broker script with a defined value by using a credit card or by debiting a suitable bank or broker account. Such a script is like a telephone card.

771. Bitcoin is best known as a pure digital currency.[347] This cryptocurrency is based on 'coins' generated through a mathematical algorithm that is progressively being solved in blocks to generate coins using computer power. The bitcoin movement is non-government and is decentralized. Bitcoins offer anonymous transactions (although not guaranteed) because all bitcoin transactions between wallets can be viewed on the decentralized blockchain database. The value of the bitcoin in March 2014 was about USD 825.00 and its value fluctuates based on supply and demand and market sentiment. The bitcoin index value for the end of December 2018 amounted to USD 3,689.56.[348]

772. The infrastructure around cryptocurrency markets is vulnerable to hackers, fraudsters and thieves. The Australian Transaction Reports and Analysis Centre (AUSTRAC) is aware that digital currencies may become attractive to criminal groups and together with other law enforcement agencies is 'actively monitoring

345. BC Neuman and G. Medvinisky, *NetCheque, NetCash, and the Characteristics of Internet Payment Services*, 1(1&2) *J Electronic Publishing* (January), DOI: https://doi.org/10.3998/3336451.0001.126.
346. Scott Worden, *Micropayments and the future of the Web* (1998), at https://cyber.harvard.edu/fallsem98/final_papers/Worden.html.
347. *See* Tom Simonite, *What Bitcoin Is, and Why It Matters. Can a booming 'crypto-currency' really compete with conventional cash?* (2011), at https://www.technologyreview.com/s/424091/what-bitcoin-is-and-why-it-matters/.
348. *See* Statista Report 2017 at https://www.statista.com/statistics/326707/bitcoin-price-index/.

developments across the range of digital currencies currently available in Australia'.[349] A discussion on anti-money laundering initiatives is discussed below.

IV. Digital Cheques

773. Similar techniques can be used to send electronic digital cheques and bills of exchange across the Internet. The Internet cheque message contains the same information as would appear on a paper cheque and is digitally signed. That is, it is encoded by encrypting the message with the drawer's private key. It is then sent to the payee. When the payee's bank collects the cheque for the payee, this is marked on the cheque message, and that message is encoded with the drawer's banks private key, which provides proof of payment.

§3. Security and Control of Payments Systems

774. No matter how clever the protocols and no matter how convenient to use, an Internet payments system will not be used unless there is widespread confidence in the system. 'Confidence' in the payments system is more than just confidence in the cryptographic methods deployed. The user must be certain that payments ordered will be delivered and that a payment that appears to be complete is in fact completed.

775. Financial institutions such as banks are qualified to play the role of a CA in the sense of security mechanisms such as SSL and SET. Financial institutions may do these first for their customers as well as offer such security as a service. In a broad sense, both security and trust infrastructures are within the scope of financial activities.

I. Characteristics of Payments Systems

776. Any payments method usually involves multiple financial institutions. There may be other institutions involved such as credit unions and building societies. Given the deregulation of the financial industry but also because of the other non-bank services that are being provided by such institutions. Payments by cheque that involves multiple financial institutions have been the pattern of payment but may also be made by direct credits – the creditor has a standing instruction with a financial institution to make payments to the debtor's bank or other financial institution account. Transactions may also involve bank-to-bank and bank-to-non-bank institutions and vice versa. The transfer of credit from one institution to the other

349. *See* Rohan Pearce, *Money Laundering Using Virtual Worlds, Bitcoin on Watchdog's Radar*, Computerworld (15 Aug. 2012), at http://www.computerworld.com.au/article/433634/money_laundering_using_virtual_worlds_bitcoin_watchdog_radar/.

implies the payment of a debt owed by one to the other (as discussed in *Foley v Hill* (1848) 2 HL Cas 28; 9 ER 1002; and *Joachimson v. Swiss Bank Corp.* (1921) 3 KB 110).

777. Transactions may also involve institutions outside the payments system such as the European GIRO scheme. A GIRO transfer is a payment transfer from one bank account to another bank account and instigated by the payer and not the payee.[350] In the UK the giro service was originally known as National Giro operated by the post office. The European GIRO system is one where it is not necessary to have an existing account with a financial institution to initiate a GIRO payment.

II. Clearing and Settlement

778. Clearing is both an accounting process and a formal acceptance of the transferred liability. Each institutional participant in a clearing system has received large numbers of orders to make payments to each of the other participants.

779. Clearing in Australia is conducted by the Australian Payments Clearing Association (APCA), a non-listed public company limited by shares and guarantee formed in February 1992.

780. Settlement refers to the process whereby the financial institutions resolve their mutual liabilities. At the end of the clearing cycle, each institution will have many individual small liabilities toward each of the other participants. From a legal point of view, each individual payment is a separate liability. From a commercial point of view, it would be impracticable to eliminate each of these individual liabilities with a separate payment.

III. Netting Arrangements

781. 'Netting' refers to replacing a series of obligations between two parties with a single obligation that is calculated by summing all the obligations owed by each party to the other and deducting the smaller from the larger. The process is commercially referred to as 'netting out' the obligations.

782. In multilateral netting arrangements, each participant pays or receives a single payment at the end of each payment. Several legal frameworks exist for this. The simplest and most common is to use the clearing organization (or some related organization) as an agent to make and receive settlement payments based on the netting out of all obligations. The clearing rules call for payments to the agent to act as a discharge of all interparty liabilities. The legal foundation for multilateral netting is that the clearinghouse rules operate as a multilateral contract under seal as provided under section 180 of the Corporations Law 2001 (Cth).

350. 'Giro' meaning the circulation of money in Dutch, German and Italian languages.

IV. Exposure Risks

783. Where netting arrangements fail to protect transactions, the system would be exposed to several serious risks. 'Contagion' risk is the risk that the failure of a single institution may lead to liquidity problems for its commercial neighbours. The size of the daily clearing in the payments systems makes this risk a very serious one.

784. 'Systemic' risk is the risk that the previously mentioned contagion could become a plague in the financial markets. If netting arrangements were held to be valid, then both 'contagion' and 'systemic' risks become very real and serious problems. Where there are payments in the system that have not been cleared before the insolvency of a member may present insurmountable problems. It should be noted here that the netting provisions in the British Eagle case were valid regarding payments that were cleared before the insolvency (*British Eagle & International Airlines Ltd v. Compagnie Nationale Air France* (1975) 2 All ER 390).

785. The Payment Systems and Netting Act 1998 (Cth) allows the Reserve Bank Australia to exercise its powers if it considers that systemic disruption to the financial system could otherwise result. Section 16 of the Banking Act 1959 (Cth) states that in the event of a bank becoming unable to meet its obligations or suspending payment, the assets of the bank in Australia should be available to meet that bank's deposit liabilities in priority to all other liabilities of the bank. This is a depositor protection device.

V. Herstatt Risks

786. Multicurrency payment across multiple time zones has its own special risk. Settlement will normally be at different times because of time zone difference, and therefore, there is an additional level of exposure. Known as the *Herstatt risk,* the name comes from the losses associated with the collapse of the Herstatt Bank in 1974 (discussed in *Momm v. Barclays Bank International* (1977) QB 79; and in *Delbrueck & Co. v. Manufacturers Hanover Trust Co.* 609 F.2d 1047 (1979)).

VI. Application to Digital Cash

787. Many of the proposals for implementing Internet payments systems implicitly assume a single financial institution at which both the merchant and the consumer hold accounts. In such a system, there is no need for clearing and settlement arrangements. However, such a system will never be a significant payments system. To enable e-commerce on the Internet, the payments system must permit the two parties to hold accounts at different financial institutions.

VII. Control of the Payments Systems

788. The Payments System (Regulation) Act 1998 (Cth) provides for the regulation of both payments systems and purchase payment facilities by the creation of a new Payments Systems Board within the Reserve Bank of Australia (RBA). A 'payments system' is defined under the Act as a 'funds transfer system that facilitates the circulation of money' between participants. This broad definition will capture many of the electronic payment mechanisms discussed in this chapter. The powers of the Payments Systems Board within the RBA include the regulation of payments systems such as digital cash and SVCs. The Regulation also gives the RBA broad powers to regulate various details of payments systems. These powers include the right to require terms and conditions, require various access schemes, mandate standards, and establish dispute resolution procedures.

789. A New Payments Platform was developed to address a number of gaps in Australia's retail payment system that the Reserve Bank had identified in its 2012 Strategic Review of Innovation in the Payments System.[351] The New Payments Platform was launched in February 2018.[352] This is a fast payments system developed by a consortium of 13 financial institutions, including the Reserve Bank. This platform operates on a 24/7 basis and allows financial institutions to provide immediate funds availability to payment recipients, even where the payer and payee have accounts with different financial institutions. The payment messages of this platform use the ISO20022 message format and can carry much richer remittance information than the 18 characters currently available for Direct Entry payments. In addition, the New Payments Platform provides a 'PayID' service, which provides the option for a payment to be made to a registered phone number, ABN or e-mail address (instead of addressing a payment to a Bank State Bank (BSB) account number).

790. The New Payments Platform will give consumers and businesses the ability to:

- transfer money instantly between accounts at different financial institutions;
- make these payments any time of day, any day of the year;
- include more accompanying information with these payments; and
- use a PayID making it a simpler way to pay that lets the payer see the name of the person or business being paid before sending the payment.

791. The platform's transactions have been growing steadily since its launch in 2018. Over 2 million PayIDs had been created as of end September, and over 35 million payments worth about AUD 30 billion had been sent through the platform.

351. *See* Reserve Bank Australia at https://www.rba.gov.au/payments-and-infrastructure/payments-system-regulation/past-regulatory-reviews/strategic-review-of-innovation-in-the-payments-system/conclusions/.
352. *See* Reserve Bank Australia at https://www.rba.gov.au/payments-and-infrastructure/new-payments-platform/.

The average value of an payment through this platform is nearly AUD 1000, consistent with this platform being used for some larger-value business payments that previously would have gone through the previously used Direct Entry system, although most transactions are significantly smaller.

792. However, other than the facilitation of the ease of electronic payments there are other questions that need to be resolved before EPS becomes de jure such as the creation of money and counterfeiting.

793. In Australia, the Reserve Bank issues currency notes, and the Treasury issues coins. The value in the money arises in the following way. A currency note or a coin represents a liability to the issuer, but it is a liability on which no interest is paid. On the other hand, the issuer obtains normal market interests on other assets. This difference between the interest-free liability and the interest-bearing security is known as *seigniorage,* a valuable source of earnings for all governments. In so far as smart cards and digital coins replacing currency is concerned, the benefits of *seigniorage* would be lost to the government and would accrue instead to the card or coin issuer.

794. *Unclaimed monies* that languish unused in banks and financial institutions arise from forgetfulness, death, or secrecy in which the secret key to the monies has been lost and become unrecoverable. Unclaimed monies could also eventuate from not knowing that a deposit or bond has been paid. For example, a bond would be returned upon the termination of a lease, such as a tenancy on a property, or some other contractual event.

795. A digital coin represents a claim on a bank similar to the claim of a current account holder. The claim does not mature, to use a neutral term, until the coin is presented to the bank by a merchant. Clearly 'old' digital coins pose the same problem for financial institutions as dormant accounts.

796. Dormant Accounts. The precise treatment of 'old' digital coins might depend upon the implementation of the payments systems. If a 'blind' system is used, the bank may know nothing more than that there are outstanding claims on it. It is quite impossible to identify the location of these coins or the person to whom the coins were issued. The solution is to 'unblind' the digital coin, a solution that may be easy to state but difficult to achieve in practical terms. For example, what if the account holder dies and the survivors do not even know of the existence of the coins. Even if they did, they would not know the key to 'unblind' the coins. What do we do in those situations? It seems the solution is that the asset and 'wealth' also dies with the account holder, and this may, of itself, not be a good thing because some asset is now lost.

797. Dormant accounts cause considerable inconvenience for the banker and represent a generally unproductive relationship. Legislation to transfer dormant account monies to the Crown or government authority is in place to release tied-up assets. Dormant accounts are subject to section 69 Banking Act 1959 (Cth).

798. Money laundering is the concealing of the source of funds that one is aware of that comes from serious crime. In this formulation, the state of mind required is knowledge (*mens rea*), although this knowledge can be inferred from objective facts. The second component is that the source of funds must be from serious crime. However, what is serious crime is undefined and elastic and may vary from jurisdiction to jurisdiction. Serious crime can include large-scale IP theft through to references to tax evasion and illegal gambling. Moreover, serious crime need not be committed in the same jurisdiction as the money laundering. Thus, in money laundering, the existence or the source of income is disguised to make it appear legitimate. The laundering task is simplified if money can be laundered or smuggled out of the country. If the destination country is one with 'good' bank secrecy laws such as Switzerland, then the laundering task is easier again. Once money is safely lodged in a secure foreign account, it can be reimported under the guise of bank loans, fees for services, or payments for non-existent goods. This activity then legitimizes the money, and it enters mainstream commerce.

A. Australian Solutions

799. Some Australian solutions to the problems of counterfeiting and money laundering are found in the Financial Transaction Reports Act 1988 (Cth) that requires 'cash dealers' to report certain information to the AUSTRAC. The Proceeds of Crime Act 1987 (Cth) imposes criminal penalties on a person who engages in money laundering. However, note that the critical words in these pieces of legislation include 'significant cash transactions' (meaning transactions of greater than AUD 10,000) and 'reasonable grounds to suspect', but not 'reasonable grounds to believe'. The latter may be an exercise of semantics but there are very important differences between those phrases.

800. The Australian regime to fight money laundering and terrorism financing is supported by legislation under the Anti-Money Laundering and Counter-Terrorism Financing Act 2006 (Cth) (AML/CTF Act). AUSTRAC is the anti-money laundering regulator with a specialist financial intelligence unit. The AML/CTF Act provides a means to help detect, deter and disrupt money laundering.[353] The belief is that the money 'laundered' may be used to finance terrorism and other serious financial crimes. The AML/CTF Act also provides measures for Australian government bodies and international counterparts with information, support cooperation and collaboration among reporting entities of AUSTRAC, promote public confidence in the Australian financial systems and help fulfil Australian international obligations whilst addressing matters of international concern.

801. Other financial practices on the Internet are regulated by specific legislation. For example, ASIC has developed proposals to regulate offers, invitations, and advertisements in relation to securities dealings on the Internet. For example, the

353. *See* Australian Parliament House web portal at: https://www.aph.gov.au/About_Parliament/Parliamentary_Departments/Parliamentary_Library/pubs/BriefingBook45p/MoneyLaundering.

ASIC recently obtained an injunction against an owner and operator of a website that gave out investment advice on the grounds that it was publishing share market advice without a licence. This case shows that Internet chat room operators have obligations to meet. One example is that of the 'pump and dump' scams which involve pumping false information to get share prices up and then dumping the stock. This is easily achievable when many thousands of people may be reached via a simple e-mail broadcast.[354]

802. The Internet has provided easy ways to move money from investors' pockets to that of promoters. Many online financial scams advise their customers to open accounts at legitimate online money transfer services such as PayPal or digital gold currency E-Gold. These services were founded principally to facilitate e-commerce payments by acting as financial intermediaries between buyers and merchants. However, these services can unwittingly facilitate the funding of scams without requiring cash to be sent through the mail.

803. PayPal's user agreement clearly states that its services cannot be used for any illegal purpose or activity. Although E-Gold describes itself as an offshore market for the buying and selling of gold, backed by precious metal reserves the company maintains overseas, in practice the system allows users to transfer money among themselves almost as though they are writing cheques.

B. e-Crime

804. DigiCash and similar schemes claim that their systems are not suited to money laundering, tax evasion, electronic ransom demands, or other criminal activity. The justification for this claim is that although the payer is anonymous, the recipient of the money has no anonymity at all. The recipient can only deposit the digital coins with the bank that issued them. Therefore, the argument continues, the bank and the authorities know that the payee has received funds. Further, since the payer has the 'blinding factor' that guarantees anonymity, the payer is always able to prove the source of the funds.

C. Other Criminal Activities

805. There are also other forms of criminal activity. While hypothetical, there is the possibility of crimes such as home raids where DigiCash stored on home computers is forcibly transferred by the home raiders. The problem of hackers into computer networks is already well known, and it is not too far in the future that these activities will spill onto cybermoney heists. In addition, the problem of fraudulent

354. B. O'Riordan, *Watchdog Ready to Bite Hard on Web Share Scams*, Australian Financial Review, 29 (8 Jun. 1999).

participants in the digital cash schemes through disguised identities (such as hijacked or stolen identities) may become problematic for electronic payments systems around the world.

§4. Australian Regulatory Responses to E-Cash

806. In Australia, there have been over twenty domestic reviews of e-commerce. In addition, several regulators are currently investigating the likely impact of e-cash on sectors of the economy and on groups of people.[355] For example, comprehensive reviews of fifteen Commonwealth Acts regulating the financial sector have or are about to occur. The most significant review was the Financial Systems (Wallis) Inquiry 1996. The report concluded that e-commerce should be subject to regulation to ensure the safety and integrity of the payments system. It noted that regulatory and legislative changes will be required in Australia simply to allow for electronic commerce.

807. The growth of e-cash portends a fundamental shift in payments methods. The potential of transferring funds instantaneously by any means makes it difficult for governments to monitor or regulate. E-cash raises other regulatory issues and dilemmas. Customers can choose between different currencies. This could result in loss of revenues from tax avoidance and loss of income earned by central banks (seigniorage). There are also issues of crime such as money laundering discussed previously and the question of privacy of such transactions. If there is going to be a close monitoring of all electronic activity, people may feel that their privacy has been invaded. The advent of digital cash and other forms of electronic money may render government-issued media of exchange obsolete. The overall impact of e-cash, however, will depend on the pace and direction of technological change and response to this by consumers, businesses, and governments.

808. It is to be noted that the Financial Sector Reform (Amendments and Transitional Provisions) Act 1998 (Cth) (FSR) deals with financial markets and financial products and proposes to harmonize the regulation of the financial industry through uniform licensing requirements. While aimed primarily at breaking down the regulatory distinctions between securities, futures, derivatives, and other financial products, the proposed reforms impact on e-payments due to the proposed broad definition of a 'financial product' and the uniform regulation of 'financial service providers'. Such a definition is broad enough to capture payments systems providers, electronic cash issuers, and smart cards. The FSR will also impose stringent POS disclosure requirements that could also impact on e-payments schemes.

355. Electronic Commerce Task Force 1996, pp. 130–135.

§5. CONCLUSION

809. The development of e-commerce, including privately issued e-cash, will depend on the pace and development of technological change, its acceptance by consumers and businesses, and the responses of government regulators in Australia and overseas. The likely impact of e-cash is probably modest according to the Bank for International Settlements (BIS), an international financial institution owned by central banks that fosters international monetary and financial cooperation and serves as a bank for central banks.[356]

810. However, e-cash will affect the way economies operate. Governments have incentives to retain their monopoly over the issuing of currency, chiefly to ensure stability of the financial system, while they also benefit from additional revenues from *seigniorage* and in some cases inflation. They also have incentives to reform regulations to encourage the use of e-money, while also ensuring that it does not have unintended consequences such as undermining the tax base. However, poorly designed regulatory responses by governments could unnecessarily impede the use of e-cash, resulting in the loss of economic activity in the financial, retailing, and other sectors and a loss of tax revenues to countries with better regulatory environments.

356. www.bis.org.

Chapter 4. Consumer Protection of ICT Users

§1. Introduction

811. Australia does not have any specialized legislation dealing with consumer law issues in a cyber environment. The ordinary consumer protection laws that govern traditional forms of commerce apply equally to e-commerce. The ACCC's website highlights pyramid selling schemes (earn money by recruiting others to the scheme), get-rich-quick scams, phoney prizes and lotteries and others. Other IT related scams include identity theft, phishing, remote access scams, false billing, and threats to life and arrest or other.[357]

812. Australians lost more money to scammers in 2017 than in any other year since the ACCC began reporting on scam activity. According to the ACCC's ninth annual Targeting Scams Report, more than 200,000 scam reports were submitted to the ACCC, Australian Cybercrime Online Reporting Network (ACORN) and other federal and state-based government agencies in 2017. Total losses reported were AUD 340 million – an AUD 40 million increase compared to 2016. Scamwatch received almost 33,000 reports of these threat-based impersonation scams in 2017. Over AUD 4.7 million was reported lost and more than 2,800 people gave their personal information to these scammers.[358]

§2. Overview of Consumer Protection Regimes

I. In General

813. Consumer protection in Australia is predominantly governed by both federal and state legislation. Statutory consumer protection is necessary because of the nature of contract law in Australia. Traditional contract law, informed by the free market economic theory of the nineteenth century, depended upon the notion of 'freedom of contract' and hence upon the principle (often fictitious) of 'equality of bargaining power'. The massive advances since the end of the twentieth century in manufacturing, distribution, advertising, and consumption of goods and services, however, have meant that this concept of the individual contract has been inadequate to protect the consumer.

357. www.accc.gov.au.
358. https://www.scamwatch.gov.au/news/australians-lost-340-million-to-scammers-in-2017. The ACCC encourages the public to visit www.scamwatch.gov.au to report scams so we can warn others about them and learn more about what to do if they are targeted by scams.

814. The three most important statutory schemes of consumer protection in Australia are the state Sale of Goods Acts,[359] the CCA,[360] and the state Fair Trading legislation.[361] There is also a considerable body of specialized State legislation that affords the consumer protection in specific areas of activity.

II. CCA and Fair Trading Legislation

815. There is a vast array of case law and legislation governing consumer contracts. The most important of these are the CCA and its counterpart in the Fair Trading Act adopted in each of the States. The application of the CCA to material posted on a website has been affirmed by the Australian courts.

816. In *ACCC v. Abel Rentacar Pty. Ltd.* ((1999) FCA 314) for example, it was found that advertisements on the web stating without qualification that cars could be hired for AUD 29 per day were misleading, and the Court ordered them removed from the Internet website operated by the respondent. Similarly, the TPA was held to apply in *ACCC v. Internic Technology Pty. Ltd.* (1998) 818 FCA where the ACCC sued Internic for operating a website that made false, misleading, and deceptive representations as to the nature of its domain name registration services. It was found that the site 'www.internic.com' operated by Internic was misleading because it falsely represented that the site was affiliated with InterNIC, which was the sole body authorized to issue domain names and which had a website, 'www.internic-.net'.

817. The most powerful and far-reaching provisions of these Acts are the prohibitions against conduct which is 'misleading and deceptive or likely to mislead or deceive'.[362] Importantly, the misleading and deceptive conduct provisions do not require evidence of intention or motive. It is adequate that the conduct took place. Nor must anyone be misled. The conduct need only be determined to be 'likely to mislead or deceive'. In making this determination, the courts will consider all of those to whom the representation was made, including the astute, the gullible, the intelligent, and the disabled.

818. An example of the misleading and deceptive provisions applying to an Internet scam occurred in October 2002. The ACCC filed proceedings in Federal Court against Mr Richard Chen for operating a website that allegedly fraudulently

359. *Sale of Goods Act* 1923 (NSW); 1972 (NT); 1896 (Qld); 1895 (SA); 1896 (Tas); 1895 (WA); *Sale of Goods Ordinance* 1954 (ACT); *Goods Act* 1958 (Vic).

360. The CCA has been the most comprehensive consumer protection initiative in Australia. Constitutional limitations upon Commonwealth power restricted the scope of the CCA with the result that the states and territories enacted their fair trading legislation in order to close the gaps in the federal scheme. The Fair Trading Acts mirror many of the provisions of the CCA.

361. *Fair Trading Act* 1987 (NSW); 1987 (WA); 1989 (Qld); 1985 (Vic); 1990 (Tas); *Consumer Affairs and Fair Trading Act* 1990 (NT).

362. *Competition and Consumer Act* 2010 (Cth) s. 52 Misleading or deceptive conduct in Sch. 2 Part 2-2 s. 18.

imitated the Sydney Opera House official site. The Federal Court found Mr Richard Chen, a resident of New York, misled and deceived consumers by operating websites that imitated the Sydney Opera House official website and offered tickets for events at the Opera House without approval. An injunction was issued. The decision follows ACCC action with the assistance of the International Consumer Protection and Enforcement Network (ICPEN) and the US Federal Trade Commission.[363]

819. Not only do the CCA and Fair Trading Acts provide for a broad scheme of relief, but they also extend the Acts' application to a wider group of people than would have been possible at common law. Part VI Enforcement and Remedies section 75B(1) Interpretation of the CCA, for example, provides that a person involved in a contravention includes a person who has been in any way, directly or indirectly, knowingly concerned in or a party to the contravention. While knowledge required by section 75B(1) is actual knowledge, where there is a combination of suspicious circumstances and a failure to make enquiry, such knowledge may be inferred as in *Compaq Computer Australia Pty. Ltd. v. Merry* (unreported), Federal Court, 14 August 1998.

III. CCA and Australian Consumer Law (2010) (Cth) (ACL)

820. Use of Schedule 2 of the CCA contains the Australian Consumer Law 2010 (Cth) may eliminate the need to consider whether a manufacturer who has supplied defective goods including electronic goods is in breach of warranty. These sections may have application where a manufacturer fails to inform potential users of a product that the goods are dangerous or makes some statement or claim to the product that may mislead or deceive the public.

IV. CCA and Enforcement, Remedies and Statute of Limitations

821. One of the most significant advantages of bringing an action under the CCA, as opposed to common law or the original Sale of Goods Act, is the variety and flexibility of available remedies. The remedies are listed as follows.

- *Loss or damage:* Schedule 2 section 236.[364]
- *Fine:* Section 79, with certain exceptions.[365]

363. Australian Competition and Consumer Commission, *Global Consumer Scams: The ACCC's International Role* (2003), Canberra. *See also* https://www.accc.gov.au/media-release/court-declares-imitation-sydney-opera-house-website-illegal.
364. A criminal conviction is possible for a breach of the *Australian Consumer Law* 2010 Sch. 2 of the CCA; however, the Court has the discretion to dismiss charges under s. 19B(1) of the *Crimes Act* 1914 (Cth). This may be based on factors such as age, health, mental condition, triviality of the offence, extenuating circumstances, or expediency.
365. Schedule 2 s. 122 compulsory recall of consumer goods, s. 133D power to obtain information, Sch. 2 s. 128 Notification requirements for a voluntary recall of consumer goods.

- *Injunctions*: Section 80 Schedule 2 Part 5-2 Division 2. A civil penalty, either prohibitive (ordering to stop doing something) or mandatory (an order to do something such as corrective advertising).
- *Corrective advertising* or disclosure of information: Section 80 Schedule 2 Part 5-2 Division 2.
- *Ancillary orders*: Section 87 Schedule 2 Part 5-2 Division 4 Subdivision A to compensate, prevent, or reduce damage suffered or likely to be suffered by a person.
- *Rescission*: Section 131C treats the contract as void.
- Prosecutions may only be brought by the ACCC, a person authorized by them, by the relevant Minister, or person authorized by the Minister.[366]
- The statute of limitations for matters under Schedule 2 section 236 and 137F CCA.

V. CCA and Defences

822. Under Part V of the TPA, a person held to have contravened the Act for unfair practices has various defences open to them based on the civil onus of proof. Section 85 Schedule 2 Part 4-6 (Defences) of the CCA provides that a valid defence will be available where the proceeding was due to a reasonable mistake, or due to reliance on information supplied by another person or was beyond their control where they took reasonable precautions to avoid the contravention.

VI. Other Consumer-Related Commonwealth Legislation

823. In general terms, Australia is a world leader in e-securities and e-bonds as evidenced by the following by the establishment of ASX's Stock Exchange Automated Trading System (SEATS) and Clearing House Electronic Sub-Register System (CHESS) and ASIC's electronic lodgement and search facility.[367]

824. In addition to the broad scope of the Fair Trading Act in each State and Territory, legislation also exists which deals with specific areas and applies concurrently with the federal provisions.[368] The States and Territories have legislated in a variety of specific areas such as food, drugs and poisons,[369] textiles,[370] footwear,[371] furniture,[372] and motor vehicles.[373]

---

366. Section 163A Declarations and Orders.
367. *Corporate Law Economic Reform Program Act* 1999 (Cth) which commenced on 13 Mar. 2000.
368. *See Fair Trading Act* 1987 (NSW); 1987 (WA); 1989 (Qld); 1985 (Vic); 1990 (Tas); *Trade Standards Act* 1979 (SA); *Consumer Affairs and Fair Trading Act* 1990 (NT); *Consumer Affairs Act* 1973 (ACT); *Consumer Affairs Act* 1972 (Vic); *Consumer Affairs Act* (WA); *Sale of Hazardous Goods Act* 1977 (Tas).
369. *See, e.g.*, (a) *New South Wales: Banana Industry Act* 1969; *Bread Industry Act* 1969; *Dairy Industry Act* 1915; (b) *Victoria: Abattoirs and Meat Inspection Act* 1973; *Bread Industry Act* 1959; *Broiler Chicken Industry Act* 1975; *Dried Fruits Act* 1958; *Filled Milk Act* 1958; *Fruits and Vegetables Act* 1958.

§3. Consumer Law Governing the Quality of Goods and Services

825. Terms as to the quality of goods and services are implied into consumer contracts by statute such as pertaining to goods, correspondence with description; fitness for purpose; merchantable quality; guarantee as to acceptable quality implying a condition of merchantable quality; and sale by sample.

826. The implied conditions under the CCA also apply to the sale of goods by way of sale, exchange, lease, hire and hire-purchase. Some State legislation also implies terms into contracts for supply of goods other than by sale.[374]

827. Pertaining to Services the guarantee of the CCA implies into every contract for the supply of services a warranty that services will be rendered with due care and skill and that materials supplied with those services will be reasonably fit for the purpose for which they are supplied.[375] There is, however, an exception where the consumer is not relying on the corporation's skill.

§4. Consumer Credit

828. Many purchases of computer equipment and software may be made on credit. The Australian government with the help of State governments has undertaken a comprehensive Reform Package to deliver on the first phase of the Council of Australian Governments' (COAG) agreements of 2008. Under this Package the Commonwealth is to assume responsibility for the regulation of consumer credit. The legislation governing this is the NCCP,[376] which includes the National Credit Code (NCC) as Schedule 1 to the Act. The NCC replicates and replaces previous state-based consumer credit codes and the Uniform Consumer Credit Code (UCCC) and it continues to apply to the conduct of Australian credit licence holders.[377] ASIC is responsible for administering the NCCP. The NCC was a part of a larger reform

370. *Textile Products Labelling Act* 1954 (NSW); *Trade Standards Act* 1979; *Goods (Trade Descriptions) Act* 1971; *Clothing and Fabrics (Labelling) Act* 1973 (WA); *Factories and Shops Act* 1960 (Qld); *Consumer Affairs (Children's Night-Clothes Regulations* 1977 (Vic).

371. *Trade Descriptions (Footwear) Regulations* 1973 (NSW); *Trade Standards Act* 1979 (SA); *Footwear Act* 1918 (Tas); *Footwear Regulations* 1950 (Vic); *Footwear Regulations* 1974 (WA); *Consumer Affairs Regulations* 1973 (Qld).

372. *Bedding and Upholstered Furniture Regulations* (NSW); *Factories and Shops Act* 1960 (Qld); *Trade Standards Act* 1979 (SA); *Consumer Affairs Act* 1972 (Vic); *Trade Descriptions and False Advertisements Act* 1936 (WA).

373. *Motor Traffic Regulations* (NSW); *Traffic (Miscellaneous) Regulations* 1968; *Motor Car Regulations* 1966 (Vic); *Vehicle Standards Regulations* 1977 (WA).

374. *See, e.g., Goods Act* 1958 (Vic), ss 103–107; *Consumer Transactions Act* 1972 (SA), s. 8(2)–(6); *Hire Purchase Act* 1959 (Tas), s. 9; 1961 (NT), s. 9; 1959 (Qld), s. 5.

375. Schedule 2 s. 60 CCA.

376. *See National Consumer Credit Protection Act* 2009 (Cth) available at: http://www.comlaw.gov.au/Details/C2014C00118.

377. *Consumer Credit Act* 1994 (Qld); *Consumer Credit Act* 1994 (NSW); *Consumer Credit Act* 1995 (SA); *Consumer Credit Act* 1995 (NT); *Consumer Credit Act* 1995 (ACT); *Consumer Credit Act* 1995 (Tas); *Consumer Credit Act* 1996 (WA).

process that introduced a licensing regime for lenders and brokers which includes obligations such as responsible lending and mandatory external dispute resolution (EDR) scheme membership.[378]

§5. Voluntary Codes

829. Australia has tended to adopt a light touch regulatory philosophy that encourages the development and implementation of codes to a specific. Several codes of conduct are relevant to consumers in an e-business environment. These include:

- Smart Card Code of Conduct and Electronic Funds Transfer Code of Conduct (www.asic.gov.au).
- Telecommunications Codes including Customer and Network Fault Management; Customer Information on Prices, Terms and Conditions Electronic Funds Transfer (EFT) Code of Conduct (www.acif.org.au).
- Internet Industry Association Code of Conduct (www.iia.net.au). Content provisions have been approved to comply with the 1999 amendments to the Australian Broadcasting Services Act 1992 (Cth). The provisions relating to advertising, privacy, and complaints handling have not yet been passed.
- Commonwealth Government's Model Code, Building Consumer Sovereignty in E-commerce – A Best Practice Model for Business (https://treasury.gov.au/publication/the-australian-guidelines-for-electronic-commerce). Based on the OECD Consumer Protection in E-commerce Guidelines, the code has provisions regulating advertising on the Internet, spamming, and other conduct.

830. While most codes are voluntary in that they do not have the force of law behind them, as noted earlier, Part IVB Industry Codes of the CCA makes provision for an organization to adopt a code that is binding with some or all the provisions to be prescribed under the CCA. Similarly, the Commonwealth Broadcasting Services Act 1992 (Cth) provides that once the ABA directs an ISP or content host to comply with a registered code, it is legally required to do so. The ABA has approved the IIA's Content Regulation Code of Practice (version 6.0).

§6. International Standards for Consumer Protection in Cyberspace

831. In April 1998, the Commonwealth government held its E-Commerce Enabling Australia Summit. In preparation for that important meeting, the National Advisory Council on Consumer Affairs prepared a report entitled Consumer Protection in Electronic Commerce: Principles and Key Issues. That report stressed that while e-commerce offers the potential of enabling Australian marketers to tap into

---

378. *See* Australian Securities and Investments Commission (2014) advice at http://www.asic.gov.au/asic/asic.nsf/byheadline/Consumer-Credit-Code?openDocument and at: https://asic.gov.au/regulatory-resources/credit/.

new markets, this would not occur without an adequate legal infrastructure of consumer protection that will engender consumer confidence in this new medium of delivery goods and services. The global nature of the problem and the coordinated response being developed is exemplified by the OECD Guidelines for Consumer Protection in Electronic Commerce (1999), which were strongly influenced by Australian developments in this area as well as those such as the EU's Distance Selling Directive.[379] The aim of EU legislation in the field of distance selling is to put consumers, who purchase goods or services through distance communication means, in a similar position to consumers who buy goods or services in shops.

I. Consumer Protection in Electronic Commerce

832. In May 2000, the Australian Government implemented the OECD's 1999 Guidelines for Consumer Protection in the Context of Electronic Commerce, in the form of a BPM. It is hoped the BPM will be adopted by Australian businesses (as well as traders outside Australia dealing with Australian consumers) and industry associations in their codes of conduct. This international approach has taken a positive step toward global cooperation in order to advance consumer protection by establishing and maintaining confidence in the electronic marketplace including independent seals of assurance schemes to develop appropriate standards.

II. Australian E-Commerce BPM

833. The BPM sets the standards for consumer protection in e-commerce. It is a voluntary model code of conduct for dealing with consumers online, underpinned by legislative requirements such as the CCA. Since its development, there have been important changes in the way consumers use the Internet and e-commerce. In 2003, the BPM was the subject of a discussion paper produced by the Expert Group on Electronic Commerce.[380]

834. The Australian Treasury Guidelines for Electronic Commerce (2006) is intended to enhance consumer confidence in e-commerce. These Guidelines provide information to businesses on how to deal with consumers when engaged in B2C e-commerce.[381]

379. Directive 97/7/EC of the European Parliament and of the Council of 20 May 1997 on the protection of consumers in respect of distance contracts available at http://eur-lex.europa.eu/LexUriServ/LexUriServ.do?uri=CELEX:31997L0007:en:NOT.

380. *See* Treasury at https://treasury.gov.au/publication/the-australian-guidelines-for-electronic-commerce.

381. *See also* the Government's Business Entry Point website at www.business.gov.au. These Guidelines update and replace the Australian E-Commerce Best Practice Model released in May 2000.

835. Businesses wanting to work in the electronic marketplace must recognize opportunities to develop innovative methods in terms of delivering products and servicing customers. A self-regulatory approach is possible with the adoption of international standards of best practice models (BPMs), which are endorsed by government, business, and consumers.

Chapter 5. ICT and Civil Procedure

§1. Introduction

836. One of the major advantages of e-business is that long distance trading, even trading across national borders, is greatly facilitated. In fact, e-business can take place even when one party is unaware of the location of the other party. This situation contrasts greatly with that of traditional transactions where jurisdiction is determined either by the physical presence of the party in that jurisdiction or the presence of physical property within that jurisdiction. In the case of e-business, its feature of being able to reach across multiple jurisdictions gives rise to many legal uncertainties about which jurisdiction's laws will apply and under what circumstances. For example, if a consumer in Australia orders a book or tennis racquet from a website in Topeka, Kansas, sent from a warehouse in Chennai, what law applies? This in turn poses a problem for Internet sites because owners of those sites can never be sure when their site might subject them to the laws of any country or state. This uncertainty about what substantive and procedural laws apply to an e-business transaction and how those laws should be applied by the courts is one of the remaining major impediments to the wide-scale adoption of Internet commerce. In fact, the situation may arise that an Internet trader may be sued in numerous jurisdictions at the same time, for essentially the same act. Alternatively, as in the case of Yahoo, the same activity may be found to be legitimate in one jurisdiction, but a criminal offence in another.

837. Similarly, law enforcement bodies have great difficulty in policing their jurisdiction when e-business activities, including some fraudulent or other illegal activity, can so readily invade the jurisdiction and evade law enforcement efforts. Unlike a manufacturing plant or other forms of traditional commerce, an entire website could be moved and established elsewhere in a matter of hours. In the case of Internet transactions, the jurisdictional problem is further exacerbated by the fact that a website from which a transaction emanates may have elements stored on multiple computers located in several jurisdictions.

838. To date there have been few Australian decisions in this area, and Australian courts have looked especially to the US for guidance. For this reason, reference is made in this section to the leading US cases on jurisdiction resulting from Internet activity.

§2. Jurisdiction: General Principles

I. Definition

839. Jurisdiction refers to the power of any government's laws and court system to bind a party or make a judgment in relation to a party or particular matter. Jurisdiction may be limited by geography, by the subject matter that the court may deal with, by the type of relief that can be sought, and the point of law or fact to be decided. The limits of a court's jurisdiction are usually defined by statute.

II. General Versus Specific or Special Jurisdiction

840. A distinction is often made between general and specific jurisdiction. *Specific jurisdiction* refers to the authority over a person for the limited purpose of deciding claims that have some important connection to the forum in which the court is situated. *General jurisdiction* refers to the authority to hear all claims against a given defendant regardless of the claim's connection to the forum. So far, no court (in deciding whether website activity in a forum subjects one to the jurisdiction of a court in that forum) has found jurisdiction over other activity not situated in the forum and unrelated to the website activity in question.

III. Jurisdiction Clause

841. In many commercial cases, the parties themselves through an express stipulation in a contract may provide that any dispute between the parties arising out of the contract must be resolved by a court in a designated jurisdiction. However, if the contract is silent as to jurisdiction or it is not otherwise clearly indicated by the parties, the court will have to apply normal jurisdictional principles with a clear case to be made out that the exercise of jurisdiction is warranted.

IV. Territorial Restrictions on Laws

842. Except for a few cases such as Australian citizens or companies acting abroad, the laws of a State normally do not have application outside of the territorial boundaries of that State. This fact makes the Internet a very difficult challenge because an Internet transaction can cross the borders of numerous countries in a matter of seconds. In this sense, it is said that the Internet can be a lawless frontier. At the same time, it is also true that the problem with Internet transactions is that too many laws apply. This is because the transmission of the digital information may be subject to every one of the jurisdictions through which that information may flow. This territorial nexus is seen in criminal law statutes that typically require there to be a territorial nexus with the State. This means that either the defendant must be located there or one of the elements of the offence occurred there. This also means that the same conduct may give rise to legal consequences in more than one State.

V. In Personam and In Rem Jurisdiction

843. Another important, but technical, distinction is based upon personal jurisdiction as opposed to jurisdiction over the thing itself, that is, 'in rem' jurisdiction.

It is not possible to bring an action against the person without giving that person notice, that is, personal service of process. However, where the 'thing' or 'res' is situated in the jurisdiction, a court may determine and exercise its jurisdiction over the 'res' even though personal jurisdiction may be absent. A good example is real estate, where a court will have no difficulty finding jurisdiction because the thing itself (the 'res') is physically located there. The question in an ICT context is whether a court can exercise its 'in rem' jurisdiction over items that are 'virtually' located in that jurisdiction, for example, a domain name. In other cases, the presence will be partly physical and partly virtual, for example, a web server.

844. In cases where personal jurisdiction is required, a case cannot be heard in a court where process cannot be served on the defendant. Thus, the general rule is that no step can be taken against defendants until they have been served with an originating process. This general rule applies to cases in which the court is said to be exercising its jurisdiction in personam. Service of process is seen as necessary in order to ground the court's jurisdiction. Note that even if the court has jurisdiction, it may decide that the forum is an inappropriate one and that on policy grounds the case should be heard elsewhere.

VI. Subject-Matter Jurisdiction

845. In addition to jurisdiction over the person, the court must also have the power to decide that type of case, that is, subject-matter jurisdiction. In some cases, the jurisdiction is limited by the type of case. For example, one could not attempt to get a divorce in a Small Claims Court. In other cases, the factor limiting the court's jurisdiction is the amount in dispute. Again, taking the example of the Small Claims Court, if the jurisdictional limit is disputes involving AUD 5,000 or less, then one could not file a case seeking AUD 10,000 in compensation.

§3. Jurisdiction in an ICT Context

I. In Australia

846. In *Macquarie Bank v. Berg* ((1999) N.S.W. S.C. 526), Macquarie Bank sought an injunction against Berg, a disgruntled former employee, who established a 'lemon' site through which he made allegedly defamatory statements about his former employer. The Court refused to exercise jurisdiction over Berg in relation to the injunction because it could only be enforceable within the territorial limits of NSW. Practically, there was no way to limit such an order to a particular jurisdiction. To impose the injunction on a website would be in effect to impose NSW law on the rest of the world, something her Honour in her discretion declined to do.

847. *Gutnick v. Dow Jones Inc.* ((2001) V.S.C. 305 (28 August 2001)) involved the following facts. In November 2000, Joseph Gutnick (P), a well-known Melbourne identity, filed defamation action in Victorian Supreme Court against Dow

Jones & Co. (D), a Delaware Corporation located in the US. D is the publisher of the print and online editions of Barrons Magazine. The defamation related to various statements made about the plaintiff in the 30 October 2000 issue of Barrons. D argued: (1) the Victorian court had no jurisdiction; (2) there was improper service of process; and (3) the US and not Victoria was the most convenient and appropriate forum. It was undisputed that an article is published when it becomes capable of being comprehended by a reader.

848. According to the Court, P could have filed the case in one of two bases: tort (libel) occurred in Victoria (place of publication) or it was committed in New Jersey but that damage was caused in Victoria. D also contended that Victoria was an inconvenient venue. The Victorian Court disagreed, holding that Victoria was the most appropriate venue because: (1) the alleged defamatory matter was published in Victoria; and that P is domiciled in Victoria, has a business in Victoria; and that (2) P sought to vindicate his reputation in the place where his reputation is most well known. The *Gutnick* decision was recently affirmed on appeal to the High Court of Australia (HCA) (*Dow Jones & Company Inc. v. Gutnick* (2002) H.C.A. 56 (10 December 2002)).[382]

849. Jurisdictional issues have also come into play in considering the extraterritorial effects of statutory regimes involving areas such as online securities, financial institutions, and other vendors of such instruments that have many opportunities available to them online. However, advertising such products on the Internet may lead to uncertainties, the most obvious of which is whether such an offering complies with the regulatory dictates of various jurisdictions.[383] Information on a website about various financial offerings may indeed be a 'public offer' and subject to the laws of those jurisdictions reached by the website. In Australia, the offer of securities on the Internet and accessible from Australia means that Australian law will apply.[384]

850. Australian guidelines indicate there are four circumstances when the ASIC does not intend to act upon an advertisement of securities online:

(1) When the advert is not targeted at persons in Australia.
(2) When it contains an appropriate disclaimer.
(3) Where the advert has no impact on investors in Australia (depends on facts of the case).
(4) Where there is no misconduct.

---

382. http://eresources.hcourt.gov.au/showCase/2002/HCA/56.

383. *See* S. Goueff, *Offering Financial Services on the Web: Experiencing the World Wide (Legal) Web*, 2(2) World Internet Law Report 26 (February 2001).

384. Australian Securities and Investments Commission Policy Statement No. 141, issued on 2 Mar. 2000.

II. A Technological Solution?

851. Technology also holds out some hope of a solution. New technology is being developed which can allow a business to select their customers and jurisdictional reach of their website. Coming from the other direction, software may also allow consumers to designate the countries, laws, or protections desired, and an expert system will match those preferences with websites that meet the specified criteria. For B2B commerce, contract will remain king. In other words, the parties will continue to specify in their contractual arrangements what laws are to govern the relationship.

III. The Internet: A New and Separate Legal Frontier?

852. Another proposal for reform is to assign Internet law disputes to their own territory, that is, to cyberspace. In other words, perhaps the industry should move to a form of self-regulation, using cyber courts and other mechanisms to resolve disputes. Indeed, such a regime could be enforced by key players such as ISP who require agreement to the regime as a condition for use of the Internet. While this approach is appealing in its simplicity, it is difficult to imagine that a traditional court would give up its jurisdictional powers, especially when the welfare of its citizenry is at stake and where such emotive moral issues as gambling and online pornography are involved.

§4. Venue

853. Also relevant in such matters is the issue of appropriate venue and choice of laws. Even if a court exercises jurisdiction, it may refuse to do so if it finds that the forum is inconvenient. The issue of venue was raised in Australia in the *Gutnick* case (discussed above). The existence of a website was not enough to support a finding of proper venue under the Federal venue statute in the district of a trademark plaintiff's residence where there was no showing that the defendant otherwise targeted the forum. For the court to have held there was no venue would have been to violate the basic principle of restricting venue to places where the defendant could reasonably expect being taken to court and constitute a substantial change to federal law.

§5. Choice of Law

854. Assuming a court has jurisdiction over the parties, the next procedural question to be resolved is what law to apply to resolve the issues in contention. Parties to an electronic or other contract can choose the law that will apply to the contract in question. If the contract does not state expressly the law to be applied, then it may be possible to imply what law the parties intended to apply. The general rule of most states is that the courts should honour the parties' choice of law unless it would violate a fundamental policy of the state. An example might be a situation where there is an unequal bargaining position where a NSW Court might insist on applying the Contracts Review Act 1980 (NSW).

§6. Conflict of Laws

I. Nature of the Conflict

855. If the parties do not agree what law should apply, there may be a conflict of laws. For example, in relation to a contract, should the court apply the law of the place where the offer was made, where the contract was accepted, or on some other criterion? To help resolve such issues, there is a body of case law to give courts guidance on such matters. Where the rules of more than one state might be involved, Australian courts will usually apply the same choice of law rules as they would apply to international disputes.

II. Categorizing the Cause of Action

856. The choice between foreign law and the law of the forum state is traditionally made by first categorizing the cause of action, for example, as a tort, contract, property, or succession matter. It will then apply one or more connecting factors which indicate the state's or country's law to be applied. For example, if an issue is categorized as being one of succession to movable property, the common law choice of law rule is that the court should apply the law of the deceased's domicile at the time of death. In the case of immovable property, the forum should apply the laws of the place where the property is located.

III. Applying the Conflict Rule

857. In the case of contracts, where the parties to a contract do not chose a governing law, the applicable law, for most aspects of contracts, is the law of the jurisdiction with the 'closest and most real connection' with the case. Among the connecting factors that will be weighed by the court include (1) the place where the contract is made; (2) the place of performance; (3) the domicile, residence or business address of the parties; and, the nature of the subject matter of the contract.

858. Generally, the courts have not given greater weight to one factor over another. This in turn has led to criticisms that the rules are too vague and in cases where the factors are evenly balanced, too uncertain and unpredictable. Sometimes, too, it is arguable that there can be more than one 'proper law' of the contract. For example, the essential validity of one part of the contract can be governed by any law, and the validity of another part of the contract can be governed by a different law.[385]

IV. Recommendations for Reform

859. While common law choice of law rules has worked reasonably well, there have been abuses. For example, some plaintiffs engage in forum shopping, picking jurisdictions where they know the law will be more favourable to their case. In other cases, the choice of law rules is unduly complex and unclear. A case in point is tort law. The traditional rule is that the wrong must be actionable both in the place where it occurred as well as the forum where the case is being brought. This forces a plaintiff to overcome two obstacles and often invites confusion about what law applies. Another problem is that legislative provisions of any statute may run counter to the choice of law rule. For example, the laws of a statute may say that contracts of one type will be governed by the laws of State A. Yet, the choice of law rules may say that the laws of State B apply because that State has the closest and most real connection. These and other problems suggest the need for Commonwealth legislation to develop uniform rules with respect to the choice of law determinations. Arguably, the Commonwealth could enact such legislation pursuant to section 51 (XXV) which allows the Commonwealth to make laws with respect to: 'The recognition throughout the Commonwealth of the laws, the public Acts and records, and the judicial proceedings of the State.'

860. Another approach would be to have all Australian States and Territories adopt a model code or to have an amendment to the Constitution giving the Commonwealth Government the power to make laws with respect to principles of choice of law and the development of procedural rules, including uniform conflict of laws rules.

861. On an international front, there have also been moves to remedy conflicts of law by means of international agreement. For example, see the Preliminary Draft Convention on Jurisdiction and Foreign Judgments in Civil and Commercial matters adopted by the Hague Conference on Private International Law (HCPIL).[386]

§7. Discovery and Rules of Evidence

862. Australia, like the US, has procedural rules that permit the parties to litigation to 'discover' material facts and information relevant to the issues set forth in the pleadings.

---

385. This issue has arisen in Australian cases. *See, e.g.*, *Weckstrom v. Hyson* (1966) V.R. 277, 282.
386. HCPIL on 30 Oct. 1999, www.hcch.net/e/conventions.

863. Whether e-mails are admissible as business records was considered by Justice Austin in *ASC v. Rich* [2005] NSWSC 741 where he held that e-mails between the Chief Operating Officer of OneTel Europe and a non-executive director of One-Tel Ltd were excepted from the hearsay rule, as they were business records within the definition in section 69 of the Evidence Act 1995 (Cth). In *Aqua-Marine v. Reef Fisheries (No 4)* [2011] FCA 578 a Federal Court of Australia adopted a similarly broad approach and held that an e-mail was admissible under section 69 of the Act.

864. Increasingly, parties are seeking not only relevant paper documents, but also electronic documents, including e-mails stored on a computer. E-mails have also played an important role in several insider-trading cases. Even as Bill Gates discovered in the Microsoft antitrust matter, e-mail messages may linger in the deep recesses of the computer's memory, even though they have been deleted.

865. In some cases, a discovery order may relate to preserving the relevant web pages that existed at the time parties have been put on notice that the web pages are subject to pending litigation. In *Pennar Software Corp. v. Fortune 500 Systems Ltd.* (N.D. Cal., No. 01-01734EDL, 25 October 2001) the Court's jurisdiction was at issue where the US District Court imposed sanctions on the defendant in the form of payment of the plaintiff's attorney's fees.

866. Unfortunately, evidence laws in Australia have tended not to keep pace with other developments, for example, the recognition of electronic transactions. For example, the general rule is that secondary documents are not admissible if the primary document is available. However, with an electronic document, there are numerous copies, each identical with the other. Some argue that in the case of an e-mail the 'original' is the original data message in the sender's computer, the recipient only receiving a copy. In most cases, whether the electronic document will be admitted into evidence will depend upon the foundation that can be laid for that document. Thus, in *Buterea v. Director of Public Prosecution for the State of Victoria* (1987), 164 C.L.R. 180, the HCA held that the best evidence rule would not apply to exclude an audiotape copy where a foundation had been laid regarding the original tape, the accuracy of the recording process, and of the taped copy.

§8. Dispute Resolution

I. Use of Technology by Australian Courts

867. Courts in Australia have for some time been active in their use of technology.[387] The development of Australia's first permanent privately hosted electronic arbitration room located in Sydney, but able to be connected to everywhere – a joint venture between Auscript and Counsel's Chambers comprised of a fully networked room with facilities for electronic evidence, document imaging, video conferencing, webcasting, chat facilities, real-time transcription, and point-to-point data lines

387. https://www.fedcourt.gov.au/law-and-practice/practice-documents/practice-notes/gpn-tech.

to access external services.[388] Most courts now have video links. In criminal custody and sentencing matters, the case can be heard via direct link without the inmate having to leave prison. Video testimony by witnesses is also now common. Digital recording systems have replaced cassette tapes. Sensitive microphones now track a speaker automatically. This use of technology has also brought about new rules for evidence and procedure. The web portal established by the Federal Court of Australia is recognized as one of the best in the world.

868. An interesting international use of IT by the courts is the Western Australia-Singapore Co-mediation Programme in which a Western Australia judge and a Singapore judge mediate and provide an early neutral evaluation of the strengths and weaknesses of each party's case. The NSW Law Society predicts that online chat rooms may replace pretrial hearings in many courtrooms within two years. This would save a lot of congestion and waiting around and substantially reduce the costs.[389] Indeed, just as different arbitration systems have competed against each other for international dispute resolution business, it is likely that we will see court systems offering their services to a global marketplace. This would be a natural extension of Australian legal services – a major export growth area for Australia.[390]

II. Mediation and Arbitration

869. Legal costs, time, and effort make litigation an unattractive means of resolving commercial disputes in many cases. In addition, courts may not be conversant with e-business and technology issues everywhere, and even where a judge does have some such knowledge, he or she may not appreciate the nuances of different businesses. For these reasons, both courts themselves and parties independently have turned to mediation and arbitration.

870. Arbitration is the process of referring a dispute to an arbitrator as an unofficial judge to make decisions that the parties have agreed to accept as binding and final upon them. Only disputes able to be tried in civil courts can be arbitrated. In Australia, arbitration is regulated by essentially uniform legislation in each jurisdiction except Queensland.[391] International arbitration and the enforcement of foreign awards are governed by the International Arbitration Act 1974 (Cth).

871. NSW and Victoria have established centres with interstate facilities for settlement of commercial disputes. The Australian Centre for International Commercial Arbitration (ACICA) was opened in Melbourne in 1985, and the Australian Commercial Disputes Centre (ACDC) opened in Sydney in 1986. ACDC focuses on alternative dispute resolution, and ACICA focuses on domestic and international

388. https://www.auscript.com/en-AU/.
389. S. Johanson, *Net Challenges the High Cost of Justice*, Age Online (4 Jan. 2001).
390. Judge Peter Blaxell, *The Future Role of Australian Courts on Resolving International Disputes*, 76 Reform 12 (Autumn 2000).
391. *Commercial Arbitration Act* 1984 (NSW); 1984 (Vic); 1986 (SA); 1985 (WA); 1986 (Tas); 1985 (NT); 1986 (ACT). *See Arbitration Act* 1973 (Qld).

arbitration. ACICA is available for arbitration held under the UNICITRAL Rules, the Rules of LCIA, and other rules of the parties' choice such as those set out in the commercial arbitration legislation. In other jurisdictions, ACICA operates through the facilities of the Institute of Arbitrators Australia.

872. Mediation or third party assisted facilitation of disputes is also very popular in Australia and used by both courts as well as independently. Dispute resolution processes stemmed from a perceived need to explore possibilities of dispute settlement. Mediation as a process within Alternate Dispute Resolution (ADR) has become a viable alternative dispute resolution process. This legitimization of alternative processes has evolved from an acceptance of the legal profession and the wider community that disputes can be resolved in a constructive rather than a confrontational way. Combined with this is the advancement of technology which has introduced yet another level to ADR – online mediation. As this concept, is still in its infancy, it remains to be seen whether communication between parties involved in intense conflict can be helped or hindered by a mediation process conducted electronically.

873. Online mediation is recognized, however, as potentially offering many advantages unavailable in traditional dispute resolution. Perhaps more importantly, it has the scope to evolve as an important venue for the future resolution of certain types of conflicts. In order to reduce the disputes, the Government has legislated for codes of conduct both voluntary and mandatory. It is recommended that firms adopt a dispute resolution scheme or lock into an existing industry one. There is no reason why these schemes, still in their infancy, may not operate in cyberspace. The National Alternative Dispute Resolution Advisory Council (NADRAC) (April 2001) report entitled *A Framework for ADR Standards: Report to the Commonwealth Attorney General* to the Attorney General's Department (AGD) has provided many suggestions.

874. In Australia, a range of ODR sometimes referred to as e-DR programmes and initiatives has been adopted. This is a significant development because it suggests that people are working out the best ways to use IT and find ways of resolving disputes that best fit the needs of each group, whether in business, consumer relations, or government. Such ADR developments are also providing answers to groups who are worried about the cost, inconvenience, language and cultural barriers, and risk of being subjected to jurisdiction faced by those who are engaged in e-business. Online ADR seems especially suited for global consumer disputes where the amount in dispute is small and jurisdiction and conflict of laws questions are prevalent. Such systems play a vital role in giving greater confidence in e-business. An important component in all of this is the need for consumer and business education about programmes, codes, and the benefits as well as the limits of ADR.

875. In Australia, NADRAC is turning its attention to the growing popularity of online ADR. This includes the use of IT to resolve disputes, including video conferencing, e-mail, artificial intelligence systems, and the Internet. It also includes the use of IT to resolve disputes in such areas such as domain names, IP, e-commerce, and ISP service.

876. While it is recognized that some government regulation is probably necessary and desirable, this should not come at the expense of hindering innovation. At the appropriate level, government has a role to play in ensuring fairness, low cost, transparency, efficiency, and impartiality of various ADR systems. One area in which there is little agreement is the extent to which various ADR processes should be binding or mandatory. It is also recognized that disputes arise in a legal context. Therefore, there is a need for law reforms to examine not only the technological issues, but also other legislation such as telecommunications, privacy, contract law, laws regarding confidentiality and privilege, enforceability issues, consumer law protection, legality of digital signatures, proof of informed consent, insurance, and risk management. Australia, in common with other jurisdictions, has much work to do before such issues are resolved. Australia also recognizes that for the Internet, international cooperation is necessary.

877. An innovative use of ODR in Australia is the Settlement Online Systems (SOS), an interactive online service, which provides double-blind, confidential, password protected, and automated dispute resolution.[392] The service allows parties to a dispute to have secure access 24/7 to a real-time settlement procedure and provides parties with a quick 'without prejudice' settlement negotiating tool.

392. www.settlementonlinesystems.com.au.

Part V. Non-contractual Liability: Roles and Responsibilities

Chapter 1. Civil Obligations: Negligence

§1. Introduction

878. Tort law is an important part of the law of obligations, giving relief, in the form of compensation, to those who have suffered loss arising out of the wrongful actions of others. Tort law is built on the body of decided cases that established precedents for both its form and application and has evolved over time.

879. In Australia, courts are bound by the decisions of higher Australian courts, ultimately the HCA. In making their decisions, Australian courts may give weight to the decisions of courts in foreign jurisdictions. This may be particularly so where the issues arising before the court are novel, as in the context of e-business or the Internet.

§2. Nature of Tort

880. A tort is an act or omission that is unauthorized by law and independently of contract, trust, or other fiduciary duty: A tort infringes:

- some absolute right of another; or some qualified right of another causing damage; or some public right resulting in substantial and particular damage to some person beyond that which is suffered by the public generally; and
- gives rise to an action for damages at the suit of the injured party.[393]

881. The word 'tort' derives from the word for 'wrong' and now consists of a miscellaneous group of actions providing redress for unlawful interference with an individual's person, property, and importantly in an e-business context, in certain circumstances, economic interests.[394]

393. P.F.P. Higgins, *Elements of Torts in Australia* 1 (Butterworths 1970).
394. Clive Turner, *Australian Commercial Law* 823 (LBC 1999).

882. As with the law of contract, tort law depends on the body of decided cases for both its form and application. Again, as with contract, there are few reported cases dealing directly with the field of e-business, and any analysis must examine the adaptation of existing law developed through traditional commercial activity.

883. Tort law is a branch of the law of civil obligations, where legal persons, both natural persons and corporations have legal obligations to refrain from causing harm to another person and if harm is done to repair or compensate for it. Socially, the function of tort is to shift loss sustained by one to the person who is deemed to have caused it or is responsible for it happening and to spread the loss over an enterprise or even the whole community.[395]

§3. Liability and Jurisdiction in Tort

884. Liability in tort may be individual or several, where it is considered that there exists concurrent liability. However, such liability may be limited by the common law of contract through the inclusion of an appropriate clause into a contract or through the application of contribution on the part of the 'victim'.[396]

885. The general legal principle governing a tortious act is that the law of the place where the tort occurs is usually applied. When a website publishes defamatory or misleading information, the state or nation where the victim is located may assert jurisdiction if the tortfeasor, who committed the tortious act, directed the wrongful activity through the Internet and into the plaintiff's state or nation.

886. However, with the increasing influence of the Internet, determining the actual location of where the tort occurred may be difficult to establish.

§4. Categories of Tort

887. Whilst the categories of torts have previously been considered to be 'infinitely various',[397] that capacity for change has slowed, and any new category of tort will be unusual today. The universally understood major groups of tort include:

- trespasses or direct interferences with the person or property;
- occupation or possession of land;
- breach of public and statutory duties;
- interference with domestic relations;
- negligence for a breach of a duty to take reasonable care;

395. David M. Walker, *The Oxford Companion to Law* 1224 (Clarendon Press 1980).
396. In *Schumann v. Abbott* (1961), SASR 149, two inquiry agents who entered premises seeking evidence of adultery were held to be joint tortfeasors as a result of common design and therefore equally liable, even though the extent of their participation differed.
397. *Chapman v. Pickersgill* (1762) 2 Wils. K.N. 145, at 146.

– misrepresentation; and
– intentionally causing damage to economic interests.

§5. Intentional Torts

888. In e-business law the categories of tort most relevant are those involving intent, negligence and wrongs of strict liability.

I. Definitions

889. Intentional torts include trespass to the person, assault and battery, false imprisonment, trespass to goods, and conversion, that is, the unlawful exercise of control over the goods of another. Intentional torts involve the perpetrator having the necessary mental element, foresight of the possible end, and a desire on the part of the perpetrator to seek to attain it. Intention of itself is an insufficient foundation in a claim for tort, and it is only where there is a connection between intention and an act aimed at attaining that end, which results in loss to the victim, that an intentional tort is committed.

890. Courts in the US have considered whether denial of service attacks and virus attacks constitute trespass or conversion. In *eBay Inc. v. Bidder's Edge Inc.*, 100 F. Supp. 2d 1058 (N.D. Cal. 2000), the Court held that it was trespass to gather data from a 'free' website if their terms and conditions of service prohibit access except in furtherance of the website owner's business. eBay sued Bidder's Edge based on the common law action of trespass to chattels. The chattel in this case was eBay's site, and the infringement took place by Bidder's Edge use of a 'robot' or 'spider' to automatically search the site, capturing information that could aid a person in finding the best bargain. The issue was whether eBay could stop Bidder's Edge from using its 'spider' to fetch information off eBay's site. Bidder's Edge argued unsuccessfully that the doctrine should not apply.

891. On a policy basis, it is arguable that eBay was, in effect, using the action to get greater legal protection for information than is otherwise protected by copyright law. It is also arguable that the reasoning in the eBay case discourages free access and open competition and that by aggregating information about bids on the Internet, spiders and robots perform a pro-consumer function by providing information about the lowest price. This reasoning is not entirely supportable, since businesses such as eBay rely in part for their effectiveness on 'being the marketplace'.

892. Cases of this sort may be influential in Australian courts. The reasoning, however, has been questioned on legal and policy grounds.

– A website is not land, and there was no demonstration by eBay of any harm incurred by the robot or spider of Bidder's Edge gathering intelligence from

eBay's site. It should also be noted that the doctrine of trespass to chattels provides relief to the possessor of the chattel, not its owner. Arguably, the only persons with the standing to bring an action were other customers of eBay.
- Further consideration is that the US equivalent of the Australian *ETA* legislation differs slightly from the Australian law. In effect, in Australia there is a requirement for consideration to pass to make website terms binding.

893. Another example of conduct in cyberspace that imports notions of trespass is 'cybersquatting'. Typically, cybersquatting is the term used for acquiring an Internet domain name which is likely to be commercially valuable, but which is not based on the acquirer's own identity or business identity. For example, if a person named Smyth acquired the domain name www.macdonald.com.au in the hope of being able to sell it to the MacDonald's fast-food chain. Domain name disputes are generally not the subject of civil law in Australia, but rather fall to be determined by the ICANN dispute resolution process, which is, in effect, contractual. Nevertheless, where the domain name is in turn used as part of an attempt to deceive or mislead, it may be a cause of action.

II. Fraudulent Misrepresentation

894. Fraud and misrepresentation are feature in e-business. The e-business platform has provided an opportunity for unscrupulous operators to engage in fraudulent misrepresentation by relying on consumer gullibility and on the relative anonymity of the electronic medium. It is able to deliberately or fraudulently misrepresent the physical, performance, or qualitative attributes of goods, sight unseen.

895. The lesson here for those involved in e-marketing is that a statement that is knowingly made, which is untrue and is relied upon by the other party to their detriment, may invoke not only the criminal law, but also the relevant consumer protection laws of Australia.[398]

III. Defamation

896. Defamation is concerned with the protection of an individual's reputation from falsehoods. Defamation law in Australia is a matter of common law in some jurisdictions and statute in others.[399]

897. The usual remedy in a defamation case is an award of damages. Where appropriate, a court may also grant an injunction to restrain publication.

398. A party falsely represented the seating capacity of a restaurant business in negotiations for its sale, and this resulted in a contravention of ss 52 and 53 of the former *Trade Practices Act* 1974 (Cth). *See Henjo Investments Pty Ltd v. Collins Marrickville Pty Ltd* (1988) 79 A.L.R. 83.

399. *See Defamation Act* 1974 (NSW). New South Wales, ACT, Victoria, South Australia, Western Australia, and the Northern Territory apply common law principles of defamation. Tasmania and Queensland have codified their defamation laws.

898. In Australia, defamation law distinguishes between publishers and distributors. Publishers are liable for republication of defamatory material because they are deemed to have acquired knowledge of the content provided by third parties through the process of editing and producing the publication for sale. This is true for online publishing as well as print-based publishing.[400]

899. However, an ISP that merely and innocently distributes or transmits defamatory material previously published by someone else is liable only if they knew or had reason to know that the material was false and defamatory. Libraries and booksellers are normally viewed as distributors, as are newsagents. A common carrier such as a telephone company is not normally liable for defamatory material carried by their equipment.

900. Defamation is a cause of action that arises where a person publishes material from which imputations are drawn which damages the reputation of another. At common law, a case of defamation is made out against the defendant where it is shown merely that the matter complained of is defamatory (defamation), refers to the plaintiff (identification), and has been published to a third party (publication). It is unnecessary for the plaintiff to prove that the matter was untrue or that it caused any damage. Where defamation is made out, there are defences available that include justification and privilege.

901. There have been cases alleging the use of the Internet for defamation, all of which seem to serve to illustrate the cross-jurisdictional difficulties that the Internet creates for law enforcement. In *Macquarie Bank Ltd. & Anor v. Berg Simpson J* of the NSW Supreme Court refused to grant an injunction against an alleged defamatory Internet website that was based in an offshore jurisdiction.[401]

902. The High Court in *Dow Jones and Company Inc. v. Gutnick* in 2002 considered that the place of tort in respect to defamatory material on the Internet was in fact where the material is downloaded.[402] Although the implication of this is that authors who published material online may be the subject of proceedings in foreign jurisdiction, even though the material may not be offending the law of the jurisdiction where the material was posted.

903. The development of a branch of the Internet devoted to the provision of negative publicity, known popularly as 'lemon sites', has until recently been a thorn in the side of corporations with a major web presence. Court decisions in Australia and the US have cancelled the registration of domain names which bear an objective similarity to those protected by law as being the property of other parties. Some websites are primarily protest and parody sites or have registered Internet addresses based on trademarked corporate names.

---

400. *See Gutnick v. Dow Jones & Co., Inc.* (2001) VSC 305 (28 Aug. 2001), later affirmed by the High Court.
401. (1999) N.S.W.S.C. 526.
402. (2002) 210 C.L.R. 575.

904. Between January and August 2000, arbitrators have ruled in favour of trademark holders in nine out of eleven domain name disputes involving '. . . sucks' variations on corporate names, according to records on ICANN's website.[403] Two such cases involving Internet sites are *Lucent Technologies v. Lucentsucks.com* and *Bally Total Fitness v. Faber*. In the *Lucentsucks* case a website was intended to confuse customers into thinking the site is associated with the company. However, the site offers pornographic photographs and services and infringes Lucent's trademark. This was also the case in the *Bally* example.[404]

IV. Passing-Off Goods

905. An action in passing-off is an action designed to prevent a trader from taking the goodwill of a business by 'passing-off' their business as that of the plaintiff. This is often done through the defendant's imitation, to some degree, of the name or business getup of the plaintiff. The imitation does not necessarily involve the copying of protected IP, but rather the creation of an impression that is likely to mislead or confuse, for example, the registration of a domain name *McDonalds* by persons who have no association with the well-known fast food chain restaurant. The practice is described as 'cybersquatting' with the intention of profiting from the rules permitting the registration of domain names on a first come first served basis. After acquiring the registration of the domain name, the cybersquatter will then on-sell the registered domain name at a ransom profit to the corporation that operates in that name.

V. Trespass

906. Are 'hackers' and those breaking into servers that host websites guilty of trespass? In Australia, the burden of proof on a charge of trespass to the person is on the defendant.[405]

§6. Negligence

I. General Civil Remedy

907. Negligence as a second broad category of torts is concerned with protection of person, property, and economic interests from damage caused by another person's failure to take reasonable care.

403. www.icann.org/.
404. *Lucent Technologies, Inc. v. Lucentsucks.com,* 95 F.Supp.2d 528, 54 U.S.P.Q.2d (BNA) 1653 (E.D. Va. 2000); and *Bally Total Fitness Holding Corp. v. Faber*, 29 F.Supp.2d 1161 (C.D. Cal. 1998).
405. *Marion's Case* (1992) 175 C.L.R. 218, per McHugh, J., 310–311.

908. The post-industrial common law treatment of liability in tort for the manufacture of dangerous products is largely a by-product of the Industrial Revolution. Prior to this time, there was no general doctrine of liability to consumers for the safety and quality of products.

909. Various court decisions, however, gradually carved out exceptions to this general rule of legal protection for manufacturers. The first exception was for cases involving fraudulent misrepresentation. In *Langridge v. Levy* (1837), 2 M&W 519, 150 ER 863, the defendant sold a gun while deliberately misrepresenting its safety. The purchaser's son was able to recover damages on the basis that he had relied upon the representation regarding its safety.

910. A second exception was established in *Dixon v. Bell* (1816), 5 M&S 198, 105 ER 1023, where the Court held the defendant liable for entrusting, without any warning regarding its danger, a loaded gun to a girl servant who shot the plaintiff's son.

II. Doctrine of Negligence

911. The doctrine of negligence developed with the landmark case of *Rylands v. Fletcher* (1865), 3 H&C 774. In this case, a landowner was held strictly liable when water escaped from his land and flooded a mine shaft on the adjoining property.

912. A second important case is that of *Donoghue v. Stevenson* (1932), A.C. 562 which established the principle that a manufacturer could be held liable to a consumer for the negligent manufacture of a product, even though there was no contract between the manufacturer and the consumer.

913. This basic doctrine of negligence has been extended in subsequent cases to cover manufacturers generally, as well as the manufacturers of component parts, product distributors, assemblers, retailers, and importers. Indeed, as our scientific knowledge grows and consumer expectations have risen, the scope of duty required in negligence has similarly expanded to enable plaintiffs to recover damages for injuries resulting from a wide variety of product defects such as asbestos, contaminated blood transfusions, cigarette smoke, faulty software or hardware, and others.

914. A claim in negligence therefore requires the following elements to be made out:

- Existence of a duty of care owed by a tortfeasor to the person harmed.
- Standard of care appropriate to the circumstances of an ordinary reasonable and prudent person.
- Foreseeability of damage to a 'neighbour' as a consequence of the breach.

915. The standard of proof required in a negligence action is that the plaintiff must prove all the elements of negligence by a preponderance of the evidence.

916. In addition to situations in which the existence of a duty of care can be demonstrated on the facts, there are situations where a recognized duty of care exists. Such as:

- Professional persons and their clients.
- Persons making negligent misstatements who possess a special skill or knowledge and the person to whom it was made reasonably acted on it to their detriment.
- Employers with respect to safe systems of work.
- Bailees of goods.
- School authorities.
- Drivers of a motor vehicles.
- Manufacturers.
- Suppliers of dangerous goods.
- Builders extending to later owners of the property.[406]

III. Negligent Misstatement

917. Although the principle established in *Donoghue v. Stevenson* has been extended to cover an increasingly wide range of cases, a plaintiff was still only able to recover actual damages to his or her person or property. Mere economic loss was not recoverable. This limitation was removed in the decision of *Hedley, Byrne & Co. Ltd. v. Heller & Partners Ltd.* (1963), 3 All ER 575, where the Court enunciated the principle that one could be held liable for negligent misstatement which resulted in mere economic loss, as opposed to damages to one's property or person. In *Junior Books Ltd. v. Veitchi Co. Ltd.* (1983), 1 A.C. 520, it was thus held that the plaintiff was able to recover for a defectively laid floor, which caused no physical injury but did result in maintenance costs which were so high that it was cheaper to replace the floor. The Court allowed recovery of the cost of a new floor plus profits lost while the plaintiff's business was temporarily closed.

918. In Australia, the landmark case *Caltex Oil (Aust.) Pty. Ltd. v. The Dredge 'Willenstad'* (1976), 136 C.L.R. 529 where the High Court found that Caltex was entitled to recover the economic losses it suffered when a pipeline owned and operated by Australian Oil Refinery Pty. Ltd. was damaged because of the respondent's negligent navigation.

919. While the doctrine of negligent misstatement in Australia must be distinguished from cases of professional negligence involving advice, they both require that there be a relationship of reliance, in the latter category, based on professional relationship. An issue that arises in the electronic world is the extent to which liability may arise from reliance on information posted on a website. Such liability may not be limited to economic loss, but to physical injury, given the large number of websites that offer information relating to health and well-being.

406. *Bryan v. Maloney* (1995) 182 C.L.R. 609.

IV. Defences

920. It is a defence against a claim of negligence that the injury complained of is too remote from the alleged cause. A principal criterion for negligence is that there must be some causal connection between the breach of the duty of care and the damage suffered. There must be some damage, and that damage must be proximate in law to the defendant's act or omission. The test that is now applied was laid down in *Overseas Tankship (UK) Ltd. v. The Miller Steamship Co. Pty. Ltd. (The Wagon Mound No. 2)* (1967), 1 A.C. 617), under which only the amount of loss directly attributable to the defendant's negligence is recoverable at law. If there should be some intervening action, the doctrine of *novus actus interveniens* allows for the defence as this connection and proximate cause has been broken. Another defence is that the plaintiff voluntarily assumed the risk (*volenti non fit injuria*). This is a complete defence, but often difficult to prove.

921. At common law, contributory negligence was a complete defence against all non-intentional torts. However, all Australian jurisdictions have introduced apportionment legislation making contributory negligence only a partial defence to such claims. In most jurisdictions, the apportionment legislation is applied to claims of negligence, breaches of statutory duty of care, and public or private nuisance.[407]

922. In all jurisdictions except SA, contributory negligence will be a defence to a contractual duty of care that is concurrent and coextensive with the duty of care in tort. This is often the case in the delivery of professional services such as in *Astley v. Austrust Ltd* (1999) 197 CLR 1 where solicitors were found to have a dual duty in contract and tort to take reasonable care in providing legal advice to their client.

923. The SA legislation uses the term 'fault' rather than wrong and does not refer to 'concurrent and coextensive contractual and tortious duties of care'. Rather, the legislation defines 'fault' as a breach of either a duty of care in tort, a contractual duty of care, or a statutory duty of care. 'A duty of care' is defined as 'a duty to take reasonable care or to exercise reasonable skill (or both)'. The legislation, however, does not offer protection against claims that are not in contract and tort. Thus, where a claim is based upon a breach of fiduciary duty or under the misleading and deceptive provisions (section 52) of the TPA, then the relevant legislation will not apply.

§7. Breach of Statutory Duty

924. State and Commonwealth statutes establish standards that impose a duty on manufacturers. A person injured as a result of a breach of these standards has a cause

407. *See, e.g., Law Reform (Miscellaneous Provisions) Amendment Act* 2000 (NSW); *Wrongs (Amendment) Act* 2000 (Vic); *Tortfeasors and Contributory Negligence Amendment Act* 2000 (Tas); and *Law Reform (Miscellaneous Provisions) Amendment Act* 2000 (ACT).

of action against the manufacturer or other person who breaches the regulation either through the legislation itself as a breach of statutory duty or may be implied. Some statutes create strict liability and do not allow the defendant to raise the issue of the plaintiff's contributory negligence (such as the provisions in the Statutory Duties (Contributory Negligence) Act 1945 (NSW)).

925. In *John Pfeiffer Pty. Ltd. v. Canny* (1981), 36 A.L.R. 466, the Court held that a statutory duty arose from a regulation that mandated precautions to be taken in the use of tools of trade.

926. Statutory duties also flow from company law. The increased risks to security created by online activity has given rise to a responsibility of directors to ensure that an effective e-security framework is in place. Lost valuable information through negligence can also result in damages such as huge business disruption expenses. The Corporations Act 2001 (Cth) (sections 180 through 184) imposes various duties upon Company Directors.

§8. REMEDIES

927. The intention of damages awarded at common law is to provide compensation by pecuniary means on the assumption that restitution is often impossible to achieve. Assessment may be made as an estimate of damages. This means that in e-business, the courts are more inclined to issue an order for the payment of money than to make some sort of order as to conduct intended to remedy a tortious situation. It goes without saying that money is easier to extract through the seizure of goods and monetary reserves than to supervise some specific court-ordered conduct in which circumstance the party concerned will be at the least unhelpful and, at worst, obstructive to delivery.

Chapter 2. Liability of Network Service Operators and ISP

§1. Introduction

928. The question here is whether network service operators and ISP are liable for defamatory materials placed by system users on their systems. The legal liability network service operators and ISP may be fraught given that they are easier to locate. An ISP may either be the primary actor in engaging in the conduct or may be an innocent secondary participant. In the latter case, a subscriber may post defamatory content on the Internet, the ISP will neither ordinarily have no knowledge of the defamatory nature of the material, nor be in a position to control it.

929. Globally, ISP have resisted legislation that would hold them liable as a common carrier. It is argued that they are more like bookshops, libraries, or postal workers in that they would not have knowledge of the content of the books on their shelves or on memories of servers leased to third parties. However, to the extent ISP, their employees, or agents have knowledge or exercise control or gain a direct financial benefit from the information, they may be primarily liable. Establishing this fact is a matter of proof and evidence.

§2. Statutory Duty

930. ISP may be liable under various statutory schemes. In Australia, the most important of these schemes involves the CCA and its counterpart in the Fair Trading Acts of the various States and Territories. For purposes of this discussion, it is important to note that these statutory claims, for example, misleading and deceptive conduct in breach of section 18 of the CCA, are independent of claims based upon contract and tort law. Thus, an exclusion clause in a contract cannot be relied upon to defeat a claim of a breach of the CCA. Similarly, a defence of contributory negligence cannot override the defendant's duty not to engage in proscribed actions such as misleading and deceptive conduct.

931. When an ISP or other service provider engages in deceptive or misleading conduct, the ISP can be liable. Less certain is whether an ISP or other service provider may be held liable when the conduct is engaged in by another party, but using the facility (i.e., the Internet, e-mail, and other services) provided by the ISP.

932. Other statutory obligations may be created by administrative bodies charged with supervision of the industry. For example, the ACMA governs the classification of content on the Internet and has established a co-regulatory scheme with ISP for classification of content and handling complaints in relation to offending material. ACMA promulgates guidelines for ISP so that consumers can obtain consistent and comparable information so they can make informed decisions when choosing an ISP. Following the Telecommunications Service Inquiry Report 'Connecting Australia' (Besley Report)[408] ISP will be required to provide in detail the price, performance help, communication, and security in a standard format to their clients.

§3. Defamation Action

933. The defence of innocent dissemination was argued in the High Court in *Thomson v. Australian Capital Television.*[409] That case involved a rebroadcast of a television programme. It was not accepted by the Court that the second broadcaster was a 'mere conduit' for the programme.

934. In the absence of any direct authority in Australia as to whether this defence would apply to a network service operator or ISP, it is likely that Australian courts would find persuasive cases in the US that have come to this conclusion. In *Stratton Oakmont, Inc. v. Prodigy Service Co.*,[410] for example, the plaintiff, a securities investment bank was successful in holding the defendant liable for allegedly defamatory statements made about Stratton by an unknown Prodigy subscriber on Prodigy's financial bulletin board called 'Money Talk'.

935. This case may be contrasted to *Cubby v. CompuServe.*[411] CompuServe was sued for allegedly defamatory statements made about the plaintiffs on CompuServe's 'Rumorville' bulletin board. It was held that CompuServe was merely a distributor because it had no more editorial control over bulletin board material than a library, bookstore, or newsstand.

936. The innocent dissemination defence is likely to be strictly construed. Thus, once a network service operator or ISP learns of the existence of defamatory material being placed on the system by its system user, it must act promptly to remove the material or risk losing the defence. This was the outcome in the UK case of *Godfrey v. Demon Internet*, in which Godfrey had notified the ISP for Demon of the offending material and demanded that it be removed.[412] By ignoring the request and not acting promptly, Demon was held to have waived the defence of innocent dissemination.

937. In the decision *Dow Jones and Company Inc. v. Gutnick* (2002), H.C.A. 56, the Court had to consider whether a person who had been defamed by an online article could sue in a jurisdiction different to the jurisdiction where the offending material was uploaded. The HCA held that Mr Gutnick could litigate his claim in

408. Australia Department of Communications, Information Technology and the Arts, Telecommunications Service Inquiry (Australia) (Besley Report) 2000.
409. (1996), 141 A.L.R. 1.
410. 1995 N.Y. Misc. LEXIS 229 (N.Y. Sup. Ct. 1995).
411. 776 F. Supp. 135 (S.D.N.Y.) 1991.
412. (1999) Case No. 1998-G-No 30 in the High Court of Justice, Queen's Bench Division, 26 Mar. 1999. Available at www.courtservice.gov.uk/godfrey2.htm.

Australia, since Australia was where the circle of people in which his reputation was likely to be damaged by the article and that was where the damage was suffered.

938. Given the growing concern among network service operators or ISP of the prospect of being found liable for carrying or hosting material of which they were not aware, the Australian Commonwealth government established a new regulatory scheme to resolve the issue. The Broadcasting Services Amendment (Online Services) Act 1999 (Cth) amended the Broadcasting Services Act 1992 and eliminated the need of using strict liability legislation. If an entity falls within the definition of an 'Internet content host' (network service operator) or an ISP under the Act, they do not need to actively monitor content. Instead, they will be notified by the ACMA if there is prohibited material. If they are not notified, then arguably they can escape liability under State or Territory law.

939. Section 91 of Schedule 5 of the Broadcasting Services Act 1992 provides that a law of a State or Territory, or a rule of common law or equity, has no effect to the extent to which it:

- subjects an Internet content host or ISP to liability (whether criminal or civil) in respect of hosting Internet content in a case where the host was not aware of the nature of the Internet content; or,
- requires an Internet content or Internet host to monitor, make inquiries about, or keep records of, Internet content hosted by the host.

940. This scheme is broad enough to apply to State and Territory laws and common laws that might impose liability on the network service operator and ISP for unwittingly carrying defamatory material with the effect of creating a defence in relation to defamation. For example, under the Defamation Act 2005 (NSW) section 32, a defence to defamation is that the defendant neither knew, nor ought reasonably to have known of the defamation, and the lack of knowledge was not due to the defendant's negligence.

§4. Negligent Provision of Information

941. It is unclear how Australia would treat a claim that the ISP was negligent in the provision of information that was defamatory or in breach of some other law. In *Zeran v. AOL* plaintiffs sought to avoid the safe harbour provisions of the US Communications Decency Act by alleging that the defendant was negligent in distributing defamatory information.[413] The argument was that section 230 of the Act

413. The decision was affirmed on appeal. *See* https://caselaw.findlaw.com/us-4th-circuit/1075207.html (129 F.3d 327 (4th Cir. 1997)). Section 230 of the Communications Decency Act of 1996 (a common name for Title V of the Telecommunications Act of 1996) is a landmark piece of Internet legislation in the US, codified at 47 U.S.C. § 230. Section 230(c)(1) provides immunity from liability for providers and users of an 'interactive computer service' who publish information provided by third-party users. *See* B. Fitzgerald, *Internet Service Provider Liability, in Going Digital 2000* 309 (A. Fitzgerald et al. eds, Prospect Media 2000).

dealt only with publication and not distribution. The Court held that section 230 was a general immunity against distribution and that to hold otherwise would defeat the very purpose of the section 230 provision.[414]

§5. Liability in Special Contexts

942. Network service operators and ISP may also be liable for chat rooms and websites dealing with financial advice. Pursuant to Chapter 7 of the Corporations Act 2001 (Cth), ASIC established a single licensing regime for financial service providers. The Act introduced a new licence for those who carry on financial service businesses in Australia, and it replaces existing licence systems that applied to new entrants after 11 March 2002. 'Financial service' is defined broadly and includes the provision of financial product advice. The provision of financial product advice includes the giving of recommendations or statements of opinion that may influence a person in deciding on a financial product. However, the mere interpretation of information will not constitute product advice. Financial product is broad and covers facilities through which a person makes a financial investment or manages a financial risk or incorporates securities, including shares and debentures. Therefore, this may capture websites and chat rooms dealing with financial advice. If an ISP just acts as a mere conduit and does not exercise control, then it will not be said to be providing the advice. Misleading and deceptive conduct provisions apply.[415]

§6. Conclusion

943. The liability of a network service operator or an ISP may be difficult to determine. In Australia, the major defence is to argue that the network service operator and ISP is a mere distributor and that the conduct involved was only an innocent dissemination. It also seems likely that network service operators and ISP must take seriously any notices of offending material and act promptly lest a court find that they are no longer entitled to rely on the innocent defence plea. To the extent that the ISP has any direct or indirect knowledge of the offending material, exercises or has the right to exercise any control over the material, or has any financial interest in the publication, then it is likely that the ISP may be found liable. Whether an ISP server could successfully rely upon Schedule 5 of the Broadcasting Services Amendment (Online Services) Act 1999 (Cth) as a defence to a defamation claim is untested.

944. Finally, it is important to note that many other countries do not have the same level of protection for network service operators and ISP and may find that they are deemed 'publishers' and therefore will be liable for defamation regardless of any motive underlying their actions.

---

414. *See also Doe v. AOL* at https://caselaw.findlaw.com/fl-supreme-court/1495838.html.
415. S. Brandone, *Licence to Chat*, elawpractice.com.au, December 2001, no. 9, 33.

Chapter 3. Product Liability

§1. Introduction

945. Consumer protection laws are aimed at ensuring that there are high standards of safety and protection for consumers in relation to goods and services they acquire. The law achieves safety standards and protection by requiring sellers and manufacturers to attain a high standard of care. The CCA and the respective State and Territory legislation provide this protection.

§2. Product Safety Laws

946. Computer hardware and software products are also subject to product safety and liability laws. Product safety laws are an integral part of product liability law, concerned with imposing minimum levels of safety to prevent injury or harm arising from the use of those products. The CCA, Volume 3, Schedule 2, Part 3.3, sections 129 through to 137 provides a comprehensive scheme covering a wide range of standards.[416]

947. Sections 104–108 of the CCA generally states that it is an offence to supply a product that does not comply with safety standards, is unsafe, or has been banned.

948. It is an offence under section 106 of the CCA to supply goods which do not comply with a prescribed safety standard or are subject to an unsafe goods order or banning order that are intended to be used by a consumer or likely to be used by a consumer.

949. In the context of e-business, an issue arises as to whether the liability of a manufacturer of software for design defects, such as may be found in medical expert systems (MES), is strictly liable or on a negligence standard. The definition of goods under section 2 for the purposes of Part 1, Schedule 2 of the CCA includes software within the definition of 'goods'. However, the information contained in software is not specifically covered in the definition. Software and the information contained within them are not easy to categorize as 'goods'. There has also been limited judicial consideration on the issue, given that the CCA generally regulates goods and services in the same way.

950. The issue is whether the application of the product liability provisions to any expert system gives rise to the threshold question of whether an injury can be said to be caused by the system itself, in the sense that the injuries in question arise not from a direct physical exposure to the system, but through reliance by the injured party, whether or not professionally mediated, on the information produced

416. Equivalent State legislation may be found in *Fair Trading Act*, for example, Division 1, Part III and Division 1, Part IV *Fair Trading Act* 1987 (NSW).

or contained within the system. In particular, the injury itself is usually one arising from the diagnostic error in reliance on the system. Finally, the issue is the classification of the defect, whether it is a manufacturing defect or a design defect. It is arguable that the provisions relate to conscious design defects.

Part VI. Privacy Protection

Chapter 1. Regulating Personal Information and Data Protection

§1. Introduction

I. Definition of Privacy

951. Privacy means different things in different contexts. At its simplest level, it means bodily privacy, protecting the integrity of the individual. It can also relate to privacy of communications or territorial privacy, to be free from surveillance and observation.[417] It can also relate to body privacy, for example collection of DNA or other health information. In another context it relates to information privacy, that is, the protection of personal information in terms of its collection, security, storage, use, and disclosure. Personal information is generally defined as information which on its own or together with other information would enable a living individual to be identified. Privacy can also mean different things to different groups. Thus, today's younger people, having grown up in a world of social media, texting and mobile phones are not as sensitive about personal privacy as an earlier generation.[418]

952. The Australian Law Reform Commission's (ALRC) report on privacy laws in Australia reflected that

> *Information privacy touches almost every aspect of our daily lives, including our medical records and health status, our finances and creditworthiness, the personal details collected and stored on a multiplicity of public and corporate databases, and even the ability to control the display and distribution of our own images.*[419]

---

417. There has been an increased focus on the national security environment since September 2001 and an accompanying array of legislation increasing the powers of enforcement agencies such as the *Surveillances Devices Act* 2004 (Cth). A chronology of legislation is listed on the Australian Parliament's website at www.privacy.org.au/Resources/APH-Lib-terrorism-071008.htm.
418. *See* S. Turkle *Alone Together* (Basic Books 2011).
419. https://www.alrc.gov.au/publication/for-your-information-australian-privacy-law-and-practice-alrc-report-108/.

953. However, there is no statutory definition of privacy in Australia. Rather, there is legislation at Commonwealth,[420] State and Territory[421] levels that protects various forms of privacy.[422]

954. Other legislation also contains privacy protection provisions relevant to entities or practices. In relation to the Internet and other telecommunications services, ISPs and telephone service providers are required to comply with the privacy protection provisions of the Telecommunications Act 1997 (Cth), the Telecommunications (Interception and Access) Act 1979 (Cth) (TIAA), and the Spam Act 2003 (Cth), to name a few.

955. Civil action right of privacy? It is unclear whether there exists in Australia, a common law tort or civil action for a breach of privacy as summarised by the ALRC summarized the position in 2007.[423]

956. Most recently, the issue of a tort of privacy was raised in Supreme Court of SA's case, *Sands v. South Australia*.[424] In that case, plaintiff Derick Sands, a suspect in a murder case, alleged that, in breach of his privacy, a person within the SA Police Force had leaked his name to the media. The SA Supreme Court held that the High Court's endorsement in Lenah Game Meats remain in need of further development before it could be held that such a common law action existed in Australia.

957. The High Court in *Australian Broadcasting Corporation v. Lenah Game Meats Pty. Ltd.* (2001), H.C.A. 63, did not rule out the possibility that a future court might find in favour of the existence of a general right of privacy (per Kirby J). Two subsequent State cases *Grosse v. Purvis* (2003), Q.D.C. 151, and *Jane Doe v. ABC & Ors* (2007), V.C.C. 281, have potentially opened the door to this cause of action. Although there is no specific 'right of privacy', at common law, privacy can be protected in specific contexts under the umbrella of other doctrines such as negligence and contract.

---

420. At Commonwealth or federal level, for example, there are the *Privacy Act* 1988 (Cth); *Telecommunications Act* 1997 (Cth); *National Health Act* 1953 (Cth); *Data-matching Program (Assistance and Tax) Act* 1990 (Cth); *Crimes Act* 1914 (Cth); *Anti-Money Laundering and Counter-Terrorism Financing Act* 2006 (Cth); and *The Healthcare Identifiers Act* 2010 (Cth).
421. In the state of NSW for example there are the *Privacy and Personal Information Protection Act* 1998 (NSW); *Health Records and Information Privacy Act* 2002 (NSW); *Freedom of Information Act* 1989 (NSW); *State Records Act* 1998 (NSW); *Criminal Records Act* 1991 (NSW); *Surveillance Devices Act* 2007 (NSW); *Workplace Surveillance Act* 2005 (NSW); *Telecommunications (Interception and Access)* (New South Wales) Act 1987 (NSW); *Access to Neighbouring Land Act* 2000 (NSW); and *Crimes (Forensic Procedures) Act* 2000 (NSW).
422. Australian Law Reform Commission, Discussion Paper 72 (2007), Review of Australian Privacy Law.
423. *Ibid.*
424. *Sands v. State of South Australia* [2013] SASC 44.

II. Privacy, Technology and the Internet

958. Technological developments have made the concept of privacy both more relevant but with an increased concern regarding protection. Individuals engage in many day-to-day transactions that are recorded or monitored. In many cases, this is uncontroversial. The individual concerned does not really care who knows the details. However, that is not always the case. Information resulting from these transactions may be valuable and useful information. In addition, while the individual may not care who is aware of the details, they may object to the way in which the details are being passed on or the consequences of that. For example, if their personal details are sold to third parties or the consequences of passing on the information subject the individual to unwanted direct advertising.

959. The expansion of technology has made personal information more accessible in that it can be collected, stored, retrieved, and transferred more readily. Practices such as data mining – using information about consumers to suggest trends or patterns, creating a purchasing profile, or to analyse buying preferences for advertising purposes – are now more common.[425] Information in this sense may be extremely valuable, and this requires adequate protections to ensure that consumers have control over their own information. Business can inspire confidence in the use of e-commerce and electronic service delivery by ensuring that personal information is adequately protected.

960. The growth of the Internet has heightened concerns about privacy. The ease of intercepting and duplicating information in digital format makes using the Internet a high-risk activity for the exposure of personal information. It is often difficult when working online to be sure with whom you are dealing. Even if you are sure of the identity of an online seller, a website and e-commerce business is easily moved from one jurisdiction to another. The transboundary nature of the Internet also poses difficulties for consumers who worry that the privacy protection afforded by consumer laws in their jurisdiction may not be enforceable against an Internet retailer who operates from another jurisdiction.

961. However, it is not just the consumer who is concerned about privacy risks; businesses are also concerned for two major reasons. As the Internet crosses many jurisdictional boundaries, there is a fear that the e-tailer will be subjected to whatever laws apply to any consumer in any jurisdiction. Identifying and managing the legal risks in this environment is extremely difficult. At the same time, e-tailers understand that consumers must have confidence in the Internet if its full potential is to be realized, and significant effort has been put into this through various security and other encryption methods.

425. V. Estivill-Castro, L. Brankovic & D. Dowe, *Privacy in Data Mining*, in *Privacy Law and Policy Reporter* 44 (1999).

962. In an electronic environment, privacy concerns also relate to the freedom to communicate or undertake transactions without unwarranted intrusion by government and regulators. There has been an increase in government surveillance such as workplace surveillance measures. Employers can now monitor and gather information on their employees through e-mail, telephone and computer monitoring, video surveillance, drug and alcohol testing, and the use of identity cards – blurring the lines between achieving the organizational outcomes of a business and the employees' right to work without undue interference.

963. Generally, it is accepted that an employer has a right to control what an employee does during work hours and the uses that are made of work facilities. However, it becomes a privacy issue when the employee is unaware of what information is being collected, the uses that will be made of it, and is unable to verify whether or not the information is accurate. The Privacy Commissioner has issued useful guidelines on privacy and workplace e-mail and web browsing[426] and some jurisdictions have passed legislation that place limits on the surveillance of employees by employers.[427]

III. Privacy Abuse

964. Technology, especially in an e-commerce environment, has been used as a tool to abuse individuals' privacy and leave personal information vulnerable. One example of IT practices that lead to potential privacy abuse is the use of data collection technology. When using the Internet, the individual leaves behind a trail of information. 'Cookies' generally assign a unique number to an online visitor for the purpose of recognizing repeat visits and tracking online behaviour. So, too, chip cards and geo-tracking devices that are used to collect and pass on information. Service providers now use mobile phone data to monitor and collect, in real-time, the sending of e-mails, trace where people browse on the Internet, and checking the destination of mobile telephone calls but not its contents without the use of a warrant.[428]

965. Once data has been collected by one organization, it is possible for that data to be shared among others. Credit records, health records, loyalty programmes, and other personal records are enormously valuable in that a profile of a user can be constructed and used for direct marketing or other commercial purposes.

966. One area in which the potential for this practice has caused concerns is that of genetic information. Highly sensitive genetic information, such as blood samples, is collected for a variety of reasons, generally in a health context. The information is not only valuable as a unique identifier, but also useful to organizations outside

426. Issued on 30 Mar. 2000. *See* www.privacy.gov.au/issues/p7_4.html.
427. *See, e.g., Workplace Surveillance Act* 2005 (NSW). http://www.austlii.edu.au/au/legis/nsw/consol_act/wsa2005245/.
428. Warrants are still required to access the contents of communications.

this context. For example, to determine whether to employ a person, determining insurance premiums and marketing of products to groups with certain predispositions, and for research purposes.[429]

967. Studies of privacy and technology suggest that privacy is still a major concern to online users. A Unisys Security Index poll undertaken by Newspoll in 2009 estimated that almost 9 million Australians are very or extremely concerned about misuse or unauthorized access to their personal information including: 8.8 million Australians are concerned about other people obtaining and or using their credit cards or debit card details, 5.2 million Australians are very or extremely concerned about their computer security when it comes to viruses and unsolicited e-mails, and 5.7 million Australians are very or extremely concerned about the security of shopping or banking online.[430]

968. The use of online social media and networking sites has increased dramatically in recent years. This raises an interesting issue of the line between voluntarily creating profiles and sharing personal information and to protect privacy. The dilemma would appear to be that while privacy may be at risk in social networking sites, information is willingly and voluntarily provided.[431]

969. An earlier study by the Privacy Commissioner into community attitudes toward privacy reported that technological developments have increased privacy concerns.[432] Thirty-six percent of Australians indicated that they would not deal with a company or charity because of concerns over its protection or use of their personal information. There is a concern that Internet businesses seem to require individuals to provide more personal information than businesses require for over-the-counter purchases. Many people believe that this information may be reused for another purpose or sold to direct marketers.[433]

970. The Australian Bureau of Statistics (ABS) annual Internet Activity Survey provides interesting survey. In the 2016–2017 survey report, the proportion of households with access to the internet at home has been steadily climbing since 20042005 but remained constant between 2014–2015 and 20162017 at 86%. In 2016–2017, 14% of connected households with children aged 5–14 stated a child had been exposed to inappropriate material and 5% of these households stated a child aged 5–14 had been subject to cyber-bullying. In 2016–2017, 5% of internet

---

429. The Australian Law Reform Commission and Australian Health Ethics Committee's 2003 report, *Essentially Yours – The Protection of Human Genetic Information*, contained 144 recommendations relating to the legal, ethical, and social implications of genetic technologies. As a result, the Human Genetics Advisory Commission was established as an independent expert advisory body.

430. This poll is undertaken twice a year and presents a social indicator regarding how safe consumers feel on key areas of security. *See* https://www.unisys.com/unisys-security-index-2018.

431. For a more detailed discussion, *see* R. Gross & A. Acquisti, *Information Revelation and Privacy in Online Social Networks (The Facebook Case)* 2005 at https://www.researchgate.net/publication/221342233_Information_revelation_and_privacy_in_online_social_networks_The_Facebook_Case.

432. This study by the Wallace Consulting Group is undertaken every three years. *See* reports for 2001, 2004, and 2007 at www.privacy.gov.au/business/research/index.html#1b.

433. *Ibid.*

users stated they had experienced abuse of personal information and 9% of internet users stated they had experienced damage or loss caused by a virus or other computer infection.[434]

971. While not alleviating such concerns, they can be somewhat allayed where organizations and agencies provide privacy assurances through a comprehensive privacy policy. The purpose of a privacy policy is to clearly communicate the personal information handling practices of an agency or organization. Privacy policies enhance the transparency of the operations of the entity and give individuals a better and more complete understanding of the sort of personal information an agency or organization holds and the way it handles that information. A good privacy notice is generally considered to be one that is easy to find, easy to read, and comprehensively explains all online information practices. It should also provide an opportunity to make informed decisions about the collection and use of information, provide access to personal information to ensure accuracy, and have security procedures to limit access.[435]

IV. Balancing Interests

972. Those operating in an e-commerce environment should realize that privacy must be balanced with other commercial needs. The privacy protection scheme adopted by Australia and reflected in the specific privacy policy of any organization needs to measure the rights of the individual with the benefits or need to use personal information. Clearly, data is an asset, and data sharing is a way of cutting costs. The outsourcing of data processing means a contractor can share and cross match data held for different clients.[436]

973. While acknowledging the legitimate concerns of private citizens, governments must also be able to collect information and data so that legitimate government interests can be pursued. There are compelling public policy arguments that privacy issues should be overridden in some cases where there are significant issues such as health and an ageing population, regulation of pornography, child abuse, and tax fraud.

974. The individual's right to privacy must therefore be balanced with other rights, for example, the implied right to freedom of speech.[437] There is also a need to balance the tension between the individual and society. Privacy advocates may speak of privacy in terms of a human right while other groups warn of an Orwellian

---

434. ABS Internet Activity Survey ABS catalogue number 8146.0. http://www.abs.gov.au/ausstats/abs@.nsf/PrimaryMainFeatures/8146.0?OpenDocument.

435. A Better Business Bureau Program at https://www.bbb.org/privacy-policy.

436. N. Waters, *Rethinking Information Privacy – A Third Way in Data Protection?*, Privacy L. Pol. Rptr 6 (2000).

437. *See* C. McLeod, *Excessive Privacy Laws Undermine Democracy*, 11(2) *Press Council News* (May 1999). *See also* C. McLeod, *When Privacy Laws Undermine Democracy*, Privacy L. Pol. Rptr 37 (1999).

nightmare in which 'big brother' usurps individual freedom. However, a more realistic and workable notion is a balance between the two. A smart business model is one that recognizes that unless consumers are confident in the electronic medium, its potential will never be fully realized.

V. Australia's International Obligations

975. The Internet operates in an international environment. Australia's obligations in relation to privacy protection also stem from various agreements and covenants to which Australia is a signatory. A fundamental expression of these international obligations is the Universal Declaration of Human Rights (UDHR), adopted in 1948, which includes Article 12:

> No one shall be subjected to arbitrary interference with his privacy, family, home or correspondence, nor to attacks upon his honour and reputation. Everyone has the right to the protection of the law against such interference or attacks.

976. International Cooperation. The OAIC participated in the global privacy enforcement network's first international privacy sweep. The OAIC released the results of the sweep which included a review of the privacy policies of almost fifty websites most used by Australians. The review included assessing privacy policies against the new transparency requirements amended in the Privacy Act 1988 (Cth) which came into effect on 12 March 2014.

977. Australia is also influenced by regional and international privacy developments including the Organization for Economic Cooperation and Development's (OECD) 1980 *Guidelines on the Protection of Privacy and Transborder Flows of Personal Data* that articulated basic privacy principles to protect personal data.

978. To a large extent, these are reflected in Australia's current privacy legislation. The OECD also urged Member States to pass legislation to encourage and support self-regulation. The OECD Guidelines were recently updated in 2013.[438] A Member country should refrain from restricting transborder flows of personal data between itself and another country where (a) the other country substantially observes these Guidelines or (b) sufficient safeguards exist, including effective enforcement mechanisms and appropriate measures put in place by the data controller, to ensure a continuing level of protection consistent with these Guidelines.

979. Any restrictions to transborder flows of personal data should be proportionate to the risks presented, the sensitivity of the data, and the purpose and context of the processing.

438. http://www.oecd.org/internet/ieconomy/privacy-guidelines.htm.

980. Also influential were various European developments and the passage by the United Nations of Guidelines for the Regulation of Computerized Personal Data Files.[439]

981. Australia acceded to the OECD Guidelines in 1984, and privacy legislation was passed in 1988.[440] The Privacy Act 1988 (Cth), updated in 2014, was passed in compliance with Australia's obligations under Article 17 of the International Covenant on Civil and Political Rights 1966 (which is almost identical to Article 12 of the UDHR).

982. In 1995, the European Union (EU) passed a Data Protection Directive protecting personal information and harmonizing privacy laws among its Member States. The Directive requires that the laws of Member States protect personal information in both the private and public sectors. That legislation must feature provisions to block transfers of information to non-Member States that do not provide an 'adequate' level of protection.[441]

983. Since 1995 the EU has been covered by national comprehensive information privacy laws governing the private sector that are based on the EU directives – Directive 95/46/EC (Data Protection Directive) and supplemented by other directives such as the Directive 2002/58/EC (ePrivacy Directive) for Electronic Communications,[442] Directive 2015/1535/EC for Information Society Services and Directive 2009/136/EC with rules about the use of cookies.

984. The Data Protection Directive (95/46/EC) concerns the protection of individuals in terms of the processing of personal data and on the free movement of such data. The Data Protection Directive establishes eight key legal principles governing data protection including fair and lawful processing; purpose limitation and specification; minimal storage term; transparency; data quality; security; special categories of data; and data minimization.

985. The Directive on Privacy and Electronic Communications (ePrivacy Directive) sets out the rules on how providers of electronic communication services, such

439. Guidelines for the Regulation of Computerized Personal Data Files, as adopted by General Assembly resolution 45/95 of 14 December 1990 at http://www.unhchr.ch/html/menu3/b/71.htm.
440. Roger Clarke, *A History of Privacy in Australia* (October 1998), at www.rogerclarke.com/DV/OzHC.html#ContI.
441. Caslon Analytics Privacy Guide, June 2007 archived at the National Library of Australia at https://catalogue.nla.gov.au/Record/3415577.
442. Directive 2002/58/EC was amended by Directive 2006/24/EC as a result of an ECJ ruling on its validity. *See Grand Chamber Digital Rights Ireland Ltd. (C–293/12) v. Minister for Communications, Marine and Natural Resources* at http://eur-lex.europa.eu/legal-content/EN/TXT/HTML/?uri=CELEX:62012CJ0293&rid=1 and Commission of the European Communities Directive 2009/136/EC of the European Parliament and of the Council of 25 November 2009 amending Directive 2002/22/EC on universal service and users' rights relating to electronic communications networks and services (Cookie Directive).

as telecoms companies and ISPs, should manage their subscribers' data. It also guarantees rights for subscribers when they use these services.[443] The ePrivacy Directive and the General Data Protection Regulation (GDPR) provide the legal framework to ensure digital privacy for EU citizens. The ePrivacy Directive is in the process of alignment with the new data protection regulation.[444]

986. A draft GDPR was published in January 2012 proposed reforming the legal structure for privacy protection in the EU to address several pressing issues. The goal was to eliminate inconsistencies and fragmentation in national laws; to provide better and heightened protection for individuals and to update the law to address contemporary issues. The EU GDPR came into force on 25 May 2018.[445]

987. Australian e-commerce businesses can be expected to increasingly exchange data with trading partners overseas. However, this is problematic where Australia cannot assure other countries, such as those in the EU, that its privacy protection meets acceptable international standards. Based on two current exemptions in Australia's privacy legislation, the employee records exemption and small business exemption, the EU does not currently consider Australia to have adequate privacy safeguards. The US also adopted a different approach to the EU and introduced a safe harbour framework based on the adherence to seven privacy principles – notice, choice, onward transfer, security, data integrity, enforcement, and access.

§2. Commonwealth Privacy Act

I. Scope of Privacy Act

988. The Commonwealth Privacy Act 1988 (Cth) applies to 'personal information' rather than to commercial data, except credit information. The protection provided under the Act is in addition to any IPR or protections that may exist in that information, for example, confidential information. Personal information is defined in section 6 of the Act as:

---

443. Directive 2002/58/EC of the European Parliament and of the Council of 12 July 2002 concerning the processing of personal data and the protection of privacy in the electronic communications sector (Directive on Privacy and Electronic Communications) Official Journal L 201, 31 Jul. 2002 P. 0037–0047.

444. *See* Proposal for a Regulation of the European Parliament and of the Council concerning the respect for private life and the protection of personal data in electronic communications and repealing Directive 2002/58/EC (Regulation on Privacy and Electronic Communications), COM/2017/010 final – 2017/03 (COD)(http://eur-lex.europa.eu/legal-content/EN/TXT/?uri=CELEX:52017PC0010); https://ec.europa.eu/digital-single-market/en/online-privacy. The draft regulation was adopted on 10 Jan. 2017. *See* https://ec.europa.eu/digital-single-market/en/proposal-eprivacy-regulation.

445. Commission of the European Communities 2016 Regulation (EU) 2016/679 of the European Parliament and of the Council 27 April 2016 on the protection of natural persons with regard to the processing of personal data and on the free movement of such data, and repealing Directive 95/46/EC (General Data Protection Regulation).

information or an opinion (including information or an opinion forming part of a database), whether true or not, and whether recorded in a material form or not, about an individual whose identity is apparent, or can reasonably be ascertained, from the information or opinion.

989. Administration of Commonwealth Privacy laws is carried out by the OAIC as an independent Australian Government agency established under the Australian Information Commissioner Act 2010 (Cth).

990. In November 2012 Federal Parliament passed the Privacy Amendment (Enhancing Privacy Protection) Act 2012 (Cth) which significantly reforms the Privacy Act 1988 (Cth) (Privacy Act).

991. The Privacy Act 1988 (Cth) updated in 2014, regulates the collection, maintenance, use, transfer, and disclosure of personal information by the private sector (large organizations with an annual turnover of more than AUD 3 million) and the Federal Government.[446] Both public and private sectors are subject to the APP. The Act also has extraterritorial application.

A. New Privacy Law

992. In the Privacy Amendment (Enhancing Privacy Protection) Act 2012 (Cth) Australia introduced major reforms to the previous privacy laws to reflect a growing concern about the importance of privacy, the role of privacy policies and the challenge of protecting privacy, especially in new contexts such as mobile computing. [447] The changes came into effect in March 2014.

993. The Privacy Amendment Act applies to businesses with annual turnover in excess of AUD 3 million; or businesses that are private sector health service providers, such as a general practitioner, private hospital or clinic; or smaller businesses specified in the Act. The APP do not apply to small business.

B. Summary of New Provisions

994. The Act creates a unified set of thirteen APP that will apply to both Commonwealth agencies and private sector organizations. These new principles replace the eleven IPP that currently apply to the public sector and the ten NPP that applied to the private sector.

995. The thirteen principles are as follows:

---

446. The Act applies to the Australian Capital Territory and the Northern Territory governments.
447. The full legislation with new provisions added (Act No. 119 of 1988 as amended, including amendments in the *Federal Circuit Court of Australia (Consequential Amendments) Act* 2013 (Cth)) at http://www.comlaw.gov.au/Details/C2014C00076/Download.

(1) Collection:
- *APP 1*: entities will be required to publish privacy policies dealing with a range of matters from how the entity will handle complaints from individuals about their personal information, to whether the entity is likely to disclose personal information to recipients overseas and the other countries in which the recipients of the personal information are likely to be located.
- *APP 2*: individuals will have the option of communicating via a pseudonym, or anonymously, where it is lawful and practicable to do so.
- *APP 3*: agencies and organizations will generally be able to collect sensitive information if it is reasonably necessary for (or, in the case of agencies, directly related to) its functions or activities and otherwise only in prescribed circumstances.
- *APP 4*: unsolicited personal information will continue to be protected by entities in accordance with the APPs, and otherwise is to be destroyed or 'de-identified' if not needed for a legitimate purpose.
- *APP 5:* there are more prescriptive notification requirements which apply to the collection of personal information.
- *APP 10*: entities must ensure the quality of the personal information they collect.

(2) Use and Disclosure:
- *APP 6:* covers use or disclosure of personal information and outlines the circumstances in which an APP entity may use or disclose personal information that it holds.
- *APP 8:* requires that before an entity discloses personal information overseas it must take reasonable steps to ensure that the recipient of the personal information does not breach the APPs.[448] Entities may seek to comply with this requirement by entering into a contractual relationship with the overseas recipient imposing responsibility for compliance with the APPs.
- *APP 10:* requires entities to ensure the quality and relevance of the personal information they use and disclose.

(3) Government Information:
- *APP 9*: adoption, use or disclosure of government related identifiers–outlines the limited circumstances when an organization may adopt a government related identifier of an individual as its own identifier, or use or disclose a government related identifier of an individual.

(4) Direct Marketing:
- *APP 7:* introduces a specific direct marketing principle, which imposes additional restrictions on the use and disclosure of personal information to promote or sell goods and services directly to individuals.[449]

(5) Security:

---

448. Section 16C of the Act gives effect to a new 'accountability approach' to cross-border data flows of personal information in line with the APEC Privacy Framework.
449. The new direct marketing requirements found in APP 7 do not affect the operation of the *Spam Act* 2003 (Cth) nor the *Do Not Call Register Act* 2006 (Cth), which continue to apply.

- *APP 11:* requires entities to protect personal information against interference which may or may not involve loss or misuse, or unauthorized access, modification or disclosure of information (e.g., interference resulting from a computer system attack).

(6) Access and Correction:

- *APP 12* and *APP 13:* require entities to allow individuals to access and correct their personal information within certain timeframes (thirty days). If requested by the individual, then the entity will be responsible for notifying any corrections to other entities.

C. Other Provisions

996. 'Personal information' is defined broadly and includes information such as names, addresses, financial information, sensitive information (e.g., health, religion), e-mail addresses or any other 'information or an opinion about an identified individual, or an individual who is reasonably identifiable'. The amendments primarily apply to businesses that have an annual turnover of more than AUD 3 million.

997. Information Commissioner and Penalties. Under the new amendments, the Australian Information Commissioner has enhanced powers to resolve privacy issues, such as investigating privacy breaches on its own motion, accepting enforceable undertakings, seeking civil penalty orders, declaring compensation orders and conducting privacy performance assessments. Individuals or corporations that seriously interfere with a person's privacy or repeatedly interfere with a person's privacy are liable for fines of up to AUD 340,000 (for individuals) or AUD 1.7 million (for corporations).

998. Privacy Codes. The new Privacy law also includes provisions under which the Australian Information Commissioner can develop binding codes of conduct, such as Australian Privacy Principle Codes (APP Code) and a Credit Reporting Code. Under the new legislation, some entities will be bound by APP Code. An APP Code will not replace the APP but operate in addition to the requirements of the APPs and must be registered with the OAIC. The new legislation also contains provisions for the development of a code of practice about credit reporting.

999. Privacy breach notification. The Australian government effective March 2014 has introduced mandatory data breach notification laws. These new laws force companies to notify their customers when they had suffered a data breach. Previously, aside from e-Health related information, there were no laws in place to enforce these kinds of notifications, leading to a situation where only large-scale data breaches are revealed to the public. From a business standpoint, too, notifying consumers of breaches builds trust and helps to minimize reputation loss associated with such breaches.[450]

1000. Privacy Disputes: External dispute resolution. The Information Commissioner, under section 35A can recognize EDR schemes to handle specific privacy-related complaints. The OAIC has issued guidelines for EDR schemes on the matters the Commissioner must consider whether to recognize an EDR scheme and the steps EDR scheme should take to apply for recognition. By way of example, the TIO EDR Scheme was to receive, investigate, facilitate the resolution of, make decisions and recommendations for, and report on, complaints about acts or practices of TIO members that may be an interference with the privacy of an individual under subsections 13(1) and/or 13(2) of the Privacy Act 1988 (Cth).[451]

1001. Jurisdiction and Extraterritoriality. The Act's extraterritorial application means that where an Australian organization is dealing with information about Australians then the Act applies to conduct no matter where it occurs, that is, within or outside Australia.

1002. Similarly, a foreign corporation that collects information in Australia or then moves that information overseas is still required to apply the safeguards required in the Act. If personal information is sent stored or processed overseas, for example contracted out to a cloud provider, the businesses must take reasonable steps to ensure that the overseas cloud provider complies with the privacy principles. If the Act is breached, then the Australian business may be held liable.

1003. Under a new section 16C of the Privacy Act 1988 (Cth), an entity will be taken to breach the APP if it discloses personal information to an overseas recipient who is not bound by the APP but does an act or engages in a practice that would breach an APP if it applied.

1004. Entities may seek to minimize the risk of liability under section 16C through their contractual relationship with the overseas recipient, for example, by including express obligations on the recipient to comply with the APP and using indemnities to reapportion liability for an interference with the privacy of an individual.

---

450. *See* OAIC's Data Breach Notification: A guide to handling personal information security breaches, at: www.oaic.gov.au/privacy/privacy-resources/privacy-guides/. *See also* OAIC's Guide to information security, *'Reasonable steps' to protect personal information* at www.oaic.gov.au/privacy/privacy-resources/privacy-guides/.

451. https://www.oaic.gov.au/privacy/privacy-complaints/external-dispute-resolution-schemes/.

II. Privacy and the Private Sector

1005. Responding to growing consumer concerns about privacy and international developments such as the EU's directives on privacy,[452] the Australian Government amended the Privacy Act 1988 (Cth) to extend its application beyond Commonwealth agencies to include the private sector. The Privacy Amendment (Private Sector) Act 2001 (Cth) came into effect on 1 July and extended the reach of the Privacy Act 1988 (Cth) to all businesses with an annual turnover of AUD 3 million or more.

1006. The Privacy Act 1988 (Cth) does not apply to State and Territory public sector agencies, although some Australian States have introduced their own privacy legislation, for example, Privacy and Personal Information Protection Act 1998 (NSW) and Information Privacy Act 2000 (VIC) State and Territory laws dealing with privacy will therefore continue to operate so long as they are consistent with the Commonwealth law. Other laws protecting confidential information will continue to operate, such as common law trust principles, breach of confidence, equitable duties of confidence, and confidentiality inherent in specific relationships (such as banker-customer and lawyer-client).

III. Importance of Consent

1007. One of the most important risk management tools in relation to privacy is obtaining a person's voluntary and informed consent to the collection and use of their personal information. Poorly drafted consent clauses are likely to be ineffective, especially where the consent is given in an online environment where proof of consent is difficult to establish. APP 7 of the Privacy Act 1988 (Cth) generally requires organizations to obtain the consent of individuals to use their personal information for an unrelated secondary purpose. While there are some exceptions to this, including the 'direct-marketing exemption', the general rule is that consent must be obtained unless the secondary use is related to the primary purpose of collection and the individual would reasonably expect their information to be used for this secondary purpose.[453]

1008. In general, the normal legal principles of consent will prevail. For example, if there is a disparity in bargaining positions or other unfair advantage, then the consent agreement may be deemed to be unconscionable. Consent must be voluntary and given with full knowledge of the actual matter agreed upon. However, where an individual agrees to a very broadly worded clause, there may be instances where the consent is not binding. Arguably, the use of broad language in

452. For example, Commission of the European Communities 2016 Regulation (EU) 2016/679 of the European Parliament and of the Council 27 April 2016 on the protection of natural persons with regard to the processing of personal data and on the free movement of such data, and repealing Directive 95/46/EC (General Data Protection Regulation). The GDPR provides the local law that restricts the flow of data to another country unless there is adequate protection within that country.

453. L. Gamertsfelder & P. Sivanesarajah, *Consents Too Broad, Too Bad*, 14 eLaw Practice 47 (2002).

a consent clause does not provide the person with full knowledge of the proposed use of the personal information. Additionally, consent obtained from a child is likely to come under special scrutiny by the courts.

1009. While the Privacy Act 1988 (Cth) requires the individual's consent to particular handling of their personal information, the Guidelines to the Act recognize that for clarity and transparency 'bundling' of consent with some precautions is permitted so that a business does not have to have a massively long and cumbersome matrix that 'unbundles' the consent by requiring approvals covering every single possible use of personal information.

A. Automated Collection by Cookies

1010. The Guidelines to the Act also make it clear that not every use of a cookie or other tracking device will require a consent. Many cookies simply collect general information, for example, how many times the site is visited, that does not identify or reasonably identify users. Approval and the ability to opt out will only be required where the information gathered would enable the website owner to identify or reasonably identify visitors to the website.

B. Behavioural Ads

1011. However, online behavioural advertising that uses personal information will be caught by the Privacy Act 1988 (Cth) and is considered 'direct marketing' where it uses personal information (APP 7).

C. Cyber Attack

1012. The Guidelines also make it clear that the fact that where a company has taken reasonable steps to secure its information, but notwithstanding those steps a site has been hacked into, this will not constitute an illegal disclosure of personal information subjecting the site owner to liability for the unauthorized access or criminal act of another.

IV. Data-Matching and Data Sharing Guidelines

1013. Data-matching involves bringing together data from a variety of sources for the purpose of comparison and is generally the provenance of government agencies, but may also occur in corporate groups with diverse, but complementary, business activities. Data-matching is used by agencies (who are subject to the Privacy Act 1988 (Cth)) to identify people for further action or investigation. For example, records from Centrelink, Department of Veteran Affairs (DVA) and the ATO may be compared to identify people who are being paid benefits to which they are not entitled or people who are not paying the right amount of tax. The Privacy Commissioner recognizes that data-matching poses a threat to personal privacy because it is a powerful administrative and law enforcement tool which analyses information about large numbers of people for public policy purposes.[454]

1014. The Data-Matching Guidelines are issued under section 27(1)(e) of the Privacy Act 1988 (Cth).[455] These non-binding guidelines have general application to Commonwealth agencies governed by the Privacy Act 1988 (Cth). With or without a request from a Minister or an agency, the Privacy Commissioner may examine proposals for data-matching or data linkage concerned with an interference with the privacy of individuals (section 27(1)(k)).

1015. The Data-Matching Program (Assistance and Tax) Act 1990 (Cth) regulates data-matching as between specific agencies, such as Centrelink, the ATO, and the DVA. The Act distinguishes between 'source agencies', 'matching agencies', and 'assistance agencies'. The purpose of the data-matching legislation is to prohibit unrestrained matching or creation of a comprehensive databank on citizens. For example, section 6 of the Data Matching Program (Assistance and Tax) Act 1990 (Cth) provides that a maximum of nine data-matching cycles are permitted in any one year, with only one cycle to be in operation at any one time. Other restrictions cover the storage of data and set time limits on when the data must be examined and investigated and the requirement to notify persons whose benefits are to be impacted, to name a few.[456]

1016. Data Sharing: Agencies are sometimes given express authority to share information, especially in circumstances where such sharing is required in order to carry out a valid legislative purpose. An example is the Australian Sports Anti-Doping Authority (ASADA) which in August of 2013 was granted new powers as a result of the passage of the Australian Sports Anti-Doping Authority Amendment Act 2013 (Cth) (the Amending Act).[457]

1017. The primary objective of the Amending Act is to provide ASADA with additional investigative powers to identify those athletes, and athlete support personnel, using prohibited performance enhancing substances and methods. This legislative move comes in the wake of the Australian Crime Commission's February 2013 report, Organised Crime and Drugs in Sport, which, among other things, found that there is (or is suspected to be) widespread use of prohibited performance enhancing substances by professional athletes in a number of sports in Australia and that traditional analytical testing of athlete urine and blood samples by ASADA is not effective in detecting increasingly sophisticated doping practices.

---

454. For more information, *see* OAIC portal at https://www.oaic.gov.au/privacy/other-legislation/government-data-matching/.
455. *Data-Matching Program (Assistance and Tax) Act* 1990 (Cth).
456. *See* G. Hughes, *Government Data Matching to Continue*, 68 L. Inst. J. 68 488 (1994).
457. S. Meade & S. Miller, *Australia: New powers for ASADA to investigate possible anti-doping violations* (3 Aug. 2013). *See* http://www.mondaq.com/australia/x/255948/Sport/New+powers+for+ASADA+to+investigate+possible+antidoping+violations.

1018. ASADA has information sharing programs in place with bodies such as the Therapeutic Goods Administration and the Australian Customs and Border Protection Service. The Amending Act broadens these information sharing arrangements by amending the Australian Postal Corporation Act 1989 (Cth) to enable Australia Post to provide information or documents to the CEO of ASADA so long as the provision of the information or documents is for the purposes of the administration of the National Anti-Doping Scheme

V. Privacy Codes

1019. Industry and specific industry sectors may draft their own privacy code. At the very least, a privacy code must be consistent with the APP and must be approved by the Privacy Commissioner.[458] This allows some flexibility in how organizations approach their privacy obligations but, at the same time, ensures that minimum enforceable standards apply to the protection of personal information.

VI. The Privacy Commissioner

1020. The Privacy Act prohibits 'interferences with privacy'.[459] Under the Privacy Act 1988 (Cth), organizations must take reasonable steps to prevent a malicious or unintentional loss of personal information they hold.

1021. There are two avenues for handling complaints. The first applies in those situations where there is no approved industry code with its own complaint handling process. It involves the Privacy Commissioner's hearing of the complaint under powers given by Part V of the Privacy Act 1988 (Cth). The Privacy Commissioner has wide powers to conciliate or make determinations, for example, that the organization complained against 'should perform any reasonable act or course of conduct to redress any loss or damage suffered by the complainant' or that the complainant is entitled to compensation for a particular amount by reason of the practice complained about.[460] If the organization or person complained about refuses to comply with the Privacy Commissioner's determination, then there must be a full rehearing on the merits in Federal Court.[461]

1022. The second avenue is to hear the complaint pursuant to an approved code, with the body designated to hear the complaint having the same determinative powers as the Privacy Commissioner. If the defendant does not comply, recourse can be had to the Privacy Commissioner or the Federal Court.

---

458. Section 18BB(2) sets out the matters the Commissioner must be satisfied are met before a privacy code may be approved.
459. Section 13.
460. *Ibid.*
461. *Privacy Act* 1988, s. 52(1)(B)(b)(ii).

VII. Other Commonwealth Legislation Impacting Privacy

1023. In addition to the Privacy Act 1988 (Cth), several other statutory regimes at the national or Commonwealth level also regulate various aspects of privacy. These include: Telecommunications Act 1997 (Cth); National Health Act 1953 (Cth); Crimes Act 1914 (Cth); Anti-Money Laundering and Counter-Terrorism Financing Act 2006 (Cth) (AML/CTF); Anti-Money Laundering and Counter-Terrorism Financing Regulations 2008 (Cth), (the Regulations) and the Anti-Money Laundering and Counter-Terrorism Financing Rules and the Healthcare Identifiers Act 2010 (Cth).

1024. The AML/CTF regime was implemented to combat the threats that money laundering and terrorism financing pose to national security and the integrity of key sectors of the economy, and to bring Australia into compliance with international AML/CTF standards developed by the Financial Action Taskforce.

1025. On 4 December 2013, the Commonwealth government announced a review of Australia's AML/CTF laws, as required by the Act. The review is led by the AGD and AUSTRAC, the review addresses issues relevant to entities currently regulated under the AML/CTF regime, including the regulatory burden created by the AML/CTF, enforcement and reporting. The review also considered whether the regulated population should be expanded to include entities not currently regulated under the AML/CTF regime, including lawyers, accountants, real estate agents and trust and company service providers.[462]

A. *Financial Data*

1026. Financial information is especially sensitive and the need for security of such data is high. The Australian Prudential Regulation Authority (APRA) issued the final version of the new prudential practice guide in 2013, 'Prudential Practice Guide CPG 235 – Managing Data Risk' (Data Guide).[463] The Data Guide aims to assist financial institutions, general and life insurance companies and superannuation funds regulated by APRA (Entities) to manage their data risks. This final version of the Data Guide has few changes from the draft released in December 2012. The Data Guide complements APRA's earlier IT security guide, Prudential Practice Guide CPG 234 – Management of Security Risk in Information and Information Technology (IT Guide).

462. The issues are discussed at https://www.homeaffairs.gov.au/about-us/our-portfolios/criminal-justice/crime-prevention/anti-money-laundering-counter-terrorism-financing.

463. https://www.apra.gov.au/draft-prudential-practice-guide-ppg-235-managing-data-risk.

B. Health Records

1027. The PCEHR established the framework for an online electronic health records system, and a register of consumers, healthcare providers and parties involved in the technological implementation and maintenance of the PCEHR system. The Act supplemented by a set of PCEHR Rules.

1028. The PCEHR Act creates an opt-in system, whereby an individual will have to register as a consumer before creating a 'shared health summary' in conjunction with their nominated healthcare provider. The Act's provisions reflect the intention that consumers will be able to control the extent to which and circumstances in which the information in their health records is accessed.[464]

§3. Privacy Legislation in the States and Territories

1029. At the state level, NSW has passed the Privacy and Personal Data Protection Act 1998 (NSW), and Queensland has passed the Invasion of Privacy Act 1971 (Qld). The NSW legislation permitted the development of private privacy codes to be approved by the State Privacy Commissioner. Victoria has introduced the Information Privacy Act 2000 (Vic) and the Health Records Act 2001 (Vic), and Western Australia has passed the Surveillance Devices Act 1998 (WA) which regulates the installation and use of data surveillance devices in a civil or criminal proceeding.

1030. Most states, like the Commonwealth, also have an Ombudsman, where a person can file a complaint against a government agency for breach of privacy principles. However, where there is a legislative privacy regime and a Privacy Commissioner, such as in the Commonwealth and NSW, the complaint is likely to be referred to that body.

§4. Related Laws

1031. While the Commonwealth Privacy Act and State legislation and industry codes provide the broad framework for the protection of data on individuals, there also exist common law doctrines and statutory provisions that may have an indirect effect in that they may be used in some contexts to protect one's privacy. In brief, these include:

– *Contract Law.* If privacy is important, there is no reason that one cannot contract for its protection and provide appropriate remedies should the contractual provisions be breached.
– *Negligence.* Depending on the context, several possibilities exist in enforcing a duty of care in relation to the protection of information. For example, a party who

464. http://www.yourhealth.gov.au/internet/yourhealth/publishing.nsf/Content/pcehr-governance#.UtXm4rS3WOc.

undertakes the duty of storage and controlling use of data can be held liable if they are negligent in the performance of these duties.
Corporations Law. Civil and criminal remedies exist for those who are involved with unauthorized dealings in company books and records stored on a computer (Corporations Act 2001 (Cth) section 1307).

- *Australian Consumer Law* provides that 'A person shall not in trade or commerce engage in conduct that is misleading or deceptive or likely to mislead or deceive.'
- *Interference under Contract.* Originating in the context of employment contracts, this doctrine has now been extended to cover any contractual obligation.
- *Confidentiality.* This common law right seeks to protect information given and received in confidence and those who wrongfully violate that confidence. If a customer provides an online seller with private information, for example, customer account details, this information may qualify as 'confidential', and the doctrine of confidentiality could be used to stop a party from violating the confidentiality of such information.
- *Conversion.* This involves the wrongful interference with the goods of another. Software is one of the most common online purchases. Given that software can in some circumstances be classified as 'goods', the taking or interference with software which contains personal information could trigger a cause of action for conversion, that is, the intentional and unlawful interference with goods belonging to another.
- *Other and Context-Specific Legislation.* For example, the Corporations Law 2001 (Cth) would govern the keeping of and access to corporate records. In the employment setting, legislation such as the Workplace Video Surveillance Act 1998 (NSW) and the Workplace Surveillance Act 2005 (NSW) are relevant to privacy in an online environment.
- *Trespass.* This old tort has been extended to cover a broad range of applications in the digital environment. Originally, it involved the wrongful entry onto land belonging to the plaintiff. Today, it could cover unauthorized access to information stored on a computer or on a website such as the 'hacking' and intrusion into websites.
- *Defamation or Damage to One's Reputation.* Cases in Australia and overseas have involved e-mail defamation or defamation based on content displayed on a website.[465]
- *Statutory IP Rights.* Various IP remedies may come into play where the disclosure violates trademark, copyright, or other IP rights. Copyright laws apply to a digital environment. Trademarks are often displayed on a website. Indeed, the multimedia nature of most commercial websites involves most aspects of IP law, and in some factual contexts, a breach of privacy may also involve a breach of IP law.
- *Procedural Avenues.* In some cases, the breach of privacy may be prevented as soon as it is detected, for example, by requesting an injunction, and claiming legal

465. *See, e.g., Dow Jones and Company Inc. v. Gutnick* (2002) 210 C.L.R.

privilege. Another important procedural avenue when Government is involved is the Freedom of Information Act 1982 (Cth)[466] (FOIA) and in most States and Territories.[467]

The Ombudsman. Privacy complaints can also be made to State and industry ombudsmen, although where there is a privacy legislative scheme, the activity would probably be referred to the Privacy or Information Commissioner.[468]

§5. Industry Codes

I. Industry Codes

1032. Subject to any applicable provisions of the Privacy Act 1988 (Cth) in relation to approved codes, in addition to legislative regimes that mandate a minimum level of privacy protection, industry codes recommend the imposition of privacy standards as a condition of membership to their organization. One of the most influential and best known of these codes is the ADMA code of practice.[469] The ADMA Code[470] contains specific standards relating to data protection in direct marketing contexts in both a paper and an electronic environment. The ADMA code of practice adopted the OECD Guidelines for Consumer Protection in E-commerce.[471]

1033. The ADMA code of practice applies only in B2C contexts and provide a blueprint for government as they formulate and implement consumer protection for e-commerce. The ADMA and OECD Guidelines provide a blueprint for private sector to develop self-regulatory codes and best practice regimes. The codes are also designed to help consumers determine expectations for fair business practices.

1034. Depending upon the technology used in direct marketing, other codes of conduct may also be relevant to consumers in an e-business environment. These include, for example:

– EFT Code of Conduct.[472] The EFT Code is a code of practice which sets out rules about how electronic funds transfers should work, what the business must do,

466. *Freedom of Information Act* 1982 (Cth).
467. *See Freedom of Information Act* 1989 (NSW); 1982 (Vic); 1992 (Qld); 1991 (SA); 1992 (WA); 1989 (ACT); 1991 (Tas).
468. *See Ombudsman Act* 1976 (Cth), *Ombudsman Act* 1974 (NSW); *Ombudsman Act* 1973 (Vic); *Ombudsman Act* 1972 (SA); *Ombudsman Act* 1978 (Tas); *Ombudsman Act* 1989 (ACT); *Ombudsman (Northern Territory) Act* 1977 (NT); *Parliamentary Commissioner Act* 1974 (Qld); and *Parliamentary Commissioner Act* 1971 (WA).
469. www.adma.com.au.
470. https://www.adma.com.au/sites/default/files/ADMA-Code-of-Practice-01.pdf.
471. OECD Council Concerning Guidelines for Consumer Protection in the Context of Electronic Commerce adopted 9 Dec. 1999 by twenty-nine OECD members, https://www.oecd.org/sti/consumer/oecdguidelinesforconsumerprotectioninthecontextofelectroniccommerce1999.htm.
472. http://www.asic.gov.au/eftcode. *See also* http://www.mastercard.com/ca/company/en/security_risk.html.

their rights and responsibilities, and what happens if something goes wrong. Businesses may choose whether to sign up to the Code.
Telecommunications Codes including Customer Information on Prices, 'Terms and Conditions' and 'Customer and Network Fault Management'.[473]
– Commonwealth Government's Model Code, *Building Consumer Sovereignty in Electronic Commerce – A Best Practice Model for Business.* Based on the OECD Consumer Protection in E-commerce Guidelines, the code has provisions regulating advertising on the Internet, spamming, and other conduct.[474]
– IIA Code of Practice.[475]

II. Third-Party Verification

1035. The Australian government has placed a heavy reliance on the private sector to regulate itself. One result of this is the growth of website verification services that assure consumers that the website bearing its seal is audited to ensure specified consumer safeguards. In the case of TRUSTe, to get the right to apply their seal of approval, a website must include a comprehensive privacy statement.

§6. Non-legal Means of Privacy Protection

I. Technical Solutions

1036. The major protector of an individual's privacy may come not from the law, but from technology itself. The greater use and availability of encryption software itself provides access to ensure a greater level of privacy protection. Software such as Pretty Good Privacy (PGP) is based on what is known as asymmetric encryption. The sender encodes a message with a public key, which the recipient, who must also have PGP, has access to. The recipient can only encode the message with their private key. In addition, the sender can digitally sign their message so that the recipient can see whether the e-mail is from the person it purports to have originated from.[476]

II. Education

1037. Education, especially of vulnerable groups such as children, will also play an important role in privacy protection. Enforcing privacy laws may be difficult because of the attitude of children in relation to giving such information displayed

473. https://www.commsalliance.com.au/Documents/all/codes/c513.
474. https://www.oecd.org/sti/consumer/oecdguidelinesforconsumerprotectioninthecontextofelectroniccommerce1999.htm.
475. www.iia.net.au.
476. A free version can be downloaded from www.pgpi.com.

in, for example, social networking sites. Many parents and children do not realize that firms are gathering information about consumer preferences using such devices as cookies.

§7. CONCLUSION

1038. The impact on privacy by new technologies will also be significant now and in the future for the emerging global economy and especially the pervasive e-business environment. However, it must be acknowledged that getting consistency of privacy protection across all jurisdictions is very difficult to achieve, although not an impossible task. These developments indicate that privacy is likely to be firmly on the e-commerce agenda for quite some time to come. Privacy is a subject-matter which will remain on the agenda of Australian law reformers.[477]

§8. FREEDOM OF INFORMATION LEGISLATION

I. Commonwealth FOI Act

1039. One of the most important aspects of this legislation is that it enables an affected person to find out what information is held about them by government agencies. Administered by the OAIC, the Commonwealth FOIA aims to give to members of the public rights of access to official documents of the Commonwealth government and its agencies.[478]

1040. Australia is both a democratic society as well as an information society. Australians expect to be fully informed about the government's actions, decisions, and policies. Increasingly, they also expect to be able to participate in and influence government policy-making and to scrutinize government decision-making. With the information revolution taking hold, Australia is also an information society in that information has and will take an increasingly central place in society. The ability of all Australians to participate in society is linked to their ability to have access to that information. In general terms, a person who wishes to obtain access to a document usually makes a request in writing to the relevant government agency giving all details necessary to identify the subject document. Commercially valuable documents and confidential business information are generally exempt from disclosure.

1041. Australia established an OAIC in November of 2010. Reforms to the *FOIA* and the passage of the Australian Information Commissioner Act 2010 (Cth) introduced fundamental changes to the way information held by government are managed and accessed by members of the public.

---

477. Richard Leder and Christie Jones, *Australia: Invasions of Privacy' Reforms: Protecting Privacy at the Expense of Freedom of Expression*, Corrs Chambers Westgarth, Newsletter (6 May 2014).

478. *See also* the *Archives Act* 1983 (Cth) which provides for the archiving and access to Commonwealth records.

1042. The Information Commissioner undertakes merits review of decisions by agencies and Ministers to refuse access to documents. The Administrative Appeals Tribunal (AAT) provides a second layer of merits review. This structural reform has resulted in a higher profile for both privacy and FOI and helped to promote understanding and awareness in the community and the public sector.[479]

1043. The FOIA is concerned with access to government information, and arguably, that increases public participation, leading to increased discussion, comment, and review of government activity. The FOIA gives individuals the legal rights of access to government documents, subject to exemptions.

1044. Exemptions and the public interest test. As a result of recent reforms many of the exemptions in the FOIA are now subject to a new single public interest test that is weighted toward disclosure. These 'conditional exemptions' include the exemptions for deliberative processes, agency operations, Commonwealth-State relations, personal privacy, business information, research and the economy. Access to a conditionally exempt document can only be denied if in the circumstances, access at that time would, on balance, be contrary to the public interest.

1045. To guide agencies in deciding the balance of public interest, the FOIA lists factors favouring disclosure and factors that are irrelevant. Factors favouring disclosure include the objects of the FOIA, informing debate on matters of public importance, promoting effective oversight of public expenditure and allowing a person access to their own personal information.

1046. Factors which cannot be considered include potential loss of confidence in or embarrassment to the government, and the high seniority of the author of a document. A decision maker must address the public interest factors in giving reasons for a decision to deny access.

1047. Access to archival records. Much government information is eventually released to the public when it reaches the open access period under the Archives Act 1983 (Cth). The open access period is being reduced from thirty years to twenty years, over a ten-year period commencing on 1 January 2011. The open access period for Cabinet notebooks is being reduced from fifty years to thirty years.

II. State and Territories FOI Acts

1048. Every jurisdiction except the NT has passed FOI legislation.[480] The objects of the FOIA are to enable the public to participate more effectively in governing the State and Territories and to make the persons and bodies that are responsible for State and Territories more accountable to the public.

---

479. For latest FOI reforms and developments, *see* https://www.oaic.gov.au/freedom-of-information/.
480. *Freedom of Information Act* 1982 (Cth); *Freedom of Information Act* 1982 (VIC); *Freedom of Information Act* 1989 (NSW); *Freedom of Information Act* 1989 (ACT); *Freedom of Information*

1049. Applicants who wish to have an FOI access decision reviewed can seek internal review by the agency or go directly to the Information Commissioner. This means that agencies need to ensure the best possible access decision is made at first instance. Information Commissioner reviews will provide a simple, practical and cost-efficient system for external merits review. Most reviews will be carried out without holding a formal hearing. Agencies and ministers must use their best endeavours to assist the Information Commissioner to make the correct and preferable decision.[481]

Act 1991 (TAS); *Freedom of Information Act* 1991 (SA); *Freedom of Information Act* 1992 (WA); and *Freedom of Information Act* 1992 (QLD). For latest versions of the legislation in each of the States and Territories, *see* https://www.oaic.gov.au/freedom-of-information/the-foi-act/other-foi-jurisdictions/.

481. https://www.oaic.gov.au/privacy/your-privacy-rights/.

Chapter 2. Privacy in Telecommunications

§1. Introduction

1050. In the context of telecommunications, many of the same laws that govern personal privacy apply equally to privacy in telecommunications.

§2. Telecommunications Act

1051. The telecommunications legislative regime contains provisions that relate to the protection of information. The Telecommunications Act 1991 (Cth) regulates service providers, such as phone companies, who are required to maintain confidentiality. Exemptions from this requirement exist to cover situations of an emergency or to meet the needs of criminal law enforcement. The Privacy Commissioner has the responsibility of monitoring compliance with the Act. The various participants in telecommunications are classified according to whether they are carriers or service providers, with most provisions of the Act dealing with carriers. Carriers include those who own the telecommunications infrastructure, the network units, which include the transmission facilities and line links to establish connections between various points across the country.

1052. Service providers are of two types: CSPs and content service providers. Carriage service providers supply a 'listed carriage service' to the public utilizing a network unit provided by one or more of the carriers. A 'listed carriage service' is one with at least one of its points located in Australia. While many provisions of the Telecommunications legislation apply to CSPs, most of these deal with CSPs who operate a 'standard telephone service'.

1053. Content service providers use the listed carriage service to provide a 'content service' to the public. A content service can involve educational, entertainment, information, or other material. ISPs are CSPs, while anyone operating a website is arguably a content service provider. The Broadcasting Services Amendment (Online Services) Act 1999 (Cth) uses the same definitions, likewise regarding ISP as CSPs.

1054. 'Eligible' CSPs must subscribe to the Telecommunications Ombudsman scheme.

1055. Carriers and CSPs must protect the confidentiality of communications. The disclosure or use of protected information is authorized in limited circumstances (e.g., disclosure or use for purposes relating to the enforcement of the criminal law). An authorized recipient of protected information may only disclose or use the information for an authorized purpose. Certain record-keeping requirements are imposed in relation to authorized disclosures or uses of information.

1056. Section 112 of the Telecommunications Act 1997 (Cth) provides for the development of industry codes and standards in a range of consumer protection and privacy areas. Under sections 117 and 134 of the Telecommunications Act 1997 (Cth), the Information Commissioner must be consulted on codes and standards which cover privacy. The codes are voluntary, but the ACMA has the power to direct entities within its jurisdiction to comply with a code.

1057. The industry code that deals with privacy in the telecommunications industry is the Telecommunications Consumer Protection Industry Code provides the code of conduct for privacy in the telecommunications industry.

1058. Part 13 of the Telecommunications Act 1997 (Cth) sets out rules for carriers, CSPs and others in their use and disclosure of personal information. What constitutes personal information will vary, depending on what can reasonably be ascertained.

1059. The Telecommunications Act 1997 (Cth) contains provisions designed to safeguard the privacy and confidentiality of customer information, including contents of communications, carriage services supplied to customers, and affairs and personal particulars of customers.[482] Carriers and CSPs must do their best to prevent telecommunications networks and facilities from being used to commit offences. The disclosure or use of protected information is authorized in limited circumstances (e.g., disclosure or use for purposes relating to the public interest and the enforcement of the criminal law). An authorized recipient of protected information may only disclose or use the information for an authorized purpose.

1060. The TIAA prohibits the interception of communications passing over a telecommunications system. It specifies the circumstances and conditions in which telecommunications can be lawful intercepted including for maintenance of telecommunication services and law enforcement.

§3. Other Legislation

1061. Depending upon the context, many other Commonwealth, State and Territory laws as well as common law doctrines are relevant to the privacy protection of telecommunications. For example, one may be under a contractual obligation to keep information private or under a duty of care to do so. In other circumstances, the information may be confidential, and the use of unsecure telecommunications to send the information may be actionable. In other cases, it will be the content of what is communicated that will be involved, for example, using telecommunications to conduct online gambling or to send prohibited content such as child pornography.

1062. In commercial contexts, the Australian Competition and Consumer Law 2010 (Cth) Schedule 2 operates against conduct that is misleading and deceptive,

482. *Telecommunications Act* 1997 (Cth) Section 270.

likely to mislead or deceive, or in breach of specific practices such as pyramid sales. If the conduct involves the sale of securities, then laws governing the sale of securities online will come into play.[483]

§4. Criminal Laws

I. Commonwealth Criminal Laws

1063. The Cybercrime Act 2001 (Cth) also has implications for privacy. One of the most controversial aspects of the Cybercrime Act 2001 (Cth) is its expanded powers of investigation.[484] These powers include allowing a magistrate to make an assistance order that requires a specified person (including the owner of a computer system) to provide such information and assistance as is necessary and reasonably practicable to enable access to copying, or printing of data. Computer equipment and storage devices can be examined off-site where it is more efficient and effective to do so. Officers can copy all data on a computer if some of the data contains evidential material or if there are reasonable grounds to suspect it contains such material. Search warrants can be used to access data accessible from the search premises (including data not physically stored at the search premises).[485]

1064. The Act also allows for 'assistance orders' whereby a magistrate may order an individual or company to surrender passwords or keys to facilitate an investigation. No protection is given of commercially sensitive data.

II. State and Territory Criminal Laws

1065. The States and Territories have also initiated criminal law reforms that account for advances in telecommunications as in the Commonwealth federal legislation. NSW has passed legislation based on *the* Model Criminal Code Project (Crimes Amendment (Computer Offences) Act 2001 (NSW)). The Crimes (Computers and Forgery) Amendment Act 1989 (NSW) created new computer-specific offences, including 'unlawful access to data in computer' and 'damaging data'. A more severe penalty occurs where the unauthorized access to data concerns data that the offender knows or ought reasonably to know relates to:

---

483. *See* Australian Securities and Investments Corporation (ASIC) which has initiated policy initiatives, including Interim Policy Statement 162: Licensing of Internet discussion sites; Policy Statement 141: Offer of securities over the Internet; and Policy Statement 107: Electronic Prospectuses issued on the Internet or on the computer networks or CD-Rom or floppy disk.

484. In fact, some fear that the Act goes too far and would catch otherwise innocuous uses of information technology and lead to government harassment and interference in what should be legitimate activity. *See, e.g.,* Electronic Frontiers Australia (EFA) comment on the Cybercrimes legislation, https://www.efa.org.au/Issues/Privacy/security.html.

485. *See* Joint Committee on National Crime Authority, investigation on law enforcement implications of new technology, https://www.aph.gov.au/Parliamentary_Business/Committees/Joint/Former_Committees/acc/completed_inquiries/1999-02/itlaw/index.

- confidential government information in relation to security, defence or intergovernmental relations; or
- the existence or identity of any confidential source of information in relation to the enforcement or administration of the law; or
- the enforcement or administration of the criminal law; or
- the maintenance or enforcement of any lawful method or procedure for protecting public safety; or
- the personal affairs of any person (whether living or deceased); or
- trade secrets; or
- records of a financial institution; or
- information (other than trade secrets) that has a commercial value to any person that could be destroyed or diminished if disclosed.[486]

1066. In Victoria, the Crimes (Computers) Act 1988 (Vic) amended the provisions dealing with 'obtaining property by deception' by adding a new section 81 that provides that 'deception' includes: 'an act or thing done or omitted to be done with the intention of causing: (1) a computer system; or (2) a machine that is designed to operate by means of payment or identification – to make a response that the person doing or omitting to do the act or thing is not authorized to cause the computer system or machine to make'.

1067. Similar reforms are found in the Summary Offences Amendment Act 1989 (SA), Criminal Law Amendment Act 1990 (WA), Criminal Law Amendment Act 1990 (Tas); Crimes (Amendment) Act (No. 4) 1985 (ACT), and on the Commonwealth level in amendments to the Crimes Act 1914 (Cth).

§5. Industry Codes

1068. The Telecommunications Act 1997 (Cth) encourages the development of industry codes and gives the ACA the power to prepare a legally enforceable industry standard if no acceptable code is developed by industry.

1069. These industry codes generally must be consistent with the APP.

1070. One of the most influential codes is that of the IIA. Its members include telecommunications carriers, content providers and publishers, web developers, e-commerce traders and solutions providers, hardware vendors, system integrators, banks, insurance underwriters, Internet law firms, ISPs, and education and training institutions.[487]

486. *See generally* M. Jackson, *Hughes on Data Protection in Australia* Ch. 6 (2d ed., Lawbook Co., 2001).
487. https://www.commsalliance.com.au/Documents/all/codes/internet_and_mobile_codes.

§6. SPECIFIC APPLICATIONS

I. Spam Legislation

1071. One of the major problems of telecommunications privacy is how to control spam or unwanted advertising. Many experts believe you can never eliminate all spam.[488]

1072. It has been estimated that up to one-third of all Internet traffic is monopolized by spam.[489] With the growth of the Short Message Service (SMS) and other applications (apps) in the mobile-marketing industry, the problem of spam is likely to become even worse.

1073. Australia has passed anti-spam legislation in the form of the Spam Act 2003 (Cth) and the Spam (Consequential Amendments) Act 2003 (Cth). The Spam Act 2003 (Cth) regulates unsolicited commercial electronic messages in Australia. Commercial electronic messages can be e-mails, SMS messages, Multimedia Messaging Service (MMS) messages, instant messaging messages, or any other similar messages.

1074. The Spam Act 2003 (Cth) sets out that commercial electronic messages must have the following features:

- *Consent.* The message must be sent with the recipient's consent. They may give express consent, or consent may be inferred from their conduct and 'existing business or other relationships'.
- *Identify.* The message must contain clear and accurate information about the person or organization that authorized the sending of the message.
- *Unsubscribe.* The message must contain a functional 'unsubscribe' facility to allow the recipient to opt out from receiving a message from that source in the future.

1075. Financial penalties for breaches of the Spam Act 2003 (Cth) are severe and the maximum penalties for ancillary liability are the same as those for direct liability. Repeat offenders, however, will be more severely penalized, with organizations liable to pay up to AUD 1.7 million per day. The penalty provisions of the legislation came into force in 2004. At that time, Australia was tenth in the ranking of spam-relaying countries for e-mail spam, according to the Sophos list. For the 2008 calendar year, Australia had fallen to thirty-second.[490]

---

488. *See, e.g.*, E.E. Clark, *Spam, Courts and Crusaders*, 15 eLaw Practice 44–46 (July 2002) and M. Mangalindan, *Cut the Spam and Win Big*, Australian Financial Review 38 (24 Jun. 2002).
489. *Ibid.* Mangalindan. *See also* Report on Spam, www.noie.gov.au.
490. *See* Sophos website at https://community.sophos.com/products/unified-threat-management/f/mail-protection-smtp-pop3-antispam-and-antivirus/93858/how-to-lookup-ip-to-see-if-blacklisted.

1076. From 28 December 2012, the value of a penalty unit for calculating financial penalties increased from AUD 110 to AUD 170. The penalty unit value had not been adjusted since 1997. The civil penalties that apply for contraventions of the Spam Act 2003 (Cth) are calculated using penalty units. This means that all financial penalties calculated using penalty units under the Spam Act 2003 (Cth) are higher for breaches of the legislation that occur on or after this date.

1077. The Act provides a range of enforcement options and the ACMA determines an appropriate action on a case-by-case basis. Formal warnings are used by the ACMA to indicate concerns about alleged contraventions and allow for the business or individual to take compliance action to prevent any future contraventions. For example, the ACMA gave McDonald's a warning in December for breaching the Spam Act 2003 (Cth). The warning related to McDonald's role in causing unsolicited commercial electronic messages to be sent through a 'send-to-friend' facility and its role in causing a commercial electronic message to be sent without a functional unsubscribe facility.

1078. 'Send-to-friend' facilities usually operate by allowing visitors to a company's website to nominate a recipient (the friend) to receive a pre-determined e-mail from the company, but which appears in the sender and reply-to addresses to come from the visitor's e-mail account. For example, McDonald's 'send-to-friend' promotion allowed visitors to e-mail links for McDonald's-themed games to their friends.

1079. Under the Spam Act 2003 (Cth), commercial electronic messages cannot be sent without express (or reasonably inferred) consent from the recipient of the message. The Act restricts companies from sending, or causing to be sent, a commercial electronic message unless the company has obtained this consent. Even if the company is not itself regarded the sender of the message, companies can still face ancillary liability for aiding, abetting, procuring or counselling the sending of unsolicited commercial e-mails.

1080. Commercial electronic messages are required to include information which clearly and accurately identifies the company and offer an unsubscribe option to allow recipients to opt out from receiving commercial electronic messages.

1081. Enforceable undertakings may be offered to the ACMA at any time and provide the opportunity for a business or individual to formalize its commitment to compliance with the Spam Act 2003 (Cth). The ACMA may also give an infringement notice in relation to civil penalty provisions. In addition, the ACMA can lodge proceedings in the Federal Court, including seeking an injunction. The legislation sets out penalties of up to AUD 1.1 million a day for repeat corporate offenders.

1082. In December 2008, the ACMA commenced its first court action against a number of defendants.

1083. In the only previous proceeding brought by the ACMA under the Spam Act 2003 (Cth), the Federal Court in 2006 ordered Clarity1 Pty. Ltd. and Mr Wayne Mansfield to pay AUD 4.5 million and AUD 1 million, respectively, for sending unsolicited e-mails and for using harvested address lists. In May 2009, the ACMA was granted interlocutory orders in the case. These orders required the respondents to refrain from a variety of activity involving the use of dating websites, including the use of fictitious profiles, using photographs without permission, and contacting website users.[491]

II. Combatting Spam

1084. One possible solution to fight spam is to file a complaint with the Privacy Commissioner. In some cases, consumer crusaders are coming to the rescue in the form of individuals and groups who have devoted considerable time in educating the public or fighting spam. Examples of groups devoted to fighting spam including Junkbusters, The Network Abuse Clearing House (www.abuse.net), Coalition Against Unsolicited Commercial e-mail (CAUCE), and Coalition Against Unsolicited Bulk E-mail (www.caube.org.au). These groups have helped to raise public consciousness about the problem of spam.

1085. In other cases, technology is providing a partial solution to the spam problem. For example, software now exists that constantly updates its spam list via a full-time data centre monitoring the company's system to combat spam attacks. Postini Corp. offers a service that routes companies' e-mail through a computer system using a set of statistical techniques to define spam.[492] Unfortunately, such technological solutions often tend to be of limited use and run the danger of keeping out legitimate e-mail messages.

1086. The industry itself has taken steps to combat spam. Examples include the ADMA and the IIA Code of Practice that prohibit spam.

1087. Regulatory agencies such as the ACCC also have a role to play in educating the public, conducting Internet sweeps, initiating representative actions, approving industry codes, and ensuring that consumer views are considered. In some cases, the sending of unsolicited e-mail (e.g., the use of a false originating address or a false or misleading subject line in an e-mail message) may constitute action that is misleading and deceptive or likely to mislead or deceive and thereby be in breach of the TPA and its counterpart in the Fair Trading Acts of the States and Territories.[493]

491. https://www.acma.gov.au/media-releases-0.
492. M. Mangalindan, *Cut the Spam and Win Big*, Australian Financial Review, 38 (24 Jun. 2002).
493. An example is the action in the US against domain name selling giant VeriSign (thanks to an AUD 21 billion stock purchase of Network Solutions in March 2000) which had been sending bulk e-mail that appeared to be an expiry and renewal notice for their domain name. A US Federal Court ordered the distribution stopped, ruling that this e-mail could mislead consumers into renewing

1088. Common law actions may also be applicable. For example, in *Intel Corp. v. Hamidi*, Cal. No. S103781, review granted 27 March (2002), the California Supreme Court granted review of lower court decision that upheld a claim of trespass to chattels claiming as damages the time its employees had to spend reading and blocking spam e-mail messages sent from an outside party. In some cases, those who bombard another with spam may be in breach of increasingly broad cybercrime laws.

1089. On an individual level, education and sound responsible e-mail use is probably the best protection. Users should not open e-mails that they suspect and identify as spam. Users should never click on boxes requesting further information and certainly should never accept what is on offer via spam e-mail.

1090. Assuming one can find the offender, it is also possible to use procedures such as small claims courts and tribunals as well as group actions against unwanted spam. Another strategy is to use a separate Hotmail or Yahoo! account for online purchases. If that account is attacked with spam, one can always abandon it and set up another one without exposing the personal mailbox. If you register your own domain name, you can use different e-mail addresses for different accounts.[494]

III. Cookies

1091. Cookies are files sent over the web to the PC of a user. The cookies usually contain the name of the user and profile information, such as a record of clicks made in surfing the Internet and can be read back by the information provider. Some cookies can track consumer behaviour across sites and privacy and consumer advocates contend that this should not be allowed without first gaining the consumer's permission.

1092. In July 2002 the EU passed Directive 2002/58/EC which provided permission for websites to install cookies in the browsers of users. Users must be given notice plus an opportunity to opt out. In December 2009 the EU amended the Directive to provide that users must provide their consent before websites can download non-essential cookies onto the user's machine via the browser (2009/136/EC). On 25 May 2011 all EU countries were required to implement the Directive. This was extended for a year given only three EU countries had met the deadline. The Directive applies to all organizations that download cookies onto the machines of users based within and without the EU. UK organizations could be subject to enforcement notices and actions, and potentially a fine of up to GPB 500,000.

1093. An ethical website will inform consumers about the fact that a cookie is placed on the consumer's PC and what the content is. Cookies should not contain

---

their domain name with a new supplier. In Australia, the ACCC took similar action against the Internet Name Group that had engaged in similar conduct in relation to consumers.

494. Visit www.whowherelycos.com and have your e-mail address removed. E.E. Clark, *supra* 44–46.

sensitive data such as credit card numbers. The use of cookies and other tracking devices may have legal consequences. Some cookies are utilized only for the session in which the online transaction takes place in order to make the site more customer-friendly. However, cookies may also be used to collect personal information without the individual's consent.

1094. Analysis of the APP suggests that the use of cookies may breach the Privacy Act 1988 (Cth). The APP provide that collection of information must be fair and not unreasonably intrusive. An example given of unfair collection is 'collecting an individual's mouse trail' or websites visited such as cookies or web bugs without telling the individual.

1095. Depending on the circumstances, other APP may also apply. For example, the APP provide that an organization must take reasonable steps to protect the security of information and organizations should provide the option of interacting anonymously whenever it is lawful and practical to do so.

1096. Some implications of spam legislation in general include: (1) cases where consumer awareness or concern about cookies is not high. (2) The recency of Australia's privacy law, government authorities do not have the resources to sufficiently monitor compliance with the new law. (3) The longer term trend where businesses will need to be increasingly sensitive to consumer privacy and that will include cookie use. Privacy and other consumer issues will be key ingredients to building consumer trust in this new e-commerce environment. (4) Education of both businesses and consumers about legal compliance in this new area of commercial activity is required. Useful guidelines for both business and consumers can be found on key government and industry websites.[495]

IV. Web Bugs, Spiders, Data Aggregation or Screen Scraping and Data Mining

1097. Bugs, spiders, and other data aggregation and mining devices involve the process of grabbing information from another's website and incorporating it into one's own without permission or any agreement from the other party.[496] A web robot or 'spider' is a software program that roams the Internet, gathering information from searchable web databases.

1098. The use of web bugs, spiders, and data mining devices may give rise to legal complaints including, copyright violation, trespass, fraud, unjust enrichment, and in some cases even criminal law violations. It is also possible that a court may find that such conduct is misleading or deceptive or likely to mislead or deceive in breach of the Australian Consumer Law 2010 (Cth). A second possibility may be to

495. https://www.ipc.on.ca/privacy-individuals/your-privacy-and-big-data/.
496. *See* Major Canadian Report on Data Mining Office of the Information and Privacy Commissioner of Ontario, www.ipc.on.ca/english/pubpres/sum per cent5Fpap/papers/datamine.htm.

use contract law, putting on the website 'No Trespass Signs' and strongly worded 'Conditions of Use' policies for all who access the site. Enforcing such provisions, however, may not be easy.

V. Unauthorized Access to E-Mail

1099. A common element of much of e-commerce is the use of e-mail. E-mail is particularly vulnerable because it is written in Simple Mail Transport Protocol (SMTP) that is encoded in plain text with American Standard Code for Information Interchange (ASCII), which in turn is readable by most computers.

1100. Unauthorized access to someone else's e-mail can give rise to a host of legal issues, depending on the context. If the information is confidential, a breach of confidence action could be brought. If the information is protected by contract, then contract remedies would ensue. If one intercepted the e-mail, then the TIAA may come into play.

1101. If the conduct involved unauthorized access to a computer, then various criminal acts could even come into play. For criminal matters, see the Crimes Legislation Amendment Act 1989 (Cth) which amended the Crimes Act 1914 (Cth), outlaws wrongful gaining of access to computers,[497] altering data,[498] or impeding access to computers.[499] The Crimes Act 1914 (Cth) also prohibits the use of communications for improper purposes, the intentional or reckless causing of communications in the course of carriage to be received by a person or service other than to whom it was directed, and the wrongful sending of signals to satellite without lawful authority or excuse.[500]

1102. Monitoring the e-mail and Internet use of employees is also arguably a breach of the Telecommunications Act 1979 (Cth). The Act prohibits the interception of communications passing over a telecommunications service (section 7).

1103. It is unlikely that retaining e-mails and storing them on a server or other digital storage device would breach the Act. This is because storing messages is unlikely to constitute electromagnetic energy passing over a telecommunications system. Storage is not itself part of the communication. An employer's computer network may be viewed as a 'telecommunications service' – a system for carrying communications by either guided or unguided electromagnetic energy. There has so far been no case in Australia that has decided the issue of whether the screening of e-mails would constitute an infringement of the Telecommunications Act 1979 (Cth). A key issue is whether employees are advised of the screening. It should be part of the employment contract and accepted as a condition of employment.

---

497. *Crimes Act* s. 76B and D.
498. *Ibid.*
499. *Ibid.*
500. *Ibid.*

§7. Conclusion

1104. Fundamental structural changes are occurring in relation to privacy and telecommunications. Not only is there a need to balance business efficacy and consumer expectations, but there is also the question of whether the online environment is sufficiently unique to require special privacy protection. The more conservative view is that online and traditional commerce should be subject to the same legal regime; that in the end, privacy is privacy is privacy. Given the broad language encompassed in the privacy principles as well as the flexibility inherent in Australian Consumer Law Act 2010 (Cth) (ACL), this makes sense. This structural change also suggests a different mind-set. No longer will the regulatory regime be focused primarily on government a collection of information. Privacy is of concern generally, and both public and private sector organizations should comply with public and consumer expectations. This, in turn, means that more attention should be given to finding out what consumers want and expect in relation to safeguarding their privacy.

1105. It is observed that countries and firms that have an adequate level of privacy protection will have a marketing edge and competitive advantage in the emerging global economy. Regulators and industry seem now intent on working together to lift the privacy bar. The Privacy Code of the IIA is an example of the recognition that the wide adoption of the Internet by consumers depends upon building and winning the trust and confidence of consumers that their privacy expectations will be met. This bar will increasingly be enforced by sanctions, whether from legislation, the Privacy Commissioner, industry code, or other source.

1106. Firms will have to get a lot more serious about knowledge management, especially as it concerns collecting of information on customers and purchasing information from third parties. One example of an area where this will be required is the integration of policies that cover the increasingly common 'bricks and clicks' environment.

1107. It may be expected that in future organizations will apply the same privacy protection policies advertised online to the off-line environment as well. This means that policies, practices, audit checks, information systems, and customer must work together with a degree of integration and consistency that many organizations have yet to achieve. All firms will have to inculcate a strong culture of privacy protection. This will mean that people at all levels of the organization must understand the importance of privacy and compliance with privacy laws and customer expectations about privacy. This privacy is also being extended to mobile applications to reflect the rapid growth and development of m-commerce.

1108. When collecting data, businesses will have to be far more purposeful in thinking about what data they need, where they are collecting it, how it is stored, how it is maintained and kept accurate, and so on. A state-of-the-art and customer-focused privacy policy will become a business asset and will be used by businesses as a marketing tool. Clear communication with customers about privacy needs and expectations will become increasingly important.

1109. More firms are now hiring a Chief Privacy Officer to oversee and manage an organization's privacy policy. Getting a privacy policy is one thing; making it work is another. Increasingly, major corporations are appointing privacy officers. Businesses and governments are coming to recognize that privacy policies are not static instruments. They will have to be reviewed from time to time to ensure they remain up-to-date and that they comply with the law and meet the overall needs of the organization.

1110. Technology will continue to be both a problem and a solution. Technological advances such as geo-tracking will continue to challenge privacy boundaries. At the same time, new technology will also come to the aid of consumers and enhance the level of privacy protection.

1111. Finally, it must be acknowledged that getting consistency of privacy protection, especially across all jurisdictions, is very difficult to achieve. Yet, international standards must, of necessity, emerge. Otherwise, when strict spam laws such as Australia's are enacted, spam sources simply move to another country, although this does not mean Australian citizens receive less spam mail.

1112. As Internet and e-commerce grows, Australian privacy regulation will have to meet international standards. The only constructive way forward is to keep pushing for a global convergence of privacy regulation. As concluded by a recent Federal Trade Commission report,[501] it is not desirable for each country to impose a separate privacy regime. Any other course of action would 'encourage a race to the bottom, reducing protection on a global scale'. It would also frustrate law enforcement efforts, impede informed decision-making by consumers, and deprive consumers of meaningful access to judicial recourse. Eventually, we will need an international agreement if global online business is to become a reality.

501. A Federal Trade Commission Report, Consumer Protection in the Global Electronic Marketplace: Looking Ahead (2000), at https://www.ftc.gov/reports/consumer-protection-global-electronic-marketplace-looking-ahead.

Part VII. Cybercrime Law Enforcement

Chapter 1. Legal Developments in Cybercrime

§1. Introduction

1113. Legal developments in computer-related crime raises the traditional difficulty of not only having to match what appear to be causes of action established in another century but also in overcoming the challenges posed by the digital medium. While prosecution and evidential requirements have largely been overcome by the creation of new, technologically advanced methods of policing and detection, there have been advancements in the field of cryptology and other methods of masking digital criminal activities. Whereas computer crime has traditionally involved the illegal entry into and manipulation of computer systems, cybercrime increasingly involves activity on the Internet and crossing multiple national and international borders and jurisdictions. The latter issue of jurisdiction brings greater levels of complexity in detection and enforcement. Governments at all levels in Australia have also struggled to attain an appropriate level of human skills, computer systems and other resources to keep up with the rapidly growing and increasingly technical nature of these various new forms of criminal activity.

§2. Definition of Criminal Acts and Punishment

1114. A crime (or offence) is a legal wrong that can be followed by criminal proceedings that result in punishment of the perpetrator of the crime.[502] This definition of crime is the basis of criminal law of the Australian and other common law legal systems. A criminal proceeding is different to a civil proceeding in that the criminal law requires the perpetrator to be found guilty of the offence beyond reasonable doubt.

1115. The legislature determines criminal acts based on factors that define a criminal act. The first is that the act must be injurious to the public in general. The second is that the act must be of a moral wrongdoing.[503]

---

502. H. Disney, *Criminal Law* 27 (2d ed., Stevens & Sons 1983).
503. P. Brett, L. Waller & C.R. Williams, *Criminal Law; Text and Cases* (7th ed., Butterworths 1993).

1116. When a person commits a crime, that person does so with the necessary elements of criminal culpability such as deliberately intending to commit the act, being reckless, or negligent in committing the act.

1117. Punishing the perpetrator of the criminal law has three competing aims: (1) to provide retribution to the victims and others of the crime, (2) to deter others from committing the crime, and (3) to reform criminals. Retribution theory provides that a crime is a wrong that justifies the infliction on the criminal of a certain amount of punishment. The deterrence theory is that the punishment deters people from committing crimes. The reformative theory sees crime as a social disease for which a cure can and should be found.

§3. Sources of Criminal Law

1118. As a federal common law system, the criminal laws of Australia are found in Commonwealth legislation,[504] the legislation of the States[505] and Territories,[506] and in the decisions of the Courts. While the original colonies had received common law and statutory criminal law from the UK, most Australian jurisdictions today have adopted their own criminal laws.

1119. There has been an increasing tendency for Australian legislation, such as the TPA, the Corporations Law 2010 (Cth) and IP laws to include a mixture of civil and criminal remedies rather than relying on just one type of remedy, thereby bridging the traditional divide between the two. But this creation of a situation whereby different standards of proof may be required for a different part of the same prosecution has itself created significant difficulty both for litigants and for State prosecutors.

1120. In general, criminal offences can be classified according to their degree of seriousness. Indictable offences are more serious and usually are triable before a judge and jury. Summary offences are less serious and are usually tried before a magistrate.

§4. Principles of Criminal Liability

1121. A series of principles underlie the criminal law in Australia and are relevant to its application to e-commerce, and to IP law and cyberspace in general. The principles being:[507]

504. *See, e.g., Crimes Act* 1914 (Cth); *Criminal Code Act* 1995 (Cth).
505. *See, e.g., Crimes Act* 1900 (NSW) as amended; *Criminal Code Act* 1899 (Qld); *Crimes Act* 1958 (Vic); *Criminal Law Consolidation Act* 1933 (SA); The Criminal Code; and *Criminal Code Act* 1913 (WA).
506. *See, e.g.,* the Australian Capital Territory which follows the *Crimes Act* 1900 (NSW), as amended in the laws of the Territory.
507. D. Walker, *The Oxford Companion to Law* 317 (Clarendon Press 1980).

- there shall there be no crime unless the law specifies the conduct done as such hence immoral, antisocial or evil conduct is not criminal unless it falls within a category of crime;
- criminal provisions must be clear and unambiguous to give fair warning of what conduct is liable to penalty;
- criminal statutes must be interpreted strictly and not extended by analogy; and
- unless a statute directs it, a criminal provision must not be retrospective, thereby penalizing what was innocent when it was done.

§5. Establishing Criminal Liability

1122. The criminal law carries with it a significantly greater range of sanctions than does the law of torts. On conviction, a court may make orders ranging from financial penalties through to custodial sentences, with the potential severity mandating a stringent and complex legal process. In addition, to establish a criminal offence, there must be temporal coincidence of the mens rea (intention to do wrong) and actus (or action which constitutes the offence charged) by the accused.

1123. Criminal intent is an important issue where prosecution is attempted under the criminal law for computer and computer-related crime. It will be seen that many of the earlier computer fraud cases brought in Australia and elsewhere failed because the State or Crown could not establish intent and/or could not show that the act alleged had, in law, occurred. The distinction is made that information on a computer was used but nothing was taken and so no crime has been committed. Other decisions stretched the existing law by finding that the defendant in using the computer without permission had stolen electricity.[508]

1124. Unauthorized access to another's computer system, especially where there is no deletion or alteration of data, is generally actionable under common law provisions dealing with fraud, forgery, theft, damage to property, and similar doctrines such as trespass. Every Australian jurisdiction has reformed its criminal laws to accommodate designated harms caused by computer crime.

§6. Capacity

1125. The rule at common law is that children under the age of seven could not commit a crime because it is assumed, they could not form the necessary intent. Today, by statute this has been raised to the age of ten in most Australian jurisdictions. Between 10 and 14 a child can be convicted of a crime if it can be shown that the child knew the act was wrong.

508. *See generally* Lim, Yee Fen, *Cyberspace Law: Commentaries and Materials* Ch. 7 (Oxford University Press 2002); R.A. Brown, *Computer-Related Crime in Australia*, in *Essays on Computer Law* 217–223 (G. Hughes ed. Longman Professional 1990).

1126. The Acts Interpretation Act 1901 (Cth) together with similar State and Territory Acts define a 'person' as including a corporation.[509] Corporations may also be liable for crimes. To make the corporation liable, the act must be done by someone with appropriate authority where the acts of that official are taken as the acts of the corporation.

§7. Criminal Procedure

1127. At the Commonwealth level, offences in the Criminal Code Act 1995 (Cth) and the TIAA cover crimes directed at computers and ICT, such as unauthorized access and distributed denial of service (DDoS) attacks. These offences are based on model provisions agreed to by all jurisdictions. The Criminal Code also includes offences for the misuse of telecommunications services for criminal purposes, such as the online distribution of child exploitation material. These offence provisions are supported by a range of powers which can be exercised by law enforcement and national security agencies in the detection, disruption and investigation of those offences.

1128. Commonwealth, State and Territory laws have offences for crimes directed at computers and ICT. States and Territories have primary responsibility for laws dealing with online versions of personal and property crimes, such as stalking, theft and fraud. Legal frameworks for State and Territory agencies to detect, disrupt and investigate offences also exist.[510]

1129. The criminal procedure governing criminal matters varies depending upon the governmental agency involved and on the seriousness of the alleged crime. Criminal prosecutions differ from civil cases in that Crown or public prosecutors bring the criminal action on behalf of the State or public. Private citizens become involved in criminal matters, for example, when they file a complaint with the police.

1130. Criminal procedure typically commences with an investigation, which in the case of computer offences may involve highly skilled computer forensic investigators. One of the major difficulties in relation to computer crime is the challenge of forensic investigation.[511] The US Department of Justice report identified four major challenges in relation to forensic evidence collection and analysis:[512]

(1) Finding *evidence* in the 'information ocean'.

509. http://classic.austlii.edu.au/au/legis/cth/consol_act/aia1901230/.
510. *Ibid.*
511. B. Etter, *The Forensic Challenges of E-crime*, Current Commentary No. 3, 10/2001, Australasian Centre for Policing Research, Adelaide, 2001.
512. US Department of Justice, *Electronic Crime Needs Assessment for State and Local Enforcement*, National Institute of Justice Research Report, NCJ 186276, March 2001, Washington, DC.

(2) *Anonymity*. Computer networks permit persons to easily maintain anonymity and most web surfers have a ‘handle’, a false name or identity.
(3) *Traceability*. Refers to how difficult it is to establish the source and destination of communications on computers and communication networks, such as the Internet. Traceability is becoming even more difficult because of the proliferation and easy availability of multiple communications providers as well as faking identities of service providers.
(4) *Encryption*. As a vast majority of data and communications will be encrypted. Encryption can hinder law enforcement investigations and increase costs because of the problems associated with cracking the encryption.

Chapter 2. Cybercrime: Substantive and Procedural Law

§1. Introduction

1131. Australian government and industry are generally positive about the growth and development of e-commerce. At the same time, it must be realized that technology is but a tool. Like any tool, it can be used for good or for ill. Computers can play various roles in criminal conduct: as a weapon, as a tool, or as a storage facility for criminals. As weapons, they are used to inflict damage or steal information. The law is concerned with achieving a balance that promotes the benefits of modern technology while at the same time minimizing the potential harm. Indeed, so powerful are today's technological developments and so inter-connected is the world, that public interest considerations today loom larger than ever in discussions of the best way forward. The cybercrimes identified here are examples only, and no attempt has been made to be exhaustive.

§2. Definition and Reach of Cybercrime

I. Definition

1132. There is no universally accepted definition of *cybercrime*. In Australia, the term 'cybercrime' is used to describe both:

(1) crimes directed at computers or other ICTs (such as hacking and denial of service attacks); and
(2) crimes where computers or ICTs are an integral part of an offence (such as online fraud, identity theft and the distribution of child exploitation material).[513]

1133. The National Plan to Combat Cybercrime (2013) provides a consistent strategic direction for agencies involved in combatting cybercrime.[514] This is a national commitment to ensure a safe and more secure digital environment for all Australians with key principles that underpin the approach. An initiative under the Plan is the ACORN that will make it easier for the public to report cybercrime, get the information they need to protect themselves and ensure agencies can respond more quickly.[515] The ACORN will also give a clearer picture of the scope and nature of cybercrime affecting Australians and enable better operational and policy responses.[516]

513. *See* Australia (2013) *National Plan to Combat Cybercrime* at http://apo.org.au/node/35312. (APO = Analysis and Policy Observatory)
514. *Ibid.*
515. *See* Online scams or fraud https://www.acorn.gov.au/learn-about-cybercrime/online-scams-or-fraud.
516. Australia (2013) *supra*. *See also* Australian Commonwealth AGD, *National Plan to Combat Cybercrime* (2013), Canberra: AGPS. *See* Appendix B. Summary of Initiatives.

1134. Responsibility for combating the different forms of cybercrime in Australia is shared between Australian Government law enforcement agencies state and territory agencies. All jurisdictions have criminal laws directed at the various forms of cybercrime. In addition to formal legislation and case law, there are also 'soft law' mechanisms to combat cybercrime such as industry codes, codes of best practice, and best practice guidelines which also seek to prevent or aid in the fight against cybercrime.

II. Nature and Extent of Cybercrime

1135. There are no reliable statistics regarding the amount of cybercrime occurring within Australia. However, given the high levels of connectivity and computer and mobile use in Australia, the level is both significant and increasing. This is evidenced in various reports and studies undertaken in Australia.

1136. According to Australia's National Plan to Combat Cybercrime:

- The number, sophistication and impact of cybercrimes continues to grow and poses a serious and evolving threat to Australian individuals, businesses and governments.
- Although it is difficult to quantify the total costs, evidence from operational agencies suggests that economic costs of cybercrime in Australia are substantial. As many instances of cybercrime go unreported, it is difficult to give an accurate figure. However, non-government estimates put the cost of cybercrime in Australia as high as AUD 2 billion annually.
- Other costs of cybercrime cannot be quantified. No dollar value can reflect the harm caused to victims by the distribution of child exploitation material or the compromise of personal information, or the emotional hardship of being left financially destitute.
- Online criminals can commit crimes across multiple borders in an instant and can target large numbers of victims simultaneously. Tools that have many legitimate uses, like high speed Internet, peer-to-peer file sharing and sophisticated encryption methods, can also help criminals carry out and conceal their activities. Despite these challenges, cybercrime and requires a long term, sustained response from Australian governments.[517]

1137. The Computer Emergency Response Team (CERT) Australia Cybercrime Security Survey 2012 found that:

- Over 20% of organizations are aware of or experienced a cyber incident in the previous twelve months, with 20% of these organizations experiencing more than ten incidents. Of the organizations which know they experienced cyber incidents, 17% suffered from loss of confidential or proprietary information, 16% encountered a DDoS attack, and 10% financial fraud.

517. *Ibid.*

- Over 44% reported the incident to a law enforcement agency, whereas only 13% sought a civil remedy through action from legal counsel.
- Over 20% chose not to report the matter to a law enforcement agency because of the fear of negative publicity.
- The most common responses as to why incidents were successful, were that they used powerful automated attack tools, or exploited unpatched or unprotected software vulnerabilities or misconfigured operating systems, applications or network devices.
- Over half of all organizations have increased their expenditure on IT security in the previous twelve months.[518]

1138. Some examples of computer-related crimes include ransom-ware, DDoS, and data corruption. In ransom-ware the attacks are on encrypted files on the compromised system.[519] The attacks either locks out the victim from the desktop environment and/or the encrypted files in the system backups. The victim is then asked to pay a fine using a payment or money transfer service to obtain the codes to unlock the computer and/or decrypt the data.

1139. In some instances, the ransom-ware may include scare-ware that displays a fake warning screen which claims that the victim's computer has been associated with criminal activity. This tactic is to discourage the victim from reporting the attacks to law enforcement agencies or to CERT. The severity of the damage varied across target organizations. In the worst case about fifteen years' worth of critical business data was lost.

1140. DDoS has been used either to bring attention to events or as a protest or for extortion. The attacker would threaten an attack against a company's website unless a payment was made. Such an attack not only disrupts the company's online activities via its website, but it can also stop clients from doing business with them online. The targets are chosen carefully especially those with websites with the most processing so that it would be difficult to take down the site easily.

1141. An example of the modification of data was reported in 2009 at a Western Australian government department. Two men who were contractors to the department were sharing information regarding an illegal access to the departmental operating system. They created malicious software and commands to hack network security controls to crack a file that would reveal user-names and passwords of departmental staff. They were charged with conspiracy to cause an unauthorized modification of data held in a computer using a carriage service, contrary to section 11.5(1) of the Criminal Code 1995 (Cth). At trial the two were found guilty by a court.

---

518. Australian Government, Cybercrime & Security Survey Report 2012. University of Canberra. https://trove.nla.gov.au/version/192779314.

519. *Ibid.*

1142. The Australian Institute of Criminology's (AIC) nationwide survey assesses the prevalence and nature of computer security incidents experienced by Australian businesses. The report by the Australian Business Assessment of Computer User Security (ABACUS) assesses the effectiveness of information technology security measures in Australian businesses. The survey highlighted that:

- Given that the average Australian household owns a PC or laptop or both (1.61 computers per household in 2009) the opportunity for cybercrime to occur at home is considerable.[520]
- Businesses are at risk. Fourteen per cent of Australian businesses experience one or more incidents of cybercrime in 2006–2007.[521]

1143. Unfortunately, computer crime often goes unreported for many reasons: Business victims fear the loss of control over the cost and direction of the case. Many victims fear the bad public relations – letting others, especially customers or clients, know that their system has been breached. There is also the fear of potential legal liability for loss of customer data and the possible reduction in shareholder value that may be a consequence of a serious breach of security.

§3. Commonwealth Cybercrime Legislation

I. Commonwealth Cybercrime Laws

1144. The Cybercrime Act 2001 (Cth) passed on 27 September 2001 amended the Criminal Code Act 1995 (Cth) through the addition of new updated computer offences based upon the January 2001 Model Criminal Code Damage and Computer Offences Report developed through Commonwealth, State, and Territory cooperation. The Act also repeals the existing offences in Part VIA of the Crimes Act 1914 (Cth), enacted in 1989 and predating existing technologies. The Cybercrime Act 2001 (Cth) provides for enhanced investigation powers relating to the search and seizure of electronically stored data by amending the Crimes Act 1914 (Cth) and Customs Act 1901 (Cth).

1145. Under the Cybercrime Act 2001 (Cth), the new offences include:

- Access or modification of computer data and impairment of electronic communications.
- Unauthorized modification of data. This would catch a person who is reckless as to whether their actions will impair data, for example, circulation of a virus.
- Unauthorized impairment of electronic communications, for example, denial of service attack.

---

520. Paul Skelton, *The 2009 Digital Atlas of Australia* (2009), at https://connectedmag.com.au/2009-digital-atlas-australia/ (6 May 2009).

521. Kelly Richards, *Australian Business Assessment of Computer User Safety Survey* (2009), at https://aic.gov.au/publications/rpp/rpp102.

- Unauthorized access or modification of restricted data, for example, giving password to someone.
- Unauthorized impairment of data on a Commonwealth computer disk or credit card.
- Possession or control of data with intent to commit a computer offence.
- Producing, supplying or obtaining data with intent to commit a computer offence. It is targeted at a situation where preparatory action is taken but the intended offence is not completed.

1146. The Cybercrime Act 2001 (Cth) includes offences that carry penalties of up to ten years, covering: hacking, distribution of viruses, denial of service attacks, unauthorized access with intent to commit a serious offence, misuse of a limited authority, for example, an employee using limited access rights to enter the system and fraudulently transfer funds, and development, supply, or possession of viruses or hacking programs.

1147. The jurisdiction of the Cybercrime Act 2001 (Cth) is very wide. The legislation covers offences where the conduct constituting an offence occurs partly in Australia, where conduct occurs on board an Australian ship or aircraft, and where the person committing the offence is an Australian citizen or an Australian company. In recent years, this has been extended to cover acts committed outside of Australia, but which have consequences within Australia.[522]

1148. The Cybercrime Act 2001 (Cth) has been criticized by some as being too vague and over-reaching. However, the limited number of prosecutions to date suggests that the government has been restrained and conservative in its enforcement.

1149. Another of the most controversial aspects of the Act is its expanded powers of investigation. These include allowing a magistrate to make an assistance order that requires a specified person (including the owner of a computer system) to provide such information and assistance as is necessary and reasonably practicable to enable access to make a copy or print the data. Computer equipment and storage devices can be examined off-site where it is more efficient and effective. Officers can copy all data on a computer if some of the data contains evidential material or if there are reasonable grounds to suspect it contains such material. Search warrants can be used to access data accessible from the search premises (including data not physically stored at the search premises).[523]

---

522. *See Cybercrime Act* 2001 (Cth) s. 15.1.
523. *See also* Joint Committee on National Crime Authority, investigation on law enforcement implications of new technology, https://www.aph.gov.au/Parliamentary_Business/Committees/Joint/Former_Committees/acc/completed_inquiries/1999-02/itlaw/index; EFA comment on the Cybercrimes legislation, https://www.efa.org.au/Publish/efasubm-acc2003.html.

1150. In addition to specific legislation dealing with cybercrime, many other Commonwealth laws may be applied to contexts involving computer-related crime. For example, there are criminal sanctions for more serious breaches of the Cybercrime Act 2001 (Cth)[524] and the TPA.[525]

II. State and Territory Cybercrime Laws

1151. Like the Commonwealth, most of the Australian States and Territories also have passed specific computer crime legislation.[526] Like the Commonwealth cybercrime legislation, NSW has also passed legislation based on the Model Criminal Code Project.[527] The Crimes Amendment (Computer Offences) Act 2001 (NSW) seeks to address three categories of activity:

(1) intentional and unauthorized access or modification of computer data, or impairment of electronic communication to or from a computer, irrespective of whether there is any intention to commit a serious indictable offence;
(2) processing, producing, supplying or obtaining data with intent to commit computer offences; and
(3) intentional and unauthorized access or modification of restricted computer data, impairment of data held in computer disk, credit card or other data storage devices.[528]

1152. In most Australian jurisdictions, the criminal provisions governing fraud now cover both deception in relation to a person and also deception of a computer or machine leading to falsification of computer-stored data, credit cards, and ATM cards.[529] Similarly, the provisions dealing with falsification of documents, which previously applied only to written documents, now cover electronic documents such as data stored on a computer or ATM card.[530] The criminal laws in most jurisdictions have also been amended to include unlawful access to a computer and hacking. In addition, traditional criminal laws dealing with theft, forgery, trespass, and burglary may also be applied to cybercrime contexts.[531]

1153. Queensland is notable for its adoption of a broad definition of cybercrime in its Criminal Code and Civil Liability Amendment Act 2007 (Qld). This broad

---

524. Note that the *Copyright Act* 1968 (Cth) defines 'literary work' as including 'a computer program or compilation of computer programs' (s. 10).
525. *See Trade Practices Act* 1974 (Cth), ss 53–65, which create offences relating to consumer protection. *See also* equivalent legislation in the Fair Trading Acts of most jurisdictions.
526. *See, e.g., Crimes Act* 1958 (Vic), s. 197; *Crimes Act* 1990 (NSW), ss 194, 201; *Criminal Code* WA, ss 441–443, 455; *Criminal Code* (Tas), ss 267–269.
527. *Crimes Amendment (Computer Offences) Act* 2001 (NSW).
528. The New South Wales Act is similar to the UK's *Computer Misuse Act* 1990 at https://www.legislation.gov.uk/id/ukpga/1990/18.
529. *See, e.g., Crimes Act* 1958 (Vic), s. 81(4); *Criminal Code* (Tas), s. 257B.
530. *See, e.g., Crimes Act* 1914 (Cth); *Crimes Act* 1958 (Vic), s. 83A; *Criminal Code* (WA), s. 443.
531. *See, e.g., Criminal Code* (WA), s. 473, in which 'forgery' is defined in such a way that it would cover alteration of computer records.

wording would arguably include all crimes included in the Commonwealth legislation, and its broad wording is designed so that it is technologically neutral and less likely to need updating to account for advances in technology.

1154. Section 408E of the Queensland Act defines *computer hacking and misuse* as the act of a person who uses a restricted computer without the consent of the computer's controller to commit an offence. The maximum penalty is two years imprisonment. He conditions for penalty includes:

- If the person causes or intends to cause detriment or damage, or gains or intends to gain a benefit, the person commits a crime and is liable to imprisonment for five years.
- If the person causes a detriment or damage or obtains a benefit for any person to the value of more than AUD 5,000, or intends to commit an indictable offence, the person commits a crime and is liable to imprisonment for ten years.
- It is a defence to a charge under this section to prove that the use of the restricted computer was authorized, justified or excused by law.

1155. Under the Queensland legislation:

- *Benefit* includes a benefit obtained or delivered to any person.
- *Computer* means all or part of a computer, computer system, or computer network and includes, for example, all external devices connected to the computer in any way or capable of communicating with each other as part of a system or network.
- *Controller* means a person who has the right to control the computer's use.
- *Damage* includes both damage to any computer hardware or software as well as for the alteration, addition, removal, loss, or other damage to information.
- *Information* includes data, file, document, or computer language or coding.
- *Restricted computer* means a computer for which a device or a particular sequence of electronic impulses is necessary in order to gain access, and the controller withholds or takes steps to withhold access to the devise, or knowledge of the code or of the sequence or of the way of producing the code or the sequence from other persons or restricts access to the device or code or sequence to a person or class of persons authorized by the controller.
- *Use* of a restricted computer includes accessing or altering any information stored in, or communicate information directly or indirectly to or from, the restricted computer, or cause a virus to become installed on or to otherwise affect, the computer.

1156. The Queensland legislation was also amended to make it easier to deal with the growing problem of identity theft.

§4. TELECOMMUNICATIONS CRIME

1157. The Commonwealth Crimes Act 1914 (Cth) (Part VIIB and Part 10.6) makes it a criminal offence to interfere with telecommunications, including computer services, the Internet, and computer systems. The Act makes it an offence to interfere with e-mail, tamper with data messages, or cause a telecommunications message to be sent to an unauthorized person.[532] It is also an offence to use a carriage service to menace or harass another person or use a carrier in a way that would be regarded as offensive to a reasonable person.[533] It is also an offence to tamper with or interfere in any way with a facility operated by a carrier.[534]

1158. The Criminal Code 1995 (Cth) makes it an offence to do anything with the intention of dishonestly obtaining a gain or causing a loss to a CSP in connection with the supply of a carriage service. It is also an offence to knowingly risk such a loss.[535] There is also an offence of general dishonesty in relation to a CSP.[536] The Crimes Legislation Amendment (Telecommunications Offences and Other Measures) Act (No. 2) 2004 introduces measures dealing with such issues as child pornography, child abuse material, sexual predation, and dishonesty in relation to financial matters. These various provisions are discussed below.

§5. SPECIFIC CYBERCRIMES

I. Theft

1159. Australia, like most countries, has criminal offences against a person that commits theft. The elements of the offence of theft may be different in different jurisdictions. However, the notion that it is not socially acceptable to steal or take someone else's property, is a notion that underpins the framework of the criminal offence of theft. In Australia, the Crimes Acts, generally, define theft as an offence where a person steals property belonging to another person with the intention of depriving that person of the property in a dishonest manner. Property can be defined as both tangible and intangible things. Theft is sometimes a very difficult to prove where the article alleged to have been stolen is either intangible or has minimal individual value.

532. *Criminal Code* 1995 (Cth), s. 85ZD.
533. *Ibid.* at s. 85ZE.
534. *Ibid.* at s. 85ZJ.
535. *Ibid.* at s. 474.
536. Dishonesty is defined in terms of the ordinary usage of the term to all.

II. Computer and/or Internet Fraud

A. *In General*

1160. With the passage of the Crimes Legislation Amendment (Telecommunications Offences and Other Measures Act (No. 2) 2004 (Cth), Australia has in place a broad criminal code to deal with a range of Internet crimes. The changes in the Act apply not just to computers or even only to the Internet, but also to television and radio services. This is because CSP is defined broadly in section 7 of the Telecommunications Act 1997 (Cth) to include a 'service for carrying communications by means of guided and/or unguided electromagnetic energy'.

1161. The first part of the Crimes Legislation Amendment (Telecommunications Offences and other Crimes Act (No. 2) 2004 (Cth) spells out three broad offences: (1) a person is guilty if that person does anything with the intention of dishonestly obtaining a gain from a CSP by way of the supply of a carriage service; (2) a person is guilty of an offence if the person does anything with the intention of dishonestly causing a loss to a CSP in connection with the supply of a carriage service; or (3) it is an offence if a person dishonestly causes a loss to a CSP or dishonestly causes a risk of loss and the person knows or believes the loss will occur, or if there is a substantial risk of a loss occurring.

1162. Schedule 3 of the Crimes Legislation Amendment (Telecommunications Offences and other Crimes Act (No. 2) 2004 (Cth) deals with financial information offences. Section 480.4 makes it an offence to dishonestly obtain or deal in personal financial information without the consent of the person to whom that information relates.

1163. Criminal fraud is classified as an offence involving deceit, which has traditionally required the involvement of the human mind to establish *mens rea.* This proved extremely difficult to achieve under pre-digital era legislation and common law, as the following case shows. In the case of *R v. Gold and Schifreen*, charges of forgery were brought against the defendants following their unauthorized access to a public database and electronic mail service.[537] It was observed by the Court that there was no such thing as an electronic document, and that even if there was such a thing, the argument in that case was tautologous as it amounted to an assertion that the computer had deceived itself.[538]

1164. The problem which the Gold case raised, that of the impossibility of equating electronic transactions completely with their pre-digital counterparts under the then existing law. In Australia, most provisions for forgery-type offences have

537. *R v. Gold & Schifreen* [1987] 3 All ER 618, [1988] 2 WLR 984, [1988] AC 1063, [1988] 2 All ER 186, HL 21 Apr 1988. The defendants had hacked a remote computer system by the unauthorized use of the passwords and IDs of other users of the system. They had been charged under the *Forgery and Counterfeiting Act* 1981 (UK) of uttering a false instrument and convicted.

538. www.bus.orst.edu/faculty/brownc/lectures/crime/crime.htm.

now been amended to admit the causing of a computer or other machine to respond to a false statement or document as if it were genuine.[539]

1165. Computer crime can be helpfully categorized into two broad categories where the computer is the target; and where the computer is the instrumentality of the crime.

1166. The first category generally involves such offences as the theft of IP directly (copyrighted materials, patent and trademark information), trade secrets, and marketing information (such as customer lists, pricing data, and marketing plans) or blackmail based on information gained illegally from computerized files (such as medical information, sexual preference, personal history). This may also include techno-vandalism where unintentional or incidental damage is done to files, not so much to profit, but for the challenge inherent in it.

1167. The second category typically involves the criminal introducing a new code to manipulate the computer's analytical processes to facilitate the crime. Crimes in this category include fraudulent use of ATM cards and accounts, the theft of money from accrual, conversion, or transfer accounts, credit card fraud, fraud from computer transactions (stock transfers, sales, or billings), and telecommunications fraud.

B. Computer Fraud as a Civil Wrong

1168. Fraudulent activity may be both a civil wrong and criminal conduct. Thus, the State may prosecute for a violation of the public duty to obey the law, while the individuals or companies who are the victims may similarly sue to rescind a contract that may be involved and to recover damages. Another important distinction between civil and criminal wrongs is that the standard of proof that must be met for a civil wrong (balance of probabilities) is much lower than that required for a criminal prosecution (beyond any reasonable doubt). This means that for the same act, an individual may be innocent of the criminal offence, but found liable for the civil wrong of fraud and deceit or misrepresentation.[540]

1169. Australia enjoys one of the highest Internet usages in the world. This increase in online activity has also brought with it increased Internet fraud, and to combat fraudulent practices, the ACCC has been proactive in combating Internet fraud. The ACCC has been proactive in raising consumer awareness and conducting sweeps in search of illegal activity, especially illegal pyramid schemes, securities fraud, and other forms of misleading and deceptive conduct. It has also been

539. *Crimes Act* 1914 (Cth), s. 63(3); *Crimes Act* 1900 (NSW), s. 250; *Crimes Act* 1900 (ACT), ss 135A–135E; *Criminal Code Act* 1924 (Tas), s. 278; and *Criminal Law Consolidation Act* 1935 (SA), ss 212, 234–235.

540. The US criminal and civil trials of O. J. Simpson came to different verdicts on essentially the same evidence, with only the standard of proof varying this difference.

proactive in initiating litigation against specific practices as well as bringing enforcement actions against businesses on behalf of consumers.[541]

1170. Another context in which fraud has been a problem is that of online securities. A case in point involved Rentech, a US registered IT company.[542] On 8 and 9 May 1999, messages were posted on bulletin boards operated by Yahoo! and Raging Bull. The messages stated Raging Bull was about to release news of patented technology that would greatly increase its value. This resulted in a dramatic increase in the value of the stock. The US Securities and Exchange Commission (SEC) received complaints about the spam message. Raging Bull denied knowledge and that in fact the messages were false and misleading. The SEC found that the postings came from Australian servers and with the cooperation of ASIC were traced to Houmouzis and Loughnan, who made AUD 17,000 from the increase in shares via a broker in Canada. Houmouzis and Loughnan were charged and convicted of making statements and dissemination of information that was false or misleading and likely to induce the purchase of securities. They were also charged with indictable offences under the Crimes Act 1914 (Cth).

1171. Given the global nature of the electronic marketplace the ACCC and ASIC in Australia have been active participants in international fora where such issues as privacy, cross-border law enforcement, hacking, and security issues have been addressed.

III. Identity Theft

1172. On the Internet, one can find out a great deal of information about a person, making it easier to have one's identity stolen.[543] According to Australian Federal Police (AFP), 25% of frauds reported involve the assumption of false identities.[544] Identity encompasses the identification of natural persons (living or deceased) as well as the identities of bodies corporate. The term identity fabrication describes the creation of a fictitious identity while identity manipulation describes the alteration of one's own identity. Identity theft is the theft or assumption of a pre-existing identity with or without consent and whether, in the case of an individual, the person is living or deceased. Thus, identity crime describes activities or offences where a perpetrator uses a fabricated identity, manipulated identity or a stolen/assumed identity to facilitate the commission of a crime(s).

1173. Recent estimates by the ABS for 2016 indicate that identity crime costs Australia upwards of AUD 1.6 billion each year, with the majority (around AUD 900 million) lost by individuals through credit card fraud, identity theft and scams.

541. *ACCC Journal*, December 1999, 69ff.
542. *See* US Securities Exchange Commission Litigation Release 16532 (2000) at https://www.sec.gov/litigation/litreleases/lr16532.htm.
543. *See* Australian Federal Police at https://www.afp.gov.au/what-we-do/crime-types/fraud/identity-crime.
544. *Identity Theft Grows: Apathy Main Culprit*, Canberra Times 13 (17 Jun. 2002).

More alarmingly, identity crime continues to be a key enabler of serious and organized crime, which in turn costs Australia around AUD 15 billion annually.[545]

1174. A Celent Communications (2001) 'Identity Theft and Its Effect on the Financial Services Industry' report found that many identity thefts occurred by careless use of wallets and people throwing away pre-approved credit card offers without shredding them.[546] Identity theft cases cost an average of AUD 17,000 each. A KPMG Forensic Accounting Report found that fraudulent purchase orders made over the Internet and trafficking in credit card numbers was common in Australia. False Internet shopfronts are also on the rise.[547]

1175. At the same time, there are critics who argue that the extent and harm from identity theft is exaggerated with some studies showing that the amount of identity theft to be much smaller than reports suggest and that most people who report identity theft suffer no or little loss.[548]

1176. For ISP, the most common crime is fraudulent use of Internet accounts. For example, people sitting in chat rooms get user names and passwords from children or young people. The imposter then uses the name and password to initiate Internet sessions. The amendments to the Identity Crime and Other Measures Act 2011 (Cth) expanded the scope of existing identity crime offences, as well as enacted new offences for the use of a carriage service in order to obtain and/or deal with identification information.

1177. The Identity Crime and Other Measures Act 2011 (Cth):

- created new offences relating to air travel and the use of false identities;
- improved the operation of the Law Enforcement Integrity Commissioner Act 2006 (Cth);
- clarified that superannuation orders can be made in relation to all periods of a person's employment as a Commonwealth employee, not only the period in which a corruption offence occurred; and
- increased the value of a penalty unit and introduce a requirement for the triennial review of the penalty unit.

1178. At the state level, some Australian jurisdictions have amended their cybercrime legislation to a make it easier to deal with the issue of identity theft. Section 408D of the Queensland Criminal Code Act 2007 (Qld), makes it a misdemeanour,

545. *See* ABS for detailed statistics on identity and personal fraud 2014–2015, Catalogue Number 4528.0 Personal Fraud, 2014-2015.
546. Celent Communications (2001), at https://www.celent.com/insights/925352159.
547. K. Nicholas, *Rising E-Fraud Takes the Credit*, Australian Financial Review 52 (26 Sep. 2001). *See also* KPMG Forensic Accounting at https://home.kpmg/au/en/home/services/advisory/risk-consulting/forensic.html.
548. B. Keane, *Cybercrime Much Rarer Than We're Told*, Crikey (31 Oct. 2012), at http://www.crikey.com.au/2012/10/31/ cybercrime-rarer-and-less-costly-than-were-told/.

punishable by up to three years imprisonment, to obtain or deal with another's identification information for the purpose of committing or facilitating the commission of an indictable offence. The offence is committed irrespective of whether the entity or person whose identity is assumed is alive, in existence, or consents to the information being obtained or dealt with. The Act extends to contexts where a person misuses the identification to facilitate the commission of an offence outside Queensland that would be an indictable offence if it were committed in Queensland. Identification information and body corporate are specified in section 408D(7).

§6. Common 'Mischiefs'

1179. The following section discusses a number of common 'mischiefs' encountered in cyberspace. This is not an exclusive list but all of these activities would now be caught under the provisions of recent cybercrime legislation, discussed previously.

I. Hacking or Cracking

1180. Hacking or cracking is a large-scale misuse of the Internet, and although it seems motivated by greed or desire to permanently deprive someone of their property (the classic definition of theft), it can nevertheless have devastating effects through a variety of attacks, all of which are considered criminal offences.[549] Hackers enter a system either to prove that they can do it (ego boosting), to steal the property of others, or more maliciously, to place a virus which aims at destroying large amounts of data and preventing the system from operating. Once a hacker gains access to a computer system, they can browse through files, read private information and inflate user privileges, install trap doors (for later undetected access), or plant logic bombs.[550]

II. Criminal Code: Commonwealth, State and Territories Models

1181. Commonwealth, State and Territory laws dealing with computer crime have been characterized as diverse in policy and piecemeal in application.[551] With the implementation of the Commonwealth Criminal code provisions provided by the Cybercrime Act 2001 (Cth) uniformity has been achieved in NSW, Victoria, SA and the ACT, with the NT law based loosely on this model.

549. T. Krone, *Hacking offences* (2005). High tech crime brief No. 5. Canberra: Australian Institute of Criminology, https://aic.gov.au/publications/htcb/htcb005 and T. Krone T. *Hacking motives* (2005). High tech crime brief No. 6, Canberra: Australian Institute of Criminology, https://aic.gov.au/publications/htcb/htcb006.

550. R. Rezka, *Viruses and Computer Games*, Business to Business Magazine (1997).

551. *See* Model Criminal Code Officers Committee (MCCOC), *Damage and computer offences* (2001). MCCOC report, Canberra: AGD.

1182. There are various levels of offences for the Commonwealth, NSW, Victoria, SA and the ACT legislation. Access alone is not prohibited and an intention to obtain a benefit or advantage is insufficient to constitute an offence. The exception is in the NT, section 276B of the relevant Act.

1183. There are four levels of criminal liability based on the defendant's intention or the manner access to data is secured. The four levels are (1) accessing data or impairing an electronic communication with the intention to commit a serious offence (with an offence attracting a maximum penalty of at least five years);[552] (2) impairing or modifying data or impairing electronic communications if done with the intent to cause or with recklessness to harm or inconvenience; (3) possession, control, production or supply of data with the intent to commit any of the above offences. Recklessness is insufficient; and, (4) accessing data that is subject to an access control restriction.

1184. The remaining three jurisdictions of Western Australia, Queensland and Tasmania have quite different laws to regulate unauthorized access offences as described below.

A. *Western Australia*

1185. In Western Australia, section 440A of the *Criminal Code* introduced in 1990 under the heading 'unlawful operation of a computer system'.[553] The section refers to a person who 'without authorization' accesses 'information stored in a restricted access system' or who 'operates' such a system 'in some other way'. A restricted access system is defined as a computer system or a part or application of a computer system that is accessible only by using a code that is held by the person in control of the computer system or made available on a restricted basis. This provision is particularly suited to the situation of someone hacking a computer from outside. However, it introduces considerable difficulty in determining when initially authorized access becomes unauthorized either by exceeding initial permissions or by the subsequent use of data or information accessed.

B. *Queensland*

1186. The Queensland *Criminal Code* 1899 (Qld) amended in 1997 defines 'computer hacking and misuse' as the use of a restricted computer without the consent of the computer's controller.[554] A restricted computer is defined as one that

552. In the Northern Territory the intention required is to cause loss or damage or to gain a benefit or advantage.
553. *See* WA, *Criminal Code* 1913 (WA) at https://www.legislation.wa.gov.au/legislation/statutes.nsf/main_mrtitle_218_homepage.html.
554. Queensland *Criminal Code* 1899 (Qld) s. 408E. Computer hacking and misuse at http://www5.austlii.edu.au/au/legis/qld/consol_act/cc189994/s408e.html.

requires a 'device, code or sequence of electronic impulses' to gain access. There is a penalty scale of two to ten years maximum term of imprisonment depending on whether: (1) an offender simply uses a computer, (2) causes detriment or damage, or gains or intends to gain a benefit, or (3) the detriment, damage or gain is valued at more than AUD 5,000.

C. *Tasmania*

1187. The Tasmanian law requires intention and a lack of 'lawful excuse', in relation to damaging (or destroying, erasing or altering) computer data or simply accessing a computer or system of computers without authority. Uncertainty is introduced as 'lawful excuse' is undefined.

D. *'Unauthorized' Access*

1188. To determine whether a hack is authorized or not is complicated. This determination requires information of whether: (1) a computer owner has any data access policy; (2) whether and how that policy is communicated to others; (3) how accessible a computer is; and, (4) how accessible are the files, directories and other information on that computer.

1189. These complexities include questions of contractual or moral rights, or of implied consent, or the limits of a consent once given.

1190. The ICT environment today is characterized by the interconnection of devices via local area networks (LAN) and global connectivity via the WWW. There may be automated and free exchange of information between computer systems via the use of a 'cookie'. A cookie is a piece of data inserted by one computer on another so that the first computer can 'recognize' that other computer on a subsequent occasion. However, cookies can also be used to track, monitor and report on other Internet activity conducted on the second computer. A cookie with this capacity is sometimes referred to as *spyware*. Spyware is relatively common and someone surfing the net may not realize, in agreeing to the terms of a download, that they are consenting to such a cookie being placed on their computer.[555]

E. *Privacy*

1191. In the NT there is an offence of unlawfully obtaining confidential information. Otherwise, Australian anti-computer hacking laws are concerned with computer security rather than issues of privacy. Where unauthorized access to data that

555. R. Barrett, *Free software is the lure, online surveillance is the reality*, Consumer web watch news (2002), at http://www.consumerwebwatch.org/news/articles/spyware.htm; and BBC, *US moves to rein in spyware*, BBC News (18 Jun. 2004), at http://news.bbc.co.uk/1/hi/technology/3818057.stm.

are subject to access control is prohibited, the relaying of confidential information obtained through authorized access is not.

F. Computer

1192. The laws in Queensland, Tasmania and Western Australia specifically refer to systems or networks of computers within the definition of computer, while the other jurisdictions refer to a computer.

1193. The Cybercrime Act 2001 (Cth) does not define a 'computer'.

1194. The use of digital technology in everyday machines and appliances is ubiquitous and the ordinary meaning of computer must be applied. An individual computer may or may not be connected to other computers and an increasing array of devices are capable of being connected either physically or using wireless technology. Interconnected computers can be hacked internally or externally and the WWW itself might be considered a single computer. Computers that are not connected to other computers nevertheless can be 'hacked' by someone directly accessing that computer.

1195. Under the Cybercrime Act 2001 (Cth) unauthorized access to data is an offence where there is an intent to commit a crime. So is the case of the modification or impairment of data if accompanied by an intention to cause harm or inconvenience. Other offences under the Commonwealth model are based on breach of access restrictions in relation to data. Only in Tasmania is the law framed without reference either to the intention of the hacker, or to access restrictions on the computer being hacked.

1196. Australian anti-hacking laws require an intent to commit a serious offence, or cause harm or inconvenience. Such requirements raises a high barrier for the successful prosecution to evidence that a specific hacking incident is criminal. On the other hand, the category of recklessness as to harm or inconvenience caused by hacking invokes a standard of reasonably foreseeable consequences.[556]

1197. The only effective defence against such attacks is not the law but tight system management involving the frequent changing of passwords, carrying out frequent audits targeting suspicious logins or attempted logins, and good training or management for staff. Frequently backing up of records to a remote site is an essential part of any harm minimization strategy.

556. *See* Krone (2005) *supra.*

III. DDoS

1198. 1194 DDoS attacks, such as those launched early in 2000 against major e-commerce players eBay, Yahoo, and Amazon.com and a variety of e-traders and other Internet users, caused losses estimated to run into the tens of millions of dollars. These attacks occur when the access of firms is interrupted. This attack is achieved by flooding servers with fake or untraceable messages that clog up their processing, for anything from a few minutes to a few days. Such stoppages cause severe damage both to the earnings of the target business and to the confidence of their customers.

IV. Viruses

1199. Viruses are the curse of the Internet era. These are small codes that can attach themselves to and reproduce themselves on programs and files in unsuspecting computers and are capable of execution either on command or on the occurrence of a specific event. Although favoured by small-time hackers, who are extremely difficult to locate and successfully prosecute, these are also used by businesses to damage their competitors.

1200. A sinister version of the virus is the ‘worm’, a program that travels from one computer to another without attaching itself to the operating system of the computer that it infects and that can later infect the operating system of any computer that uses a file taken from the infected computer. The case of *United States v. Robert Tappan Morris* makes an interesting study in terms of traditional criminal law requirements in the face of massive publicity and public anger.[557] In that case, the defendant was convicted under the Computer Fraud and Abuse Act of 1986, 18 U.S.C.S. §1030(a)(5)(A), for releasing a worm which caused computers at various educational and military sites to cease functioning.

V. Password Sniffing

1201. Password sniffers are programs that monitor and record the name and password of network users as they log in, jeopardizing security at a site. Whoever installs the sniffer (usually through a low-level access break-in to the host computer system) can then impersonate an authorized user and log in to access restricted documents and undertake restricted processes.

---

557. *United States v. Robert Tappan Morris*, 928 F.2d 504 (2nd Cir. 1991).

VI. Spoofing

1202. A major cyber threat to Australian businesses is e-mail-based impersonation scams targeting key personnel. The scheme involves cybercriminals mimicking business owners and executives through phishing e-mails (discussed below). Criminals typically pose as personnel in positions of authority and ask victims to perform money transfers, pay invoices, or to send the attacker sensitive data. The ACCC's Scamwatch reveals that Australians reported over AUD 4.7 million in losses caused by impersonation attacks in 2017, and estimates that 2,800 Australians were tricked into giving up personal information.[558]

1203. Spoofing is the act of disguising one computer to electronically 'look' like another computer in order to gain access to a system which would normally be restricted. E-mail spoofing is when an attacker (cybercriminal) forges an e-mail so that it appears the e-mail has been sent by someone else. This is either done so that the entire name and e-mail address of the sender is a forgery, or in more straightforward cases, just the name of the sender.

1204. The ThreatMetrix Digital Identity Network detected attacks during real-time analysis and interdiction of fraudulent online payments, logins and new account applications. The Network analysed over 81 million Australia-New Zealand (ANZ) transactions, revealing that the 138% the growth in the percentage of financial services attacks originating from ANZ is higher than any other region around the world. Out of the 81 million ANZ transactions analysed, more than 16 million bot attacks occurred in the region, a 33% increase when compared to Q1 data.[559]

VII. Pagejacking

1205. Pagejacking is the copying of a page by an unauthorized person(s) to filter off traffic to another site. Pagejacking forces an Internet user to go to another site (usually a pornographic one) and blocking the 'exit' and 'back' functions so that they are unable escape.[560]

---

558. *See* ACCC Scamwatch at https://www.scamwatch.gov.au/news/australians-lost-340-million-to-scammers-in-2017 and https://www.scamwatch.gov.au/about-scamwatch/scam-statistics. *See also* Ironbastion Impersonation Scams at https://blog.ironbastion.com.au/email-impersonation-scams-phishing-what-your-staff-can-do/.
559. LexisNexis® Risk Solutions 2018, *Australia hotbed for cybercrime*; new report.
560. https://www.ftc.gov/news-events/press-releases/2001/02/internet-pagejacker-settles-ftc-charges. *See also* The President's Working Group on Unlawful Conduct on the Internet and The EFA shows identity spoofing as most prevalent attack vector in the ANZ region (22 Oct. 2018), at https://www.prnewswire.com/news-releases/australia-hotbed-for-cybercrime-new-report-shows-identity-spoofing-as-most-prevalent-attack-vector-in-the-anz-region-300735029.htm; and FTC Asks Court to Hold Internet Pagejacking Defendants in Contempt: Previous FTC Order Barred Phishing, Pagejacking, and Mousetrapping at https://www.ftc.gov/news-events/press-releases/2008/01/ftc-asks-court-hold-internet-pagejacking-defendants.

VIII. Phishing and Key Logging

1206. Phishing involves tricking or baiting someone into disclosing their passwords and other account information in order to perpetrate a theft or other criminal activity. This may be done, for example, by sending an e-mail with a fake letterhead or asking the victim to click on a link that takes them to a fake site and asks them to log in with their password and other details. A related technique is keylogging. In this case there is no direct contact with the victim, but a Trojan or other malware is hidden on the victim's computer and the software captures the user's keystroke information.

1207. Malware, is the short form for malicious code that can take the form of viruses, worms or Trojan horses that infect electronic devices.[561] These infections become part of a 'blended attack' relying on social engineering. The latter is the ability to manipulate someone to doing something they would not normally do. Malware include a remote administration tool (RAT) that is used to access a computer's camera, microphone and install other types of malware; keyloggers to monitor for passwords, credit card details and e-mail addresses; ransom-ware used to encrypt private files and then demand payment in return for the password; botnets for DDOS attacks and other illegal activities; crypto-miners that use your computer hardware to mine cryptocurrency and which slow your computer down; and, hijacking or defacement attacks to deface a site or embarrass you by posting pornographic material to your social media.

1208. *Spear phishing* is an e-mail or electronic communications scam targeted towards a specific individual, organization or business. Although often intended to steal data for malicious purposes, cybercriminals may also intend to install malware on a targeted user's computer.

1209. So far in 2017, the ACCC's Scamwatch has received more than 11,000 reports of phishing scam, with nearly AUD 260,000 lost.[562] Phishing scams are the most common scam reported to Scamwatch – reports are 63% higher than the next most popular category. Statistics also show that older Australians (those aged 65+) are particularly vulnerable to this scam and that e-mail or the phone are the scammers' preferred tool of the trade for contacting potential victims.

1210. A keylogger is a function which records keystrokes on a computer. At this basic level, a keylogger seems harmless. In the hands of a hacker or a cybercriminal, a keylogger is a potent tool to steal information. Keyloggers track the keystrokes to intercept passwords and other sensitive information typed on the keyboard. This gives hackers access to PIN codes and account numbers, passwords

561. R. Matthews & K.N. Lovell, *Don't click that link! How criminals access your digital devices and what happens when they do*, The Conversation (11 Feb. 2019), at http://theconversation.com/dont-click-that-link-how-criminals-access-your-digital-devices-and-what-happens-when-they-d0-109802.

562. ACCC Scamwatch at https://www.accc.gov.au/media-release/dont-fall-for-a-scammers-phishing-bait.

to online shopping sites, e-mail ids, e-mail logins, and other confidential information. When the hackers get access to the users' private and sensitive information, they can take advantage of the extracted data to perform online money transaction from the user's account. Keyloggers can sometimes be used as a spying tool to compromise business and state-owned company's data.

1211. To gain access hackers may use phishing. This method fakes an e-mail from a legitimate company to fish for passwords and credit card numbers. Sometimes, these e-mails contain attachments which download programs (Trojans) stealthily into your computer once you click on them. Another method is where the hacker researches on an intended victim beforehand in order to find weaknesses in a victim's online habits.

1212. In a twist on an e-mail scam, this is one where the message purports to have been sent from a hacker who has compromised your computer and used your webcam to record a video of you while you were watching porn. The e-mail threatens to release the video to all your contacts unless you pay a Bitcoin ransom. The e-mail also references a real password previously tied to the recipient's e-mail address. The passwords may have been compromised by a data breach at a server that the recipient subscribed to previously.[563]

§7. CYBERSTALKING AND CYBER-BULLING

1213. Stalkers use the Internet to 'wilfully, maliciously and repeatedly follow or harass another person and who makes a credible threat with the intent to place that person in reasonable fear for his or her safety, or the safety of his or her immediate family'.[564] Harassment online is at least as harmful as the more traditional variety. Harassment undertaken online or through the transmission of threats by electronic messaging systems are a criminal offence.

1214. The stalking provisions in the criminal code of most jurisdictions define stalking in general terms with the courts left to apply the general language to specific contexts, such as using the Internet to stalk and harass.[565] Victoria and the NT use statutory language that specifically includes 'telephoning, sending electronic messages to, or otherwise contacting the victim or any other person'.[566]

1215. Cyber-bullying violates both criminal and civil laws in Australia. Cyber-bullying has often arisen in school contexts involving young people who misuse technology such as texting to bully one of their peers. However, before someone is

563. Allan Turner, *Latest online scam aims to prick porn watchers' guilty conscience*, at https://www.smh.com.au/technology/latest-online-scam-aims-to-prick-porn-watchers-guilty-conscience-20170815-gxwvxl.html (15 Aug. 2017).
564. J. Rosenoer (1996), *Cyberlaw The Law of the Internet* 193 (Springer).
565. *See, e.g., Criminal Code Act* 1913 (WA); *Criminal Code* 1924 (Tas), s. 192.
566. *Crimes Act* 1953 (Vic), s. 21A; *Criminal Code* Act 1983 (NT), s. 189.

criminally liable, they must be capable of being deemed by the law to be responsible for their actions. Those cyber-bullies who are under 10 years of age will not be liable for their actions, while those aged between 10 and 14 will only be liable where it can be proven beyond reasonable doubt that they understood that they should not have committed the offence. Accordingly, any offender over 14 years will be criminally liable.

1216. The possible heads of liability for cyber-bullying include:

- Misuse of Telecommunications Services (Commonwealth Offence). The Criminal Code Act 1995 (Cth) makes it a criminal offence to misuse telecommunication services. Where cyber-bullying involves the abuse of Internet and phone services, Commonwealth, State and Territory telecommunications laws may be relevant.
- Assaults, Intimidation and Harassment at School (NSW). NSW is one of the few Australian jurisdictions to enact legislation specifically directed at bullying in schools. In its terms, these laws also include cyber-bullying.[567]
- Criminal Laws Dealing with Assault. The criminal laws governing assault are also wide enough to include various forms of cyber-bullying. However, under Queensland, Tasmania and Western Australia statutes, words or images sent online are insufficient to, alone, make out a threat. Also, the geographic distance between assailants and their targets in most cyber-bullying contexts may make it difficult to prove that a threat creates an apprehension of fear of a present or immediate harm. Also, under the legislation of some states, mere use of words or images posted or sent online are insufficient of themselves to constitute a threat under assault laws.

1217. Another possible issue is whether mere psychological harm is enough. The Australian High Court has recognized psychiatric harm as a form of damage warranting compensation in *Gifford v. Strang Patrick Stevedoring.*[568] A similar interpretation could be applied to Australian criminal statutes, so that where cyber-bullying leads its target to suffer a recognizable psychiatric illness, a criminal charge could follow.[569]

---

567. *Crimes Amendment (School Protection) Act* 2002 (NSW).
568. *Gifford v. Strang Patrick Stevedoring Pty Ltd* (2003) 214 CLR 269.
569. *See generally* D. Butler, S. Kift & MA Campbell, *Cyber bullying in schools and the law: Is there an effective means of addressing the power imbalance?*, 16 eLaw Journal: Murdoch Electronic Journal of Law 90 (2010).

§8. ONLINE GAMBLING

I. Extent of Gambling in Australia

1218. Gambling in Australia is a major economic activity. 'Australians bet around AUD 574 million (approximately 86%) on sport and racing through Australian online operators and AUD 92 million (approximately 14%) is currently bet on sport and racing by Australians through unregulated overseas websites.'[570]

1219. Video slot machines (pokies) were introduced into almost every bar, hotel, and club in Australia in the 1990s. In 1999, the Productivity Commission estimated that the Australian gambling industry provided an economic benefit somewhere between AUD 2.3 and AUD 3.2 billion. However, gambling has also proven to be a significant social problem. For example, it is estimated that there are some 290,000 problem gamblers, annually costing society from AUD 940 million to AUD 2.9 billion. In a few short years, gambling has outrun illicit drugs (AUD 890 million) and perhaps even alcohol (AUD 2.4 billion) as a major social problem. It is estimated that gambling is behind one suicide every fortnight in the state of Victoria.[571]

II. Interactive Gambling Act

1220. The Interactive Gambling Act 2001 (Cth) was passed on 28 June 2001 and commenced operation in January 2002. The Act applies to all interactive gambling service providers, whether in Australia or located offshore and whether Australian or foreign owned. A penalty of AUD 1.1 million for corporations and AUD 220,000 for individuals applies for each day of contravention. This Act imposes a new layer of regulation over State and Territory gaming, wagering, and lotteries enactments. Many of these State and Territory provisions already relate to online interactive gaming. The goal of the legislation is to prevent the further growth of gambling and protect consumers. The Act creates a broad offence where any of the customers of the service are resident in Australia.

III. Interactive Gambling Act Reforms

1221. The Interactive Gambling Act regulates the provision of interactive gambling services in Australia.[572] Key reforms that came into effect on 13 September

570. C. Barry, *The downside of regulating sports betting*, Canberra Times (12 Mar. 2013) at http://www.canberratimes.com.au/comment/the-downside-of-regulating-sports-betting-20130312-2fxfz.html.
571. R. Morais, *The Stakes Get Higher*, Forbes Global 24–27 (29 Apr. 2002).
572. https://www.legislation.gov.au/Series/C2004A00851.

2017 are designed to combat illegal offshore gambling through stronger enforcement and disruption measures. These reforms are complemented nationally by consistent consumer protections. One significant Interactive Gambling Act reform is the clarification of the prohibition of 'click-to-call' in-play betting services while place based betting services are not prohibited.

IV. National Consumer Protection Framework

1222. The National Consumer Protection Framework is intended to help empower individual gamblers to minimize problem gambling. It includes a national self-exclusion register for online wagering, a voluntary opt-out pre-commitment scheme for online wagering and a prohibition on lines of credit betting offered by wagering providers, together with other measures.[573]

1223. The ACMA may, on its own initiative, or in response to a complaint, investigate whether a person has contravened a provision of the Interactive Gambling Act. A complaint may be made to the ACMA under section 16 of the Interactive Gambling Act. Examples of prohibited interactive gambling services include online casino-style games, online slot machines and online wagering services that accept in-play bets on sports events.

1224. A 'prohibited interactive gambling service' is defined in section 5 of the Interactive Gambling Act as a gambling service where:

- the service is provided in the course of carrying on a business; and
- the service is provided to customers using any of the following:
  - an Internet carriage service;
  - any other listed carriage service;
  - a broadcasting service;
  - any other content service; and
  - a datacasting service.

1225. Regulated interactive gambling service is defined in section 8E of the Interactive Gambling Act. The services refer to those that are excluded from the definition of a prohibited interactive gambling service but includes telephone betting services and online wagering services (other than those offering in-play betting). Such services cannot be provided to customers in Australia without a licence granted by an Australian state or territory licensing authority.

573. http://pandora.nla.gov.au/pan/65939/20171219-1410/www.mhs.gov.au/media-releases/2017-09-08-gambling-ministers-agree-stronger-online-gambling-protections.html.

V. Enforcement

1226. The ACMA has a range of powers to deal with breaches of the Interactive Gambling Act, including the power to:

- issue formal warnings (sections 58 and 64A of the Interactive Gambling Act);
- issue infringement notices for contraventions of the Interactive Gambling Act (section 64C of the Interactive Gambling Act);
- apply to the Federal Court or Federal Circuit Court for civil penalty orders for contraventions of the Act, and/or injunctions (sections 64B and 64D of the Interactive Gambling Act);
- refer a matter to the AFP for investigation, or to the Commonwealth Director of Public Prosecutions, in connection with criminal offence provisions.

1227. The ACMA is responsible for enforcing broadcasting licence conditions prohibiting the advertising of interactive gambling services, as set out in the Broadcasting Services Act 1992 (Cth) and imposed on broadcasting licensees by section 61FD of the Interactive Gambling Act.

VI. Penalties

1228. The Interactive Gambling Act has criminal offences and civil penalty provisions.

1229. If a person is found guilty of an offence under the Act, the penalty is 5,000 penalty units per day the offence continues (up to AUD 1,050,000) or up to five times that for a body corporate (up to AUD 5,250,000). The civil penalty for a contravention of the Interactive Gambling Act is up to 7,500 penalty units per day the offence continues (up to AUD 1,575,000) or up to five times that for a body corporate (nearly AUD 7,900,000).

1230. The ACMA can apply to the Federal Court or Federal Circuit Court for a civil penalty order.

VII. Role of ACMA

1231. The ACMA is responsible for investigating valid complaints about online content, including Internet and mobile phone content, and enforcing Australia's anti-spam law. The ACMA carries out compliance and enforcement activities under the Interactive Gambling Act 2001 (Cth) plus related legislative and other instruments, including industry codes of practice.[574]

574. https://www.acma.gov.au/about-interactive-gambling-act.

A. Interactive Gambling Industry Code

1232. The Internet industry also plays a role in managing the potential for problem gambling among Australians through the development of an industry code. The Interactive Gambling Industry Code was registered by the ACMA in December 2001 under section 38 of the Interactive Gambling Act. It is the responsibility of the Communications Alliance.[575]

1233. The code provides a mechanism for ISP to meet their legal obligations in dealing with designated Internet gambling matters, including a scheme to deal with notifications by the ACMA of prohibited content. A complaint may be made to the ACMA about a breach of the code under section 17 of the Interactive Gambling Act.

1234. Some limited exemptions are given to sports betting and lotteries other than instant or Keno style. The lottery exemption protects Lotto services such as Tattslotto, Oz Lotto and Super 6, Powerball, and Keno, but not electronically generated lotteries. The aim is to allow existing lotteries to use electronic means but not to allow new forms of electronic lottery. However, these exemptions given to animal races and sporting events do not apply to overseas wagering operators, who will be prohibited from offering their services to Australians. Telephone betting services are also exempted from the legislation. So are television game shows such as 'Who Wants to be a Millionaire', which involves some form of payment; however, the Minister may impose conditions on such mediums and will monitor them.

1235. Note finally that the definition of gambling refers only to 'games of chance'. It does not capture interactive games such as trivia games or arcade games, which are regarded as games of skill.[576]

1236. Under the Interactive Gambling Act, Australian-based operators are prohibited from providing an interactive gambling service to customers physically present in Australia. The reach of the Act also covers designated countries declared by the Minister. The idea is that such countries will have reciprocal legislation.

1237. The Act also prohibits advertising of interactive gambling services on broadcast media, Internet, and print publications, consistent with the Tobacco Advertising Prohibitions Act 1992 (Cth). This will have an impact on carriers, ISP, publishers, broadcasters and datacasters. Even if a party is not the author or publisher of the advertisement, but merely authorizes an interactive gambling service advertisement to be broadcast in Australia (apart from an accidental broadcast), it

575. http://commsalliance.com.au/Publications/all/codes/interactive_gambling_code and also http://www.communications.gov.au/online_safety_and_security/online_gambling/interactive_gambling_industry_code.

576. Even if certain activity is excluded from the Commonwealth act, it may still be caught by a State or Territory prohibition.

can still be held liable. Organizations and associations receiving any form of financial benefit (e.g., membership fees) are also prohibited from maintaining an Internet directory of members offering interactive gambling services, including a URL address or hyperlink of the site.

1238. Defences are provided under the Interactive Gambling Act. Evidence of 'reasonable diligence' can include the following factors on whether:

- customers had a contractual relationship with an explicit condition that the customer not use the service while in Australia;
- customers were informed that online gambling is prohibited in Australia;
- the operator required customers to provide personal details and whether those details showed the customer was not personally present in Australia; and
- there exists network data that shows the customer was not physically present in Australia at the time.

VIII. Gambling Reforms

1239. Digital technologies are rapidly changing Australia's gambling industry. The 2015 Review of Illegal Offshore Wagering (the Review) noted that online wagering is the fastest growing gambling segment, with over AUD 1.4 billion gambled online each year.[577] Digital technology is also enabling operators to reach our phones, our televisions, our home computers at any time of the day or night. The Review also noted that Australians are losing between AUD 64 million and AUD 400 million every year betting in illegal offshore sites, and this means tax revenue is also lost. In the online world, the proportion of problem gambling is three times higher than in other forms of gambling.[578]

1240. An investigation on the feasibility of other disruptions measures to curb illegal offshore gambling activity, including voluntary ISP blocking and financial payment blocking is being undertaken and a final position is expected by 2019. A feature of the legislation is that the Government has indicated it will use its banking powers under the Constitution to prohibit Australian entities from facilitating financial transactions with overseas Internet gambling operators. Thus, if an Australian uses a credit card to fund an online deal with a foreign operator, the contract will not be enforced, and the bank will default on payment. The overseas gambling outfit when forced with debts that it cannot enforce may soon tire of the Australian market. The negative upshot of this provision is that it may provide incentives for gamblers to turn to other forms of payment that will be more difficult to police.

---

577. https://www.dss.gov.au/communities-and-vulnerable-people/programmes-services/gambling/government-response-to-the-2015-review-of-the-impact-of-illegal-offshore-wagering.
578. https://www.dss.gov.au/communities-and-vulnerable-people/programs-services/gambling/betting-restrictions-and-online-wagering-in-australia-a-review-of-current-knowledge-report. *See also* The *Betting Restrictions and Online Wagering in Australia: A Review of Current Knowledge* a report prepared by the Australian Gambling Research Centre (AGRC), Australian Institute of Family Studies (AIFS), and commissioned by the Department of Social Services (DSS).

§9. OBSCENITY AND PORNOGRAPHY

I. Summary of Issues

1241. The issues surrounding censorship are similar to the gambling debate with the exception that there is probably less agreement about the harms of pornography, especially non-violent erotica. The basic issue comes down to enforceability. How can Australia effectively regulate Internet content as an island in the world Internet community? Notwithstanding the difficulty, a bipartisan proposal has mooted the implementation of some type of national filter in the form of content standards.[579]

1242. Those who doubt the constitutional validity, practicality, and workability of a national content control regime argue that the best control lies not with the States and Territories, but with parents who can exercise supervision and adopt available technology that can bar access to the sites.[580]

II. Online Privacy Protection of Children

1243. Research conducted by the ABA found that most adults believed using the Internet involved some risk, with the main areas of perceived risk being:[581]

- financial dangers such as fraud and credit card number theft (54%);
- personal data misuse and privacy issues (45%);
- content exposure concerns (39%); and
- viruses (21%).

1244. The most common concern over content was the perceived risk of children accessing unsuitable content (27%). Access to pornographic material and the receipt of such content through unsolicited e-mails or accidental discovery were the major concerns. The difference in the level of regulation of the Internet compared with other media was a recurring theme raised by parents, when asked why they were concerned about access on the Internet.[582]

579. *Coalition announces some sort of Internet filter ... and immediately backs down*, Sydney Morning Herald (5 Sep. 2013), at http://www.smh.com.au/federal-politics/federal-election-2013/coalition-announces-internet-filter--and-immediately-backs-down-20130905-2t7nb.html. *See also* http://www.zdnet.com/au/australian-opposition-vows-to-implement-internet-filter-by-default-7000020270/.

580. EFA, an anti-censorship group, recently issued a Freedom of Information request to the ABA seeking to find out what kind of information the Government was banning and what it was planning to ban as a result of complaints and its subsequent assessment of sites as Restricted or R-Rated. *See* https://www.efa.org.au/FOI/foi_aba_2000.htm. *See* EFA Internet Censorship Laws in Australia at https://www.efa.org.au/Issues/Censor/cens1.html.

581. *See* ABA Internet@home online at https://www.abs.gov.au/AUSSTATS/abs@.nsf/Lookup/4102.0Main+Features60Jun+2011.

582. *Ibid.*

1245. New provisions under the Crimes Legislation Amendment (Telecommunications Offences and Other Measures) Act (No. 2) 2004 (Cth) concern child abuse and pornography on the Internet; using a carriage service for child pornography material; to possess, control, produce, supply, or obtain child pornography material for use through a carriage service; use carriage service for child abuse material; circumstances in which an ISP or Internet content host may be liable under the Act; sexual predation, that is, using a carriage service to procure or groom a child for sexual purposes; and, provisions, where the victim must be under 16 and the perpetrator 18 or over.

1246. As the Australian Government continues to develop its regulations under the Telecommunications Act 1997 (Cth) legislation and specific legislation such as the Enhancing Online Safety for Children's Safety Act 2015 (Cth) as well as industry codes seek to grapple with the issue of use of the Internet by children.

1247. The Office of the eSafety Commissioner was established in 2015 by the Enhancing Online Safety for Children's Safety Act 2015 (Cth) to coordinate and lead the online safety efforts across government, industry and the not-for-profit community as an independent statutory office.[583] The Office operates a world-first reporting scheme to deal with serious cyber-bullying that affects Australian children.[584]

1248. Other extensive legislative reform protecting children from online pornography and other harms involve amendments to the Telecommunications Offences and Other Measures Act (No 2) 2004 (Cth) and the Crimes Legislation Amendment (Sexual Offences Against Children) Act 2010 (Cth).

III. Industry Codes and International Cooperation

1249. The protection of children has been a major feature of industry codes, for example, that of the IIA. Child pornography is also dealt with by the Convention on the Rights of the Child as well as through such measures as the UNICEF-sponsored 'Optional Protocol on the Sale of Children, Child Prostitution and Child Pornography', which came into force in January 2002.[585] Negotiated over a number of years with governments, experts and NGOs, the Optional Protocol seeks to raise the standards in protecting children from all forms of sexual exploitation and abuse.

§10. Suicide-Related Material

1250. The Criminal Code Amendment (Suicide-Related Material) Offences Act 2005 (Cth) amended the Criminal Code by creating new offences that deal with the

583. https://www.legislation.gov.au/Details/C2015A00024/ and https://www.esafety.gov.au/.
584. https://www.esafety.gov.au/reportcyberbullying.
585. *See* UNICEF https://www.unicef.org/crc/index_30204.html.

use of a carriage service to counsel, induce, or promote suicide. The Act also makes it an offence to use a carriage service to access material, transmit material, or make material available if it promotes or provides instruction about a method of suicide and it was intended to have that effect.

§11. Anti-vilification Laws

1251. Australian States and the Commonwealth also have anti-vilification laws in place that prohibit, for example, use of a web posting that constitutes religious or racial vilification.[586]

1252. In May 2009, Holocaust denier Fredrick Toben was sentenced to jail for contempt of court for ignoring a 2002 court ruling that prohibited him from publishing his anti-Jewish rants on the Internet.[587]

§12. Anti-Terrorism Laws

1253. As part of its response to the threat of terrorism, Australia has taken measures such as new laws that could apply to terrorist activity. These new laws involved the creation of approximately 100 new offences that do not fit the normal realm of domestic criminal law. These offences dealt with terrorism, genocide, crimes against humanity, war crimes, and other international criminal activity that derived from international legal origins. These new laws included the Suppression of the Financing of Terrorism Act 2000 (Cth); Criminal Code Amendment (Suppression of Terrorist Bombings) Act 2002 (Cth); Telecommunications Interception Legislation Amendment Act 2002 (Cth); Security Legislation Amendment (Terrorism) Act 2002 (Cth); Criminal Code Amendment (Terrorism) Act 2003 (Cth); and the Crimes Legislation Amendment (Telecommunications Act) 2004 (Cth).

1254. The Australian Security Intelligence Organization (ASIO) was given the power to question anyone whom they believe may have information on terrorism, including those who may not be involved in terrorist activity. ASIO is also given the power, in serious cases, to detain people for up to forty-eight hours without legal representation. The Government amended the Criminal Code to insert terrorism offences. These relate to 'terrorist activity which was defined as an act or omission that constitutes an offence under the UN and other international counter-terrorism instruments, or an act committed for a political, religious or ideological purpose designed to intimidate the public with regard to its security and intended to cause

---

586. *See* Racial vilification law in New South Wales – Final report. *See also* B. Swartz, *Couple Jailed for Contempt in Vilification Case*, The Age (21 Feb. 2008) at https://www.parliament.nsw.gov.au/lcdocs/inquiries/2260/Racial%20vilification%20law%20in%20New%20South%20Wales%20-%20Final.pdf.

587. www.abc.net.au/rn/lawreport/stories/2009/2573443.htm.

serious damage to persons, property or infrastructure.' The Criminal Code also covered ancillary conduct such as aiding, abetting, conspiracy, attempt or incitement. The offences carry a maximum penalty of life imprisonment.[588]

1255. The Government has also enacted new 'anti-hoax' laws.[589]

1256. The Financial Transactions Reports Act 1988 (Cth) was amended to ensure the reporting of possible terrorist-related financial transactions and international funds transfers.

1257. The TIAA was amended to permit access to unread e-mails where another form of lawful access to the system or device capable of displaying the communication is held by the relevant agency. Terrorism offences are included in the definition of 'class 1 offences' for purposes of telecommunication warrants.[590]

1258. Overall, these reforms in the area of counter-terrorism provided enhanced Commonwealth powers and a consolidation and strengthening of Commonwealth agencies that deal with these issues. On 6 October (2002), the Government implemented the United Nations regulations to block financial transactions that might assist terrorists. The Government also took steps to enhance the powers of the ASIO by creating a new general offence of terrorism and an offence related to preparing for or planning terrorists acts and allowing terrorist property to be frozen and seized.

1259. Australia has also improved the accuracy of domain name registrant data. The 'Whois' data – information about those who have registered an Internet domain name – can potentially be useful for tracking terrorists.

---

588. Media Release, AGD, *Upgrading Australia's counter-terrorism capabilities – Amended* (18 Dec. 2001), at https://www.ag.gov.au/NationalSecurity/Counterterrorismlaw/Pages/Australiascounterterrorismlaws.aspx.

589. *Criminal Code Amendment (Anti-hoax and Other Measures) Act* 2002 (Cth).

590. *Ibid. See also* M. Bryan, *Computer Crime Rate Doubles*, Australian Financial Review, 33 (21 May 2002).

Chapter 3. Cybercrime Law Enforcement and Criminal Procedures

§1. Introduction

1260. In general terms, Australian law enforcement efforts in relation to cybercrime have involved four major strategies. The first is putting into place regulations and legislation that enable the law enforcement agencies to tackle the major problem areas for example the Cybercrime Act 2001 (Cth).

1261. A second strategy is the formation of strategic partnerships in the fight against crime. These partnerships include the law enforcement agencies to work with industry, federal government to work with their state and local counterparts, and national governments to work with each other internationally.

1262. A third major strategy is education, both in regard to knowledge to prevent the crime occurring in the first place as well as assistance in helping to solve cybercrime.

1263. Finally, governments have been working to provide greater resources in order to increase the capacity to combat computer-related crime. For example, the Commonwealth government has established a world leading system called 'Crimtrac', which maintains databases such as the National Automated Finger Print Identification System and the National Investigation DNA database. In addition, the AFP and the police forces of the various States and Territories have established Cybercrime Units.

1264. Another important development within Australian policing is the decision by the Australasian Police Ministers' Council (APMC) to establish an Australian Hi-Tech Crime Centre (AHTCC). The Centre is hosted by the AFP and co-located with its Transnational Crime Coordination Centre (TCCC). The focus of such a centre is on serious, organized, and multi-jurisdictional crime with a hi-tech dimension.

§2. Need for Cooperation between Industry and Police

1265. Law enforcement agencies around the world would be united in their view that ICT industry does not do enough itself to protect its networks. It seems that notwithstanding the increase of attacks on computer systems, many firms do not seem to value their security. Since the attack by the 'I Love you' virus and even more so after the events of 9/11 in the US, governments have been more active in protecting security and working with the private sector to take preventative action.[591] The clear

591. For example, the Department of Justice in the US has been far more vocal about the need for improved security. It has established its website www.cybercrime.gov to provide information to the public about the extent of the problem and what can be done about it.

message is that law enforcement agencies cannot do it alone. In other words, government and industry must work closely together to share information and protect the information and other infrastructures from terrorists and related threats.[592]

1266. Firms must be proactive in protecting their networks and have an action plan in place to minimize the damage and assist police in the conduct of their investigations. The security plan should give some attention beforehand of what enforcement agencies should be contacted, how the data might be recovered, and how the security breach in the system will be patched or remedied. More fundamentally, a security breach must be reported. Unfortunately, too many firms remain under the misguided belief that reporting a security breach will cause them further commercial damage. Yet, law enforcement agencies are more astute these days about protecting the reputation of a firm who reports a security breach, and the failure to report merely plays into the hands of those who would commit such crimes. Some companies have gone the other way and want their name associated with a high publicity arrest to send a warning to future criminals that they will be caught and dealt with. Finally, developing a security policy is one thing; it is another to regularly test and evaluate it.

§3. Preventative Private Action Against Cybercrime

1267. In addition to cooperating with police, the private sector must change its attitude about the importance of security. Although there has been a considerable amount of discussion about the importance of security, that discussion has yet to result in actions that redress the problem.

1268. In terms of remedies, after changing user attitudes, the most cited barriers to improving security tend to be management of software upgrades and bug patches.

1269. In some cases, technological solutions are the answer. For example, the System Administration, Audit, Networking, and Security Institute (SANS) a non-government research and education organization, provides an update of the top twenty cyber vulnerabilities most often exploited by hackers and includes a list of top products that scan for leading cyberflaws.[593] The list was compiled by the Federal Bureau of Investigation's National Infrastructure Protection Centre, the General Services Administration's Federal Computer Incident Response Centre, and SANS. The SANS site points to the ten most commonly exploited vulnerabilities to Unix and to Windows systems, together with step-by-step instructions on how to correct security flaws. Similarly, agencies such as AGIMO assist businesses and governments about security and other e-business or e-government issues.[594]

---

592. This was the overriding message also of the US Presidential Commission on Critical Infrastructure Protection (Marsh Commission) 1997 at https://fas.org/sgp/library/pccip.pdf.
593. www.sans.org/top20/.
594. www.agimo.gov.au.

1270. Industry groups also play an important role in preventing cybercrime and improving the quality of service generally. For example, the IIA provide guidance about filters and has developed a code of best practice for ISP and others in the industry. It is estimated that piracy costs the Australian CD-ROM-based music, business, and games software industry AUD 200 million per year.[595] Other examples of industry codes include the Direct Marketing Model Code of Practice, the Insurance Council of Australia Code of Conduct, and the Asia Pacific Smart Cards Forum Code of Conduct.

§4. International Developments

I. International Cooperation

1271. Cybercrime protection will not happen internationally unless developing countries get some help in terms of law enforcement capabilities. Thirteen countries, including Australia and the US, have signed a memorandum of understanding in n2001 to cooperate to help stop the threat posed by cross-border Internet fraud.[596] The project has two aspects. The first is a public website to provide general information about consumer protection in the signatory countries. The second is a private website designed to promote international cooperation.

II. Racist Websites

1272. Parliamentarians from the forty-three nations of the Council of Europe want transatlantic efforts to block racist websites. Modern technology needs safeguards, and one of those should be to ban hate speech. A report has found that there are currently 4,000 race-hate sites, including 2,500 in the US, compared to only 160 in 1995.[597] The Council of Europe approved text of a cybercrime protocol outlawing racist speech on the Internet.

III. Convention on Cybercrime

1273. The Council of Europe has approved the Convention on Cyber-Crime on 19 September 2001. The treaty was approved by the forty-three Member States and ratified by Australia in 2010. The treaty creates procedural structures for police officials to pursue computer crime across national borders.[598] As of November 2013,

595. K. Nicholas, *Piracy Battle Far from Over*, Australian Financial Review, 29 (2 Jul. 2002).
596. The memorandum of understanding at the US Federal Trade Commission at www.ftc.gov/os/2001/04.
597. Racism and Xenophobia in Cyberspace at the Council of Europe website at http://www.assembly.coe.int/nw/xml/XRef/X2H-Xref-ViewHTML.asp?FileID=9540&lang=en.
598. http://conventions.coe.nt/Treaty/EN/rojets/FinalCybercrime.htm. Background Information and full text of the Convention can be found at the Council of Europe's website, www.coe.int/T/E/Communication_and_Research/Press/Themes_Files/Cybercrime.

forty-one states have ratified the convention, while a further eleven states had signed the Convention but not ratified the treaty.[599]

1274. In August 2012, the Australian Government passed the Cybercrime Legislation Amendment Act 2012 (Cth) (CLAA). The purpose of the CLAA was to enable Australia to accede to the Council of Europe Convention on Cybercrime (Cybercrime Convention), the only international treaty on cybercrime. The result of the new law is the amendment of existing Commonwealth statutes, including the Mutual Assistance in Criminal Matters Act 1987 (Cth), the Criminal Code Act 1995 (Cth), the TIAA and the Telecommunications Act 1997 (Cth).[600]

1275. The CLAA empowers Australia's law enforcement and intelligence agencies to compel carriers to preserve the communication records of persons suspected of cyber-based crimes and to request other parties to the Convention to do the same.

1276. The CLAA also expands the Commonwealth cybercrime offences. Computer crimes in Australia are set out in Commonwealth as well as State and Territory law. The cybercrime law expands the application of the Commonwealth offences under the Criminal Code 1995 (Cth) by removing the requirement that a Commonwealth computer or Commonwealth data be involved or affected, or that a carriage service be used, in the commission of the offence. The cybercrime law also extends the geographic reach of the provisions to conduct which occurs wholly or partly in Australia, on board an Australian aircraft or ship, and to the conduct of Australian nationals abroad in certain circumstances.

1277. The Convention on Cybercrime and the CLAA framework facilitate international cooperation between State parties to the Convention through the cross-border preservation and sharing of communication records.

1278. The treaty also requires signatory States to regularize criminal law so that it would prohibit unauthorized access of computer systems, unauthorized interception of computer transmissions, hacking computer systems or data, making devices facilitating such activity, and forging computer data. It also criminalizes distribution of material based on their content particularly child pornography.

1279. The Cybercrime Convention has not been without its critics. The criticisms include:

- The treaty encompasses too wide and too obscure a list of offences to be criminalized including the production and sale of any device designed for the purpose

599. List of signatories and ratifications of the treaty, website of the Council of Europe: http://hub.coe.int/.

600. Select Legislative Instrument 2013 No. 4; Explanatory Statement, at http://www.comlaw.gov.au/Details/F2013L00205/Explanatory%20Statement/Text.

of defeating computer data, computer infringement, the related rights of the Rome Convention, and the holding liable heads of corporations for computer offences.

- The treaty makes extraditable the complete list of offences. This is not practicable or workable across almost fifty countries.
- The treaty needs greater international cooperation, a single point of contact for intelligence sharing, and sharing of data prior to commission of crime and data processing to understand the implications of the gathered data.

Part VIII. Environmental Law Issues

Chapter 1. Cyber Law and Environmental Law

1280. Cyber law is driven by physical infrastructures and the processing by ICTs that result in tangible and intangible products. How these products are used and further exploited are defined by the roles and responsibilities of the various actors as producers and owners. Rules and regulations define the respective roles. Without ICT, cyber law may not exist. With it, cyber law has partly been responsible for bringing about rules and regulation to produce the many positive impacts of computers and the Internet.

1281. The Internet has brought many advances to society. However, with the maturation of ICT together with the planned obsolescence of ICT equipment there is the immediate problem of how to deal with and address the issues of waste electronic and electrical equipment (WEEE). Much of the waste materials are being dumped in land fill and in some cases are exported to developing countries for the recovery of valuable resources.

1282. This chapter outlines the growing environmental problems associated with WEEE and whether environmental law may provide some guidelines and offer lasting solutions to governing IT equipment at the end of their usefulness.

1283. After providing a working definition of e-waste and its many variant names, an outline is given to suggest how environmental law may be used to address issues arising from WEEE. Such issues include the transborder movement of hazardous materials and the role of international agreements such as the Basel Convention. Some comparisons are made in differentiating how countries are actively dealing with WEEE including Australia, the EU and UK and China. The different legislative approaches that have been developed to combat the WEEE problem are compared and a governance model proposed.

Chapter 2. Information Technology and E-Waste

1284. A UN report noted that the world produces at least 50 million tonnes of electronic and electrical waste (e waste) a year with only 20% of this is formally recycled with 80% either ending up in landfill or being informally recycled.[601] The report reveals the annual value of global e-waste was over AUD 62.5 billion.

1285. Much of the recycling is performed informally in developing countries and by hand exposing workers to hazardous and carcinogenic substances such as mercury, lead and cadmium. E-waste ends up as landfill that contaminates soil and groundwater. Improper management of e-waste results in a significant loss of scarce and valuable raw materials, such as gold, platinum, cobalt and rare earth elements. It is estimated that 7% of the world's gold may currently be contained in e-waste, with 100 times more gold in a tonne of e-waste than in a tonne of gold ore

1286. Global e-waste production is predicted to reach 120 million tonnes per year by 2050 if current trends continue,[602] according to a report from the Platform for Accelerating the Circular Economy (PACE)[603] and the UN E-Waste Coalition.[604]

1287. According to the ABS Australians are among the highest users of technology and concomitantly e-waste is becoming one of the fastest growing types of waste. Up to 2008, data show that nearly 17 million television sets and 37 million computers have been sent to landfill. Of the 15.7 million computers that reached their 'end of life' in Australia in 2007–2008 only 1.5 million were recycled – less than 10%. Annually Australians buy more than 4 million computers and 3 million television sets.[605]

---

601. UN Report, *Time to seize opportunity, tackle challenge of e-waste* (24 Jan. 2019), at https://www.unenvironment.org/news-and-stories/press-release/un-report-time-seize-opportunity-tackle-challenge-e-waste.
602. PACE, *A New Circular Vision for Global Electronics* (January 2019), at http://www3.weforum.org/docs/WEF_A_New_Circular_Vision_for_Electronics.pdf.
603. PACE is a public-private collaboration project accelerator designed to bring about the circular economy at speed and scale. It is a coalition of more than fifty leaders from business, government and international organizations. *See* http://www3.weforum.org/docs/WEF_A_New_Circular_Vision_for_Electronics.pdf.
604. The UN E-waste coalition is a group of seven UN agencies including the International Labour Organization (ILO); International Telecommunication Union (ITU); UN Environment; United Nations Industrial Development Organization (UNIDO); United Nations Institute for Training and Research (UNITAR); United Nations University (UNU) and the Secretariats of the Basel and Stockholm conventions. It is supported by the World Business Council for Sustainable Development (WBCSD), the World Health Organization (WHO) and the World Economic Forum and coordinated by the Secretariat of the Environment Management Group (EMG).
605. ABS, *Electronic and Electrical Waste Publication 4602.0.55.005 – Waste Account, Australia, Experimental Estimates 2013* (Canberra: ABS).

1288. Electronic waste (e-waste) is defined by the ABS as waste electrical and electronic equipment. Such equipment depends on electric currents or electromagnetic fields in order to function. This also includes consumer entertainment electronic equipment, office information and communications technology, household consumer appliances, lighting devices, power tools and devices used for sport and leisure including toys. E-waste is also sometimes referred to as techno-trash and techno-waste together with other variants in nomenclature.

1289. E-waste is an important and looming issue because of the negative impacts on the environment. The increased consumption of raw materials in the production of electrical and electronic equipment is coupled with the taking up of landfill space as well as the release of hazardous substances into the environment. This latter occurs when substances such as toxic heavy metals leach into soil and water plus others that contain non-biodegradable materials. Televisions and computers contain toxic materials such as lead, cadmium and mercury in its construction. These substances need to be managed safely if people and the environment are to be protected.

1290. On the other hand, e-waste may be 'mined' to recover valuable materials such as gold, silver and copper or the waste itself recycled and repurposed. Statistics suggest that the amount of gold recovered from one tonne of electronic scrap from personal computers is more than that recovered from 17 tonnes of gold ore.[606]

1291. The question has been asked as to whether e-waste is an untapped treasure?[607] In 2012 the StEP Initiative (Solving the E-waste Problem), a United Nations University (UNU) programme that aims to tackle e-waste, estimated that globally 48.9 million tonnes of electrical and electronic products were discarded. If present trends continue by 2017 the annual amount of e-waste produced around the world will reach 65.4 million tonnes.

1292. StEP recently produced the first e-waste world-map showing how much e-waste each country produces. China is shown as the leading producer in 2012 with 11.1 million tonnes followed by the US at 10 million tonnes.[608]

1293. In Togo, West Africa members of a community 'maker space' have created a 3D printer made almost entirely from electronic waste and scrap.[609]

---

606. Electronics TakeBack Coalition, *Facts and Figures on e-Waste and Recycling* (2010), at http://www.electronicstakeback.com/wp-content/uploads/Facts_and_Figures.
607. *See* Jonathan Kalan, *Is e-waste an untapped treasure?* (2010), at https://www.bbc.com/news/av/technology-26239741/making-a-living-from-toxic-electronic-waste-in-ghana (19 Feb. 2014).
608. *See* StEP initiative world map at http://step-info.org/step-e-waste-world-map.html.
609. *See* Woelab at http://www.woelabo.com/.

1294. A Ghana company FairPhone, builds phones from recycled components and non-toxic materials sourced from the digital dumping ground of Agbogloshie.[610]

1295. In Kenya, the e-Lab start-up company is tackling the African e-waste problem by transforming such waste into art, fashion and jewellery.[611]

1296. e-Waste is indeed is a treasure trove of precious metals and minerals. Recycling mobile phones alone provides about 24 kg of gold, 250 kg of silver, 9 kg of palladium and nine tonnes of copper.[612]

1297. Recovering these treasures, however, comes at a price. Low-end recyclers use acids or flame to extract the minerals that are a dangerous source of pollution. In Guiyu, China and elsewhere in India and Pakistan, there are scores of so-called cancer villages, black rivers and suffocating smog as a result of such recycling efforts. Whether this is recycling per se or dumping by another name nevertheless presages a serious issue.[613] The practices highlight an impending e-waste crisis waiting in the wings ready to break out into epidemic proportions as a result of unsustainable practices coupled with the weight of unmanageable volumes.

1298. The environmental imperative is that by reducing the environmental impact through recycling, reuse and repurposing of ICT some respite might be on offer. Being abstemious by using limited material resources, and safely and properly disposing of electronics equipment may make huge strides in avoiding environmental degradation.

---

610. *See* Fairphone at http://www.fairphone.com/2013/11/21/taking-back-phones-for-a-circular-economy-e-waste-in-ghana/.
611. http://kalan.me/2540092#.
612. *See* L Lewis, *Urban Miners' Buried in E-waste*, Australian 7 (7 Jan. 2014).
613. *See* V. Pelosi, *US cyber-waste dumped in Asia* (2002) at http://www.newint.org/columns/currents/2002/05/01/us-cyber-waste-dump-in-asia published 1 May 2002. Karnataka State Pollution Control Board at https://kspcb.gov.in/E-Waste.html.

Chapter 3. E-Waste Issues: Global and National Initiatives

1299. Among the more prominent initiatives that have been taken by the International organizations and nation states to address e-waste issues is that of the Basel Convention 1989 to manage the international movement of hazardous waste.

1300. The Basel Convention on the Control of Transboundary Movements of Hazardous Wastes and their Disposal was adopted on 22 March 1989 in Basel, Switzerland. This Convention was brought into force in 1992 and over 170 countries have signed the Convention including Australia. The Convention is an international treaty designed to reduce and regulate the movements of hazardous waste. It is a direct response to the widespread importation and dumping of toxic wastes in Africa in the 1980s.

1301. A main objective of the Convention is to protect human health and the environment against the adverse effects of hazardous wastes. Three major thrusts of the Convention include:

(1) a focus on the reduction of hazardous waste generation coupled with the promotion of environmentally sound management practices;
(2) restriction on the transboundary movements of hazardous wastes; and
(3) a regulatory system that restricts such movements.

1302. A cornerstone of the Basel Convention is the principle of prior informed consent where before an export of hazardous materials may take place the authorities of the State of export notify the authorities of the prospective States of import and transit with details of intended movements.[614]

§1. Reduction of E-Waste Generation in Australia

1303. To implement the 1989 Basel Convention the Australian government enacted the Hazardous Waste (Regulations of Exports and Imports) Act 1989 (Cth) to control the trade in specified waste materials.

1304. In Australia, the national and state and territory governments together with industry have developed the National Products Stewardship Scheme to promote and encourage recycling. Such a co-regulatory scheme has given rise to the National Television and Computer Recycling Scheme (NTCRS) funded and run by the television and computer industry. The Scheme builds on existing recycling efforts by councils, charitable and other organizations, to enable householders and small business to drop-off their unwanted televisions and computer products free of charge at selected collection locations across Australia.

614. Basel Convention 1989 at http://www.basel.int/TheConvention/Overview/tabid/1271/Default.aspx.

1305. The ACT was the first jurisdiction to offer such services to householders under the NTCRS. The ACT was also the first to implement landfill bans for computers in 2005 and televisions in 2010. The direct disposal of e-waste to landfill has been progressively banned by SA. Other Australian States have since followed suit.[615]

1306. In the co-regulatory scheme companies importing or manufacturing over a specified volume threshold of television or computer products become liable under the relevant legislation[616] and must join and fund an approved co-regulatory arrangement to provide collection and recycling services on their behalf. To date three approved co-regulatory arrangements have been operational since 2012–2013.[617]

1307. The Product Stewardship Act 2011 (Cth) came into force in August 2011 and provides the legislative framework for national product stewardship scheme. This is a key commitment by the Australian Government under the National Waste Policy and endorsed by the COAG in August 2010.

1308. This piece of legislation is supported by the Product Stewardship (TV and Computers) Regulations 2011 (Cth) which came into force in November 2011. The Regulations define the co-regulatory arrangements of responsible parties.

1309. The Regulations require industry to fund collection and recycling services to meet progressively increasing annual recycling targets, set as a proportion of the estimated total television and computer waste arising in Australia. These targets begin at 30% in 2012–2013 and increase to 80% by 2021–2022.[618]

1310. A further support mechanism to ensure consistency and guidance for the e-waste recycling industry is the Australian Standard 5377:2013 published in February 2013. This standard sets the benchmark for sound handling of waste under the scheme and is being implemented over time.[619]

1311. A total of 635 collection services – retail drop off points, local government and other waste facilities and temporary collection events were provided by the three co-regulatory arrangements at the end of June 2013. An estimated total of

615. National Television and Computer Recycling Scheme – Department of Sustainability, Environment, Water, Population and Communities (2012), at http://www.environment.gov.au/settlements/waste/ewaste/publications/index.html and *see also* ACT (2010) https://www.tccs.act.gov.au/__data/assets/pdf_file/0019/1131814/noWasteby2010strategy.pdf and South Australia (2014) http://www.zerowaste.sa.gov.au.
616. *Product Stewardship (TV and Computers) Regulations* 2011 (Cth).
617. Department of Environment (2014a), *National Television and Computer Recycling Scheme: Outcomes 2012-13* (February). *See* http://www.environment.gov.au/topics/environment-protection/national-waste-policy/television-and-computer-recycling-scheme.
618. *Ibid.*
619. Australian Standard 5377:2013 *Collection, storage, transport and treatment of end-of-life electrical and electronic equipment. See* http://www.standards.org.au/OurOrganisation/News/Documents/1430217%20E-Waste%20MR.pdf.

137,756 tonnes of televisions and computers reached end-of-life in Australia in 2012–2013. The target for the industry under the scheme was to recycle 30% of this amount. About 98.8% of this target was achieved under this arrangement. However, national data are unavailable on the amount of e-waste recycling that occurred outside the scheme in 2012–2013.[620]

1312. The disposal of mercury-containing lamps is primarily a state and local government responsibility in Australia. There is no legislation on collecting and recycling lamps. Landfill disposal of large amounts of mercury-containing lamps is forbidden in some States. There is a national voluntary scheme for recycling mercury-containing lamps from commercial and public lighting sectors.

1313. Between 2012 and 2013, 40,813 tonnes of waste televisions and computers were recycled in Australia, equivalent to 98.8% of the predefined national recycling target (41,327 tonnes for two types of waste products).[621] However, this collected amount is only 8.7% the total amount of e-waste generated for all product categories.[622]

§2. New Zealand

1314. In New Zealand, most e-waste is still going to landfill. E-waste is classified as a non-priority waste stream in New Zealand. Therefore, there is no restriction on e-waste sent to landfill, and there is no national legislation to regulate the collection and recycling of e-waste.[623]

§3. European Union and UK

1315. As with efforts in Australia, in the EU the WEEE Directive of 2012 is pertinent.[624] The WEEE Directive aims to reduce the amount of waste electrical and electronic equipment that ends up in landfill. This goal is to be achieved through changes in the electronic and electrical equipment (EEE) production cycle from product design to ease of dismantling, recycling and reuse. The provision of WEEE collection centres and processing systems is integral to this scheme.

---

620. Department of Environment (2014a) *supra.*
621. *Ibid.*
622. Department of Environment (2014b), at http://www.environment.gov.au/system/files/resources/cb4ad924-aaf8-4127-b8a1-31a30c2eca82/files/national-waste-policy-implementation-2013.pdf.
623. Government of New Zealand, *How to dispose and recycle electronic waste responsibly* (2013), at https://www.mfe.govt.nz/publications/waste/waste-electrical-and-electronic-equipment-guidance-collection-reuse-and-recycli-5.
624. Directive 2012/19/EU of the European Parliament and of the Council of 4 Jul. 2012 on Waste Electrical and Electronic Equipment (WEEE) at http://eur-lex.europa.eu/legal-content/EN/TXT/?uri=uriserv:OJ.L_.2012.197.01.0038.01.ENG.

1316. Implementation of the objective includes efforts by national and local government, EEE manufacturers and distributors, vendors and consumers. Compliance with WEEE Directive includes the mandatory participation in a Producer Compliance Scheme (PCS) that requires services that enable EEE to be effectively and economically recycled or reused so that new EEE placed on the market marked with certain information would allow for the correct disposal by the end user. Such schemes include: Distributor Takeback Scheme (DTS); Designated Collection Facilities (DCF); and Approved Treatment Facilities (ATF).

1317. In the EU there is a WEEE Directive on the transborder movement of hazardous materials and the eradication of certain hazardous substances from new EEE (the RoHS Directive).[625] Producers of EEE within the scope of the RoHS Directive are responsible for ensuring that their products meet the requirements. Further, the act of placing a product on the market is a declaration by the producer that the product complies with the Directive. The CE mark ensures such a declaration.[626]

1318. A CE mark C€

1319. The RoHS Directive draws its scope from that of the WEEE Directive with a few exceptions such as products intended to protect national security or military purposes or where electricity is not the main power source.[627]

1320. From 2016 EU Member States will have to collect 45 tonnes of e-waste for every 1000 tonnes of electronic goods put on sale during the previous three years. By 2019 the target must rise to 65 tonnes or Member States can opt to collect 85% of total e-waste generated.

1321. In the UK, Regulations implementing the WEEE Directive include the Waste Electrical and Electronic Equipment Regulations 2013 (UK).[628]

---

625. Directive 2012/18/EU of the European Parliament and of the Council of 4 Jul. 2012 on the Control of Major-accident Hazards Involving Dangerous Substances, amending and subsequently repealing Council Directive 96/82/EC at http://eur-lex.europa.eu/legal-content/EN/TXT/?uri=uriserv:OJ.L_.2012.197.01.0001.01.ENG; and the ROHS Directive on the Eradication of Certain Hazardous Substances from New Electrical and Electronic Equipment 2011/65/EU (RoHS 2) published in Official Journal L174, 1 Jul. 2011. This Directive came into force on the 21 Jul. 2011 and transposed into national law by Member States by 2 Jan. 2013.
626. The CE mark, or formerly EC mark, is a mandatory conformity marking for certain products sold within the European Economic Area (EEA) since 1985. The mark consists of the CE logo and, if applicable, the four-digit identification number of the notified body involved in the conformity assessment procedure. The CE marking is the manufacturer's declaration that the product meets the requirements of the applicable EC directives.
627. https://ec.europa.eu/environment/waste/rohs_eee/index_en.htm.
628. *See Waste Electrical and Electronic Equipment Regulations* 2013 (UK) at http://www.legislation.gov.uk/uksi/2013/3113/pdfs/uksi_20133113_en.pdf.

1322. An associated aim is to prevent illegal shipments of e-waste to poorly equipped developing countries, where workers recovering resources from WEEE are exposed to health hazards.[629]

§4. CHINA

1323. In 2011, China generated 3.62 million tonnes of e-waste made up of discarded televisions, refrigerators, washing machines, air conditioners and computers. Additionally, China was the recipient of increasing volumes of e-waste imported from around the globe. The exact volumes of such imports have been difficult to estimate and quantify because of illicit activity.[630]

1324. China has developed five key domestic policies including (1) a ban the transboundary importation of e-waste into China, (2) establishing principles for domestic e-waste management, (3) restricting the use of hazardous materials in electronic products, (4) licensing formal recyclers and setting treatment standards, and (5) establishing a national e-waste collection system and recycling infrastructure.

1325. To underpin these domestic policies legislation has been enacted, for example, the Regulation on the Administration of Recycling and Treatment of Waste Electrical and Electronic Equipment State Council No. 551 of 2011. This Regulation formalizes e-waste recycling in China by creating official e-waste collection channels, issuing treatment licences and providing subsidies to the formal sector.

1326. Other key national legislations and policies related to e-waste management in China include:

– Administrative Measures on Pollution Prevention of WEEE, SEPA No. 40 2010.
– A Catalogue for Managing the Import of Wastes, 2009.
– An Ordinance on the Management of Prevention and Control of Pollution from Electronic and Information Products, Ministry of Industry and Information Technology (MIIT) No. 39, 2007.
– Technical Policy on Pollution Prevention and Control of WEEE SEPA No. 115, 2006.

1327. However, the challenge is in the implementation and enforcement of these pieces of legislation. Substantial administrative reforms may be required especially with the transboundary shipment of e-waste, the licensing of recyclers to ensure that the standards are met, and to forbid informal recyclers from operating without the requisite licences.

---

629. BBC News Europe, *Electronic waste: EU adopts new WEEE law* (19 Jan. 2012), at http://www.bbc.co.uk/news/world-europe-16633940.
630. *See* F. Wang, R. Keuhr, D. Ahlquist & J. Li, *e-Waste in China: A Country Report* (2013), Tokyo: UNU-ISP available at http://collections.unu.edu/eserv/UNU:1624/ewaste-in-china.pdf.

Chapter 4. Role of Environmental Law in Cyberspace

1328. From a governance point of view, to mitigate the negative impacts of ICT, the role of environmental law to inform policy and practice could either be to disrupt malicious activity or through government efforts to control the production, use and disposal of ICT.

1329. From an international governance perspective, the havoc caused by intangible cyber disruptions could be characterized as a kind of transborder harm.

1330. Herein lies a difficult dilemma in that the transborder harm could be tangible as in the export of potentially toxic hardware or the dumping of WEEE and alternatively it could be intangible such as denial of service attack on a computer system.

1331. An example is the cyber disruptions that took place in Estonia in 2007. The lessons from the disruption are salutary. A 'botnet' threatened the national security of Estonia.[631] The so-called DDoS attacked websites which were suddenly inundated by tens of thousands of visits, jamming and disabling and overcrowding the bandwidths of the servers running these sites. Because of high levels of connectivity and prevalence of e-commerce and e-government services, the DDoS affected many sectors of Estonian society.

1332. Such attacks may be considered as variants of transborder harm and may be no less different from the export of potentially toxic hardware.

1333. This duality of characterization (tangible-intangible element) is a first cyber challenge in attempting to integrate cyber law with environmental law.

1334. A second cyber challenge is the role of non-state actors in transborder harm given that industry and users have as much or a greater stake than state actors. The Australian approach and indeed the Basel Convention, have designed a co-regulatory approach where all three parties have a vital stake in resolving the issues – government, industry and private parties such as users, consumers and recyclers.

1335. Lessons from environmental law in outlining the scope, the enforcement of regulation and remedies for environmental harm provide the principles for developing holistic solutions for cyberspace. Equivalents of norms and principles employed in environmental law could be used with similar effect in cyberspace.

1336. The 1930s Trail Smelter case enunciated the principle of good neighbourliness and this seems to be fully applicable in cyberspace.[632] The principle defines

---

631. *See* J. Traynor, *Russia accused of unleashing cyberwar to disable Estonia*, The Guardian, (17 May 2007) at http://www.guardian.co.uk/world/2007/may/17/topstories3.russia.
632. *Trail Smelter* (*U.S. v. Canada*) 3 R. Int'l Arb. Awards 1905 (1938 and 1941).

the role of state sovereignty as well as the responsibility of the state even where non-state actors are involved. The obiter from the Trail Smelter case suggests that States can be liable for harm from cross-border emissions. In the Internet age this cross-border principle might be applied to botnet attacks in cyberspace.

1337. The other landmark environmental law case in the late 1940s is that of the Corfu Channel litigation.[633] In this instance the legal principle is that when states are aware of activities that will harm other states, they are obliged to prevent them. There is an implied mutual obligation among states to prevent harm. The applicability of this principle in cyber law includes the omission of an action in preventing pollution and hazardous activity.

1338. While it may not be easy to identify and stop cyber pollution of the kind suggested with WEEE these issues require new laws to resolve such problems. International environmental legal norms provide the scope and are helpful in a range of activities including those undertaken by private actors. It may be suggested that environmental legal norms may provide guidelines and solutions to the current and emerging issues in cyber security, cyber conflict, and cyber defence.

---

633. *Corfu Channel* (*UK v. Albania*) 1949 I.C.J. 4 (Apr. 9).

Chapter 5. Governance and Regulatory Framework for Environmental Law

1339. Even where good environmental management legislation exists, poorly developed regulatory frameworks and weak enforcement regimes may limit their value. The need is for more effective regulatory frameworks for environmental and resource management in cyberspace.[634]

1340. One of the first steps in this regard is the need to identify key stakeholders and then to define closely the respective roles and responsibilities. The key stakeholders here may be shown in diagrammatic form below (Figure 8). After identification, specific focussed e-waste legislation may need to be developed that provides guidance, monitoring and either punitive or educational measures to help reduce the volumes of e-waste.

634. *See* Department of Foreign Affairs and Trade, *Aid and the Environment – Building Resilience, Sustaining Growth. An Environment Strategy for Australian Aid* (June 2007) at http://aid.dfat.gov.au/aidissues/Documents/environment.pdf.

Figure 8 Key Stakeholders in Managing WEEE

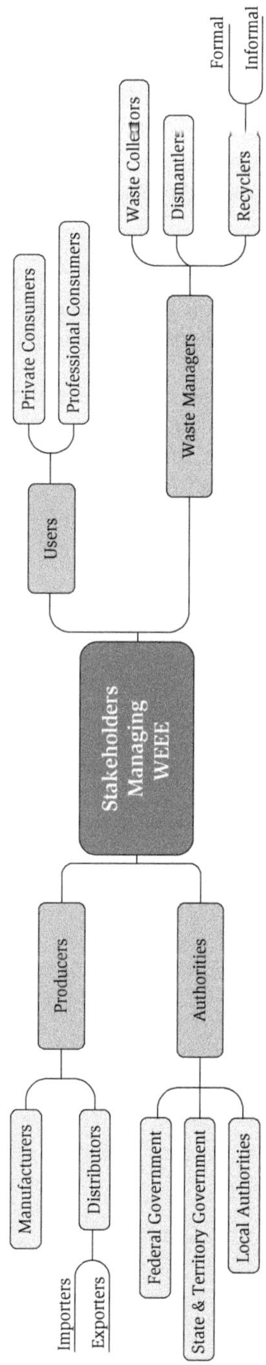

§1. Framework for E-Waste Legislation

1341. A framework for e-waste legislation should address all of the following:

- Develop clear definitions and terminology to encompass the scope of EEE and e-waste.
- Establish clear targets for e-waste legislation such as collection, reuse, recycling targets.
- Develop evaluation methods for implementing e-waste laws and treatment standards.
- Improve formal sector's collection performance including appropriate financing and subsidy schemes and methods of determining rates in the collection, logistics and treatment fees.
- Demarcate responsibilities of producers, users and other stakeholders.
- Establish monitoring systems for implementing legislation by creating feedback mechanisms and improvement of practices.
- Stimulate eco-design through other innovative legislation and raise public awareness of e-waste issues through education programmes at all levels of society.

Chapter 6. Summary and Conclusions

1342. Cyber law is both the product of, and the result from, the use of ICT. The technology provides many and varied challenges to traditional law and legal norms. Some parts of cyber law have been created as a response to these challenges in order to ensure that some rule of law exists. In this process the obsolescence of ICT equipment and infrastructure as WEEE will have an impact on the environment.

1343. Available data from around the world suggests that e-waste is a growing problem not only in terms of its volume but also in terms of its toxicity. Whilst attempts at resource recovery have been made, the results are on a small-scale and patchy.

1344. Global and national initiatives have focused on treaties, the Basel Convention, for instance, through to the reduction of waste both at source and at end-of-life. Australian examples suggest a co-regulatory approach may work. This approach will permit the funding by governments with privateers recycling e-waste. Mutually agreed targets may be set that are progressively increased in order to keep pace with the growth in volumes of WEEE.

1345. The EU WEEE Directive requires compliance with recycling, reuse and mandating that new EEE placed on the market contains certain information to allow for the correct disposal by the end user. Furthermore, the EU RoHS Directive is aimed at the transborder movement of hazardous materials and on eradicating the use of certain hazardous substances in new EEE.[635] The UK has implemented the EU WEEE Directive with domestic legislation.

1346. China has developed key environmental protection policies for the administration and recycling and treatment of WEEE. The main challenge in China and elsewhere is the implementation and enforcement of environmental legislation.

1347. Environmental law plays a vital role in mitigating the negative impacts of ICT, as well as informs policy and practice. As a start environmental law has to deal with the tangible aspects of e-waste.

1348. Environmental law norms and principles can be fashioned and reconceptualized to deal with the intangible aspects of the products of ICT such as cyber disruptions occasioned by DDOS.

1349. As a result, integrating cyber law with environmental law will need to address the tangible-intangible aspects of ICT use as well as deal with state and non-state actors.

---

635. ROHS Directive on the Eradication of Certain Hazardous Substances from New Electrical and Electronic Equipment 2011/65/EU (RoHS 2) published in Official Journal L174, 1 Jul. 2011. This Directive came into force on the 21 Jul. 2011 and transposed into national law by Member States by 2 Jan. 2013.

1350. To assist in developing a more effective regulatory framework for environmental and resource management in cyberspace, an identification of key stakeholders may provide a governance structure. Such a governance structure may permit the respective roles and responsibilities to be defined so that a focused e-waste strategy may be underpinned by relevant legislation.

1351. It is believed that international environmental norms may also provide the scope, mechanisms, guidelines and solutions for developing cyber law to a greater extent than is presently the case. To date, it appears that environmental law has been underutilized and overlooked especially in addressing problems relating to WEEE. While it may not always be easy to identify and stop cyber pollution, it may be possible to both stop malicious activity and disable botnets and sources of malicious software.[636]

636. *See* Jason Healey and Hannah Pitts, *Applying International Environmental Legal Norms to Cyber Statecraft*, 8(2) I/S: A Journal of Law and Policy for the Information Society 356–387 (2012).

Part IX. Technological Developments

Chapter 1. GIS and Cyber Law

§1. GIS in a Cyber Law Context

1352. This chapter suggests the link between cyber law and an information technology application generally described as geographic and geospatial information systems (GIS). While cyber law deals with the relationship of the Internet to technological and electronic elements a parallel consideration is how software application and information systems interface with the Internet. If cyber law is taken to include the body of law bearing on the network of networks, the Internet, then GIS is the manifestation of technology that places challenges to the law by way of the protection of information access, privacy, IPR and the response of Australian jurisdictions to these topics.[637] Much of the law is not new but involves the application of traditional laws tailored for the new technology albeit with some completely new areas of law developed to address the emergent challenges.

1353. In Australia the GIS industry is valued at more than a billion AUD dollars and represents an important segment of the Australian economy.[638]

§2. Data and Information

1354. Geographic information systems are a technology fed by data. Raw data are transformed into information through initial processing. Digital geographic data may be distinguished from numeric and other kinds of data, for example, numerical, quantitative, qualitative, derived and synthetic data which are collectively described as digital geospatial data.

1355. In the context of processing therefore, when data are 'ordered' in some way, say based on geography to make the data intelligible to humans, we then have

637. 'Cyberlaw' Encyclopædia *Britannica*. Encyclopædia *Britannica Online Academic Edition*. Encyclopædia Britannica Inc., 2014, https://www.britannica.com/topic/cyberlaw (accessed 21 May 2014).

638. ACIL Tasman (2008) at https://www.crcsi.com.au/assets/Resources/e2b13d9b-9be9-4338-ad68-b6758f759355.pdf.

the beginnings of geospatial information. This characterization of data and information may be extended to higher levels of abstraction so that from information is derived knowledge and the sum of all knowledge provides an 'intelligence' to the scheme of things. Indeed, it is sometimes claimed that 'wisdom' is the correct use of knowledge.

1356. Information has taken a central place in modern society and technology has revolutionized the way it is collected, stored and disseminated. A citizen's ability to participate in a democratic (or any) society is increasingly linked to their relative abilities to get access to that information.

§3. Definition of GIS

1357. GIS mean different things to different people ranging from the perverse to the obtuse. To some it seems to be a part of a government information system whereas to others it may seem to be a part of the 'alphabet soup' of information technology where people talk only in acronyms. However, any definition of GIS must acknowledge the important statement made by Lord Chorley (UK Department of Environment (DOE)) 1987 as 'a system for capturing, storing, checking, manipulating, analyzing and displaying data which are spatially referenced to the Earth'.[639]

639. United Kingdom, Department of the Environment (DOE) (1987) *Handling Geographic Information,* Report of the Committee of Enquiry chaired by Lord Chorley, London: HMSO at p. 132; and Tomlinson, RF (ed.) (1972) *Geographical Data Handling*, 2 vols. IGU Commission on Geographical Data Sensing and Processing for UNESCO/IGU Second Symposium on Geographical Information Systems, Ottawa.

Chapter 2. GIS and Cyber Law Legal Issues

1358. The legal issues raised by GIS technology include the following:

- Contract law – breach of contract, contract for service or goods, employees and contractors.
- IPR such as copyright and patents – licences, permits, royalty, copyright protection, third-party rights to value-added data, Crown copyright and implied proprietary authority, action by government, trade secrets and trademarks.
- Privacy issues related to intrusions into personal life and information.
- Consumer protection and tort law – liability for loss and injury, damages, for negligence, products liability, error in datasets offered for sale, sovereign immunity, mistake and misrepresentation.
- Law of evidence, GIS and maps in courts and future roles.
- Legal and regulatory environment governing access to public information and data, policy issues, privacy and data protection.

Chapter 3. GIS and the Law of Contract

§1. General

1359. Fundamental legal questions in cyber law are generated by the nature of the technology in GIS and whether a product or a service is being provided; and whether a GIS provider is a contractor or employee.

1360. Contractual issues are multifaceted and prismatic especially in relation to geospatial information products and services. These geospatial information products and services sometimes meld inconspicuously into one another and make it difficult to identify each element individually. Hence, it may be vital for geospatial analysts and practitioners to recognize the respective roles of information providers, software consultants and end users of information systems on the one hand and the software, technical support and other services on the other. A sound understanding of contract law will go a long way to good business practice to ensure effective business relationships.

1361. New developments in the delivery of geospatial information, storage, and analysis have transformed the nature of the workflow. The shift in paradigm is one that is wholly digital to one that is from the desktop to one that is virtual in the 'cloud'. Cloud computing has opened new vistas in spatial computing and geospatial analytics as users can access these resources from anywhere, at any time and share these with everyone. In addition, the introduction of crowd-sourced mapping techniques suggests that the volunteer and the 'crowd' add to the complexity of contractual relationships.

§2. Geospatial Information: Products and Services

1362. Geospatial information tools deliver both products and services. The sale of products and goods requires different contractual terms to those that offer services to the public at large. Contracts are both necessary and sufficient conditions for business efficacy for persons and agencies seeking to offer geospatial information services or products. However, at various stages before any agreement, and before contracts are signed, a person or agency may need to explore the nature of the product or service that is contemplated whether it be:

- A request for information (RFI);
- A request for proposals (RFP);
- The provision of programming services and/or licensing and leasing of software;
- The maintenance of databases, data collection, data analysis and reporting;
- The development of a GIS;
- The outsourcing of mapping functions including the collection, storage and dissemination; and
- The delivery of mapping services through mobile devices and on the Internet.

1363. Geospatial analyses using GIS has since its inception been the provision of products rather than one of services, even though the latter may also be contemplated. GIS analyses include maps and written reports and the accompanying recommendations and expert opinion on the problem at hand whether these are environmental, logistical or merely database management issues. A common feature of commissioned works is that one party can expect a document or series of documents providing both analyses as well as strategies to assist in the decision-making process. In doing so, there is an implied warranty of some form. That warranty would include the fact that the task was undertaken with all due diligence, skill and care and that the final product was delivered in a workman-like, professional manner. Furthermore, it is implied that the work was executed and that the materials supplied are of good quality and fit for the purpose for which they are given.

1364. With geospatial information analysis as a service some form of indemnity and exclusion from legal liability is usually written into the contract. These exclusions, of necessity, may include terms that avoid or limit liability arising from negligence and the subsequent damage and loss.

1365. A contract for geospatial information services will also attract tort liability arising from negligence. The liability involves a duty of care, the breach of the duty of care, causation or proximate cause, and damages. Contractual liability is more limited and narrower in scope because of the privity requirement.

1366. Where the geospatial information contract was for the provision of software – the mapping system itself, there may be difficulties in distinguishing between the supply of goods (products) and/or the provision of services.

1367. In Australia, the NSW Supreme Court considered the supply of both software and hardware as a sale of goods. In *Toby Constructions Products Pty. Ltd. v. Computa Bar (Sales) Pty. Ltd.* the court held that the sale and installation of software and hardware and the training of the purchaser's staff constituted a sale of goods.[640] The judge stated that the 'system, software included, whilst representing the fruits of much research and work, was in current jargon off-the-shelf, in a sense mass-produced'.

1368. Similarly, an English court in *Micron Computer Systems Ltd. v. Wang (UK) Ltd* treated the supply of a computer system, comprising both the hardware and software, as a sale of goods.[641]

1369. The underlying facts of each case noted above suggests whether a product or a service or even both products and services are dependent on the facts of the

640. [1983] 2 NSWLR 48 per Rogers J at p. 51.
641. Unreported 9th May 1990 (QBD).

case and what is contemplated in the contract itself.[642] Hence, in the sale of geospatial information databases, it may be necessary to specify the nature of the data product as completely as possible. This will mean specifying as far as possible what the data were collected for, what the data have been used for, what the data may be unsuitable for, and what is the coverage of the data set. Specifications will be necessary in order to ensure that the buyer knows what they are buying, what types of warranties are being given and exclusions of liabilities.

§3. Contract of Service and Contract for Service

1370. A distinction can be made between a contract of service and a contract for service. The distinction is between an employee and a consultant each attracting different legal entitlements and responsibilities.

1371. This distinction is an important one under the common law. The distinction between a contract of service and a contract for service is concerned with the hiring of personnel either as an employee or of an independent consultant.

1372. An employment contract is one under which the employer has the right to directly control the services of the employee. In an employment contract, the employer has the vested right to give directions as to the manner of performance of the work, the ownership of the products produced and the intangibles including IPR.

1373. On the other hand, an independent contractor or consultant may contract for a result. The result may be a product or the performance of an activity. The contractor or consultant may not agree to accept the directions of the employer as to the execution of the work. Hence, the consultant performs 'for service' as opposed to an employment contract where it is one 'of service'.

1374. Contractual liability and the privity of contract define roles and responsibilities of the parties. The doctrine of privity of contract defines the connection or relationship that exists between two parties in a contract. The privity of contract is a necessary element of the law to sheet home contractual liability, identify responsibilities and to make reparation for damage and loss suffered between those parties in a contractual relationship.

1375. Vendors who supply data that are discovered to be inaccurate, incomplete or misleading and which might negatively impact on persons or property could give rise to a contractual liability. Similarly, users of geospatial data may become subject

642. *See also* a comparative discussion of the different jurisdictions throughout the common law world in Commerce Clearing House Inc. (CCH) 1992 *Guide to Computer Law*, 'Computer hardware and software as goods' (CCH ¶7120), 'Hybrid transactions: Contracts including system support services' (CCH ¶7140); and 'Time-sharing and service bureau contracts' (CCH ¶7160).

to legal obligations to the provider or vendor when they fail to comply with provisions of the contract or use the geospatial products beyond the intended uses outlined in the contract. Examples of usage beyond the contract include using data incorrectly, whether intentional or otherwise, however, may be exposed to tortious liability.

1376. A contract for the provision of a geospatial service may often specify a quality standard, for example, the scale, resolution, or accuracy to some national or international benchmark. How the contract is fulfilled, such as the type and quality of the media on which the data, product or service is to be delivered or maintained, the time of delivery including the updating of the data, and the privity of the contract or the exclusivity of the data represent the terms of the contract. A vendor will have to fulfil these terms in order to avoid any form of liability. Failure to deliver any of these may put the contractor in breach of the contract.

Chapter 4. GIS and Property Rights

§1. Characteristics of Property Rights and GIS

1377. Property rights, especially those pertaining to the intellect remain an elusive and an enigmatic topic of discussion for cyber law. Depending on the context these rights are difficult to define and isolate because they are ephemeral, dynamic and ever changing. Unless these IPR are attached to some tangible element the topic is elastic and indefinable.

1378. The WIPO Convention Stockholm 1967 Article 2 (viii) defines 'IP' to include rights relating to:

- Literary, artistic and scientific works.
- Performances of performing artists, phonograms and broadcasts.
- Inventions in all fields of human endeavour.
- Scientific discoveries.
- Industrial designs.
- Trade marks, services marks and commercial names.
- Protection against unfair competition.
- All other rights resulting from intellectual activity in the industrial, scientific, literary or artistic fields.

§2. Protection of IP in Australia

1379. In Australia, IP law does not cover all the rights in the Convention's list above. The Australian approach is more piecemeal with no general protection given to cover 'all other rights' in the residual category above.

1380. The protection of IPR is both statutory and common law, derived from and closely parallel to the law of the UK. There are four distinct statutory regimes:

(1) *Copyright.* Copyright Act 1968 (Cth) protects the rights of authors in their 'work' of original creative effort. Such rights also include the right to reproduce the work and to make copies and the right to present it to the public.
(2) *Registered designs.* Designs Act 1906 (Cth) grants rights in relation to the appearance of an article provided that its features are novel or original.
(3) *Patents.* Patents Act 1968 (Cth) protects rights of inventors in their inventions provided certain threshold requirements have been satisfied such as novelty, inventiveness and utility.
(4) *Trade marks.* Trade Marks Act 1955 (Cth) protect the marks used by traders in relation to their goods and services to indicate the origin or trade connection of those goods and services.

1381. Generally, IP is concerned with the protection of ideas such as inventions, as well as the way in which ideas are expressed such as in copyright. The rationale behind such protections is that without it and the prospect of financial rewards, a person would not invest time, effort and creativity in developing ideas and to bring it to the benefit of others. Copyright, patents, designs and trademarks provide a means of protecting that investment of time and effort by preventing the unauthorized use of protected material.[643]

§3. PROTECTION OF IPR AND GIS

1382. In the spatial information context property rights are omnipresent. Geospatial information technology involves all kinds of inventive, creative and original endeavours. Such work may involve the compilation of data to build databases for map products. The data may be expressed in graphic and textual form in order to communicate ideas.

1383. Geospatial information services may be delivered in inventive ways either by methods or systems that are unique and special to spatial information systems. All these activities and delivery methods should be deemed valuable enough for the geospatial information professional to seek some form of protection from loss, theft, and inadvertent slippage into the public arena.

1384. In parallel, the geospatial information professional should seek to avoid any infringement of the rights of others and the consequent liabilities. With IPR subsisting in GIS products and services the boundaries separating what may be in the public domain and those in the private domain can best be described as 'fuzzy' and the lines easily transgressed.

1385. The potential for infringement is further exacerbated in the digital environment given the ease with which information and data may be sent over the Internet with easy replication and the production of derivative works. One example is the practical difficulty in tracing the lineage of the data or the author of the work. Tracing lineage is important in giving attribution to the work, to seeking permission, or to sheet home liability for damage for erroneous data.

I. Ownership Rights

1386. IPR are particularly relevant to GIS not only because GIS databases are very expensive to develop but also because copyright protection may be difficult to obtain for map products and even more difficult for digital GIS databases. Copyright incorporating concepts such as 'sweat of the brow' are increasingly being

643. Golvan C, *An Introduction to Intellectual Property Law* vii(Federation Press 1992).

looked at as a way of providing non-contractual protection of such databases and where ad hoc licensing or other means of protection may not be possible or practicable.

1387. In cyberspace, there appears to be a preoccupation with the copyright of maps and dynamic electronic maps produced 'on-the-fly'. The copyright debate thus far has focused on the issue of maps being 'factual' products and thereby being excluded protection since most copyright laws do not protect 'facts', only their expression. However, in cyberspace geospatial information maps are stored as files on a digital database. This very fact raises the twin dilemma as to whether these factually accurate compilations in databases can be given protection under copyright law.

1388. Even if the database were protected in some way, it is arguable that if one were to extract the facts and express these in a different graphical form, the very act of extraction and expression may not amount to an infringement of the copyright subsisting in the database because ostensibly a new product is being created.

1389. An added difficulty with using databases is that it is often very difficult, if not impossible, to separate facts from expression. Facts relate to the content of the database, and expression relating to the way the database is digitally organized and structured.

1390. There is no clarity as to how much protection existing law affords geospatial information databases. In the US the Feist case and in Australia the Desktop Marketing case raise serious problems for the copyright protection of maps and digitized geospatial information systems in databases in general.[644]

II. IPR Protection Framework

1391. The framework facilitating the protection of IPR in Australia is by common law and statute. At common law the protection of IPR in goods and services is found in goodwill or commercial reputation attached to a name, mark or trade dress (get-up).

1392. Trade secrets and confidential information are protected by the equitable action of breach of confidence.

1393. The statutory regime for the protection of IPR is with the Copyright Act 1968 (Cth). The Act deems printed and digital maps copyrightable because these are interpreted as 'literary' and 'artistic' works under section 10(1).

644. *Feist Publications Inc. v. Rural Telephone Services Company*, 111 S.Ct. 1282 (1991), 499 US 340 (1991); *Telstra Corporation Ltd. v. Desktop Marketing Systems Pty. Ltd.* [2001] FCA 612, *Desktop Marketing Systems Pty. Ltd. v. Telstra Corporation Ltd.* [2002] FCAFC 112.

1394. Literary works include a table or compilation, expressed in words, figures or symbols, whether in a visible form or not. Map data stored in an electronic database, even though seemingly a factual compilation is considered a literary work. A drawing is an 'artistic' work, which may include a diagram, map, chart or plan.

1395. The Copyright Act 1968 (Cth) also requires 'originality' in the sense that the author has expended a minimal degree of skill, judgment and labour to achieve that result.

1396. The concept of originality can be most problematic when one interprets maps as electronic databases, that is, those that store facts can be thought of as merely compilations. For a compilation to be 'original' an author must demonstrate a certain degree of skill not only in selecting the factual content but also in the expression of those facts so that the arrangement in presentation can be deemed to be a truly original product.[645] Any map thus comes within both the 'drawing' and 'literary work' definitions of the Copyright Act 1968 (Cth). This dual categorization raises uncertainty particularly in relation to statutory defences to infringement of copyright.

1397. Initially, maps, as with directories and other fact-based works, enjoyed a flexible judicial approach. Prior works could be used by a later cartographer on the basis that it was in the public interest to produce more accurate maps.[646]

1398. However, since the eighteenth century, the approach is the same as those cases involving directories and other types of works. Thus, while a later cartographer was free to make a map on the same subject as an earlier cartographer, the obligation was to do this independently and not to copy or use any of the results of work done by a predecessor. Indeed, as Page Wood V.C. indicated by way of obiter in *Kelly v. Morris* (1866) L.R. 1 Eq. 697 at 702, that it would even be impermissible for the later author to refer to the original map at all.

1399. The leading Australian map case is that of *Sands & McDougall Pty. Ltd. v. Robinson* (1917) 23 CLR 49. The High Court held that the defendant had reproduced the plaintiff's map of the Balkans, even though the former had changed the colour of the political divisions, corrected the Balkan boundaries, introduced some places which had acquired recent prominence and deleted some other places.

1400. If the Sands & McDougall verdict is the correct approach involving maps then it suggests that later map makers should steer clear of all earlier publications and begin from scratch – an altogether unpalatable and impracticable prospect.[647]

---

645. *Sands & McDougall Pty. Ltd. v. Robinson* (1917) 23 CLR 49 – a case of inventive originality.
646. *Sayre v. Moore* (1785) 1 East 316, n. 5, 102 ER 139.
647. S. Ricketson, *The Law of Intellectual Property* 210 (Law Book Company 1984).

1401. Maps are graphical representations of space whether in one, two, three or n-dimensions. The term hyper-space has been used to describe three or more dimensions. More conventionally, we may think of maps as depicting three-dimensional terrestrial space related to some feature of the earth from the mountains to the plains to the sea and deep ocean valleys. We may also divide such terrestrial space into discrete regions to depict both administrative boundaries as well as social space in terms of cultural groups.

1402. In a geospatial information context 'layers' of information superimposed on a common grid is the technique to produce a map. The map is comprised of layers may have multiple interests and rights – a fragmentation of IPR and interests – since the data in each layer may be derived from different sources and at different times. While ownership of each of the layers may be attributable to an owner, use has been made of so-called data commons and IPR statement. Data commons refer to public domain data that belongs to everyone and the IPR statement such as a copyright notice is one that asserts right of the authors, is commonly found on both the final map as well as on the digital database of the map.

1403. Thus, in GIS where a map is reduced to digital form, one of the first attributes that can become blurred by data processing is the control over the ownership of IPR in the digital data. In the past agencies have claimed copyright on the paper maps that they have provided to users. However, with digital data the task is not so easy.

1404. With traditional paper maps and books, the article including the copyright notice may be handed over-the-counter to a customer. With digital products it may be as impersonal as pressing a button to transfer the data electronically.

1405. Also, the copyright notice on a digital copy may easily be deleted with the press of a key. Even with map data that are handed over in a diskette, memory stick or other digital form, one is unable to examine the article or to preview its contents as one could do with a map or a book as the former may need access to some digital equipment.

1406. Furthermore, when one digitizes from a published map there is a strong element of ownership and possession in claiming 'my digital map' even though it is based on someone else's original.

1407. When one adds other information and performs operations on it like re-formatting and combining it with other data, the 'paternity' of the original source(s) become further blurred or may disappear after several iterations of the data. The 'offspring' now takes on a new form and new identity indistinguishable from the source data. The product could now be claimed to be an 'original' piece of work.

1408. The claim to ownership could also subsist as a 'sweat of the brow' issue where time, effort and skill have been used to produce the new product. The issue therefore is: at what stage does the new map become an 'original' and assume a new identity in order that copyright and other IPR may be claimed on its own merits?

1409. There may be no answer to this dilemma short of tracing 'paternity' and ownership at each step of the operation. This is where a metadata layer usefully describes what is being done, but also by whom, and at what stage. The final product could be one where there may be multiple copyright owners and a 'new' copyright work will conceivably be the whole of the work. Cyberspace law may have to be developed to accommodate such eventualities.

1410. In terms of maps and electronic databases it is said that the originality requirement is 'low' under Australian copyright law with little or no scope for a cartographer to create a fully 'original' result. This may be because GIS aim for accuracy and standardization in order to make the database more accessible.[648]

1411. The information in the database makes it invaluable and the arrangement, selection and the different formats that may be used gives the work enough originality. Significantly, it has been noted, with some irony, that the more comprehensive a database is, the less scope is there to lay a claim to copyright protection as an original piece of work. This is because in a comprehensive database, there may be nothing left to 'select' in order to satisfy the requirements of the Copyright Act 1968 (Cth).[649]

1412. Sellers of public and private information can invoke confidentiality restrictions on their clients, users and customers when they purchase their products. Thus, in a GIS context one can use confidential information but one may not disclose it to a third party. Sellers of such information enforce these restrictions through a contractual agreement.

III. Legal Risks

1413. The development and application of GIS in a commercial context may involve legal risks which, if ignored could result in liability and loss for a business or government entity that develops GIS and/or sells, distributes and resells or provides GIS services. For this reason, it is important that a GIS developer offering products and/or services limits and minimizes legal risks through the implementation of a legal risk management strategy.[650]

---

648. P. Eldred, *Geographic Information Systems and Copyright: Are We on the Right Road?*, WALIS News, 13–18 (March 1995) at p. 14.
649. DS Karjala, *Copyright in electronic maps*, Proceedings of the Conference on Law and Information Policy for Spatial Databases, Tempe AZ, October, NCGIA & Center for the Study of Law, Science and Technology, Arizona State University College of Law (1994), at http://www.spatial.maine.edu.tempe/karjala.html. And in 35 *Jurimetrics* J. 395–415 (1995).
650. K. Reid, E.E. Clark & G. Cho, *Legal Risk Management for Geographic Information Systems*, 7 J. L. Info. Sci. 169–207 (1996).

IV. Functional Characteristics

1414. In GIS, the data used are digital versions of maps. Other information such as various forms of indexing, cross matching, unique identifiers and other software generated markers are added to the digital maps. The information has been included to make the digital versions of maps more 'functional' within a GIS. While these have made the digital data very complex, the intent is to make the data easier to use and access through the computer and information system.

1415. The four main functional characteristics of GIS data are pertinent in this discussion include:

(1) Graphical representation (input and output data) as maps.
(2) Attribute information to make the data more meaningful.
(3) Data integration by geographical location.
(4) Spatial analysis.

1416. On any interpretation of the Copyright Act 1968 (Cth) the inescapable conclusion is that printed maps from GIS and maps stored as digital data in a database qualify for protection. The key elements of originality and reduction to material form satisfy the basic requirements of copyright. However, the very nature of the data storage technology in the form of the electronic database and as a compilation of geographical facts begs the question of whether these also attract copyright protection.

1417. Other legal issues relating to geospatial databases include duration of protection, authorship, ownership, and protection of non-original databases and rights to unfair extraction. In information technology there is doubt whether computer-produced data can lay claim to copyright protection, whether such data are original and if so, who is the author?

1418. Collated information in the form of an electronic database poses a vexed problem because the Copyright Act 1968 (Cth) makes it clear that compilations of information will be protected as a 'literary work' only if a court is satisfied that the compilation represents a suitable degree of originality.

1419. Subject to these provisos, an electronically stored database will be entitled to the same amount of protection under the Copyright Act 1968 (Cth) as a conventional database in hardcopy format.

1420. Facts, as such, are not protectable under copyright law. However, various Commonwealth jurisdictions have found ways to protect compilations under the auspices of copyright law and abundant case law exists to support this practice.[651]

651. JT Cross, *Protecting Computer Databases under the United States Copyright Laws: Implications of the Feist Decision*, in *Computers and Law* 113–127 at 113 (I. Carr & K. Williams eds, Intellect Books 1994).

1421. The Berne Convention – droit moral – protects the integrity of a creator's work. Moral rights are not transferable and remain with the author and heirs for fifty years from the year of the author's death.

1422. Moral rights relate to the right to integrity; that is, the right to object to any distortion, mutilation or other modifications which might be prejudicial to the artist's honour or reputation; the right to attribution, that is, the right to claim authorship of a work; the right to decide when a work will be published; and, the right to withdraw a work from publication.

1423. In so far as moral rights in maps are concerned, it appears that all such rights may subsist except the right of integrity. A map produced by an 'author' using GIS may object to having the subtle colours of the work reduced to 8-bits rather than the millions of colours that are available on modern computers.

1424. An author can rightly complain if the aspect ratio of the map is changed or if the work is truncated, clipped and cropped to fit into a page format that is being designed. How authors of such GIS products can ensure 'integrity' is an issue that will rear its head more and more in future.

1425. In practice, caveats that are attached to marginal information on the map as well as technical specifications placed in a box annotation may preserve details under which the original map was produced. As well this may serve to assert the moral rights of the 'author'.

1426. There are, of course, practical and legal problems that are difficult to resolve. For instance, GIS does not fit neatly into any of the specific categories of 'works' whether literary, dramatic, musical or artistic works. Yet, GIS products are the result of human creativity.

1427. Unlike other protected works, the products from GIS and the databases accompanying these are open to copying and unauthorized use with a loss of the heritage of the data after perhaps one cycle. As observed previously it is impossible to use an information system without making a copy of it first. This is radically different from traditional protected works where such copying is unnecessary.

1428. The display of data on a computer screen may constitute a reproduction in material form, as well as a 'public performance', albeit ephemeral since the display may be switched off. A print of the data stored in the computer may infringe copyright and if this were part of an electronic network, the network manager may be in breach for authorizing an 'infringement'. The dynamic nature of a database with frequent updates may make it impossible to determine when protection for the data begins.

1429. It could be concluded that electronically stored databases are no different from non-electronic databases and therefore should raise no new copyright issues. Non-original databases do not qualify for copyright protection because there may be no originality in the selection and arrangement.[652]

652. P. Lindsay, *Copyright Protection of Electronic Databases*, 4 J. L. Info. Sci. 287–292 (1993).

Chapter 5. GIS and Privacy

§1. Overview of Privacy Issues

1430. The relationship between GIS, personal privacy and the role of regulation is at best nebulous and uncertain. While tidy minds might wish a strict dividing line between what is private and what is public, there is a 'zone' of privacy. This zone delineates those parts of our lives that are private where reside strategic information about us, our financial status, health, and education. There is also another part where the private information melds into a public space.

1431. In cyberspace, geospatial information may be used to demonstrate spatial relationships and are in themselves fundamental data on geography and spatial location. But GIS may also handle a diverse range of personal information from the truly 'personal' ones through to those of a more general but sensitive nature – age, gender, height, home address, social security number, marital status, religion and so on.

1432. The tools of GIS allow personal and general information to be collected, manipulated, displayed, and transmitted cheaply, easily and speedily. However, the very capabilities of geospatial tools in information analysis and transfers have raised a multitude of novel and interesting information and personal privacy issues.

1433. In common law, the claim to privacy as a right rather than merely an 'interest' or property to be protected, is a relatively recent development. In the past the protection of privacy has been ad hoc.

1434. Geospatial technologies deployed over cyberspace are in daily use and have heightened locational information and personal privacy concerns. Thus, data taken out of context – acontextual data – and used in that sense may produce results that may be highly unjust and totally inappropriate. This could raise ethical questions and should be foremost in the thinking of geospatial information practitioners. Some would like to consider ethics as a continuum in which there is both a duality of a right and a wrong way of undertaking activities, as well as ethics, as a way of dealing with a right way and a better way of doing things. In equitable jurisdictions and civil cases there may be a claim to a right, but it is the party who has the better claim that often holds sway in a legal debate.

1435. Geospatial technologies in common use today rely on both spatial attributes as well as other personal and feature information. These have the 'ability' for tracking people, their shopping and travel habits, the places that they go to for recreation, for what duration and in some instances making an inference of the purposes of that event.

1436. In this context we consider location-based services (LBS) that rely on the key ingredients of time and space. LBS may be considered no different from geodemographics, an information technology that enables marketers to predict behavioural responses of consumers based on statistical models of identity and residential location.[653]

§2. Nature of LBS

1437. LBS have become commonplace because of the use of geo-addressing and GPS together with other mobile communication and tracking technologies that use Internet infrastructure. By inference and as an example, LBS can include the tracking of people through their use of credit card data from profiling exercises, statistical modelling, and pattern analysis. More generally, GIS using the power and reach of the Internet may peel away the veneer of privacy in terms of who we are, where we are, and what we have been doing either by way of speech, through our activities such as retail purchases or simply being at a location.

§3. Legislation and LBS

1438. There is one view that without legislation to curb the (mis)use of such data there would be anarchy. However, an equally compelling but opposing view is that there should be no legislation but rather just self-regulation by industry itself.[654]

1439. While geospatial applications based on remote sensing of the earth on regional scales, and the use of GIS in very small-scale city planning are relatively well known, the application of such technologies to home location are less prominent. In general, utility companies make use of home location data to track usage of power, gas and water, whereas social security benefit providers and licence administrators may make use of street addresses to tag locations for administrative purposes.

1440. Telecommunication services to the home via the land line provide home address information so that all phone communications to and from the home address can be recorded, stored, analysed and made available to others. Telephone traffic data may be analysed as call records for billing and invoicing purposes. The data also give paired locational information of the origin and destination of calls (dyads) that may be mined for other information.

---

653. J.D. Goss, *Marketing the New Marketing: The Strategic Discourse of Geodemographic Information Systems*, in *Ground Truth: The Social Implications of Geographic Information Systems* 130–170 (J. Pickles ed., Guildford Press 1994) and J. Goss, *We Know Who You Are and We Know Where You Live: The Instrumental Rationality of Geodemographic Systems*, 71 Econ. Geography 171–198 (1995).

654. A.F. Westin, *Privacy and Freedom* (Athenum 1967); and A.F. Westin, *Information Technology in a Democracy* (Harvard University Press 1971).

1441. More recently home telephone services have facilities such as caller id, CLI, and CND that give information of a caller, the caller's phone number, and the time of the call. Caller, line, and number identifications are now generally available and have been used by telecommunication companies, law enforcement agencies and consumers as a means of screening and tracing calls.

1442. Through broadband technology and wireless networks, telephone communications have now moved onto the Internet. The use of VOIP services means that most routine communications may be transacted over the Internet.

§4. Implications

1443. The above discussion demonstrates the issues of personal and informational privacy and the use of geospatial technologies and its implications for cyberspace law. Especially in cyberspace, the question of how invasive geospatial information technology has been or can potentially be is an important question. While the present state of development the technology cannot be said to be personal data invasive; nevertheless, there is still a need for vigilance as well as the ethical use of such technologies even if there are social benefits. The legal and regulatory frameworks governing privacy in Australia confirm that there are no constitutional impediments in preserving a right to privacy in Australia.

1444. Analyses of geospatial applications on the Internet on home location, the tracking of individuals over space, tracing financial transactions and communications has identified privacy risks inherent in the use of such technologies. The identified privacy risks may be categorized as invasive, enhancing, or sympathetic.

1445. The implications for user organizations is that geospatial technology applications are but one of different kinds of surveillance and of dataveillance. Equally, technology providers should be reminded of these sorts of privacy issues and to genuinely strive for anonymity in the use of personal information when marketing their products.

Table 4 summarizes the privacy risks when using various geospatial technologies.

Table 4 Privacy Risk Status and Geospatial Technologies

Geospatial Technologies Related to	*Applications*	*Privacy Status*
LOCATION	Utilities, benefit providers, licence	N/I
Home address:	administration	I
Fixed	Inhabitant registration systems	E
Mobile	White Pages, ex-Directory, silent numbers	E
	Reverse White Pages	I
	GPS/DGPS/AGPS*	I
	Auto-reporting mobile devices	
MOVEMENT	Transborder (passports)	N/I
Individual	Credentialed building access	I
Mass	Biometrics	I
	Transponders	N/I
	CCTV*	I
	Pattern recognition; pattern matching	N
	Intelligent Transport Systems and imposed	N/I
	identifiers (travel cards)	
TRANSACTIONS	Cheque data with magnetic ink character	N
Financial	recognition	N
Retail	Turnaround documents with optical character	N
	recognition	N
	Encoding, magnetic strips	I
	Bar coding	I
	ATMs, EFTPOS, Credit/debit cards*	E
	Loyalty schemes	I
	Smart cards, stored-valued cards	
	Real-time locater mechanisms	
COMMUNICATIONS	PSTN traffic data, call records	I
Fixed	Real-time tracing, interception	I
Mobile	Mobile telephony, pagers, analogue/digital/	N/I
	satellite phones / PDA*	N
	Personal phone numbers, ENUM*	I
	Caller id, CLI, CND*	
CONVERGENT	Voice data TCPIP/VoIP*	N/I
TECHNOLOGIES	RFID computer wear*	I
Information	EPIRB*	I
Technology	Identity tags (prisoners, children)	I
Mobile, on person		

Notes: Privacy status: E – enhancing; I – intrusive, N – neutral; GPS = global positioning systems; DGPS = differential global positioning systems; AGPS = assisted global positioning systems; CCTV = closed circuit TV; ATM = automated teller machine; EFTPOS = electronic funds transfer point of sale; PSTN

= public switched telephone network; PDA = personal digital assistant; ENUM = a communication addressing scheme over the Internet; CLI = caller line identification; CND = caller number identification; VOIP = voice over Internet protocol; TCPIP = transmission control protocol Internet protocol; RFID = radio frequency identification; EPIRB = emergency position indicating radio beacon.

Chapter 6. GIS and Liability Issues

§1. Legal liability and risks

1446. Collecting and sharing crowdsourced geospatial data carry risks and legal liabilities. Such risks depend largely on the nature of the relationship between the volunteer contributor and the user of the product. The relationship between volunteer and user could be a contractual one where either there is a privity of contract or it could merely be that of a user of the product and service. Privity of contract refers to the relation that binds two parties and recognized by law. An absence of privity may lead to no contractual liability. On the other hand, tortious liability attaches to negligent behaviour where a duty of care was owed, and that duty was breached. The requirement is that there should also be a causal link between the negligent act and the loss suffered. In the case of Volunteered Geographic Information (VGI) volunteers who may not have any specialized training or expertise in mapping or geography, mistakes and errors may be made in data collection. Hence, the threshold test for tort liability is whether there was an exercise of due diligence to the standard of a reasonable person.

I. Legal Responsibilities

1447. Any identification of the legal responsibilities of producers and users (prod-users) will require a determination of whether a VGI website and available datasets is a product, service or mere provision of information. Each characterization may attract different kinds of liabilities. Where the dataset is proclaimed as a product, there might be strict product liability legislation that may determine a cause of action for actual and/or apprehended loss. Where the dataset is part of a service or the mere provision of information, the case against liability could be that all care has been taken and that there can be no responsibility for any deficiency in the information.

II. Contractual Liability

1448. The relationship between the VGI website service provider and users expresses the 'duty' in the 'Terms of Use' contract posted on the web site together with warranties and indemnities that might be attached to the dataset. Thus, for volunteers, particular care must be exercised by not promising any type of warranty or guarantee for the data submitted. To do so might expose and heighten the risk of legal responsibility for any errors. So too should volunteers refrain from providing any indemnification for the data and information submitted to a web site.

III. Tort Liability

1449. Tort liability may arise in other ways.[655] VGI site operators may insist that users accept the terms of use of their data as a product that includes advice about any defects in the data. Tort liability could arise from the unauthorized use of copyrighted data or the inappropriate use of personal information that may contravene privacy and data protection laws.[656] Tort liability may arise when the volunteer submits information that may be inadvertent but inherently inaccurate which is used by someone and which causes harm, damage or loss.

IV. Liability of Network Hosts

1450. The liability of VGI network hosts may take the form of posting erroneous data or the use of false observations that result in injury and damage to persons who have relied on that data. Data accuracy becomes critical on hosting platforms. Who is to blame may be a difficult question as it could be the volunteer contributor, the platform owner and editor and/or the public body. The extent of this responsibility can be a complex forensic issue of tracing and deep analysis.

V. Mitigating Circumstances

1451. The extent and mitigation of the responsibility for crowdsourced geospatial data could hinge on: (1) the degree of quality control in the data it receives; (2) the editorial and filtering of data; (3) the nature of the data; and, (4) the degree of control asserted over the data. Under tort law the greater the control the greater is the responsibility and exposure to liability should anything go wrong.

VI. Volunteers as Good Samaritans

1452. In many jurisdictions Good Samaritan law may shield volunteers from liability. Good Samaritan law is not found on statute books but is a concept adopted by the courts and applied as public policy. However, public policy and practices vary in different jurisdictions.

A. Common Law Cases

1453. In common law the duty to rescue is provided by the UK House of Lords landmark case of *M'Alister (or Donoghue) v. Stevenson, HL* [1932] A.C. 562 that

655. E.S. Robson, *Responding to Liability: Evaluating and Reducing Tort Liability for Digital Volunteers*, Washington, D.C.: Commons Lab, Woodrow Wilson International Centre for Scholars, September 2012, 57 pp.
656. Robson, ES (2012), *ibid.*

gave birth to Lord Atkin's neighbour principle. Perversely, such duties could be mitigated by not undertaking rescue services and in the case of geospatial data by not providing the crowd-sourced maps. The volunteers of geospatial data could assume the role of a passive observer and not assist in a crisis to avoid any liability. Alternatively, the volunteers could discourage reliance on the information that they provide with disclaimers and other warnings. A statement to the effect that the information is not to be relied upon for use in life threatening situations could be employed.

B. US Legislation

1454. In the US, courts have taken the view that there is no duty to rescue. It has been observed that Good Samaritan laws in the US do not require a person to rescue another, even if the person could do so safely.[657] The rationalés suggest that: (1) a volunteer group that undertakes to rescue others exposes itself to liability; (2) a duty to rescue arises only when a person puts another in danger and a responsibility arises to mitigate that harm and danger; and, (3) a duty to rescue becomes mandatory where there is a special relationship between the parties.

C. European Rescue Laws

1455. Laws in much of Europe criminalize a failure to help people in peril in emergency situations. Indeed, in Germany the failure to provide first aid to a person in need of help is punishable under § 323c of the German Criminal Penal Code.[658]

VII. Other Tortious Liability

1456. Worries about tortious liability remain in several different ways: (1) crowd-sourced data might be misused; (2) volunteers could get injured when collecting the data; (3) the legal responsibility for the data are unascertained and unascertainable; and, (4) the legal status of the volunteers themselves, as a loose collective of like-minded people who wish to help, is uncertain. The US Federal statute Volunteer Protection Act of 1997 (VPA) offers some protection to a broader range of volunteers. Examples include those volunteers operating under organizational structures of a certain kind and the imposition of limits on volunteer compensation by the courts.

---

657. E.S. Robson, *Potential liability for crowd-sourced disaster response groups* (2011), at https://stipcommunia.wordpress.com/2011/09/26/potential-liability-for-crowdsourced-disaster-response-groups/ (accessed 29 Sept. 2011).

658. Public Broadcasting Service (1997) 'Online NewsHour: French Legal System', September 3, 1997 at https://germanlawarchive.iuscomp.org/?p=752 (accessed 08 Aug. 2013).

1457. Radical changes may be needed to reduce such examples of geo-liability. This is because legal liability theories governing geospatial information are largely under-developed and there is a tendency for the law to lag technology relative to resolving the growing challenges presented by new technology. The disparities between legal frameworks and policy perspectives have been made evident in the above discussion.[659]

659. T. Scassa, *Geographic Information as Personal Information*, 10 Oxford University Commonwealth Law Journal 185–214 (2010).

Chapter 7. GIS: Emerging Issues

1458. Geospatial information from the collection of spatial data, storage, analysis and its use in information systems has been transformed by 'disruptive' technologies ('innovative') and have dictated a new modus operandi.

1459. In the Web 2.0 environment the Internet is an integral part of the infrastructure. Static pages of web sites have been transformed by the addition of new information by users 'on the fly'. Sites are used and updated by collaborative and cooperative means for dialogue, creation of content, and meeting online of a virtual community. The previous era of the floppy disk and compact disc to exchange data and information has given way to the USB Flash drives, memory sticks and to cloud computing.

1460. More likely the emphasis is on 'service provision' of geospatial information however delivered. Geospatial information science has developed techniques and methodologies that deliver geospatial information systems quite simply and effectively so that today the need is for more ubiquitous geospatial information services.

1461. Geospatial information services include spatial computing for site selection, asset tracking, facility management, navigation and logistics. Ecologists use GPS to track endangered species and better understand animal behaviour while farmers use GPS for precision farming to increase crop yields and reduce costs. Educationalists use the digital virtual globe such as Google Earth to teach children about their neighbourhood and the world in an enjoyable way.

1462. The new digital environment has made nearly everyone with a mobile device a map maker and a digital recorder. Nearly every phenomenon is observable, may be captured and may be mapped. Using cell phones, GPS devices and putting information on the Internet through various social media outlets has made the spatial context all important.

1463. However, the newly minted volunteer cartographer may be untrained in GIS technology but nevertheless contributes to location-based services. The volunteers and hobbyists who contribute to 'crowd-sourced' information mapped by Google Earth Maps and OpenStreetMapping has brought GIS to the masses.

1464. While expectations of such deployment are rising so are the legal risks. The more obvious one being privacy concerns generated by the ubiquity of location-aware devices that automatically record personal movements, habits and other information linked to one's location.

1465. No less important are those concerns relating to the contributors of geospatial information and the kinds of tacit agreements they are bound by. An understanding of the contractual issues in using 'clouds' and 'crowd-sourced' information would help develop different ways of leveraging existing resources and to tailor it to the legal framework.

1466. Cloud computing is a significant shift from the way IT solutions have been implemented in the past but these present new challenges. Many of these may be overcome by using skilled personnel in contract negotiation and vendor management to contractually address the legal risks related to service levels, data processing and storage, infrastructure, security, and an institution's relationship with the cloud computing service provider.

Chapter 8. GIS: Cloud Computing and VGI

§1. Cloud Computing

1467. Cloud computing provide a means to undertake computing tasks, software, data access, data storage resources. Users of cloud computing take advantage of computing infrastructure but are not involved in the detailed technical setup. The advantages offered by cloud computing generally and to GCC analysts, users, data providers and others are unlimited. The benefits include lower costs, expanded access to products and services and to be able to do so online from anywhere in the world.

1468. Geospatial software may only be needed to be leased or paid for based on usage on a needs basis through web services. This is indeed neo-geography par excellence and the 'cloud' is poised to radically change the way geospatial analytics is performed. As an example, the US government has introduced its 'cloud first' policy for new government computing requirements.

1469. According to the US National Institute of Standards and Technology (NIST) cloud computing is a 'model for enabling ubiquitous, convenient, on demand network access to a shared pool of configurable computing resources (e.g., networks, servers, storage, applications, and services) that can be rapidly provisioned and released with minimal management effort or service provider interaction'.[660]

1470. Four service classes of cloud computing include infrastructure as a service (IaaS), the PaaS, SaaS and data as a service (DaaS). Each of these entities may overlap and may have some shared features.

1471. As the names suggest infrastructure services could include computing resources for processing, storage and networking whereas the cloud as a platform provides the environment in which organizations and agencies create and deploy applications in a web-based context. To drive some of the applications the necessary software could be made available for business applications.

1472. DaaS is the necessary component to drive either the infrastructures or the platforms and applications. Geospatial information applications require the ability to mine data, to discover data connections, to access, to manipulate and to use these for dynamic or static mapping purposes. The GCC concept satisfies the needs of geospatial analytics.

1473. A review by the AGIMO has shown that some standard terms on which many cloud computing services are offered may not meet all the legal requirements of an Australian government agency. The Better Practice Guide suggests that the

660. *See* US Department of Commerce NIST on Cloud Computing 2013 at https://www.nist.gov/document-10202.

contractual positions with providers need to be set out early in any procurement process and to negotiate agreements that are acceptable to all parties. The key legal issues addressed include protection of information, tortious liability, managing the performance, ending the arrangement, resolving disputes and other legal issues.[661]

1474. The protection of the information includes those that impinge on privacy, security and confidentiality. For these, how the records are kept and a right to audit such protection measures should be written into the contract.

1475. Compensation for data loss and the use of subcontractors are also to be monitored. Privacy obligations are paramount when moving data to the cloud. This might mean a loss of direct control over the information and in cases where the data are stored and processed outside the jurisdiction.

1476. Different means of indirect control might be available. However, it is important to ensure that the contract terms prohibit the service provider from using the data for its own purposes and that security measures are in place to protect sensitive data such as personal information. Contractual terms may include the location where the service is provided from, the level of encryption to be applied, security access protocols implemented and the physical media to store the data.

1477. Contractual liability issues relate to its limitations and indemnity clauses. Performance management cover service level agreements, response times, flexibility of service and business continuity where there are interruptions to the service and for disaster recovery. On termination of the arrangement there should be an agreement as to the circumstances when there is an end to the contract by mutual agreement, by default and the rights to termination.

1478. Where disputes surface choice of law and jurisdiction should be set out. There are other legal issues such as how to prevent and deal with harmful code, application of foreign laws, trans-border data transfers and export control and IPR ownership.[662]

§2. VGI

1479. After cloud computing VGI has taken centre stage in that this new innovation has demonstrated the power and force of 'crowd-sourced' information.[663] VGI has addressed mapping needs in crisis situations and no more better illustrated

661. *See* AGIMO (2010) at http://agimo.gov.au/files/2013/02/negotiating-the-cloud-legal-issues-in-cloud-computing-agreements-v1.1.pdf (accessed 08 Jul. 2013).
662. For detailed legal and technical discussions of cloud computing issues, *see* L.R. Lifshitz, *Understanding Cloud Computing: Legal Issues and Best Practice* (Loud Computing Law, Toronto: Federated Press 2011); and R.L. Percival, *Cloud Computing: Due Diligence Considerations* (Cloud Computing Law Workshop, Toronto: Federated Press 2011).
663. *See* M. Goodchild, *Citizens as Sensors: The World of Volunteered Geography*, 69 Geojournal 211ff (2007).

than during the Haitian earthquakes of 2010.[664] Volunteer mapping efforts that assist in relief efforts have since been used in the context of forest fires, floods, hurricanes and other disasters.

1480. VGI maps have been created through volunteers who record information using mobile devices and submit these to a website or central agency that analyses, reviews and then publishes the data on base maps provided by OpenStreetMap or GoogleMaps.[665] VGI contributors are novices and not professional map creators.

1481. While reliability and accuracy of VGI might be questioned, the timely production of near-instantaneous maps during times of crisis has proven invaluable. Nevertheless, tortious liability issues have become apparent especially where there is an endangerment of life. VGI service providers hence ensure that they do not engage in 'negligent' conduct and vet volunteer contributions.

1482. It may be difficult to determine whether a VGI website is a product, service or mere information. Hence, tortious liability may attach to negligent behaviour where a duty of care was owed and was breached and that there was a causal link between the negligent act and the loss suffered. However, as the contributors may not have any specialized training or expertise in mapping or geography, mistakes and errors may creep in. Exercise of due diligence of a reasonable person is the lower standard threshold test for any tortious liability. But liability may be unlikely for an innocent mistake.

1483. Contract do not take place in a vacuum. There are inevitably interactions between the various theories of law including tort liability, IP and legislative provisions. In many jurisdictions contract law has been codified, even the common law; and this is in response to the rise of consumer protection concerns. This may be because the parties are literally at arm's length when agreements are formed or that there might be in an unequal bargaining position.

1484. The Web 2.0 environment has now forced a re-think of contractual obligations and shifted the paradigm from the desktop to the hand-held device to the cloud. What the resulting landscape might look like in the future will largely depend on whether the law has developed to lead innovation or whether there will be a lag with the law attempting to catch up with technology. Discourse in these matters on emergent cyberspace law may only assist in promoting better practices and behaviours for the benefit of all.

---

664. *See* M. Zook et al., *Volunteered Geographic Information and Crowd Sourcing Disaster Relief: A Case Study of the Haitian Earthquake*, 2 World Health Med. Pol. 7 (2010).

665. *See* OpenStreetMap at http://www.openstreetmap.org and Google Maps at https://maps.google.com (accessed 08 Jul. 2013).

Chapter 9. Robotics Industry and Artificial Intelligence

1485. The importance of robotics to Australia is highlighted by its geography. Australia is a country with a small and ageing population and with high labour costs. To ensure its future economic success Australia will need to be proactive in the advancement of robotics and anticipate and plan for the changes that robotics will bring about in the world of work and Australian society in general.

1486. The convergence of technologies and other advances has led to a rapid growth in robotics. The pace of innovation and the connections between technologies and disciplines have continued to advance. These advances include developments in Machine Learning (ML), Data Mining, Machine Vision and Dexterity, Miniaturization and Computational Statistics. The field of Artificial Intelligence (AI) that develops algorithms that allow for the automation of cognitive tasks is beginning to realize the promise it has long held. Biotechnology, nanotechnology, neurology and many interrelated fields are beginning to map the human brain and develop the next generation of computers that can emulate human thinking. As their use increases, the cost of automation is coming down, while the speed, mobility, performance and adaptability of automated robots and other devices is improving rapidly.

1487. In general, as more data are collected, and software for big data algorithms become cheaper and more sophisticated, there will inevitably be a disrupting effect on many traditional labour markets. As modern robots become smaller, lighter and more flexible, they will be especially suited to Australia's manufacturing sector which is predominantly small-to-medium size businesses. The growth of robotics is also likely to bring about major societal changes, including reshaping the world of work, not only in manufacturing but in the services sectors as well including education, health care and other service sectors.[666]

1488. According to the International Federation for Robotics (IFR) total accumulated sales, measured since the introduction of the first industrial robots at the end of the 1960s, totalled approximately 2,470,000 units by the end of 2012. These units include the dedicated industrial robots installed in Japan up to and including 2000.[667]

1489. The Asia region, which includes Australia and New Zealand was by far the biggest market with 84,645 industrial robots sold in 2012 with China being the largest purchaser of robotics in the region. After the strong increase of 132% in 2010, sales of industrial robots again rose, by 27%, to a new peak of about 88,700 units in 2011. Between 2007 and 2012, the compound annual growth rate of robot

---

666. E. Brea et al., *An Initiative to Enhance SMC Productivity Through Fit-for-Purpose Information and Robotic Technologies*, CSIRO, Australia at https://publications.csiro.au/rpr/pub?pid=csiro:EP134792.

667. http://www.ifr.org/industrial-robots/statistics/. Note that many of the earlier robots are no longer in use. It is estimated there are a little over a million robots in active use.

supplies to Asia/Australia was about 8% on average.[668] In dollar terms the worldwide market value for robot systems in 2012 is therefore estimated to be AUD 26 billion.[669]

1490. In employment terms, a 2011 report commissioned by the IFR found that 150,000 people worldwide are already employed in the engineering and assembly of robots. This report also notes that robotics can help countries win back manufacturing previously lost to low labour cost countries, maintain the competitiveness of existing manufacturing and lead to new manufacturing.[670]

1491. Between 2014 and 2016, robot installations were estimated to increase by 6% on average per year compound annual growth rate of about 4% in the Americas and in Europe, and about 8% in Asia including Australia. The trend toward automation continues to increase the volume of robot installations. But, the rate of increase in robot sales will be more moderate. The IFR predicts the robotics industry has a bright future encouraged by global competition requiring the modernization of production facilities; energy-efficiency and new materials; growing consumer markets; decreasing life-cycles of products and increasing variety of products require flexible automation; technical improvements of industrial robots for use in the general industry and in small- and medium-sized companies; improved quality of product require sophisticated high tech robot systems; and, improved quality of work with robots taking over dangerous, tedious and dirty jobs that are not possible or safe for humans to perform.[671]

1492. An Australian researcher is similarly optimistic about the future of Australian manufacturing.[672] He submits that if Australian businesses can find the funds to support greater use of modern and soon-to-be-here technology in automation and robotics, then they can improve their competitiveness to meet the challenges of the Asian century and help to maintain employment in the manufacturing industry. A new generation of lightweight, assistive robots looks to provide SME with new options to improve their competitiveness, increase productivity and meet the challenges of high costs and a shortage of skilled workers. Seizing this opportunity, however, will require a willingness to embrace change and see robotics as an opportunity rather than a threat. It will also require highly skilled workers who can set up, maintain and operate the robotics system.

1493. The implications of all of this for Australia are clear. In the future there will be a premium on education both in terms of technical areas such as science and mathematics but also in the human and social skills areas. Government, industry and education should undertake careful analysis and planning in relation to employment

668. http://www.ifr.org/industrial-robots/statistics/.
669. *Ibid.*
670. Peter Gorle and Andrew Clive, *Positive Impact of Robots on Employment* (2011), London, Metra-Martech Limited, at Metra_Martech_Study_on_robots.pdf.
671. http://www.ifr.org/industrial-robots/statistics/.
672. Alberto Elfes, *The Conversation* (6 Feb. 2013), at http://theconversation.com/why-the-australian-manufacturing-industry-needs-the-next-generation-of-robots-11888.

and career trends. Above all, there will be a premium on the capacity for change and continued growth, learning, and re-learning. Evidenced-based decisions made from rigorous research are a must.

§1. ROBOTICS AND CYBER LAW

I. Legal Definition of Robot

1494. The law will have to have a clear definition of what exactly is meant by 'robot'? The IFR use of the term 'industrial robot' is based on the definition of the ISO as an 'automatically controlled, reprogrammable multipurpose manipulator programmable in three or more axes'. Other definitions include service robots, personal service robots and professional service robots.[673]

1495. Legal definitions would need to include the function and context within which the robots are used. For example, service robots may require a higher standard of safety given their close involvement with humans. Similarly, the use of robotics in the health and finance industries is likely to be regulated by specific provisions governing those industries. A case in point are specific provisions governing high frequency trading in the stock and shares market.[674] One may also distinguish between domestic and commercial uses of a robot. Another context is international. For example, international conventions may be developed that related specifically to the use of drones, the unmanned aerial vehicles.[675]

II. Impact on Employment

1496. A recent UK study, by the University of Oxford, Oxford Martin School, of over 700 American jobs found that in the near future up to half of those jobs would be replaced by robotics.[676] In the environment of the future it is predicted there will be far fewer middle-skilled jobs and far more low skilled jobs many of which will be highly susceptible to being replaced as a result of advances in technology, especially robotics.[677]

673. IFR at ifr.org. ISO Standard ISO8373.
674. E. Clark, *The Legal Tortoise and the High Frequency Trading Hare: The Challenge for Regulators*, 25 Austrl. J. Corp. L. 274–303 (2011).
675. http://www.ifr.org/industrial-robots/statistics/.
676. *See* C.B. Frey & M.A. Osborne, *The future of employment: How Susceptible are jobs to computerisation?* (2013), at http://www.oxfordmartin.ox.ac.uk/downloads/academic/The_Future_of_Employment.pdf.
677. http://www.oxfordmartin.ox.ac.uk/publications/view/1314.

A. *Jobs Most at Risk*

1497. The UK Report mentioned above makes the case that computerization is no longer a threat confined to routine manufacturing jobs but increasingly impacts the service sector. The report cites research from McKinsey Global Institute's estimates that sophisticated algorithms could substitute for the knowledge work of approximately 140 million people worldwide.[678] Unlike the automation of the past which replaced manual work, today's technological advances are more often replacing lower level knowledge work.

B. *Jobs Least at Risk*

1498. As one would probably intuitively guess, the Report indicates that the jobs of the future that are at lowest risk of automation include those that require human judgment, creativity and knowledge of a range of social factors that are not readily susceptible to collecting and categorizing, analyzing and developing and subjecting to an algorithm. These include most management, business, finance and upper order legal roles. It also includes higher order science and technical areas which require high levels of intelligence, creativity, experience and judgment. Also, less subject to automation are roles that require interacting with people, reading human emotions and dealing with a variety of contexts requiring sophisticated human interaction.

§2. Artificial Intelligence and Cyber Law

1499. About six decades ago John McCarthy (1959) coined the term artificial intelligence to refer to the 'science and engineering of making intelligent machines'.[679] AI is considered by many to be the possession of intelligence or the exercise of thought by machines.[680]

1500. One important meta-ethical issue often discussed is that of synthesized intelligence in intelligent machines. As noted previously, for machines to demonstrate intelligent behaviour, at a minimum such AI systems should reproduce aspects of human intelligence. During the construction of such devices, the question to ask is how ethically the machines should behave towards both humans and other AI agents? Wallach (2010) introduced the concept of artificial moral agents and poses

678. McKinsey Global Institute, *Automation and the future of work* (2017), at https://www.mckinsey.com/featured-insights/future-of-work/jobs-lost-jobs-gained-what-the-future-of-work-will-mean-for-jobs-skills-and-wages.

679. J. McCarthy, *Programs with Common Sense*, in the *Proceedings of the Teddington Conference on the Mechanization of Thought Processes*, pp. 756–791 (1995), London: Her Majesty's Stationery Office. In his paper McCarthy discussed the idea of AI using logic as the method of representing information in computer memory.

680. L.. Hauser, (n.d.) *Artificial Intelligence*, Internet Encyclopaedia of Philosophy at http://www.iep.utm.edu/art-inte/ (accessed on 4 Jun. 2015).

two fundamental questions to go with this: First, whether humanity wants computers to be able to make moral decisions and second, whether such machines (robots) if able to do so can behave morally.[681]

1501. Automation does raise awkward moral questions without any accompanying formal or legal guidelines for answers. These questions touch on machine ethics and the acceptance and deployment of autonomous systems. More prosaically Autonomous Weapons Systems Used in Conflict Zones and Citizen Use of Wearable AI Technology.

1502. ICT industry has also introduced augmented reality (AR) that refers to the use of technology to 'augment' the experience of reality in a dynamic, instantaneous, direct and indirect manner. Real-world elements and objects are augmented by computer-generated artefacts such as sound and vision in order to enhance the perception of reality.

1503. In parallel virtual reality (VR) refers to an artificial world that mimics reality by means of 'avatars' and other digital devices.[682] In information technology an avatar refers to the graphical representation of a user or the user's computer personality and character as seen in the Second Life, online virtual world.[683]

1504. The technology surrounding either AR or VR may be described as 'immersive' or 'ambient'. In immersive mode the real-world is augmented by various means. In ambient mode a projected layer of imagery is superimposed on an object or scene in the real-world to enhance the perception and the experience. Augmediated or augmented reality is open and partly immersive, perhaps described as 'ambient', where a user may be able to see through and all around a scene. The technology puts things into the user's real-world, that is, augments what the user sees.

I. Autonomous Vehicles: Driverless Cars

1505. However, the current state of AR and VR technology and its recent introduction to common use may be insufficiently mature to provide the solutions sought for navigation purposes. Wassom (2012j) has discussed the perils of AR while driving.[684] Driver distractions either in answering a mobile phone or reading and sending text messages have been recognized by road safety experts and transport researchers as the probable cause of collisions. The Detroit suburb of Troy has prohibited not only texting while driving but also making a phone call and 'any other activity that can distract a driver and affect their ability to safely operate the vehicle.

681. W. Wallach, *Moral Machines* 37–73 (Oxford University Press 2010).
682. The Hindu origin of the word *avatar* refers to a deity that has taken on terrestrial form. An epic science fiction film *Avatar* (2009) was produced by James Cameron.
683. 'Second Life' was developed by San Francisco-based Linden Lab and launched on 23 Jun. 2003. *See* W.J. Au, *The Making of Second Life: Notes from the New World* (Collins 2008).
684. B.D. Wassom, 'No augmenting reality while driving?' in *Augmented Legality* 40–42 (Bloomfield Hills, MI: Honigman, Miller, Schwartz & Cohn, LLP 2012a).

Activities under this classification include eating, grooming, reading, writing, or any other activity that prevents someone from having control of the vehicle with at least one hand on the wheel.'[685]

1506. Using an AR app on a smartphone whilst driving is a form of texting because while one may not be inputting information into an electronic device, one may have one's eyes on the display screen of the electronic device rather than concentrating on the road. The AR app by Multicellphone has developed an app that can detect 'your lane and other vehicles in front of you and provides useful information for your driving situation' but only 'in good lighting conditions during daytime for visible lane markings on highways and country roads and for detection of regular cars'.[686]

1507. The pairing of AR displays with GPS units has added a 'dynamic' element to geospatial information. However, the heads-up displays suffer the same criticism as those sending text messages whilst driving or looking at GPS display units. The legal issues are unresolved because of the 'newness' of AR technology in civilian applications.

1508. In car building technology there is already a range of accident-avoidance and driver-assist aids such as adaptive cruise control, automatic tracking, vehicle spacing distance alerts, lane-keeping and park assist. It has been suggested that there is a need for 'adjustable ethics' given that autonomous cars may become more commonplace. The ethical question is how self-driven vehicles are to react when faced with spontaneous situations that could bring about an accident. We may be dealing with unforeseen events for which no design or computer program exists. The ethicist dilemma of sacrificing an innocent person to save multiple innocent persons – the so-called trolley problem – may require the adoption of adjustable ethics.[687] The philosophical quandary this problem raises is still debated today and is a question of human morality and an example of the philosophical view called consequentialism. This promotes the view that morality is the result of the consequences of an action and that the consequence is all that matters.

II. Legal Challenges and Privacy Issues

1509. As may be discerned, the task is not easy. The legal challenge is even more perilous as a car maker could argue it should not be liable for damage as a result of user choice. Arguably the car maker could still be liable for giving user a choice in the first place. Lin (2015) proposes that there should be a code of ethical

685. https://www.michigancapitolconfidential.com/will-troys-crackdown-on-distracted-driving-spread (accessed 06 Jul. 2013).
686. http://www.multicellphone.com/6577/augmented-driving-iphone-app-brings-augmented-reality-to-your-car/ (accessed 6 Jul. 2013).
687. D. Tuffley, *Self-driving cars need adjustable ethics set by owners*, The Conversation (25 Aug. 2014) at https://theconversation.com/self-driving-cars-need-adjustable-ethics-set-by-owners-30656/ (accessed on 4 Jun. 2015).

conduct for manufacturers of robotic cars and for the authorities to introduce laws to limit a car-maker's liability in a similar way legal protection was afforded to the makers of certain vaccines for the protection of the public interest.[688] An equally potent counter-point could be that if the tools that we use, such as computers, do things for us, is that tool not an extension of ourselves? If so, then we may not also become ultimately responsible for the consequences of their use and vicariously legally liable for any damage or loss caused?

1510. In a world where AI is present and where AR technologies are omnipresent there is a need to ask how the laws and the way these are applied are to be adapted. Wassom (2012b) believes that framing the right question is the first step.[689] AR may characterize the substance of the litigation as well as the procedures that govern it. One burden of characterization is where to draw the line with fully immersive AR, for example, advertisements that seemingly float in mid-air, untethered and which appear to be painted on a physical object. A graphic example could be AR superimposing a rival hamburger icon on a McDonalds set of 'Golden Arches' each time these are encountered in the real-world. Not only are there issues of possible branding and trade mark infringements but also of unfair competition, physical property rights as well as IPR generally.

1511. In a further example, the ubiquity of AR embedded in personal wearable video recording devices may lead to accidental recordings of private conversations. Such recordings could be unintentional especially in settings where people expect privacy – the family home, bedroom, church, or reading confidential documents and e-mail. What could be worse is that these recordings might be shared in real-time and streamed live to Facebook and other social media.[690]

1512. Under the norms of privacy expectations in the English-speaking common law world the following could be infringed:

- Intrusion into seclusion – a common law tort if it is highly offensive to a reasonable person, and where no publication is necessary.
- Publication of private facts – that includes the public dissemination of obscure private facts that are not part of public records. Where it is in the public interest,

688. *See* P. Lin, *The right to life and the Martens Clause*, Paper presented to the Convention on Certain Conventional Weapons (CW) Meeting of Experts on Lethal Autonomous Weapons Systems (LAWS), at United Nations in Geneva, Switzerland on 13–17 April 2015. Charlton, A (2015) 'You or the pedestrian: Ethics of autonomous cars making emergency decisions to save lives' at https://www.ibtimes.co.uk/you-pedestrian-ethics-autonomous-cars-making-emergency-decisions-save-lives-1506685?webSyncID=127557ea-dc1a-37e3-3e96-5964c1b46ba6&sessionGUID=6bd56726-7987-2348-4bb5-7d2665c7b749 (accessed on 4 Aug. 2015).

689. B.D. Wassom, *Real laws in an Augmented Reality* (2012b), at http://www.wassom.com/the-coming-conundra-real-laws-in-an-augmented-reality.html (accessed on 21 Jun. 2012).

690. B.D. Wassom, *Invading privacy with wearable video-recorders and AR eyewear* (2012c), at http://privacyref.com/blog/wearable-recording-devices-invasion-privacy/ (accessed on 21 Jun. 2012).

publication may be permissible, but not where it may be offensive to a reasonable person if made public. Examples of such facts include those relating to health or some intimate sexual information.
- False light – defamation, slander, libel tort to protect a person's reputation.
- Eavesdropping – a tort or a criminal offence or both. This may involve making audio or video recordings of other people's conversations under circumstances where there is a reasonable expectation of privacy. An example is the surreptitious recording and broadcasting a room-mate's intimate encounter.

1513. There may be no bright lights to assist in regulating AR usage by consumers save to say that these legal boundaries are constantly shifting and are up for debate. Consumer-wearable AR and its universal adoption will shrink further our perception of what it means to be private, to have privacy and to be left alone.

1514. The privacy issues identified above have yet to be considered for wearable consumer AR recording devices. This is a new field of endeavour and the AR-VR net is cast wide and hence there will need for cautious development of the legal checks and balances. In parallel, the legal net may be described as conservative, cautious with long held precedents and deep historical roots thereby rendering it cumbersome and ponderous. But, this is not without reason as various rights, obligations and responsibilities need to be respected with care.

§3. Other Legal Issues

1515. In order to achieve clarity and certainty involved with robotics many legal issues must be resolved. For example, driverless cars are already available and have been legislated in several US States. However, the ethical standards, product liability, agency, safety standards, insurance and other legal issues will need to be resolved so that people developing this industry will have enough certainty to risk the substantial investment required.

1516. Among the legal issues that must be resolved are:

- *Balance*. The law is about conflict and the need to balance competing interests. The design of legal rules that govern robotics will need to achieve the appropriate balance between encouraging innovation through robotics and related technologies and ensuring public safety, particularly in the context of autonomous robots.
- *Agency* Issues. The law of agency is especially relevant to robotics and covers the legal principles governing the liability when one person acts on behalf of another. An example is a software-only system such as automated trading agents which have caused serious 'flash crashes' in share markets in the US.
- *Responsibility*. Given that robots will be acting autonomously or sometimes in partnership with a human, we will need to determine rules for placing ethical and legal responsibility with the appropriate party. This issue could get very tricky especially in relation to new generations of autonomous robots that are also

equipped to learn in much the same way that humans do. Although it is in the realm of science fiction now, some argue that as robots assume more and more human qualities, we will have to even consider legal rights for robots.

- The rules governing robots will have to be adapted to *widely varying contexts* ranging from robots conducting interviews, dispensing advice, looking after patients, providing transport, looking after security needs and military usage. Different contexts may require different legal and practical considerations.
- *Health, safety and employment* law issues will need to be resolved as robots enter for example the world of work and encounter new environments outside of the laboratory and contexts in which they will interact with humans, sometimes in unexpected ways and with unexpected and/or unintended results.
- *Regulatory and licensing issues* raised by robots in the home, the office, in public spaces (e.g., roads), and in specialized environments such as hospitals.
- There will be *privacy* issues especially relating to robots that are collecting or using data in personally sensitive areas such as health care delivery and national security. Other privacy issues will come about as a result of robotic intrusions, for example, drones spying on backyards and into houses where people would traditionally have an expectation of privacy.
- There will be *IP issues* to be resolved, especially given the newness of the industry and its rapid growth and development in a competitive environment.
- Where a robot is involved in a professional area such as medical diagnosis or other *professional advice*, there will be ethical and legal issues related to licensure, agency and scope of permitted activity to be resolved.
- Given a robot is a 'product' there will be *product liability* and *insurance* issues to sort out, for example with the growth of commercial drones. For example, what is the liability should a doctor deploy robotic surgery and a patient is severely injured by a malfunctioning robotic device.
- *International* issues. As the impact of robots goes across national borders there is likely to emerge the need for international agreement, an example being moves to restrict the use of drones.[691]

1517. As demonstrated by developments such as the Human Brain project, the field of robotics is likely to advance exponentially in the years ahead. An example of that potential is the establishment of a website for robots to learn from each other and share information.[692] However, the various legal issues will have to be resolved before Australia can take full advantage of this new technology.

691. R.P. Barnidge, Jr., *A Qualified Defense of American Drone Attacks in Northwest Pakistan under International Humanitarian Law*, 30 B.U. Intl. L. J. 410–447 (2012).
692. http://robohub.org/roboearth-tested-in-life-like-scenario-bbc/.

Part X. Conclusions

1518. Several themes run through this volume. The centrality of cyber law is prominent given that e-business is being mainstreamed and has become a serious challenger to bricks-and-mortar enterprises. It may be conjectured that e-business is not optional and any business that is not taking it seriously may not be in business five years hence. In the Information Age, assets are commonly intangible such as IP and the rights therefrom. The regulation of the ICT market is the focus of this book. The centrality of cyber law is assisted by the convergence of business services from legal services, to technologies such as the IOT where various electronic devices speak a common language to enhance connectivity. These developments have been described either as a revolution in information technology, telecommunications, internationalization and globalization leading to the Information Age that has led to new and emerging models of delivery for both private and public sector goods and services. Or, in the alternate the technologies have been described as disruptive. In this environment, we are witnessing the use of technology to offer services in new ways, to create new services and the creation of whole new industries.

1519. The increasing importance of comparative and international developments underscores the criticality of ensuring laws and policy frameworks are available to help support the economy. Law is an integral component of any country's e-commerce system and e-government system. Increasingly, governments are seeing an effective legal system as a source of competitive advantage. Those seeking to reform and improve their legal systems tend today to seek the best laws wherever they can be found and adapt them to their needs. An example is Australia's adoption of many US laws to govern its economic system. Similarly, courts when faced with what to do in relation to a new technology, will look for insight and guidance to other jurisdictions and cases they have decided. However, some solutions to the problems may more likely be technical and social than legal. A good example is the problem of security of signatures, something that is more likely to be resolved by developments in encryption technology than by legal reforms. Indeed, the importance of soft law is coming to the fore in the form of codes, guides, ethical standards, industry standards and the many other forms of rules that regulate human behaviour in various ways rather than through the coercive power of the state. The distributed model of Internet governance, belonging to no single country and involving stakeholders from all sectors of society, is a good example of new modes of regulation that hold valuable lessons in this new environment of the global information society.

1520. In an era of constant change, the new and burgeoning digital age is challenging many of the ways in which business and Government function. The explosive growth of the Internet and its borderless nature are dictating a profound rethinking of the nature of the relationships. These include the relationships between government, business and consumers in all its permutations. To adapt to such changes successfully organizations and the people who work in them, need to be more responsive and flexible than ever before. While the focus of the media generally has been on new technology the more substantial challenge is that of organizational change. In this everyone must be able to unlearn and challenge previously held assumptions that may no longer be true in the new century and to be agile in learning and using new paradigms.

1521. While technology may be used for good or evil, this volume has chronicled sectors of the ICT that have given rise to legal, social and political concerns. Some may require a balancing of private and public interests whereas others have advocated strict compliance and punishment. As cybercrime easily crosses jurisdictional boundaries, Australia is putting into place the infrastructure to enable investigators to cooperate with their counterparts in other countries and effectuate prosecution. The experiences therefrom have informed the development of policy and law enforcement techniques to stem the growth of such crimes. With the greater democratization of society and as the power of technology in the hands of the individual increases, it will be crucial to ensure that private and public interests are properly protected. This may mean that Western concepts of 'individualism', in some cases, may have to give way to the greater public good. Achieving this balance will be difficult, but our very survival may depend upon it.

1522. Just as cyber law had to depend upon traditional metaphors and analogies to be extended to contexts involving the Internet, so too, appropriate legal metaphors must emerge which will allow Parliaments, Courts and others to design the appropriate legal infrastructure that will provide the necessary guidance for this new industry to evolve.

1523. But the problem is that the norms that exist in the real-world do not necessarily transfer easily to the digital realm. New modes of communication have developed to accommodate the virtual digital world to the real-world.

1524. The study of cyber law portends that good and evil emanate from the use of ICT and that the legal infrastructure is there to guide behaviour, set limits and dispense punishment where loss or hurt is incurred. In the real-world such loss and injuries are real and tangible. However, in the realm of the cyber world, the losses are not so evident nor are they as palpable since these are perpetrated in the virtual world. Herein lies the paradox and the dilemmas, can the law of the land be analogized in the virtual world? This discussion canvasses various topics that review future worlds and to assess the capacity of the legal system to respond to these various malevolent intents. The summary and conclusions to this text is made by way of observations and guiding principles emanating from the discussions in the various Parts.

1525. The *first guiding principle* for cyber law is that state sovereignty or Westphalian sovereignty is that each state has exclusive sovereignty over its territory. Such a principle is enshrined in the United Nations Charter (1945) of modern international system of sovereign states which states that 'nothing should authorise intervention in matters essentially within the domestic jurisdiction of any state'.[693] Every state has an equal right to sovereignty.

1526. The *second guiding principle* is that any discussion of the regulation of the ICT Market may be considered incomplete if the trends arising from regulation is not recognized. The issue of data breaches and cyber security loom large and require attention as these arise as a result of legislation and attempts to circumvent it.

1527. In Australia, the Notifiable Data Breaches (NDB) Scheme came into effect on 22 February 2018.[694] Since the introduction of the NDB Scheme, 550 data breaches have been reported, up from 114 reported in the 2016–2017 financial year.[695] However, there has to date been no enforcement action taken for a failure to comply with the NDB Scheme. Data breaches have shone a light on inadequate and unethical data handling processes.

1528. Since the introduction of the NDB Scheme in Australia, the private health sector has continued to record the highest number of data breaches. The sector has reported a total of 109 breaches and was the only one with a higher rate of breaches attributable to human internal factors, such as employee carelessness or misbehaviour, than to external threats.[696] The Australian Digital Health Agency annual report identifies 42 data breaches in relation to the MyHealth Record system in 2017–2018, though none were malicious attacks.[697]

1529. It has been predicted that the EU General Data Protection Regulations (2018) (GDPR) will inspire other governments to update their data protection legislation.[698] Singapore, Brazil and Canada have updated their data privacy laws to keep pace with the GDPR to harmonise obligations with foreign jurisdictions.

693. Charter of the United Nations at https://www.un.org/en/charter-united-nations/.
694. *See* OAIC at https://www.oaic.gov.au/privacy-law/privacy-act/notifiable-data-breaches-scheme.
695. *See* OAIC *Notifiable Data Breaches Quarterly Statistics Report: 1 July – 30 September 2018* (30 Oct. 2018); and, OAIC, *Notifiable Data Breaches First Quarterly report* released (11 Apr. 2018).
696. Jeremy Kirk, *Australia's biggest breach offender: Healthcare sector* (1 Aug. 2018), at https://www.bankinfosecurity.com/australian-health-care-sector-reports-most-breaches-a-11267; Hamish Broadbent & Natalie Mason, *Australia: Data breaches on the rise on the health sector*, *Mondaq* (8 Oct. 2018), at http://www.mondaq.com/australia/x/743342/data+protection/Data+breaches+on+the+rise+in+the+health+sector.
697. https://www.digitalhealth.gov.au/about-the-agency/publications/reports/annual-report/Annual_Report_Australian_Digital_Health_Agency_2017-2018_Online.pdf.
698. *See* Allens, *Trend Watch: What the top ten 2018 cybersecurity trends mean for your business*, at https://www.allens.com.au/pubs/priv/priv-trendwatch-jan19.htm.

1530. Legislation and cyber security go hand in hand, and the need to protect the nation's cyber infrastructure have also been recognized. The ASIC has continued to draw attention to cyber security issues acknowledging the need for boards to have a thorough understanding of the cybersecurity landscape as a fundamental aspect of every businesses risk management strategy. In September 2018, ASIC released a report that reviewed Australian financial services (AFS) licensees' compliance with the breach reporting requirement in section 912D of the Corporations Act 2001 (Cth). ASIC was critical of AFS licensees, highlighting 'serious' and 'unacceptable' delays in the reporting of significant breaches.[699]

1531. The APRA has also indicated that ensuring entities are able to respond effectively in the event of a cyberattack is a priority. On 7 November 2018, APRA released the final version of prudential standard CPS 234, the first prudential standard in Australia that specifically addressed information and cyber security.[700] The new standard will take effect on 1 July 2019.

1532. The Australian Cyber Security Centre (ACSC) 2018 was created within the Australian Signals Directorate (ASD). This initiative was recommended in the Defence White Paper (2016) to mitigate the cyber threats directed at vital infrastructure and Australia's national security.[701] A cyber security strategy has been put in place with an overarching three-pronged strategy.[702]

1533. The Cybersafety Plan focuses on the broader social and personal risks associated with the use of computers and the Internet and the protection of children online.[703]

1534. The Commonwealth's Cyber Security Strategy outlines the vision for a secure, resilient and trusted cyber environment, and provides a framework to better address threats to computer systems and data, including systems which underpin Australia's national security, critical infrastructure and systems of national interest. This Plan recognizes existing strategies and that the best way to protect against security risks is also the most effective way of protecting against cybercrime.[704]

1535. The Cybercrime Plan involves a range of Commonwealth, State, Territory and other agencies and groups in a coordinated effort to combat cybercrime. The Cybercrime Plan supports a range of other Commonwealth Government strategies,

699. https://download.asic.gov.au/media/4879889/rep594-published-25-september-2018.pdf.
700. https://www.apra.gov.au/sites/default/files/cps_234_july_2019_for_public_release.pdf.
701. http://www.defence.gov.au/WhitePaper/Links.asp.
702. Department of Home Affairs, *Australia's Cyber Security Strategy: Enabling Innovation, Growth & Prosperity* (2016), at https://cybersecuritystrategy.homeaffairs.gov.au/.
703. Australian Government Cyber Safety Plan. Office of the eSafety Commissioner. https://www.esafety.gov.au/.
704. https://cybersecuritystrategy.homeaffairs.gov.au/.

including the National Security Strategy, NDES, Organised Crime Strategic Framework and National Organised Crime Response Plan and National Identity Security Strategy. It also supports and promotes the development of State and Territory strategies to respond to cybercrime.[705]

1536. A third guiding principle is that the study of cyber law must recognize the intangibility of property and its rights. While rights and its protection were the focus in the text there have been developments in the ICT sector which have now re-directed attention to the technology itself. Electronic devices carry and send messages as well as store these. Some of these devices may be used for malicious purposes.

1537. In Australia the Telecommunications and Other Legislation Amendment (Assistance and Access) Act 2018 (Cth) (TOLA) was passed as a way of preventing suspected terrorist activity.[706] The so-called encryption laws came into force from Dec 2018 where a suspect is compelled to provide information to enable access to the contents of locked electronic telecommunication devices. The penalties for non-compliance are made under the Crimes Act 1914 (Cth). The TOLA Act strengthens the ability of AFP to address existing and future obstacles to lawfully accessing digital content.

1538. The most significant aspect of the new law is the power granted to Australian government agencies to issue a range of notices requiring designated communication providers to undertake particular action regarding the security of their services. While debate around the TOLA has focused on the need for these new powers to combat terrorism and child abuse, the powers granted under the TOLA may be used in respect of any 'serious Australian offence' that is punishable by a maximum term of imprisonment of three years or more.

1539. The TOLA also amends a variety of legislation including the Crimes Act 1914 (Cth) and the Surveillance Devices Act 2004 (Cth) to permit Commonwealth and state law enforcement to issue, and collect evidence under, a 'computer access warrant' which allow the government agency to covertly seize and access information. These actions were previously only available to the ASIO.

1540. To ability of law enforcement agencies to interrogate the contents of an electronic device might appear to breach the contract that a device owner has with the service provider. The TOLA Act, as presently conceived in the discussion above, overrides the contractual obligations of service providers to device owners on the basis of national security concerns.

1541. A fourth guiding principle is that in the cyber world the myriad and multiplicity of characterizations cannot be foreseen and predicted. New imaginations

---

705. https://www.homeaffairs.gov.au/criminal-justice/files/national-plan-combat-cybercrime.pdf.
706. D. Murray, 'Encrypt laws force password handover', *The Australian* 2–3 Feb. 2019, p. 11.

are required to accommodate new situations and new laws developed. While contract law and electronic transactions legislation do not attract overt principles insofar as cyber law is concerned, the characterization of the cyber world is one of transferability and application from the real-world to one that is virtual.

1542. While the section on non-contractual liability identified the various roles and responsibilities in tort, a curious question may be posed to cyber law: Does cyber law extend beyond the grave? A young Canadian died of septic shock and a perforated intestine and complications related to Crohn's disease recently.[707] He was the gatekeeper of USD 265 million fortune in cryptocurrency. However, no one has access to the funds because the funds remain sealed in an online black hole with his company claiming that access to the encrypted money died with him. The company Quadriga is Canada's largest cryptocurrency exchange. The same may be said of funds left in dormant accounts and the owner may have deceased leaving behind 'old' digital coins protected by a password. Investors have launched legal action to recover the funds. But several legal conundrums remain. What is the legal position of the crypto funds and what laws govern the recovery of the money that the investors have outlaid? The law of contract suggests a link between the investors and the currency exchange. Succession law would suggest a close examination of the man's will and what is stated there. Is there a need to develop a cyber law of succession under such circumstances? How would encryption laws compelling manufacturers of electronic devices to surrender encrypted passwords work in this case? Cyber law would indeed need to be stretched to address the issues posed by this case. Dormant accounts may be subject to the Banking Act 1959 (Cth) depending on the electronic payment system used for creating and storing the digital currencies.

1543. A fifth guiding principle is that there remain pockets of uncertainty and ephemerality in legal constructs and rule in the face of developments wrought by the cyber world. It is unclear whether there exists in Australia, a common law tort of privacy or civil action for a breach of privacy. Such torts and rights have been discussed in the substantive section on this topic previously. Here the attention should be turned to global developments on the topic as well as the rights of consumers to privacy and consumer data at a local level.

1544. The 'right to be forgotten' is a concept that has been debated, enshrined in legislation and put into practice overseas especially in the EU, Argentina and elsewhere.[708] This right may be interpreted as another tool to exorcise one's digital trail and persona in cyberspace. The right to be forgotten may be a means to determine one's own life and development without being constantly reminded and stigmatized by actions performed in the past. The argument is that if 'you're not there, then there may be no privacy to protect'. The key word is 'there', meaning a presence on the Internet and in cyberspace. But, is there a 'there' there in cyberspace?

---

707. H. Tomlinson, 'Investors shut out of crypto fortune', *The Australian*, 11 Feb. 2019, p. 10.
708. A. Mantelero, *The EU Proposal for a General Data Protection Regulation and the roots of the 'right to be forgotten'*, 29(3) Computer Law & Security Rev. 229–235 (2013). doi:10.1016/j.clsr.2013.03.010.

1545. However, there are practical and operational impediments in the implementation of such a right and the proposal of such a right has sparked widespread controversy. How such a right to be forgotten may be raised to the status of an international human right with respect to access to information presents logistical difficulties. Such difficulties arise from imprecise rulings on the issue when implementing such a right. Other arguments stem from the concerns of its impact on the right to the freedom of expression vis-à-vis the rights to privacy. By extension, the argument may be taken to an extreme where the right to be forgotten may be taken to mean a censorship regime that both rewrites history and decreases the value of repositories such as the Internet. At the other extreme proponents argue that the right to be forgotten is a necessary device to stem issues such as revenge porn – the distribution of sexually explicit images or video of individuals without their permission. The key in these arguments being that one's personal online presence persists almost indefinitely if not removed by intent.

1546. Researchers from the Center for IT Security, Privacy and Accountability (CISPA) and the University of Auckland, NZ have developed a framework called Oblivion. This framework automates the right to be forgotten in a scalable, provable and privacy-preserving manner. The process automates the verification of someone's personal information that could be found in a Google search. Oblivion may assist in reducing the workload for administrators from the high volume of take-down requests to Google.

1547. The right to be forgotten may be contrasted to an individual right of consumers to bring claims for breaches of the Privacy Act 1988 (Cth) concerning their information. The ACCC document Digital Platforms Inquiry Preliminary Report was released on 10 December 2018.[709] In this document the ACCC recommended that individuals should be able to recover for financial and non-financial harm suffered because of a breach of the Privacy Act 1988 (Cth) and the APPs.

1548. Even where no privacy laws have been broken, unethical or improper handling of data revealed by a breach can exacerbate costs and damage to a person's reputation and standing. The poor handling of personal data leaves companies exposed to significant reputational damage.

1549. In June 2018, the Australian Broadcasting Corporation (ABC) revealed that HealthEngine had been sharing patient information with a law firm, on the basis it obtained express consent. Whether HealthEngine was in breach of privacy law, such practices may be interpreted as out of step with consumer expectations and perceived as inadequate and unethical. The significant negative media attention this

---

709. https://www.accc.gov.au/focus-areas/inquiries-ongoing/digital-platforms-inquiry, Digital Platforms Inquiry – Preliminary Report.pdf.

revelation attracted resulted in the company announcing that it had changed its business model to assuage concerns about the handling of consumer data.[710]

1550. The Australian government has proposed the implementation of a Consumer Data Right following the recommendations of the Review into Open Banking in Australia.[711] The Treasury Laws Amendment (Consumer Data Right) Bill 2018 will give Australians greater control over their data, empowering customers to choose to share their data with trusted recipients only for the purposes that they have authorized.[712] The Right will be implemented initially in the banking, energy, and telecommunications sectors, and then economy-wide on a sector-by-sector basis. The second stage exposure draft legislation and explanatory material has only been recently released and the outcome of this Bill will be keenly watched by consumers and industry sectors.

1551. A sixth guiding principle is that the cyber world can bring about pain and suffering just as the physical world will do. Here the hurt and damage is done as it were 'at arms-length' and yet the consequences are real and felt. In 2013 the journalist Ginger Gorman was 'trolled online' – an Internet slang to describe deliberate acts to start a quarrel or to upset people on the Internet by posting inflammatory and hurtful comments. Gorman received scores of hateful tweets, including a death threat. She was terrified, but once the attack subsided, she found herself curious. Who were these 'trolls'? How and why did they coordinate such an attack? And how does someone fight back? What can the law do to assist? Gorman wrote a book Troll Hunting where she sought to expose the world of online hate and its human fallout.[713] In criminal law it may be understood that any 'apprehension' or fear instilled onto someone may lead to a cause of action on criminal grounds. Does such a principle also apply to the virtual world where there was no face-to-face meeting nor physical contact, simply a virtual online one? If the perpetrator is identified and caught can criminal charges be effective? These are moot questions as the issues stem from the characterization of a cybercrime and how and when any accused person may be brought to justice.

1552. On the WWW, there are content that exists on 'darknets' – described as overlay networks that use the Internet that require special software and authorization to access. In this part of the Web the content is not indexed and hence cannot be found by conventional web search engines. What takes place behind the darknet remains secret. There is no way of knowing if stories of goings on and illicit online trading of prohibited drugs and other criminal activities are true. Yet, cyber law may at some stage be called upon to consider monitoring and to bring those who perpetrate crimes to task. There is no such thing as a victimless crime, it is only that

---

710. Pat McGrath, *HealthEngine app announces 'major changes' after doctor and patient backlash*, ABC (5 Jul. 2018), at https://www.abc.net.au/news/2018-07-05/healthengine-flags-major-changes-amid-patient-gp-concerns/9940232.
711. https://treasury.gov.au/review/review-into-open-banking-in-australia/.
712. https://treasury.gov.au/consumer-data-right/.
713. G. Gorman, Troll Hunting: Inside the World of Online Hate and Its Human Fallout (2019), Richmond, Vic: Hardie Grant Books, 2019.

the victims themselves do not see themselves as such and do not report it to law enforcement agencies. Without the victim reporting a crime there may be no way to bring to justice the criminal parties.

1553. A seventh guiding principle is that cyber laws and regulations may need to be transnational and cross-jurisdictional. Witness that environmental law issues are yet to be mainstreamed in the cyber world, but technological innovations may require the attention of cyber law.

1554. In Australia, the Security of Critical Infrastructure Act 2018 (Cth) took effect on 11 July 2018. The legislation creates a critical infrastructure asset register that gives the Minister of Home Affairs a 'last resort' power to direct an owner or operator of a critical infrastructure asset to mitigate national security risks. Such critical infrastructure can be targets for state-sponsored, terrorist and financially motivated hackers and attackers with serious potential ramifications.

1555. In 2018 Australia banned Chinese telecoms companies Huawei and ZTE from providing 5G technology to Australian mobile phone operators, citing 'national security risks'.[714]

1556. In April 2018, the US, UK and Australia issued a coordinated announcement that accused the Kremlin of a 'malicious Internet offensive' in 2017 that targeted 'government institutions, private sector organizations and infrastructure'.[715]

1557. Australia, Britain, Canada, New Zealand and the US, forming the Five Eyes alliance, are increasing cooperation on the issue of 'foreign interference'. Discussions to date have focused primarily on interference by China and Russia.[716]

1558. Globally, there have been increasing efforts from private organizations and governments to cooperate on sharing information and tackling cyber security issues. Industry-specific communities dedicated to the sharing of information also exist at the national and international level.

1559. An eighth guiding principle suggests that global solutions might be required even for local problems in environmental matters and in technological matters. However, global solutions bring to the fore geopolitics, world trade, multipartite agreements, treaties and conventions. In geopolitical terms there inevitably will

---

714. Byron Kaye and Tom Westbrook, *China's Huawei slams Australia 5G mobile network ban as 'politically motivated'*, Thomson Reuters (23 Aug. 2018), at https://www.reuters.com/article/us-australia-china-huawei-tech/australia-bans-chinas-huawei-from-mobile-network-build-over-security-fears-idUSKCN1L72GC.
715. Ewen MacAskill, *US and UK blame Russia for 'malicious; cyber-offensive*, The Guardian (17 Apr. 2018); and Anne Davies, *Australia joins US and UK in blaming Russian-backed hackers for cyber-attacks*, The Guardian (17 Apr. 2018).
716. Noah Barkin, *Exclusive: Five Eyes intelligence alliance builds coalition to counter China*, Thomson Reuters (12 Oct. 2018), at https://www.reuters.com/article/us-china-fiveeyes/exclusive-five-eyes-intelligence-alliance-builds-coalition-to-counter-china-idUSKCN1MM0GH.

be 'blocs' and opposing geopolitical philosophies. Technology and its use or non-use can spark alliances, alignments and restrictions on e-commerce and trade.

1560. Governments restricting the use of technology sourced from certain countries and certain manufacturers has already been mentioned above. The government bans also extend to software and apps. The Australian Defence Department has banned staff and serving personnel from downloading Chinese social media and messaging app, WeChat, on their work phones. [717] This move highlights concerns around Chinese espionage activities in Australia. It is known that WeChat has deep and well-documented security flaws. As well WeChat is subject to both 'censorship and surveillance' in China. The lack of privacy and the potential for Chinese apps to contain spyware or malicious ware was behind a decision in December 2018 by the Indian Defence Ministry to ban serving personnel from having WeChat and other similar services on their phones.[718]

1561. WeChat is pushing into Australia through its payments function, which allows Chinese tourists to Australia to shop on holidays as they do at home. In the final analysis there is the balancing and weighing up of national security concerns with economic concerns.

1562. Another source of concern is that of sovereignty and independence from foreign-based interference. It has been documented that Australia has banned the use of Chinese technology from the supplier Huawei. The Australian Department of Home Affairs articulated the rationale for banning Chinese telecommunication companies from participating in the roll out of 5G telecommunications networks by stating that 'vendors ... are likely to be subject to extrajudicial directions from a foreign government that conflicts with Australian law'.[719] China's 2017 security legislation spells out that Chinese organizations must 'support, co-operate and collaborate in national intelligence work and guard the secrecy of national intelligence work they are aware of'.[720] The Chinese 2017 National Intelligence Law requires all Chinese companies, whether government-owned or privately owned, to serve the Chinese state's interests in any matters relating to intelligence.[721] That law and others are a source of concern for Western officials who think Chinese firms have no choice to comply with Communist Party directives.[722]

---

717. A. Grigg, *Australia's Defence Department bans Chinese app WeChat*, Australian Financial Review (11 Mar. 2018), at https://ww.aft.com/technology/apps/australias-defence-department-bans-chinese-app-wechat-20180310-h0xay8.
718. A. Grigg, *WeChat's privacy issues mean you should delete China's No. messaging app*, Australian Financial Review (22 Feb. 2018), at https://www.afr.com/news/world/asia/wechats-privacy-issues-mean-you-should-delete-chinas-no1-messaging-app-20180221-h0wgct.
719. D. Uren, *It may be a bit late to slam the digital door on China*, The Australian (14 Feb. 2019), p. 12.
720. https://www.canada.ca/en/security-intelligence-service/corporate/publications/china-and-the-age-of-strategic-rivalry/chinas-intelligence-law-and-the-countrys-future-intelligence-competitions.html.
721. G. Sheridan, *We are bound to be caught up in Huawei fallout*, The Australian (31 Jan. 2019), p. 12.
722. D. Strumpf, *Huawei glitches to take years to fix*, The Wall Street Journal (11 Feb. 2019), p. 21.

1563. A ninth guiding principle is that cyber law regulation and compliance in a digital world can be complex and confusing. The world today is increasingly complex and our lives increasingly digital. In a global economy, human activity – goods and services – move across national borders. In this environment, legal compliance has grown in volume and complexity. Moreover, the regulatory context is constantly changing with liability ever more likely to extend to personal and corporate responsibility. Aggressive regulatory agencies and new procedures such as class actions and expanded discovery are making the cost of non-compliance more prohibitive than ever. The auditing of compliance whether national or transnational can prove difficult. A technical solution has been deployed in the form of RegTech regulatory technology to provide regulatory compliance.

1564. This new environment has seen greater attention by regulators and those regulated to use technology to monitor compliance. 'RegTech' is a blended term that describes the use of technologies to deliver regulatory requirements. This involves using technology to better deliver value in relation to reporting, monitoring, providing analytics and fulfilling auditing requirements. Compliance is thus able to be achieved more efficiently, more effectively and with greater transparency. The technology enables better outcomes for both the regulator and the entity being regulated. RegTech is superior to traditional systems that have been, and largely remain, paper-based, bureaucratic-centred, transaction-based, and involving many intermediaries in the regulatory chain.

1565. Evidence of the rapid adoption of RegTech is the formation of the International RegTech Association[723] to ease and accelerate the evolution of RegTech by promoting innovation and facilitating integration and collaboration, throughout the global RegTech ecosystem. Deloitte published a report on RegTech Universe in 2017 listing more than 150 RegTech startups globally.[724]

1566. A tenth and final guiding principle is that effective national cyber law and transnational laws and regulations are needed. Effective laws and strong enforcement are critical if poor consumer experiences have led to a loss of faith in e-commerce that is part of the market economy. To restore consumer trust in markets that operate fairly, effectively and to consumer benefit there must be a prevailing culture that encourages such trustworthiness. In Australia, at one stage in the early 1970s, businesses were opposed to laws that made cartels and monopolies illegal and corporate behaviour that misled consumers. However, appropriate laws are now in place and no corporate leader would say such behaviour is acceptable any longer. The ingredients include strong competition, appropriate regulation and well-informed consumers. To these ingredients should be added the aggressive enforcement of the various laws, making effective laws and policy reforms that encourage stronger competition in the marketplace. These steps would ensure that the markets are working efficiently and that consumers are treated fairly.

---

723. https://regtechassociation.org/.
724. https://www2.deloitte.com/lu/en/pages/technology/articles/regtech-universe.html and https://www2.deloitte.com/lu/en/pages/technology/articles/regtech-companies-compliance.html.

1567. In December 2017 Australia together with 67 other nations agreed to embark on a formal round of the WTO negotiations to craft a new set of enforceable global rules to govern digital trade.[725] The aim is to strengthen the trust among digital transaction partners, banning tariffs on low-value goods traded through e-commerce platforms, trade facilitation such as the recognition of digital contracts and signatures, removing barriers on cross-border data flows and forcing foreign firms to open access to their source code as a condition for trade or investment among others. At a time when the role of the WTO is being called into question, this e-commerce initiative reinforces how the WTO adds value. Australian exporters, including tech start-ups, could benefit from new global rules to reduce red tape when operating in foreign markets, helping them grow their exports. With such rules in place cyber law may develop with much vigour and can be used to rigorously pursue recalcitrants in the e-commerce world.

725. *See* Steve Ciobo, *Australia has led an initiative at the 11th World Trade Organization (WTO) Ministerial Conference (MC11) on e-commerce*, at https://trademinister.gov.au/releases/Pages/2017/sc_mr_171214.aspx.

Selected Bibliography

Beatty, J.F. & Samuelson, S.S. *Business Law and the Legal Environment.* Cengage, 2012.

Bettinger, T. *Domain Name Law and Practice: An International Handbook.* Oxford: Oxford University Press, 2014.

Bolam, P & Choi, R. 'Electronic Signatures: When Are They Effective?'. *Internet Law Bulletin* (October 2012): 118–120.

Boyle, J. *The Public Domain: Enclosing the Commons of the Mind.* Yale University Press, 2010.

Burgess, C. & Burgess, M. *The Social Employee: How Great Companies Make Social Media Work.* McGraw-Hill, 2013.

Cahoy, D. & Oswald, L.J. *The Changing Face of US Patent Law and Its Impact on Business Strategy.* Cheltenham, Glos: Edward Elgar, 2013.

Carones, S. *Australian Consumer Law.* 2nd ed. Sydney: Thomson Reuters, 2012.

Carter, J. *Carter's Guide to Australian Contract Law.* 6th ed. Sydney: LexisNexis, 2012.

Carter, J. *Contract and the Australian Consumer Law – A Guide.* Sydney: LexisNexis, 2011.

Carter, J. *Carter's Breach of Contract.* Sydney: LexisNexis, 2011.

Chaffrey, D. *E-Business and E-Commerce Management* 5th ed. Harlow: Prentice Hall, 2011.

Christensen, C., Horn, M. & Johnson, C. *Disrupting Class: How Disruptive Innovation Will Change the Way the World Learns.* McGraw-Hill, 2010.

Clark, E. & Sims, I. 'Flying into the Hurricane: Law, Policy and Practice Implications of Cloud Computing'. *Intl. J. Tech. L. Policy* 1 (2012): 135–151.

Clark, E.E. 'The Legal Tortoise and the High Frequency Trading Hare: The Challenge for Regulators'. *Australian Journal of Corporate Law* 25 (2011): 274–303.

Clarke, P. & Clarke, J. *Contract Law: Commentaries, Cases and Perspectives.* 2nd ed. Oxford: OUP, 2012.

Cohen, A.I. *Social Media: Legal Risk & Corporate Policy.* Aspen Publishers, 2013.

Craig, T. & Ludloff, M. *Privacy and Big Data.* O'Reilly Media, Inc, 2011.

Dabbah, M.M. *Competition Law and Policy in the Middle East.* Cambridge University Press, 2012.

Davis, J. *Contract: General Principles – The Laws of Australia.* 2nd ed. Sydney: LawBook Co, 2012.

Feldman, N. *Cool War: The Future of Global Competition.* Random House, 2013.

Selected Bibliography

Fitzgerald, A. 'e-Contracts'. In *Internet and E-Commerce Law, Business and Policy*, edited by B. Fitzgerald et al. Sydney: LawBook Co, 2011.

Fitzgerald, B. et al. *Internet and E-Commerce Law.* Sydney: Thomson, 2011.

Gerber, D. *Global Competition: Law, Markets, and Globalization*. Oxford University Press, USA; Reprint edition, 2012.

Goldstein, M. *Telecommunications: National Broadband Plan Reflects the Experiences of Leading Countries, but Implementation Will Be Challenging*. Diane Publishing, 2011.

Govindarajan, V. & Trimble, C. *Reverse Innovation: Create Far from Home, Win Anywhere.* Harvard Business Press, 2012.

Graw, S. *An Introduction to the Law of Contract.* 7th ed. Pyrmont NSW: Lawbook Co., 2011.

Hallbom, T.M. *Coaching in the Workplace: Coach Skills for Peak Performance.* Bringforth Publishing, 2012.

Harkins, M. *Managing Risk and Information Security: Protect to Enable*. Apress Publications, 2012.

Healey, J. & Pitts, H. 'Applying International Environmental Legal Norms to Cyber Statecraft'. *I/S: A Journal of Law and Policy for the Information Society* 8 no. 2 (2012): 356–387 and at http://moritzlaw.osu.edu/students/groups/is/files/2012/02/6.Healey.Pitts_.pdf.

Hutcheon, S. 'Cracking the cryptic world of virtual cash'. *Sydney Morning Herald*, 8–9 February 2014, p. 9.

Irani, Z. & Lov, P. *Evaluating Information Systems.* Routledge, 2013.

Jones, K. *The Doha Blues: Institutional Crisis and Reform in the WTO*. Oxford: Oxford University Press, 2010.

Kappos, D. 'Design: The New Frontier of Intellectual Property', available at http://www.nationallawjournal.com/id=1202596653483/Design-The-New-Frontier-of-Intellectual-Property?slreturn=20170203145129.

Katz, J. *Digital Signatures (Advances in Information Security)*. Springer, 2010.

Kerschischnig, G. *Cyberthreats and International Law.* Eleven International Publishing, 2012.

Kohl, U. *Jurisdiction and the Internet: Regulatory Competence over Online Activity*. Cambridge University Press; Reissue edition (University Press; Reissue edition, 2010).

Lifshitz, L.R. *Understanding Cloud Computing: Legal Issues and Best Practice.* Loud Computing Law, Toronto: Federated Press (2013).

Lipton, J. *Internet Domain Names, Trademarks and Free Speech (Elgar Intellectual Property and Global Development).* Edward Elgar Publishing Ltd. 2010.

Lipton, P., Herzberg, A. & Welsh, M. *Understanding Corporations Law*. 17th ed. North Ryde, Sydney: Thomson-Reuters, 2013.

McLauchlan, D. 'The Uncertain Basis of the Postal Acceptance Rule?'. *Journal of Contract Law* 30 (2013): 33.

Mahfood, P.E. *Homework: How to Hire, Manage and Monitor Employees Who Work at Home.* Irwin Professional Publishing, 2013.

Mason, S. *Electronic Signatures in Law.* 4th ed. Institute of Advanced Legal Studies for the SAS Humanities Digital Library, School of Advanced Study, University of London, 2017.

Merges, R.P. *Justifying Intellectual Property.* Harvard University Press, 2011.

Miller, R.V. *Miller's Australian Competition & Consumer Law Annotated 35th Edition.* Sydney: Thomson, 2013.

Mulholland, A., Pyke, J. & Fingar, P. *Enterprise Cloud Computing: A Strategy Guide for Business and Technology Leaders.* Tampa, Florida, Meghan-Kiffer Press, 2010.

Paterson, J. *Unfair Contract Terms in Australia.* Sydney: Thomson Reuters, 2011.

Percival, R.L. *Cloud Computing: Due Diligence Considerations.* Cloud Computing Law Workshop, Toronto: Federated Press, 2011.

Reveron, D.S. (ed.) *Cyberspace and National Security: Threats, Opportunities, and Power in a Virtual World.* Georgetown University Press, 2012.

Saini, R., Saini, S. & Sharma, S. 'Nanotechnology: The Future Medicine'. *Journal of Cutaneous and Aesthetic Surgery* 3(1) (2010): 32–33. doi:10.4103/0974-2077.63301.

Samovar, L., Porter, R., McDaniel & Roy, C. *Communication between Cultures.* 8th ed., Cengage Learning, 2012.

Scassa, T. 'Geographic information as personal information'. *Oxford University Commonwealth Law Journal* 10 (2010), 185–214.

Scholl, H.J. *E-Government: Information, Technology, and Transformation.* Google eBook, 2010.

Schox, J. *Not So Obvious: An Introduction to Patent Law and Strategy.* 3rd ed. CreateSpace Independent Publishing Platform, 2013.

Snedaker, S. *Business Continuity and Disaster Recovery Planning for IT Professionals.* Butterworth-Heinemann, 2011.

Solove, D.J. & Schwartz, P.M. *Information Privacy Law.* Wolters Kluwer Law & Business, 2011.

Sunder, M. *From Goods to a Good Life: Intellectual Property and Global Justice.* Yale University Press 2012.

Syngress, M.C. *Social Media Security: Leveraging Social Networking While Mitigating Risk.* 2013.

Talukder, M. Quazi, A. & Sathye, M. 'Mobile Phone Banking Usage Behaviour: An Australian Perspective'. *Australasian Accounting, Business and Finance Journal* 8 no. 4 (2014): 83–104.

Tankha, A. & Bout, L. *Trademarks – A Guide for Registering, Opposing and Appealing a Mark.* 2nd ed. Authorhouse Publishers, 2010.

Tapscott, D. & Williams, D. *Macrowikinomics: Rebooting Business and the World.* Portfolio Hardcover, 2010.

Wallach, W. *Moral Machines.* Oxford: Oxford University Press, 2010.

Wang, L., Ranjan, R. & Chen, J. *Cloud Computing: Methodology, Systems, and Applications.* CRC Press, Boca Raton, Florida 2012.

Weerakkody, V. & Reddick, C. ed. *Public Sector Transformation Through E-Government: Experiences from Europe and North America.* Routledge, 2012.

Weinstein, S., McEwan, N. & Each, N. *Electronic and Mobile Commerce Law: An Analysis of Trade, Finance, Media and Cybercrime in the Digital Age.* University of Hertfordshire Press, 2011.

Selected Bibliography

Wright, A.D. *A Necessary Evil: Managing Employee Activity on Facebook, LinkedIn and the Hundreds of Other Social Media Sites.* Society for Human Resource Management, 2013.

Wu, Q., *Competition Laws, Globalization and Legal Pluralism: China's Experience.* Hart Studies in Competition Law, Hart Publishing, 2013.

Zichermann, G. & Cunningham, C. 'Introduction'. In *Gamification by Design: Implementing Game Mechanics in Web and Mobile Apps.* Sebastopol, California: O'Reilly Media, 2011.

Index

The numbers here refer to paragraph numbers

Advertising. *See* E-marketing, consumer protection
Aggressive enforcement of laws, 1566
Alternative dispute resolution. *See* Dispute resolution
Anti-competitive Conduct, 182
Antitrust. *See* Competition
Anti-vilification. *See* Cybercrime; Torts
Artificial Intelligence, 1486, 1499
  Accident-avoidance, 1508
  Adjustable ethics, 1508
  Augmediated Reality (AR), 1504
  AR augmented reality app, 1506
  AR driver distraction, 1505
  AR litigation characterization, 1510
  AR perils, 1505
  Artificial moral agents, 1500
  AR-VR Ambient mode, 1504
  AR-VR Immersive mode, 1504
  Augmented reality, 1502
  Autonomous systems, 1501
  Autonomous vehicles, 1505
  Code of ethical conduct, 1509
  Consequentialism, 1508
  Driver-assist aids, 1508
  Heads-up displays, 1507
  Human Brain project, 1517
  Human morality, 1508
  Legal boundaries, 1513
  Legal challenges, 1509
  Limit liability, 1509
  Machine ethics, 1501
  Meta-ethical issue, 1500
  Other legal issues, 1515–1517
  Privacy expectations, 1512
  Privacy issues, 1514
  Synthesized intelligence, 1500
  Trolley problem, 1508
  VR Virtual reality, 1503
Assignment. *See* Copyright
Australia
  Asian region presence, 93
  Australian Capital Territory, 15
  Australian Economy, 29–38, 66–69
  Balance of political power, 18
  Broadband connections growth, 93
  Business Internet access, 73–75
  Business IT Use, 72
  Business online income, 75
  Business online orders, 74
  Child protection online, 87
  Cloud services spend, 94
  Constitution, 7–18
  Cultural composition, 4–6
  Cyber security indicators, 88
  Data downloads, 78–79
  Digital Economy key indicators, 70–75
  Digital infrastructure investment, 92
  E-government transformation, 91
  Employment, 69
  Family Court, 20
  Farm products, 31–32
  Federal Court, 21–24
  Federation, 13
  Fishing industry, 35
  Free enterprise economy, 39, 40
  G-20, 37
  GDP, 68
  General background, 1–41
  Geography, 1–3
  Global financial crisis, 66
  Global outlook, 41
  Government formed, 17–18
  Growth markets, 91–96
  Heritage Economic Freedom Index, 30
  Home Internet devices, 85

Household use of IT, 82–90
Indigenous population, 5
Internet access, 89
Internet subscribers, 76
Judicial power, 19–24
Labour Party, 26–27
Legislation, 11–12
Liberal-National Party coalition, 26–27
Major economic parameter statistics, 67–69
Manufacturing exports, 34
M-Commerce growth, 96
Mobile handset subscribers, 80–81
Mobile health, 95
Northern Territory, 15
Online activities, 90
Other political parties, 27
Political parties, 25–27
Political system, 7–18
Population, 28
Pre-Election Economic and Fiscal Outlook, 67
Service industries, 33
Social and cultural values, 39–41
Trading partners, 36
World Trade Organization, 37
Australian Cyber Security Centre, 1532
Australian Federal Police, 1537
Australian Legislation
Acts Interpretation Act (1901), 1126
Anti-Money Laundering and Counter-Terrorism Financing Act (2006), 800, 1023
Australia Act (1986), 16
Australian Competition and Consumer Law (2010), 1062
Australian Consumer Law (2010), 415, 577, 820
Australian Information Commissioner Act (2010), 989, 1041
Australian Postal Corporation Act (1989), 1018
Australian Sports Anti-Doping Authority Amendment Act (2013), 1016
Australian Wine and Brandy Corp Act (1980), 400–402
Banking Act (1959), 785
Broadcasting Services Act (1992), 159, 225
Broadcasting Services Amendment Online Services Act (1999), 938, 1053
Circuit Layouts Act (1989), 331
Commonwealth Broadcasting Services Act (1992), 830
Competition and Consumer Act (2010), 158, 658, 748, 815, 930, 945
Copyright Act (1968), 261, 284, 471, 1393
Copyright Amendment Digital Agenda Act (2000), 263
Copyright Amendment Moral Rights Act (2000), 268
Copyright Amendment Parallel Importation Act (2003), 355
Corporations Act (2001), 639, 742, 745, 1031
Crimes Act (1914), 1067, 1101, 1144
Crimes Amendment (Computer Offences) Act (2001) NSW, 1065, 1151
Crimes Computers Act (1988) Victoria, 1066
Crimes Computers and Forgery Amendment Act (1989) NSW, 1065
Criminal Code Act (1995), 1127, 1144, 1158
Criminal Code Amendment Suicide-related Material Offences Act (2005), 1250
Criminal Code and Civil Liability Amendment Act (2007) Queensland, 1153
Criminal Law Amendment Act (1990) Tasmania, 1067
Criminal Law Amendment Act (1990) WA, 1067
Customs Act (1901), 1144
Cybercrime Act (2001), 1063, 1145
Cybercrime Legislation Amendment Act (2012), 1274–1277
Data matching Program Assistance and Tax Act (1990), 1015
Designs Act (2003), 266
Electronic Transactions Act (1999), 650
Electronic Transactions Act (2001) Qld, 685
Electronic Transactions Amendment Act (2011), 502
Electronic Transactions Regulations (2000), 663
Enhancing Online Safety of Children's Safety Act (2015), 1247
Family Law Act (1975), 20
Federal Court of Australia Act (1976), 21

Financial Sector Reform (Amendments and Transitional Provisions) Act (1998), 808
Financial Transactions Reports Act (1988), 799
Freedom of Information Act (1982), 1039
Hazardous Waste Act (1989), 1303
Health Records Act (2001) Victoria, 1029
Identity Crime and Other Measures Act (2011), 1177–1178
Information Privacy Act (2000) Victoria, 1006, 1029
Interactive Gambling Act (2001), 1220
International Arbitration Act (1974), 870
Invasion of Privacy Act (1971) Queensland, 1029
National Consumer Credit Protection Act (2009), 742, 828
Patents Act (1990), 264
Payments Systems Regulation Act (1998), 788
Payment Systems and Netting Act (1998), 785
Personally Controlled Electronic Health Records Act (2012), 141, 1027–1028
Privacy Act (1988), 658, 757, 981
Privacy Amendment Enhancing Privacy Protection Act (2012), 990–991
Privacy Amendment Private Sector Act (2001), 1005
Privacy and Personal Data Protection Act (1998) NSW, 1029
Privacy and Personal Information Protection Act (1998) NSW, 1006
Proceeds of Crime Act (1987), 799
Product Stewardship Act (2011), 1307
Product Stewardship Regulations (2011), 1308
Records Act (2001) Victoria, 1029
Sale of Goods Act, 577
Sale of Goods Act (1932) NSW, 578–580
Security of Critical Infrastructure Act (2018), 1554
Spam Act (2003), 954, 1073
Spam Consequential Amendments Act (2003), 1073
Summary Offences Act Amendment Act (1989) SA, 1067
Surveillance Devices Act (1998), WA, 1029
Telecommunications Act (1991), 151, 1051
Telecommunications Act (1997), 152, 161, 954, 1246
Telecommunications and Other Legislation Amendment Act (TOLA) (2018), 1537
Telecommunications Consumer Protection Act (1999), 159, 209
Telecommunications Interception and Access Act (1979), 954, 1060, 1127, 1257
Telecommunications Offences and Other Measures Act (2004), 1158, 1160, 1245
Trade Marks Act (1995), 267, 414
Trade Practices Act (1974), 316, 414, 1119
Australian Prudential Regulation Authority, 1527
Australian Securities and Investment Commission, 1526
Australian Signals Directorate, 1531

Balance private public interest, 1521
Bans software and apps, 1560
Borderless Internet, 1520
Breaches Privacy Act (1988), 1547
Broadcasting Services
ACMA rules on gambling content, 233
Civil and Criminal proceedings, 230
Content services, 232
Industry Codes and Standards, 228
Internet Service Provider, 227
Online provider rules, 229
Owners and operators of towers, 225
Regulating Internet industry, 227
Restrictions on services, 225
Schedule Content services, 226
Schedule Online services, 226
State or Territory applicability, 231
Synoptic view of Act, 233
Business Names
ASIC, 411, 413
Australian Business Name, 411
Australian Company Name, 411
Cybersquatting, 415
Drawbacks name registration, 412
Registration, 410
Registration authorities, 411

Index

Censorship and surveillance, 1560
Centrality of cyber law, 1518
China National Intelligence Law (2017), 1562
China security legislation (2017), 1562
Circuit Layouts
  Acts of infringement, 356–357
  Appeals, 368
  Artistic Work Copyright Act (1968), 341
  Assignment and licence, 347
  Burden of proof, 360
  Circuit layout protection other countries, 334
  CLA Circuit Layout Act Background, 332
  CLA commercial exploitation, 336
  CLA exclusive rights, 335
  CLA other IP law, 331–335
  CLA sui generis protection, 334
  CLA synoptic view, 334
  Common law defences, 361
  Defences, 358
  Eligible layout, 344
  First sale doctrine, 350
  Grey market, 355
  Groundless threats to proceedings, 365
  IC as literary work, 341
  Infringements primary, 356
  Infringements secondary, 356
  Infringement under Copyright Act, 353
  Innocent commercial exploitation, 359
  Integrated circuit (IC), 333
  IP protection for circuit layout designs, 330
  Jurisdiction, 368
  Limitation of actions, 366
  Limited exception Copyright Act, 354
  Logic instructions as program, 342
  Marking advantages, 349
  Object code circuitry protected, 342
  Parallel importation, 351
  Parallel importation software, 352
  Proof of facts, 367
  Prospective ownership, 348
  Protection criteria, 343
  Protection length of, 346
  Protection nature of, 344
  Remedies available, 363–364
  Reverse engineering, 338
  Rights to bring action, 362
  Semiconductor chip, 333
  Statutory defences, 359–360
  Treaty on IP in respect of IC (1989), 331
  TRIPS Agreement (1989), 332
  Uruguay Round GATT negotiations (1989), 332
  US Semiconductor Chip Protection Act (1985), 330
  WIPO, 331
Class actions, 1563
Collateral Issues Contract
  Agents actual authority, 638–639
  Anton Piller order, 642
  Consumer protection, 640
  Copyright assignment, 632
  Corporations Act (2001), 639
  Escrow agent use of, 634
  Escrow Internet, 635
  Escrow source code, 632
  Liability and ownership, 629
  Mareva Injunction, 643
  Minor capacity, 636–637
  Minors and agents, 636–639
  Ownership rights, 631
  Remedies injunctions, 641
  Software maintenance, 633
  Trademarks on goods, 630
Competition, 61, 118, 149, 158, 173, 190, 206, 235, 240–243, 317, 398, 429, 446, 891, 1378, 1566
Compliance. *See* Risk management, information governance
Computer access warrant, 1539
Computer chips. *See* Circuit Layouts
Consumer Data Right, 1550
Consumer Law Goods and Services
  CCA implied conditions, 826
  CCA Industry Codes, 830
  CCA services, 827
  COAG Agreement (2008), 828
  Consumer credit, 828
  E-Commerce Best Practice Model, 832–833
  EU Distance Selling Directive, 831
  International Standards, 831
  National Credit Code, 828
  OECD Guidelines Consumer Protection (1999), 831
  Quality, 825
  Treasury Guidelines E-Commerce (2006), 834–835
  Uniform Consumer Credit Code, 828
  Voluntary codes, 829
Consumer Protection Cyberspace

ACCC case law, 816–819
ACCC website and scams, 811
Australian losses to scammers, 812
Australian Stock EXchange, 823
CCA Defences, 822
CCA Remedies, 821
Clearing House Electronic Sub-register System, 823
Consumer protection, 813–814
Consumer protection statutory schemes, 814
Fair Trading Act States and Territories, 824
Internet scam, 818
Misleading and deceptive, 817
Stock Exchange Automated Trading System, 823
Consumer Protection Regulation
Consumer service guarantee (CSG), 208
CSG services, 216
CSG standard, 216
CSG when service inapplicable, 218–219
Digital data service obligation (DDSO), 213
DDSO General, 213
DDSO Special, 213
Definition universal service obligation, 210
Service time frames, 217
TCPSS Synoptic view, 209
Telecommunications Industry Ombudsman (TIO), 220–224
Telstra, 211, 214
TIO Constitution, 223
TIO Functions, 221–222
TIO Powers and responsibilities, 224
Universal service obligation (USO), 208
Universal service provider, 211
USO objective, 212
Consumer trust in markets, 1566
Contract, 534, 536, 559
Copyright, 632. *See also* Intellectual Property Rights
Critical infrastructure, 1534
Cryptography
ABN-DSC, 702
Australian Business Number, 701
Australian Standard Code of Tendering, 706
Australian Tax Office, 701
Automated approvals, 705
Certification authorities, 692, 694, 701
Definition PKI, 694
Digital certificates, 691, 694, 701–702
Digital keys, 691
Electronic procurement, 703
Electronic purchase order, 704
E-tendering, 706
Gatekeeper-accredited organizations, 691
Gatekeeper Report (1998), 691
Gatekeeper Strategy, 692
Goods and Services Tax, 701
Government Public Key Authority, 691
International Organization for Standardization, 692
International Telecommunications Union, 692
Message integrity, 696
Non-repudiation, 694, 697
OECD Guidelines on Cryptography, 692
Office of Government Information Technology, 691
Public key infrastructure (PKI), 691
PKI biometrics, 699
PKI four pillars, 695
PKI workability, 700
Public key encryption, 698
Public key technology, 691
Registration Authority, 694
Standards Australia, 692
Trust and certainty, 690
Validation authority, 694
Cyberattack, 1531
Cybercrime, 805, 906, 1180, 1210, 1211, 1269, 1554
Cybercrime Identity Theft
ABS id theft loss estimates, 1175
Anti-hoax laws, 1255
Anti-terrorism laws, 1253–1259
Anti-vilification laws, 1251–1252
ASIO, 1254, 1258
Children Online Privacy Protection, 1243
Children unsuitable content, 1244
Common mischiefs, 1179
Computer definition, 1192–1194
Convention on the Rights of the Child, 1249
Cookie, 1190
Counter-terrorism reforms, 1258
Criminal Code Act (2007) Queensland identity information, 1178
Enforceability to regulate Internet content, 1241–1242
Hacking or cracking, 1180

Identity crime, 1172
Identity fabrication, 1172
Identity manipulation, 1172
Identity theft Celent Report, 1174–1175
International Cooperation Children, 1249
Local area networks, 1190
Northern Territory unlawful obtaining of information, 1191
Obscenity and Pornography Issues, 1241
Spyware, 1190
Terrorism offences inserted into Criminal Code, 1254
Terrorist-related financial transactions, 1256, 1258
UNICEF Optional Protocol (2002), 1249
'Whois' data accuracy, 1259
Cybercrime Law
Australian Business Assessment of Computer User Security, 1142
Australian Institute of Criminology survey, 1142–1143
Computer Emergency Response Team (CERT), 1137
Cybercrime definition, 1132
Cybercrime examples, 1138
Cybercrime nature and extent, 1135–1143
Cybercrime Security Survey (2012), 1137
Distributed denial of service, 1140
Modification of data, 1141
National Plan, 1133
Online Reporting Network, 1133
Ransomware, 1138
Scareware, 1139
Cybercrime Law Enforcement
Anti-hacking laws, 1196–1197
Crime capacity of minors, 1125
Crime definition, 1114–1117
Criminal Code Model provisions, 1127
Criminal Code State and Territories, 1181
Criminal intent, 1123
Criminal law sources, 1118–1120
Criminal liability establishing, 1122
Criminal liability levels, 1183
Criminal liability principles, 1121
Criminal procedure, 1127–1130
Cybercrime legal developments, 1113
Person defined, 1126
Unauthorized access, 1124, 1188–1189, 1195
Cybercrime Legislation Australia
AFP Transnational Crime Coordination Centre, 1264
Australian Federal Police, 1263
Australian Hi-Tech Crime Centre, 1264
Council of Europe Convention on Cybercrime, 1273
Council of Europe to block racist websites, 1272
'Crimtrac', 1263
Cybercrime Act critique, 1148–1150
Cybercrime Act jurisdiction, 1147
Cybercrime Act new offences, 1145
Cybercrime Act penalties, 1146
Cybercrime Convention, 1274–1278
Cybercrime Convention critique, 1279
Cybercrime preventative private action, 1267
Cybercrime remedies, 1268–1269
Cybercrime technological solutions, 1269
Cyberflaws, 1269
Deception of persons and computers, 1152
Industry Police cooperation on Internet protection, 1265–1266, 1270
International cooperation, 1271
International MOU cross-border Internet fraud, 1271
Law enforcement education, 1262
Law enforcement resources, 1263
Law enforcement strategic partnerships, 1261
Law enforcement strategies, 1260
National Automated Finger Print Id System, 1263
National Investigation DNA databases, 1263
Queensland Criminal Code (1899) computer hacking & misuse, 1154–1155, 1186
Queensland cybercrime definition, 1153
SANS cyber vulnerabilities, 1269
Tasmania law unlawful excuse, 1187
WA Criminal Code (1990) unlawful computer operation, 1185
Cybercrime Online Gambling
ACMA gambling advertising prohibition, 1227
ACMA Interactive Gambling Act role, 1231
ACMA investigations, 1223, 1226

Australia extent of online gambling, 1218
Broadcasting Services Act (1992) gambling prohibition, 1227
Click to-call prohibition, 1221
Gambling definition, 1235
Gambling reform, 1239
Illegal Offshore Gambling Activity, 1240
Illegal Offshore Wagering Review, 1239
Interactive Gambling Act ACMA enforcement, 1226
Interactive Gambling Act Australia based, 1236
Interactive Gambling Act defences, 1238
Interactive Gambling Act limited exemptions, 1234
Interactive Gambling Act penalties, 1228–1230
Interactive Gambling Act prohibition advertising interactive gambling, 1237
Interactive Gambling Act reforms, 1221
Interactive Gambling Industry Code, 1232–1233
National Consumer Protection Framework, 1222
Place-based betting services, 1221
Prohibited interactive gambling service, 1224
Regulated interactive gambling service, 1225
Video slot machines (pokies), 1219
Cyber Crime Plan, 1535
Cybercrimes Specific
ACCC Internet fraud, 1169
ACCC Scamwatch, 1202, 1209
ANZ financial services attack, 1204
Bitcoin ransom, 1212
Carriage service provider, 1160
Computer crime categories, 1165–1166
Computer fraud civil wrong, 1168
Criminal fraud, 1163–1164
Crypto-miners, 1207
Cyber-bullying, 1215, 1216
Cyber-bullying liability, 1216
Cyber-bullying psychological harm, 1217
Cyberstalking, 1213–1214
Distributed denial of service attacks, 1198
International fora participation, 1171
Internet fraud, 1169
Keylogging, 1206, 1210
Malware, 1206–1207
mens rea, 1163
Online securities fraud, 1170
Pagejacking, 1205
Password sniffers, 1201
Phishing, 1206, 1211
Phishing spear, 1208
Social engineering, 1207
Spoofing, 1202–1203
Spoofing e-mail, 1203
Telecommunications crime, 1157
Telecommunications Offences Act financial information offences, 1162
Telecommunications Offences Act offences, 1163
Theft, 1159
ThreatMetrix Digitial Identity Network online payment fraud, 1204
Trojan, 1206, 1211
US SEC cooperation with ASIC, 1170
US Securities and Exchange Commission, 1170
Viruses, 1199
Worm, 1199
Cybercrime, Torts, 1251, 1252
Cyber Law and Environmental Law, 1280
Australian Bureau of Statistics, 1287
Basel Convention, 1283
Cancer villages, 1297
e-Waste, 1284
e-Waste definition, 1288
e-Waste global, 1286
e-Waste mining, 1289, 1296
e-Waste negative impacts, 1289
e-Waste StEP Initiative, 1291
e-Waste UN coalition, 1286
ICT equipment, 1276
StEP China, 1292, 1297
StEP Ghana, 1294
StEP Kenya, 1295
StEP Togo, 1292
Toxic heavy metals, 1289
UN Report, 1284–1286
Waste electronic and electrical equipment, 1281
Cyber law beyond the grave, 1542
Cyber law complex, 1563
Cyber Law Concepts
Australia competitive advantages, 65
Avatars, 58
Bazaar open model, 46
B2B, 43, 92
B2C, 43, 92

Index

C2G, 43
Cloud computing, 50
Convergence, 54, 56
Democratizing of innovation, 60
Digital constitutionalism, 45
Disruption, 60
Disruptive innovation, 61
E-commerce, 43
Embedded Internet, 57
Facebook community, 57
Fourth Industrial Revolution, 59
Free Libre Open Source Software, 46
G2B, 43
G2C, 43
Globalized world advantages, 63
Globalized world and Australia, 63
Globalized world disadvantages, 63
GNU General Public Licence, 46
GNU Project, 46
History of media, 62
Innovation, 60
Intelligent Web, 53
Internet, 48
Internet of Things (IOT), 54
Knowledge Information Economy, 59
Market Life Cycles, 60
m-Commerce, 49
Media convergence, 55
New forms of property, 58
Peer-to-peer computing P2P, 44
Second Life, 58
Semantic Web, 51, 53
Social media models, 47
Software cathedral model, 46
Virtual worlds, 58
Web 2.0, 52
World Wide Web, 51
Cyber Security, 1526
Cyber security issues, 1530
Cyber Security Plan, 1533
Cyber Security Strategy, 1534
Cyberspace and Environmental Law
Basel Convention, 1334
Botnets, 1331
China main challenge, 1346
Co-regulatory approach, 1344
Corfu Channel case, 1337
Cyber disruptions, 1331
Distributed denial of service, 1331
Environmental law underutilized, 1351
Environmental legal norms, 1338
EU RoHS Directive, 1345
EU WEEE Directive, 1345
e-Waste legislation framework, 1341
Governance, 1328
Key stakeholders, 1340, 1350
Non-state actors, 1334, 1349
Regulatory framework, 1339
Roles and responsibilities, 1340
Tangible-intangible aspects, 1349
Trail Smelter case, 1336
Transborder harm, 1329
Cyber threats, 1532
Cyber world characterizations, 1541

Damages in Contract
Damages assessment of, 619
Damages consequential, 615–616
Damages incidental, 617
Damages loss of bargain, 621
Damages loss of profits, 620
Damages principles, 614
Damages reliance of one party, 622
Damages remoteness at common law, 626–627
Damages special, 615
Damages US damages, 618
Interest on outstanding sums, 625
Restitution of money paid, 623
US Uniform Commercial Code, 618
Darknets, 1552
Database Protection
Approaches to compilations, 314
Author of database, 304–305
Compilations, 311
Computer produced data, 310
Contractual arrangements to protect rights, 307
Database revisions, 308
Databases minimum originality, 322
Derivative works and rights, 306
Doubt robots as authors, 305
Electronic databases, 300–303
EU Directive Databases, 307
Facts not copyrightable, 311, 313
Feist and *Telstra* cases, 312
GIS, 302
Japan data base works, 324
Maps as factual compilations, 319
Nordic countries common provision, 323
Originality, 309–310
Originality in electronic databases, 302
Sweat of the brow, 309
Technological protection measures, 317

Telstra case, 315–316
Thin copyright, 320–325
Tracing paternity in digital data, 301
Unfair competition dismissed, 317
Unresolved protection issues, 325
Data breaches, 1526
Data Matching
Australian Crime Commission Report, 1017
Australian Customs and Border Protection Service, 1018
Australian Tax Office, 1013
Australia Post, 1018
Centrelink, 1013
Data matching assistance agencies, 1013
Data matching guidelines, 1013–1015
Data matching source agencies, 1015
Data sharing Sports Anti-Doping Authority, 1016
Data sharing Sports Authority objectives, 1017
Definition data matching, 1013
Dept Veteran Affairs, 1013
Therapeutic Goods Administration, 1018
Defamation
Defamation common law, 896, 900
Defamation damages remedy, 897
Defamation definition, 896
Defamation ISP, 899
Defamation litigation, 901–902
Defamation on Internet, 901
Defamation publishers versus distributors, 898
Domain name disputes, 904
Hackers, 906
Lemon sites, 903
Passing-off actions, 905
Trespass, 906
Defence White Paper (2016), 1532
Democratization of society, 1521
Dispute resolution, 867, 872, 876
Disruptive technologies, 1518
Domain Names
Administration of, 424–433
au ccTLD, 425–427, 429
auDA, 427, 431–432
AusRegistry Pty Ltd, 429
Australian procedures, 440
Australian reforms, 446–447
ccTLD, 422
Chinese Internet Network Information Centre, 434
Community Geographic Domain Names, 435
Country code top level domain names, 419
Critique cybersquatting provisions, 445
Definition of domain names, 416–419
Dispute resolution procedure, 438–440
Domain name URL, 417
Domain name *versus* trade mark, 441–444
Federal law, 432
Generic Names Supporting Organization, 423
Generic top-level domain names, 418
Generic top-level domains, 421
Geo-ethnic terms, 452
Geo-political terms, 452
ICANN, 418
ICANN reforms, 448–454
in rem action, 439
Inter-Governmental Organizations, 452
International Non-Proprietary Names, 452
Internet Assigned Numbers Authority, 425
Open Second Level Domain Names, 436
Registration in Australia, 434
Singapore I-DNS, 434
Top-level domain, 417
Transfer protocol, 417
Typology of domains, 420–423
UDRP, 438–439
Unassignable domain name licence, 437
Uniform Domain Name Dispute Resolution Policy, 430
US Green Paper (2013), 454
US Network Solutions, 434
WIPO Second Domain Name Process, 452
Dormant accounts, 1542

E-Commerce Trust Tools
Encryption technology exports, 716–717
Hyper Text Transfer Protocol, 709
Passwords, 715
Secure electronic transaction, 709–712
Secure socket layer protocol, 708
Transport Layer security protocol, 709
Virtual private networks, 713–714
Voice over IP protocol, 709
Wassenaar Arrangement, 717
E-government, 99–100

Index

ACCC, 107
ACMA, 103
AGIMO, 104, 115, 129
APS agencies, 129
ARNECC Strategic Statement (2014), 139
ATO, 134
Australia as a Digital Economy Strategy (2013), 131
Australian Customs and Border Protection Service, 110
Consumer Affairs Div Treasury, 109
Definition e-Government, 97
Department of Communications, 102
Department of Health and Ageing, 142
Digital by default, 135
Digital Economy Conversation (2017), 132
Digital Economy Future (2009), 119
Digital Economy Future initiatives, 119
Digital Economy Strategy (2018), 130
Digital first commitment, 131
Digital Transformation Agency, 129, 136
E-Commerce Best Practice Model, 109
E-Commerce Policy Framework, 115, 117
E-Commerce Strategic Framework (1999), 116
Economist Intelligence Unit, 120
E-Conveyancing National Law, 138
E-Government Development Index, 125
E-Government Leadership, 129
E-Government major strengths, 143
E-Health legislative framework, 141
E-Health record, 140
E-Health records OAIC, 142
E-readiness, 120
Global context, 125–128
Government exemplary adopter, 114
GovShare, 129
Information Economy, 98
Infrastructure challenges, 121–124
Initiatives, 113–114
Inter-Governmental Agreement, 138
International cooperation, 124
IP Australia, 108
Legal infrastructure, 98
myGov, 133
National Broadband Network, 121–123
National Commission of Audit, 135
National Digital Economy Strategy (2011), 129
National e-Conveyancing Council, 138
National e-Conveyancing Office, 137
National e-Conveyancing System, 137
NICTA, 105
NOIE, 115
OAIC, 106
Other initiatives, 124
Promoting e-Business, 101
State governments assistance schemes, 111–112
Transformative strategy, 135
UN E-Government Survey results, 126–128
UN Global E-government Readiness Report (2004), 97
UN Public Administration Network survey, 125
WIPO Treaties, 124
World Intellectual Property Organization, 124

Electronic Banking Payment Systems
ACCC, 731
AGIMO National Smartcard Framework, 754
ASIC, 733
ASIC Regulations Guide, 745
Assurance needed, 756
Australian Privacy Principles, 758
Automated teller machine, 727
Billing practices, 757
BPAY, 736
Charge card (debit card), 746
Code of Banking Practice, 744
Commonwealth Acts consumer protection, 723
Consumer Credit Code, 748
Contractual obligations, 748
Credit card fraud, 750
Credit cards, 747, 749
Cybermoney, 727
Definition banking service, 744
Definition electronic money, 726
Definition payments system, 725
Disintermediation, 719–720
e-cash, 728
Electronic financial transaction, 724
Electronic Funds Transfer Code of Conduct, 731, 735, 737–739
Electronic purse e-wallet, 752
e-Payments Code, 740–742
Financial transactions, 718
Funds transfer instruments, 727

IIA Code of Practice, 743
Internet banking, 736
Manual signatures excluded, 734
Mastercard Cash Card, 730
Mastercard Pay Pass, 755
Near field communication, 755
Personal identification number, 732
PIN@POS proposal, 733
Point of sale transfers, 727
Quick Link, 730
Smart card applications, 753
Smart Card Code of Conduct, 752
Smart card contactless, 755
Smart card contact type, 755
Smart cards, 729–730, 752
Smart card types, 755
Stored-value cards, 729
Stored-value smart card, 751
Third-Party Assurance, 723
VisaCash, 730
Wallis Inquiry (1996), 721–722
Electronic Payment Systems, 762–764
Australian Transaction Reports and Analysis Centre, 772
Bitcoin, 764, 771
Block chain technology, 765
BPAY, 763
Cryptocurrencies, 764
Digital cash, 765
Digital cheques, 773
E-cash, 764, 767
Home banking communication interface, 760
HTTP, 760
Internet banking, 759
Internet banking protocols, 760
Internet banking risks, 760
Milli-cent, 764, 770
Net cash, 764, 768–769
SHTTP, 760
Electronic Transactions
Australia global online spend, 654
Australia online sales, 652
Australia Post online shopping, 653
Australia top export markets, 654
B2B services, 646
B2C services, 646
B2G, 647
C2G, 647
Cross-border issues, 660
e-Business, 646
e-Commerce, 645–646
e-Commerce and Internet, 651
e-Commerce heavily regulated, 658
E-commerce includes other media, 655
EDI, 646, 655
Electronic transactions legal status, 644
Expert e-Commerce Expert Group, 657
G2G, 647
i-Commerce, 646
Legal infrastructure, 656
Light touch regulation, 645
m-Commerce, 646
Private regulation on Internet, 659
UNCITRAL, 650
Web 2.0, 646
Electronic Transactions Background
Australian Government Information Management Office, 674
Click button contract, 683
Commonwealth excluded from consent provisions, 671
Commonwealth national uniform scheme, 666
Consent to receive electronic communications, 670
Digital persona, 686
Digital signature, 669, 679
Digital signature requirements, 679–680
Digital signatures foolproof, 688
Digitized signature, 669
Electronic authentication, 674
E-signature authentication versus security, 688
ETA applies to Commonwealth Acts, 662
ETA default rules, 672
ETA graphical representation, 668
ETA not addressed PKI PKAF, 686
ETA objectives, 662
ETA other laws, 673
ETA principles, 667
ETA strategic framework, 664
ETA workability, 678
EU Directive on Electronic Signatures, 689
Key differences with State and Territory laws, 666
National Electronic Authentication Council, 674
National Office for the Information Economy, 674
Objection in electronic form, 685
PKI authority assumption, 687
Regulations exemptions, 663

Settlement by e-mail, 685
Signature by e-mail, 682
Signed by digital pen, 684
Typed name accepted, 681
UNCITRAL Model Law eCommerce, 661
UNCITRAL Model Law on Electronic Signatures, 675
UN Convention CUECIC, 676–677
UN Convention CUECIC aims, 676
US E-Sign Act (2000), 689
US Uniform Electronic Transactions Act (1999), 689
E-marketing, consumer protection, 895
Encryption laws, 1537
Ephemeral legal constructs, 1543
EU Database Directive
Database right, 327
EU Directive on Databases (1996), 326
EU Software Directive (1991), 326
Licensing database rights, 329
Sui generis right, 327
EU GRDP (2018), 1529
E-Waste Initiatives
Australian Capital Territory, 1305
Australian Standard 5377:2013, 1310
Basel Convention, 1300
Basel Convention objectives, 1301
China, 1323–1327
China domestic policies, 1324, 1326
China Recycling and Treatment of Waste Regulation (2011), 1325
Collection services, 1311
Co-regulatory scheme, 1306, 1311
Council of Australian Governments, 1307
EU and UK, 1315
EU Approved Treatment Facilities, 1316
EU CE mark, 1317
EU Designated Collection Facilities, 1316
EU Distributor Takeback Scheme, 1316
EU Producer Compliance Scheme, 1316
EU RoHS Directive (2012), 1317
EU WEEE Directive (2012), 1315
Mercury-containing lamps, 1312
National Products Stewardship Scheme, 1304
National TV and Computer Recycling Scheme, 1304
National Waste Policy, 1307
New Zealand, 1314
Principle of informed consent, 1302
Recycling targets, 1309
South Australia, 1305
UK Waste Electrical & Electronic Equipment Regulations (2013), 1321
Waste TV and computers, 1313

Financial institution. *See* Electronic Banking Payment Systems
Five Eyes Alliance, 1557

5G, 1562

Foreign interference, 1557
Freedom of Information
Administrative Appeals Tribunal, 1042
Australia democratic society, 1042
FOIA access to archival records, 1047
FOIA exemptions and public interest test, 1044–1046
FOIA government information, 1044–1046
FOIA Northern Territory, 1044
FOIA review application, 1049
Information Commissioner reviews, 1042
OAIC, 1041

Geographic Information Systems (GIS)
Data, 1355
Definition GIS, 1357
Geospatial information, 1355
Industry, 1353
Information, 1355
Intelligence, 1355
Knowledge, 1355
Legal Issues GIS, 1358
Wisdom, 1355
GIS Cloud Computing and VGI
AGIMO standard terms, 1473
Cloud computing, 1459, 1466
Cloud computing Data as a service, 1470, 1472
Cloud computing Infrastructure as a service, 1470
Cloud computing Platform as a service, 1470
Cloud computing Software as a service, 1470
Compensation data loss, 1475
Contractual liability, 1477
Crowd-sourced, 1463
Disputes, 1478

Geospatial cloud computing, 1467–1468, 1472
Indirect control, 1476
Protection of information, 1474
Theories of law interaction, 1483
US NIST cloud computing, 1469
VGI crowd-sourced information, 1479–1480
VGI reliability and accuracy, 1481
VGI website, 1482
Volunteer cartographer, 1463
Web 2.0, 1459, 1484
GIS Contract Law
Cloud computing, 1361
Contract for service, 1370
Contract of service, 1370
Contractor or employee, 1359
Contractual liability, 1374
Crowd-sourced mapping, 1361
Database maintenance, 1362
Data supply vendor, 1375–1376
Delivery of map services, 1362
Development GIS, 1362
Employment contract, 1372
Exclusions, 1364
Geospatial analytics, 1361
Indemnity, 1364
Independent contractor, 1373
Legal liability, 1364
Licensing leasing, 1362
Nature of data product, 1369
Outsourcing mapping, 1362
Privity of contract, 1374
Product and services, 1360
Request for information, 1362
Request for proposals, 1362
Sale of goods, 1367–1368
Spatial computing, 1361
Tort liability, 1365–1366
Traditional geospatial analyses, 1362
Users of geospatial data, 1375
GIS Emerging Issues
Disruptive technologies, 1458
Geospatial information science, 1460
Geospatial information services, 1460
Geospatial information systems, 1460
Google Earth Maps, 1463
Legal risks, 1464–1465
New digital environment, 1462
OpenStreetMapping, 1463
Service provision, 1460
Web 2.0, 1459, 1484
GIS Functional Characteristics
Aspect ratio, 1424
Berne Convention, 1421
Categories of works, 1426
Caveats, 1425
Collated information, 1418
Compilations protected, 1420
Database protection, 1416
Data heritage, 1427
Digital data, 1414–1415
Display on computer screen, 1428
Droit moral, 1421
Ephemeral, 1428
Functional, 1414
Legal issues, 1417
Moral rights, 1422–1423
Public performance, 1428
GIS Liability Issues
Contract, 1448
Geo-liability, 1457
Inappropriate use, 1449
Legal liability and risks, 1446
Legal responsibilities, 1447
Mitigating circumstances, 1451
Network hosts, 1450
Prod-users, 1447
Rescue common law duty, 1453
Rescue European laws, 1455
Rescue German Criminal Penal Code, 1455
Rescue US no duty, 1454
Terms of use contract, 1448
Tortious liability others, 1456
Tort liability, 1449
Unauthorized use, 1449
US Volunteer Protection Act (1997), 1456
Volunteered Geographic Information, 1446
Volunteers as Good Samaritans, 1452
GIS Privacy Issues
Acontextual data, 1434
Calling line id, 1441
Calling number display, 1441
Dataveillance, 1445
Dyads, 1440
Ethical questions, 1434
Geo-demographics, 1436
GIS tools, 1432
LBS nature of, 1437
Legislation, 1438–1439
Location-based services, 1436

Personal information, 1431
Privacy as a right, 1433
Privacy as interest or property, 1433
Privacy risks, 1444
Privacy risk status summary table, 1445ff
Surveillance, 1445
Telecommunication services, 1440
Tracking people, 1435
Voice Over Internet Protocol, 1442
Zones of privacy, 1430
GIS Property Rights
Australian IP law, 1379
Australian map case, 1399–1400
Characteristics property rights, 1377
Common law, 1391
Comprehensive database, 1391, 1411
Confidential information, 1392
Confidentiality restrictions, 1412
Control of ownership, 1403
Copyright notice, 1405
Database protection, 1383
Data commons, 1402
Definition intellectual property, 1378
Desktop Marketing case, 1390
Facts from expression, 1389
Feist case, 1390
GI Professional, 1384
Hyper-space, 1401
Ideas as expressed, 1381–1382
IPR statement, 1402
Judicial approach, 1397
Layers of information, 1402
Legal risks, 1413
Literary works, 1394
Maps as factual products, 1387
Maps graphical representations, 1401
Maps on the fly, 1387
Metadata layer, 1409
My digital map, 1406
Originality, 1395–1396
Originality low, 1410
Ownership rights, 1386
Paternity, 1407
Potential for infringement, 1385
Protection framework IPR, 1391
Protection of ideas, 1381
Services delivered, 1383
Statutory regimes, 1380
Sweat of the brow, 1386, 1408
3-D terrestrial space, 1401
Trade secrets, 1392
World Intellectual Property Organization, 1378
Global solutions, 1559

Hackers. *See* Cybercrime
Handling personal data, 1548
Hardware Contract, 553–557
Computer systems changeover, 556–557
Computer systems title, 558
Computer systems warranty, 559
ICT equipment procurement, 560
ProcureIT Framework NSW, 561–564
HealthEngine, 1549
Huawei, 1555

ICT and Civil Procedures
Admissibility of e-mails, 863–866
Alternate Dispute Resolution, 872, 876
Arbitration, 870
Australian Centre for International Commercial Arbitration, 871
Australian Commercial Disputes Centre, 871
Cause of action categories, 856
Choice of law, 854
Conflict of laws, 855–858
Conflict rule application, 857–858
Definition jurisdiction, 839
Discovery order, 865
Dispute resolution, 867
Evidence laws, 866
Hague Conference Private International Law, 861
Internet separate legal frontier, 852
Jurisdiction, 836
Jurisdiction Australian guidelines, 850
Jurisdiction Australian litigation, 846–848
Jurisdiction clause, 841
Jurisdiction extraterritorial effects, 849
Jurisdiction general, 840
Jurisdiction ICT context, 846–850
Jurisdiction in personam, 843–844
Jurisdiction in rem, 843–844
Jurisdiction *res*, 843
Jurisdiction specific, 840
Jurisdiction subject-matter, 845
Jurisdiction technological solutions, 851
Law enforcement, 837–838
London Court of International Arbitration, 871
Mediation, 872

Mediation and Arbitration, 869
National ADR Advisory Council, 873, 875
Nature of conflict, 855
Online Dispute resolution, 874
Online mediation, 873
Reform international, 861
Reform model code, 860
Reform recommendations, 859
Rules of evidence, 862
Settlement Online systems, 877
Territorial restriction on laws, 842
Use of technology Australian courts, 867
Venue, 853
WA Singapore Co-mediation Program, 868
ICT and Contract Law
ADMA Code of Practice (2006), 507
Bespoke contract IPR, 529
Bespoke contract sale or hiring, 530
Bespoke customized software, 528
Bespoke force majeure clause, 531
Boilerplate clauses, 533
Box-top licences, 539
Break-seal licences, 539
Browse-wrap agreements, 543
Click-wrap agreements, 542
CLRC Report Copyright and Contract (2002), 482
Conditions post contract, 536
Consensus, 512–513
Consensus silence online, 513
Contract click-wrap, 504
Contract click-wrap cases, 525
Contract click-wrap terms, 524
Contract common law *versus* statutory, 487
Contract dispute resolution clause, 537
Contract enforceability online, 540
Contract fax then mail, 505
Contract formation US cases, 547–549
Contract ICT arbitration clauses, 538
Contract implied terms, 526–528
Contract online jurisdiction, 503
Contract online link, 524
Contract online postal rule, 503, 504
Contract representation, 521–525
Contract representation authority, 523
Contract representation timing, 521–522
Contracts e-Commerce legal issues, 551
Contract software development, 527
Contracts standard form B2B, 550
Contract terms, 517
Contract terms express, 518–519
Contract terms *versus* representation, 520
Definition electronic communication, 501
Definition of condition, 534
Disclaimers or exclusions, 492
Electronic agents untested, 500
Electronic contracts, 479
Elements of a contract, 487*ff*
ETA digital signatures, 515
EU Directive Distance Contracts, 507
Intention to create legal relations, 488
Invitation to treat online, 490
Machines accept offers, 497–498
Mass market agreements concerns, 545
Model Law e-Commerce (1996), 480
Offer and acceptance online, 489
Oral contracts, 516
Oral contracts electronically, 516
Parole evidence rule, 516
PayPal, 538
Principles of contract law, 483–486
Request for tender electronically, 495–496
Shrink-wrap agreements, 541
Shrink-wrap contracts Australia, 544
Shrink-wrap terms, 539
Statute of Frauds (1677), 514
Terms and conditions on web page, 491, 493
Terms implied by statute, 532
Ticket cases, 497
UNCITRAL Model Law Electronic signatures, 480
UN Convention CUECIC (2005), 480–481
UN CUECIC provisions, 501–502
UN Model Law Electronic Commerce functional equivalence, 506
Usefulness of definition clauses, 535
Valuable consideration, 508–511
Valuable consideration online, 511
Warranty indemnity, 534, 536
Website design acceptance of offer, 494
Web-wrap terms, 539
Written document requirements, 514–516
ICT and Copyright
Copyright, 279
Copyright exclusive right, 277
Copyright fingerprinting, 287
Copyright licensing process, 290
Copyright traps, 287

Copyright watermarks, 287
Definition literary work, 282
Different durations, 285
Digital rights management, 289
Exclusive rights, 282
Fair dealing use, 283
Grant of copyright length of time, 281
Preventing unauthorized copying, 279
Protects works, 280
Published on Internet, 286
Raster maps, 288
Right to copy, 279
Royalty, 277
Separate owners, 285
Vector maps, 288
ICT Market Regulation
Australia, 144
Population distribution, 146–147
Telecommunications, 144
ICT Regulation
ACCC public inquiry, 180
Access regime objects, 173
Access regime principles, 178
Access undertaking, 172
ACMA, 152–157
Advisory notice, 193
Anti-competitive conduct, 185, 190
Any-to-any connectivity, 175
AUSSAT Pty Ltd, 148
AUSTEL, 150
Australian Broadcasting Authority, 155
Australian Communication and Media Authority, 152
Australian Communications Authority, 155
Australian Telecommunications Commission, 148
Carriage service provider, 167, 187, 195
Carriers, 165, 187, 195
Content service provider, 167
Entities regulated, 164
Network unit, 166
Objects, 161
Regulatory Policy, 163
Service providers, 167
Synoptic views, 162
CCA Parts XIB & XIC, 159
CCA Part XIB Anti-competitive Conduct, 182–207
CCA Part XIC, 169–181
Competition notice Part A, 183, 191
Competition notice Part B, 192
Competition Notice regime, 188–194
Competition notices, 186
Competition rule, 183, 189
Core access arrangements, 176
Declared services, 170, 179
Definition carriage service, 198–199
Definition carrying communications, 201
Definition communication, 200
Definition telecommunication market, 197
Eligible territory, 174
Exemption order, 194
History of regulations, 148–160
Illegal to fix prices, 207
Listed services objectives, 173
Market definition, 204
Market power, 205–206
National Broadband Network paper (2009), 160
NBN, 169
Optus Communications, 151
Overseas Telecommunications Commission, 148
Policy imperatives of access regime, 177
Postmaster General's Department, 148
Public switched telephone network, 151
Record keeping rules, 182
Standard access obligations, 171
Telecommunications Access Forum (TAF), 180
TAF principal functions, 181
Telecom, 148–149, 151
Telecommunication market, 195–202, 207
Unacceptable conduct, 184
Individualism, 1521
Information Age, 1518
Intangible property, 1532
Intellectual Property Rights
Australia promotion of innovation, 256
Browsing, 258
Bundle of rights, 253
Copyright regime, 257
Copyright 16th C, 259
Dilemmas electronic environment, 258
Forms of expression, 258
Geographic information, 254
ICT professionals, 254
Infringements digital environment, 255
Intellectual property, 249
Moral rights, 253
Ownership of IPR, 251

Pay wall, 258
Property rights, 250
Statute of Anne (1709), 259
Sui generis rights, 253
US copyright objectives, 252
Use online, 258
International developments, 1519
Internet governance, 1519
Internet of Things (IOT), 1518
IPR Infringements
Copyright an anachronism, 475
Copyright thin protection, 476
Database Management system, 462
Defences to infringement, 466–468
Discretionary equitable remedy, 471
Fair dealing and fair use, 456, 468
Independent creation, 467
Infringements Australia, 455
IPR generic rights, 473
Licences and agreements, 477
Parallel importation, 457–460
Public interest, 466
Remedies, 470–471
Reproduction material form, 464–465
Substantiality requirements, 461–463
Territorial copyright, 457
UK confidential memo, 456
Unprotected data in databases, 463
24 x 7 information standard time, 478
IPR International
Berne Convention, 275
Conventions and Treaties, 274–276
Overview IPR Treaties, 276
Rome Convention, 275
TRIPS, 274
TRIPS Agreement, 275
WCT, 275
WIPO, 274
WPPT, 275
WTO, 274
IPR Other in ICT
Aerial photographs, 405
Atypical developments, 389–397
Berne Convention, 369
Business methods, 378–382
Cancún Ministerial Conference (2003), 399
Chinese calligraphic characters, 406
Computer-aided typography, 407–408
Copyleft movement, 389, 392
Creative Commons, 394–395
Defences to infringement, 372
Definition of work enlarged, 386
Digital rights management, 387–388
Dongle, 387
Droit de suite (*see* Moral rights)
Droit moral (*see* Moral rights)
European Patent Convention, 382
European Patents Office, 382
Exceptions to TRIPS, 398
Fonts, 406–409
FOSS for Africa, 397
Free and open source software, 389–393, 396–397
Free Software Foundation, 392
Geographical Indications, 398–402
GNU/Linux, 392
GNU Public Licence, 392
IBM, 391
ICT no moral rights regime, 371
Information protection borne on or near the fact, 376
IPR summary chart, 409*ff*
Landsat images, 405
Microsoft, 391–392
Moral rights, 369, 373–374
No rights reserved, 389
One-click patent, 379
Open Source Definition, 393
Open Source Initiative, 393
Opera in the Outback, 407–408
Patent law territorial, 384
Photographs, 403–405
Severity of penalties, 387
Sui generis right, 375, 377
terroir, 402
Thumbnail pictures, 404
TRIPS Agreement, 398
UK non-economic rights, 360
UNIX Operating System, 390
US Copyright Act non-recognition moral rights, 370
USPTO business method patent, 380
USPTO Geographic Information patents, 383
IPR Protection Australia
Business methods and systems, 265
Common law, 260
Compilation of facts, 263
Confidential information, 270
Copyright as a type of property, 261
Copyright as bundle of economic rights, 262
Copyright safeguards, 262

Design new and original, 266
Fonts, 272
Framework, 260
Geographical Indications, 269
Internet Treaties computer programs, 263
Jurisdiction oriented, 267
Monopoly rights, 264
Photographs, 271
Summary Table IPR features and protections, 273ff
Trade marks protected, 267
Trade secrets, 270
USPTO one-click patent, 265

Legal metaphors, 1522
Location-Based Services. *See* Geographic Information Systems (GIS)

Moral rights, 253, 260, 268, 369–377, 1189, 1421–1423, 1425
MyHealth Record, 1528

Negligence
Breach of statutory duty, 924–926
Contributory negligence as a defence, 922
Corporations Act (2001) Director duties, 926
Cybersquatting, 893
DDS as trespass, 890
Definition intentional tort, 889–893
Domain name disputes, 893
Duty of care in SA, 923
eBay case, 890–892
Exceptions to liability, 908–910
Fault *versus* wrong in South Australia, 923
Fraudulent misrepresentation, 894–895, 909
ICANN, 893
Negligence causal connection, 920
Negligence contributory, 921
Negligence damage proximate, 920
Negligence defences, 930
Negligence doctrine, 911–916
Negligence duty of care, 916
Negligence elements of, 914
Negligence mere economic loss, 917–918
Negligence misstatement, 917–919
Negligence of manufacturers, 913
Negligence professional, 919
Negligence standard of proof, 915
Novus actus interveniens, 920
Remedies at common law, 927
Robot, 890
Spider, 890
Tort categories, 887, 907
Tort intentional, 888
Tort law, 878
Tort law of the place principle, 885
Tort liability, 884, 908
Tort nature of, 808–883
Virus attack as trespass, 890
volenti non fit injuria, 920
Network Service Operators Liability
ACMA classification of content, 932
ASIC licensing scheme, 942
Besley Report ISP responsibilities, 932
Co-regulatory scheme with ISP, 932
Defamation action, 933–940
Defamation Act (2005) NSW defence to defamation, 940
Defamation defence untested, 943
Defamation jurisdiction, 937
Definition financial product, 942
Definition financial service, 942
Innocent dissemination, 933, 936
Internet content host, 938
ISP as common carriers, 929
Liability of ISP, 928, 931
Liability of network service operators, 928
Liability special context, 942
Mere distributor, 935
Misleading and deceptive conduct, 930
Negligent provision of information, 941
Other statutory obligations, 932
Publication *versus* distribution, 941
Regulatory scheme, 938
Regulatory scheme applicable to State and Territory, 940
Relief from strict liability, 938–939
Safe harbour provisions, 941
Statutory duty, 930–932
US cases persuasive, 934
New Global Rules, 1567
Notifiable data breaches, 1527

Oblivion framework, 1546
Organizational change, 1520

Pain and suffering, 1551
Presence on the Internet, 1544

Privacy and Spam Law
ACMA court proceedings, 1082–1083
ACMA determinations, 1077
Chief Privacy Officer, 1109
Combatting spam, 1084
Commercial e-message requirements, 1080
Common law actions, 1088
Cookies, 1091
Cookies breach Privacy Act, 1094–1095
Cookies Ethical websites, 1093
Cookies EU Directive (2002), 1092
E-mail Unauthorized access, 1099–1103
Enforceable undertakings, 1081
Enforcement options, 1077
Express consent required, 1079
Federal Trade Commission Report (2000) Privacy international efforts, 1112
Financial penalties for breaches, 1075–1076
Groups fighting spam, 1084
Individual level, 1089
Knowledge management, 1106–1107
m-commerce, 1107
Multimedia Messaging Service, 1073
Privacy protection consistency, 1111
Regulatory agencies, 1087
Send to a friend facility, 1078
Short Messaging Service, 1072
Small claims courts and tribunals, 1090
Spam Act e-message features, 1074
Spam as unwanted ads, 1071
Spam legislation implications, 1096
Special privacy protection, 1104
Storing messages, 1103
Technological solutions, 1084–1086
Web bugs, 1097, 1098
Web robot or spider, 1097
Privacy Criminal Laws
Australian Communications Authority, 1068
Cybercrime Act Assistance orders, 1063
Cybercrime Act Investigation powers, 1063
IIA Code influential, 1068
Industry Codes Telecommunications Act (1997), 1068–1069
NSW Computer-specific offences, 1065
NSW Damaging data, 1065
NSW Unlawful access, 1065
Victoria deception, 1066
Privacy Legislation Australia
AML/CTF regime, 1024–1025
APP Access and correction, 995
APP Code, 998
APP Collection, 991
APP Direct marketing, 995
APP Government information, 995
APP Security, 995
APP Use and disclosure, 991
APRA Australian Prudential Regulation Authority, 1026
APRA Data Guide, 1026
APRA Prudential Practice Guide, 1026
Asymmetric encryption, 1036
AUSTRAC, 1025
Australian Privacy Principles, 985
Behavioural ads, 1011
Best Practice Model for Business, 1034
Code of conduct Electronic Funds Transfer, 1034
Code of practice data protection ADMA, 1032–1033
Code of Practice IIA, 1034
Codes of conduct for E-business, 1034
Consent and bargaining position disparity, 1008
Consent and bundling of, 1009
Consent and cookies, 1010
Consent and privacy, 1007–1008
Credit Reporting Code, 998
Cyberattack and personal information, 1012
Definition personal information, 982, 996
External dispute resolution schemes, 1000
Financial information security, 1026
Hacking, 1031
Health Records, 1027–1028
Information Privacy Principles, 994
National Privacy Principles, 994
New Privacy Law reforms, 992–993
OECD Guidelines Consumer Protection, 1032–1033
Other Commonwealth Legislation impacting privacy, 1023–1025
Personal information broadly defined, 996
Pretty Good Privacy, 1036
Privacy Amendment Act and Australian Privacy Principles, 993
Privacy Amendment Act applies to businesses, 993

Privacy Amendment Act applies to private sector, 993
Privacy Amendment Act new provisions, 994
Privacy and private sector, 1005–1006
Privacy breach notification, 999
Privacy Codes, 998, 1019
Privacy Commissioner, 1020
Privacy complaint avenues, 1021–1022
Privacy disputes, 1000
Privacy external dispute resolution, 1000
Privacy Extraterritoriality, 1001–1004
Privacy Industry Codes, 1032
Privacy Information Commissioner, 997
Privacy Jurisdiction, 1001
Privacy laws administration, 983
Privacy Legislation States and Territories, 1029
Privacy Ombudsman, 1030–1031
Privacy penalties, 997
Privacy Protection Non-legal means, 1036–1037
Privacy Protection Technical solutions, 1036
Related laws, 1031
Software as goods, 1031
Third Party Verification, 1035
TIO EDR Scheme, 1000
TRUSTe, 1035

Privacy Protection
Australian Law Reform Commission Privacy report, 952
Data mining, 959
Definition personal information, 951
Definition privacy, 951
EU Data Protection Directive (1995), 982–984
EU ePrivacy Directive (2002), 985
EU General Data Protection Regulations (2017), 985–987
Global privacy enforcement network, 976
OECD 1980 Privacy Guidelines, 977–979, 981
Office of Australian Information Commissioner, 976
Privacy ABS Internet Activity Survey, 970
Privacy abuse e-commerce, 964–965
Privacy Australia International obligations, 975
Privacy balancing interests, 972–974
Privacy civil action right, 955
Privacy Commissioner Guidelines, 963
Privacy Commissioner study, 969
Privacy employer rights, 963
Privacy genetic information sensitive, 966
Privacy on Internet high risk activity, 960
Privacy on the Internet, 958–963
Privacy policy organizations and agencies, 971
Privacy right cause of action open, 957
Privacy right *Lenah Game Meats* case, 956–957
Privacy risk, 961
Privacy tort Sands case, 956
Privacy Unisys Security Index poll report, 967–968
Privacy *versus* freedom of speech, 974
Surveillance, 962
UN Guidelines Personal Data, 980
Universal Declaration of Human Rights, 975
US Safe Harbour framework, 987

Privacy Telecommunications
Carriage service providers, 1052
Common law privacy protection telecommunications, 1061
Conduct misleading and deceptive, 1062
Confidentiality of communications, 1055
Content service providers, 1053
Eligible carriage service providers, 1053
Industry codes and standards, 1056
Industry Code Telecommunications Consumer Protection, 1057
ISP, 1053
Personal information use and disclosure, 1058
Privacy and confidentiality customer information, 1059
Service providers, 1052

Product Liability
Classification of defect, 950
Consumer protection laws, 945
Diagnostic error, 950
Medical expert systems, 949
Product liability provisions to expert system, 950
Product safety laws, 946–948
Real-world *versus* cyber-world, 1524
RegTech Association, 1565
RegTech compliance, 1563

RegTech ecosystem, 1565
RegTech Universe, 1565
Revolution in IT, 1518
Right to be forgotten, 1544
Right to be forgotten critique, 1545
Software design defects, 949

Risk management, information governance, 111
Robotics
Asia region, 1489
Assistive robots, 1492
Australia robotic in industry, 1492–1493
Australia robotics, 1485
Computational statistics, 1486
Data mining, 1486
Education, 1493
Employment, 1490
Growth of, 1486
International Organization for Standardization, 1494
Jobs least at risk, 1498
Jobs most at risk, 1497
Labour markets, 1487
Machine learning, 1486
Machine vision and dexterity, 1486
Map human brain, 1486
Miniaturization, 1486
Robot installations, 1491
Robot legal definition, 1494–1495
Robots employment, 1496
Small to medium enterprises, 1491

Security of Payments Systems
Application to digital cash, 787
ASIC regulates securities, 801
Australian Payments Clearing Association, 779
Bank State Bank number, 789
Characteristics of Payments systems, 776–777
Clearing, 778–780
Confidence, 774
Contagion risk7, 83
Control of Payments Systems, 788
Definition payments system, 788
Digital coin claims, 795
Dormant accounts, 796–797
E-crime, 804
E-Gold, 802
Exposure risks, 783–785
Financial institution role, 775
Herstatt risks multi-currencies, 786
Home raids, 805
ISO 20022 message format, 789
Money laundering, 798
Money laundering criminal penalties, 799
Money laundering terrorism, 800
Netting, 781–782
New Payments Platform, 789–791
Online financial scams, 802
PayId service, 789
Payments Systems Board, 788
PayPal, 802–803
Regulatory responses, 806
Reserve Bank currency notes, 793
Reserve Bank of Australia, 788
Seigniorage, 793, 807, 810
Settlement, 780
Soft law, 1519
Strategic Review Payments System (2012), 789
Systematic risk, 784
Unclaimed monies, 794
Wallis Inquiry (1996), 806
Software Contracts
Applications programs choices, 569
Bespoke software, 565, 570–583
CCA (2010), 577
Contracts goods or services, 576
Hardware-software litigation cases, 572–575
ICT contracts, 556
Merchantable quality, 581
Microsoft Windows Operating System, 568
Payment price, 583
Personnel contracts, 584–585
Responsibilities of custodians, 582
Sale of Goods Act (1979) UK, 581
Skill and care services, 581
Software contract inclusions, 568
Software not term of art, 568
Supply of Goods and Services Act (1982) UK, 581
Terms of contract, 567
Software Distribution Agreements
Characteristics software distribution agreements, 593–596
Commercial off the shelf services, 608
Computer Bureau Services, 604–606
Computer software, 592
Government outsourcing ICT, 611–613

Government SourceIT Model Contracts, 607–608
ISP services, 603
ISP services access and quality of, 602
Network services, 602–603
OECD definition software agreements, 596
Privacy Commissioner outsourcing and privacy, 613
Semi-complex procurement, 610
Simple procurement, 609
Taxation issues, 595
Software Protection
Application programming interfaces, 292
Author computer program, 293
Computer program literary work, 291
Copyright formality free, 291
De-compilation reverse engineering, 295
Embedded software protection, 297
GIF, 288
Patents, 291
Protection has low threshold, 292
Right holder exclusive rights, 294
Smart phone apps, 298
Software as a service, 299
State sovereignty, 1525
Succession law, 1542
Sui generis protection, 291
Technical solutions, 1519
Trademarks as brands, 296

Telecommunications Reforms
ACCC regulated services, 240–242
ACMA, 245–248
Competition notice regime, 243
Competition regime reform, 240–243
Consumer safeguards, 244–248
Exemption to some carriers, 248
Infringement notices, 247
Minimum performance benchmarks, 246
NBN, 237–238
Pay phone removal, 245
Reforms, 234–248
Statement of Expectations, 239
TELSTRA minimum benchmarks, 244
TELSTRA Structural separation, 236–239
Transnational cross jurisdictional, 1553
Trolled online, 1551
Turnkey Contracts
Australia turnkey contracts, 591
Computer package, 590
Contract for service, 601
Facilities management servicing ICT, 599
Maintenance contracts, 597–598
Package deal contracts, 587
SA Service Level Guidelines, 600
Turnkey meaning, 586
Turnkey project, 587–589
UN Charter (1945), 1525
Virtual world, 1524
Warranty (*see* Contract)
WeChat, 1560
WeChat payments function, 1561
Westphalian sovereignty, 1525
World Trade Organization (WTO), 1567
ZTE, 1555.

www.ingramcontent.com/pod-product-compliance
Ingram Content Group UK Ltd.
Pitfield, Milton Keynes, MK11 3LW, UK
UKHW020131290926
15471UKWH00003B/407

9 789403 521022